GALLIPOLI

GALLIPOLI

by

Captain Eric Wheler Bush

ST. MARTIN'S PRESS

NEW YORK

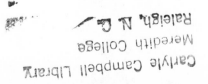

Copyright © 1975 by Eric Bush
All rights reserved. For information, write:
St. Martin's Press, Inc., 175 Fifth Ave., New York, N.Y. 10010
Printed in Great Britain
Library of Congress Catalog Card Number: 75-9470
First published in the United States of America in 1975

To

ALAN HUGH HILLGARTH
C.M.G., O.B.E., Captain, Royal Navy

Acknowledgements

If it had not been for the kindness of Messrs Harry Spanton, John Sharpe, Paul Duncan and Richard Esdale, who organised *B.I.* (now P. & O.) Educational cruises in the *Nevasa* and *Uganda*, my Gallipoli story might never have been written. This book is the result of voyages made as guest lecturer on the Campaign, when passage of the Dardanelles and a visit to Istanbul was included in the itinerary. I wish to place on record my indebtedness to all concerned.

I am particularly grateful to Captain Alan Hillgarth, Royal Navy, Blake term-mate and shipmate of the *Bacchante*, to whom this book is dedicated. He read the proofs and, as always, gave much sound advice which was taken.

Mrs George Shield, who, as Mary Kaye, was Sir Ian Hamilton's personal private secretary from 1916 and is now his literary executor (our first meeting was in Monte Carlo in 1939) also read the proofs making many helpful suggestions. She kindly gave me access to Sir Ian's personal papers including those lodged in the University of London, King's College, Military archives, where Mr Antony Grant, the archivist was very helpful.

Major H. V. Howe of Cremore, N.S.W. Australia, is a good friend to all Anzac midshipmen. He and I have corresponded for years and both my naval sons have met him. He is one of the immortal but diminishing band which took part in the first rush across the beach at Anzac at dawn on 25 April 1915. An authority on the Campaign and a member of the Gallipoli Mission, 1919, he read my Anzac story, and his help was invaluable.

Others from 'down under' to whom I am indebted include Mr W. R. Lancaster, Director, Australian War Memorial, Canberra; Miss Julia Bergen, Alexander Turnbull Library, Wellington, N.Z.; Lt-Col E. F. Allchin (10 Bn A.I.F.); Major F. A. Eustace (1st N.Z.E.F.), and Brig.-Gen. T. S. Louch (11 Bn A.I.F.).

The late Herr Hans Hommel and I first met up the Yangtse in 1932 and we remained close friends. I am much indebted to him for translations from the German, and for introductions to Cdr Rolf Güth, Führungsakademie der B.W. Hamburg; Herr Franz Hahn, Marineschule Mürwik, and Dr Friedrich Stahl, Militärchiv, Breslau, whose valuable help I also acknowledge. I thank Mr Charles Seymour for translations from the French; and Major T. Verschoyle for elucidating Turkish words and for much help in other directions.

From Turkey I would like to thank Brig. K. P. Molyneux-Carter, a former Defence and Military Attaché, Ankara; Mr Hugh La Fontaine, Istanbul; and Messrs A. Davidson and J. P. B. Hyde, the British Consulate General, Istanbul.

Valuable assistance with research was also given by Captain S. W. Roskill, R.N., Churchill College, Cambridge; Dr Ronald Hope, Seafarers' Education Service; Sqn Ldr J. H. McN. Campbell, Mrs J. D. Wyeth and Mrs P. Wakefield, Commonwealth War Graves Commission; Captain J. M. H. Cox, R.N., Naval Attaché, Bonn; the late Brig. T. N. Smith, and Lt-Col H. R. K. Gibbs, 6th Queen Elizabeth's Own Gurkha Rifles Assn; Rear-Admiral G. S. Ritchie, Hydrographer of the Navy; Miss Rose E. B. Coombes, Mr Vernon Rigby and Mr Ralph Squires, The Imperial War Museum; Captain H. R. Keate, R.N., Naval Attaché, Paris; Major T. P. Shaw, Lancashire Headquarters, the Royal Regt of Fusiliers; Mr G. O. Osbon, the National Maritime Museum; Rear-Admiral P. N. Buckley, Naval Historical Branch, M.O.D.; Lt-Col A. Joanny, the Royal Norfolk Regt Assn; Brig. S. A. Hassan, Office of the High Commissioner for Pakistan, London; Miss D. H. Gifford and Cdr G. D. Godfrey, R.N., Public Record Office; Maj.-Gen. A. MacLennan, R.A.M.C., Historical Museum Trust; Dr E. P. Hall, Research Laboratory for Archaeology, Oxford; the Director and staff, Royal United Service Institution; Major G. J. B. Egerton, South Wales Borderers and Monmouthshire Regt Museum; Lt-Col J. E. Margesson, Headquarters the Royal Regt of Wales; Lt-Cdr G. H. F. Frere-Cook, R.N., Curator, Submarine Museum, H.M.S. *Dolphin*; The Society of Authors; Mr R. G. Bird, Borough Librarian and Staff, the Tunbridge Wells Public Library, especially Miss Jean Mauldon; Mr A. E. Buss, Marriott's Photo Stores, Tunbridge Wells.

From a list of over two hundred names, several of whom are old shipmates and friends, I would like to mention the following in particular: the late Major C. J. P. Ball; the late Dr C. J. Bashall; Major E. H. W. Banner; Cdr C. R. Bax, R.N.; Captain J. S. Bethell, R.N.; Rear-Admiral Sir R. Bevan (Flag Lt to Admiral Wemyss); Lady Elizabeth Binney; the late Major M. G. Bird; Captain L. A. K. Boswell, R.N.; the Hon. Mrs Helen Bowen-Pease (Josiah Wedgwood papers); Lt-Col Edwin Bowring, R.M.; Maj.-Gen. H. D. G. Butler; Sir Olaf Caroe; Captain A. W. Clarke, R.N.; Lt (S) A. H. K. Cobb, R.N.; Mr M. C. C. Crookshank; G. E. Dale; Captain H. M. Denham, R.N.; Captain P. G. Dickens, R.N.; Mrs R. K. Dickson; Mrs Douglas Dixon; Cdr C. H. Drage, R.N.; Rear-Admiral D. A. Dunbar-Nasmith; Rear-Admiral H. T. England; Mrs Irene Fisher (George Morgan papers); Judge Sir Gerald Fitzmaurice; Miss Olga Franklin, Matron-in-Chief (Retd), Q.A.R.N.N.S.; Captain F. C. Flynn, R.N.; Lt-Cdr F. E. Garner, R.N.; Mr Martin Gilbert; Cdr P. J. Hare, R.N.; Maj.-Gen. F. C. Horton, R.M.; Captain T. A. Hussey, R.N.; Miss R. M. Jerram; Lt-Cdr P. K. Kemp, R.N.; Lord Keyes; Lord Kinross; Cdr C. F. Laborde, R.N.; the late Captain H. C. Lockyer, R.N.; Vice-Admiral E. W. L. Longley-Cook; Vice-Admiral Sir A. Mansergh; Mrs Marguerite Maund (Doughty-Wylie papers);

Captain J. Savile Metcalf, R.N.R.; the late Cdr H. F. Minchin, R.N.; Rear-Admiral H. E. Morse; Vice-Admiral Sir H. G. Norman; Captain P. J. Norton, R.N. (Waterlow papers); Vice-Admiral R. D. Oliver; the late Cdr O. G. Ommanney, R.N.; Cdr R. A. B. Phillimore, R.N.; Captain M. J. Parkes-Buchanan, R.N.; Lt-Col M. J. Perreau; the late Col E. S. Phipson, I.M.S.; Mrs F. A. Rayfield; the late Mr Ernest Raymond; the late Lt-Cdr G. K. Rylands, R.N.; Col W. A. Salmon; Col R. H. Sayer; Lt-Gen. Sir R. Savory; Vice-Admiral B. B. Schofield; Rear-Admiral B. L. G. Sebastian; the late Major R. Sinclair, R.M.; Captain W. D. M. Staveley, R.N.; the late Vice-Admiral Sir G. Stephenson; Sir Leonard Stone; Cdr H. R. Tate, R.N.; Cdr D. S. E. Thompson, R.N.; Lt-Col E. N. Thursby; Brig. C. E. F. Turner; Captain P. N. Walter, R.N.; Captain S. W. Wareham, R.N.; Lt C. Watkins, R.A.F.; Mr William Weld Forester; Captain E. F. Wettern; Lieut. W. Corbett Williamson, R.M.; Captain A. M. Williams, R.N., and Cdr H. M. Wilson, R.N.; Cdr J. B. Woolley, R.N.; Cdr R. T. Young, R.N.

I wish to express my gratitude to the authors (or their executors, trustees or representatives) and publishers for permission to include their copyright material listed under 'References'. If by any inadvertence copyright material has been included for which I have failed to obtain permission, I hope my apologies will be accepted.

I am deeply indebted to Mrs Elizabeth Bullock for competing so efficiently with the exacting task of typing and checking the manuscript, and to Mrs Sabben-Clare for helping her. I also thank Mr Arthur Banks for his splendid maps.

I thank Lieutenant-General Sir James Wilson, Deputy Colonel, Lancashire, The Royal Regiment of Fusiliers, for permission to copy for the jacket design, their painting by Charles Dixon 'The Lancashire Landing'. This gives me much pleasure because, as first Captain of the 5th H.M.S. *Euryalus*, I have been a close friend of the Regiment for thirty-four years.

I am most grateful to The Rt. Hon. the Baroness Spencer-Churchill of Chartwell, Admiral of the Fleet the Earl Mountbatten of Burma, and to Lieutenant-General the Hon. Sir Edmund Herring of Australia, for their very kind messages of good will.

Finally I salute my wife Mollie for her encouragement and patience during a long haul.

ERIC BUSH
Langton Green,
Kent

Contents

Illustrations

Maps

I

To Gallipoli

*'Stirring times those which I love to recall; for they
were the days of gallantry and enthusiasm, and were
moreover the days of my boyhood.'*
George Borrow, 1803–1881
Lavengro

'Favoured! favoured!' a chorus of voices greeted me as I returned to
the gunroom, the midshipmen's mess of the cruiser *Bacchante*. Our
Captain, 'Algy' Boyle, had just told me that I was to take charge of
the picket boat when on active service. 'Why you?' the other midshipmen demanded. 'It should be the senior while you are the
junior . . . Favoured! Favoured!' – and so it went on.

There is an old saying in the Navy that seniority among midshipmen does not count and that the most suitable get the best
jobs. Actually I had been chosen because I was the smallest and
therefore the least likely to stop bullet or shell. However, after a
few days Douglas Dixon, the senior midshipman, was detailed for
the less powerful steam pinnace, and, to my relief, the tormenting
stopped.

Our ship had arrived at Port Said on 9th February 1915 to aid in
the defence of the Suez Canal and to patrol off the coasts of Palestine
and Asia Minor.

Six months earlier than that we midshipmen – there were nine of
us – had been first-term cadets – Blake term – at the Royal Naval
College, Dartmouth. Now we were war veterans, fifteen years old,
each one of us a man while still only a child.

A naval cadet of those days joined the Royal Naval College,
Osborne, in the Isle of Wight, for two years at the age of twelve and
a half. Then followed two further years at Dartmouth and six
months at sea in a training cruiser with finally an appointment to
the Fleet as midshipman at about seventeen and a half.

When the summer term of 1914 was half over, Winston Churchill,
First Lord of the Admiralty, came down to Dartmouth to look at us.

He must have been pleased with our potential officer-like qualities because on August 1st three days before the actual Declaration of War, a pre-arranged telegram 'Mobilise!' was received there. We got away in six hours, sea chests and all, 434 of us altogether, quite an achievement. The Admiralty had appointed us to ships of the Second Fleet, where it was hoped we could make ourselves useful and continue with our training in comparative safety. But it didn't work out that way. While the fully blown midshipmen of the Grand Fleet were impatiently waiting for *Der-Tag*, the day when the German High Sea Fleet would come out and fight, we in the Second Fleet were getting all the fun and most of the casualties as well. This explanation and a few pages which follow are necessary as an introduction to this book, because 90 per cent of the midshipmen at Gallipoli were the half-trained 'warts' whose naval education had been so rudely interrupted. Some were wounded while others never came back, but we in our humble way all helped to make history.

A first ship is of great importance. It can influence your outlook on naval life and shape your future career. Looking back now, I realise how fortunate we were to serve under Captain Boyle. A younger son of the Earl of Shannon, he was a bachelor, an ex-gunnery officer and a strict disciplinarian. We were scared stiff of him, but we had to admit that he was always efficient and sometimes very kind.

In harbour one day early in the commission the ceremony of hoisting the Colours was about to take place. The marine guard had paraded aft on the quarter-deck. Captain Boyle with the Officer of the Watch and the Midshipman of the Watch were in attendance.

'Eight o'clock, Sir!' reported the signalman.

'Make it so!' ordered the Captain; and the bugler sounded off, the guard presented arms and everyone on the upper deck stood to attention, facing aft, officers saluting.

Then the trouble started. 'Sound the "Carry on"!'

'What the devil are you doing on watch wearing a dirty shirt?' roared the Captain to the Midshipman of the Watch.

Poor Jack Phipps. We had to do our own washing, and he was adrift without one clean shirt to wear. After another midshipman had been found to relieve him, Phipps descended crestfallen to the chest-flat where he found the Captain's valet waiting for him with one of the skipper's own white shirts, beautifully laundered.

A midshipman of the First World War received the princely sum of 1s 9d a day, while his parents were required to pay the Admiralty a further £50 a year towards his education. We were allowed a wine-bill of 10s a month (no spirits), and we had to make a contribution towards our messing. If we put a foot wrong we had our backsides beaten – and why not? The punishment was quickly over. As for shore-going, there was little opportunity except occasionally for recreation. We were approaching adolescence, and sex was beginning to raise its head, but as we seldom saw girls they were seldom discussed, which gave peace of mind. We youngsters lived odd lives with death sometimes round the corner, yet we were surprisingly happy.

Captain Boyle must have had a difficult task commanding a ship's company made up largely of officers dug out for the war, and of reservist ratings. Only a few officers and a few key ratings were still on the Active List plus a handful of seamen boys from H.M.S. *Ganges* who, like ourselves, were about fifteen years of age or only a few months older. The Marine Detachment was half Royal Marine Light Infantry, known as Red Marines, and half Royal Marine Artillery, or Blue Marines, affectionately referred to as 'bullocks' because of their size. Amalgamation, with the overall title of Royal Marines, did not take place till 1923.

Our reservists had many trades and included postmen, dozens of them, and members of the Fire Brigade, a carry-over from the days of sail when seamen spent much of their time in the rigging. We had nineteen ex-policemen including Leading Signalman Ryan, a tall, chunky fellow with a drooping moustache (yes, a reservist could keep his moustache up if he so wished). Ryan loved to talk to us midshipmen. Perhaps he had young sons of his own. A conversation with him always ended the same way: 'See this scar?' he would say, holding up his thumb. 'Bitten by Miss Sylvia Pankhurst, I was, while trying to arrest her.'

We had joined the *Bacchante* at Sheerness, and on August 4th the day war was declared, we went out on patrol with our sister ships the *Euryalus, Aboukir, Hogue* and *Cressy*. Eight days later, on August 12th I celebrated my fifteenth birthday by keeping the middle watch, midnight to 4 a.m.

Our first excitement was the Battle of Heligoland Bight on August 28th. The Huns lost a few ships, but none of ours were sunk. Our squadron did not actually get engaged but after the battle was over we embarked casualties and German prisoners. Our P.M.O., Staff Surgeon Murray Levick, and his medical staff were kept busy, but he was accustomed to emergencies, having served with Captain Scott in the Antarctic.

It was an experience to watch badly wounded sailors being carried on board, some of them laughing and joking. I was not shaken exactly – just impressed.

We took them to Sheerness, then returned on patrol. On September 17th we docked at Chatham, followed by *Euryalus* four days later. On September 22nd while coaling ship and preparing for sea, we intercepted a wireless message to say that our sister ships the *Aboukir*, *Hogue* and *Cressy*, had been sunk by a U-boat. Casualties were very heavy. Many of our Blake Term were in the *Aboukir* and *Hogue* while some from the Greynvile Term were in the *Cressy*, and more than half of them all were lost.

The sinking of these three ships with the loss of so many ex-Dartmouth cadets – children, really – caused an outcry in the Press. A section of the British public could not understand how we boys could be of any use on board a ship in the grim business of war and demanded our recall to the College. But those most concerned, as is often the case, stuck up for us. On September 30th, *The Mother of a Dartmouth Cadet* wrote to the Editor of the *Morning Post*, 'If my son can best serve England by giving his life for her, I would not lift one finger to bring him home. If any act or word of mine should interfere with or take from him his grandest privilege, I could never look him in the face again.' Brave words, but typical of all our parents.

As far as our gunroom in the *Bacchante* was concerned, you may be sure we all prayed that we would not be sent back to the College. We reckoned that if this did happen it would be unfair, because we were really not much younger than those seamen boys who were already serving in most ships of the Fleet.

We lived on tenterhooks for several weeks, but finally, in the absence of any definite news, we began to feel more secure.

Winston Churchill did not in fact speak on the subject until 16th November 1914, when he was called upon to defend Admiralty policy. 'The decision to send the naval cadets from Dartmouth to sea in time of war,' he said, 'was arrived at a considerable time ago. It was felt that young officers of their age would be of great use on board His Majesty's ships, and that they would learn incomparably more of their profession in war than any educational establishment on shore could teach them. They are a regular part of the ship's complement.'

Churchill had set out his views in more detail when he replied to a letter from Lord Crewe on 1st October 1914. What he wrote is worth repeating: 'It wd be a vy harsh measure to deprive these young boys of an experience wh they will always look back to, & from wh their professional value is sensibly increased. We have had piteous appeals from the parents to allow their boys to go. I am assured they render useful services . . . I have satisfied myself that

naval opinion supports the present Admiralty practice. I asked that
it shd be carefully re-considered; but we were found united in keeping the lads at sea to take their chance. . . .'[1]

After a call at Malta for coal and a run ashore, we in the *Bacchante*
arrived at Port Said on 9th February 1915. Our presence there was
needed, as also that of the *Euryalus* which was ahead of us by a few
days. The Turks had made, at 3 a.m. on February 3rd, a brave attempt
to cross the Canal into Egypt at a point near Tussum, five miles
north of the Great Bitter Lake. Their boats were made of galvanised
steel, each capable of holding about thirty soldiers. They had been
hauled across the Sinai desert mounted on wheels, no mean feat. At
Tussum the banks are fifty feet high, so that nothing was detected
till the enemy was launching the first boat and sliding others down
the slope. It was dark with little moon, but the 62nd Punjabis, who
held this part of the line, saw them and opened fire. Most of the
boats had to be abandoned but three did succeed in crossing, although their occupants were promptly killed or made prisoners.
Next day, February 4th, a considerable body of the enemy was found
entrenched on the east bank. They showed a white flag but opened
fire as soon as our men advanced. However, they were soon overwhelmed. Among the killed was a German major.

If meant as a serious attack it was made with inadequate force
and inadequate preparation and was never within measurable distance of success. The only wonder is that it was not punished more
severely. There was no real pursuit on our part, not even a serious
attempt to harass the retreat towards El Arish. Yet the Turkish losses
must have been at least 2,000, besides a number of men drowned in
the Canal. Our own casualties amounted to some 150. This victory
had the unfortunate effect of giving our troops a false impression of
the fighting qualities of the Turkish soldier, which was to prove a
handicap at Gallipoli.

After coaling ship on February 9th by native labour – a rare treat for
us! – we embarked Major the Hon. Aubrey Herbert (brother of the
Earl of Carnarvon who discovered Tutankhamen's tomb in 1922),
interpreter in Turkish and Arabic, as Military Intelligence Officer.
Then off we went to bombard the Turkish fort at El Arish on the
Sinai coast. Continuing north we closed Joppa (now Tel Aviv –
Jaffa) but found nothing to interest us there except that our Fleet
Paymaster James Cox purchased a boat-load of oranges for the

ship's company. They were sold on board at twelve a penny. I bought a suitcase full, with dire results.

There followed visits to Haifa and Beirut, where we watched an American cruiser taking off refugees. Finally we fetched up at Alexandretta (Iskenderun), where our Captain took over the duties of Senior Naval Officer, Syrian Coast, from H.M.S. *Doris*, Captain Frank Larken.

The main purpose of our visits to these ports was to obtain intelligence through contacts made by Aubrey Herbert. It soon became clear that the Turks were expecting an Allied landing somewhere along the coast. To them and to a section of British opinion, such an attack seemed the obvious way of relieving Turkish pressure on Egypt and on Mesopotamia (now Iraq). It was while we were at Alexandretta that the Allied Fleet began, on 19th February 1915, the bombardment of the Outer Forts of the Dardanelles. This did not affect us, at least for the time being.

The railway line from Constantinople (now Istanbul) passed south through Asia Minor and Syria, close to the shore at Alexandretta. Here there was a branch-line by Jonah's Pillar, the old Syrian Gates, a point on shore near where, according to legend, Jonah was disgorged by the whale. The line had already been cut and rolling stock destroyed by a landing party from the *Doris*, which left us with the task of watching the coast road, where wagons loaded with artillery wheels were said to pass north for the Turkish army. By day we patrolled the coast. After dark we lay at anchor keeping the road in the beam of a searchlight.

One forenoon the long-expected carts arrived crawling along the foreshore, each drawn by a pair of bullocks. Captain Boyle hated the idea of firing at the defenceless drivers so ordered a warning shot to be placed ahead of the convoy. The Turks immediately left their oxen and dived into a ditch, while their beasts went slowly forward alone, like automata. We now fired a second round which injured a leading animal. Poor thing, how it bellowed and struggled. The sight was too much for its driver, who emerged from the ditch, cut the bullock free and then, grasping the harness of its fellow, made an attempt to lead the procession. Again a warning shot was fired 'across his bows', but the driver went steadfastly on to what he must have known was certain death. In the end he was left lying by his oxen and their broken carts. We had given him every chance. If the admiration of our ship's company could reward a dead Anatolian for his courage the reward was his. We loathed the whole thing.

Next day an Anatolian Turkish official representing the local Governor came off to see the Captain. His get-up was a dark brown suit rather the worse for wear, a coloured shirt none too fresh, a tie badly knotted and out of place and of course the inevitable fez. On his great flat feet he wore a pair of unpolished brown boots.

After much salaaming and bowing from the boat, he mounted the accommodation ladder and stepped on to the quarter-deck.

'Hoş geldiniz – you are welcome,' said Aubrey Herbert interpreting for the Captain, who looked, as always, very regal in his blue uniform with medal ribbons, telescope under left arm, right hand at the salute. After hand-shakes all round the three disappeared down the after hatch-way into the Captain's cabin.

What went on between decks I do not know beyond the fact that when Aubrey Herbert expressed Captain Boyle's regret over the death of the Anatolian the official remarked that it was an incident beneath his dignity to notice.

'Allahaismarladik – farewell,' said Aubrey Herbert, as the blighter went down the gangway into his boat. We were glad to see the back of him.

Threat of a further attack on the Suez Canal brought us again to Port Said where news reached us of the failure of the Navy's grand attack on the forts at the Dardanelles on March 18th. Transports full of troops now passed north through the canal in ever increasing numbers. We cheered them as they went by. It was clear that there was going to be a landing.

On April 9th we were recalled to Port Said. Next day we put to sea in company with our old friend the *Euryalus*. Bowing to the statue of de Lesseps at the end of the long breakwater, we shaped course for Port Mudros, to play our part in the Gallipoli campaign.

Making passage of the Karpathos Strait, by Rhodes, island of the Knights of St John, then through the Dodecanese, we entered the Aegean Sea. With Mytilene (now Lesbos) showing up on our starboard hand, and Skyros to port, we set course on the final leg of our journey.

At 1.50 p.m. on April 12th we passed Kombi Point, Lemnos, and anchored in the crowded harbour. We had joined the flag of Vice-Admiral John de Robeck, Commander-in-Chief, Eastern Mediterranean Fleet.

2

A Naval Beginning

'There must be a beginning of any great matter, but the continuing unto the end until it be thoroughly finished yields the true glory.'
Sir Francis Drake to Lord Walsingham,
17th May 1582

When war with Germany began on 4th August 1914 it was generally expected that she would walk over France in a few weeks. Alternatively, if she did not do that our Russian ally, by sheer weight of numbers, might roll all the way to Berlin, arriving there before Christmas. As it turned out neither of these two things happened. The Germans failed – though they only just failed – to accomplish what was expected of them. Then the Russian steam-roller, though it did incalculable service by causing the Germans to detach troops to their Eastern Front, ran out of steam. The two sides had become fairly well balanced, until Turkey, three months later, came in on the side of the Central Powers.

We had been on good terms with Turkey for many years but had lost favour there recently and Germany had not been slow to take up the role of her friend. A British Naval Mission was in Constantinople from 1912, under the direction of Rear-Admiral Arthur Limpus who was appointed Naval Adviser to the Turkish Government. His relations with the Turks were cordial, and his mission had won considerable esteem, until in 1913 a German Military Mission, led by a Prussian General of Cavalry called Liman von Sanders, arrived with a large staff. Von Sanders at once began to act as a kind of Inspector-General of Turkish forces, which was well calculated to put Admiral Limpus's nose out of joint.

Relations were not improved when the Allies refused Turkey loans which Berlin hastened to advance, and the final blow came when we cancelled delivery of two Dreadnought battleships which were being built in Great Britain for the Turkish Navy. The cost of these two ships (£3,680,650) had been met in part by gifts from peasants and from other patriotic Turks. Although not yet actually commissioned, they had already been named *Reshadieh* and *Sultan Osman I*, and Turkish seamen specialists were standing by the ships while still in dockyard hands. When completed the *Reshadieh* was re-named H.M.S. *Erin*, with Captain the Hon. Victor Stanley, our skipper at Dartmouth, in command; and the *Sultan Osman I* the *Agincourt*, Captain Henry Montagu Doughty of Theberton Hall, Suffolk, a brother of Lieutenant-Colonel C. H. M. 'Dick' Doughty-Wylie, V.C., of V Beach fame. Both ships fought at Jutland.

Needless to say, German diplomats took instant advantage of the anger caused by this cancellation, and their next diplomatic move was decisive.

At the end of July 1914 the new German battle-cruiser *Goeben*, with the light cruiser *Breslau*, had entered the Mediterranean. The *Goeben* mounted ten 11-inch guns and had a secondary armament of twelve 5·9s. Her designed speed was twenty-seven knots, although actually she could only do twenty-four, but she was superior in arma-ment to any capital ship we had in the Mediterranean at that time, while the *Breslau* with twenty-seven knots was superior to our light cruisers in speed, though not in gun-power. Both ships were under the command of Rear-Admiral Wilhelm Souchon, an officer of marked ability.

On August 2nd the *Goeben* and *Breslau* arrived at Messina, on the north-east coast of Sicily. Two days later they left to bombard Bone and Phillipeville in order to interfere with the transport of French troops from Tunisia to the Western Front. Arriving back in Messina early on the 5th they immediately began to coal. It took them two days and a night to complete to full capacity.

Admiral Souchon had received a wireless message from Berlin on the morning of the 4th informing him that an alliance had been concluded with Turkey on August 2nd (not known to the Allies until much later), and instructing him to proceed to Constantinople with all dispatch. At about the same time the Italians told Souchon that in view of Italy's neutrality his ships would be interned if they did not shove off when coaling was completed.

Accordingly, at 5 p.m. on August 6th, Souchon, having made his Will, duly put to sea, bands playing, ships cleared for action. He very skilfully evaded our fleet and reached Constantinople on August 10th.

While infuriated Allied Ambassadors demanded immediate intern-ment, the wily Kaiser played his trump card. He nominally sold (or presented) to Turkey these two valuable warships. On 16th August 1914, in the presence of Sultan Mehmed V and with much handclapping, both ships were enrolled in the Turkish Navy. The German ships' companies exchanged their uniform caps for the fez and embarked a few Turkish officers and ratings to justify the ships wearing the Turkish ensign. Rear-Admiral Souchon was appointed Commander-in-Chief, Turkish Fleet.

This clever piece of diplomacy was followed by the promotion of General Liman von Sanders to the post of Military Commander-in-Chief. Fresh loans were advanced, and a Pan-Islamic movement was fostered in Asia Minor, Egypt and Persia and attempted in Northern India. Rumours were also spread that the Kaiser had adopted the Islamic faith.

Turkey's reactions, however, were not immediate. Possibly the Sultan was still clinging to his respect and affection for England, feelings shared by a large number of his subjects, among whom tradition has always died hard. But at this period in history the Young Turk party – the War party – dominated the scene. Convinced that the Central Powers were going to win the war, they had visions of the British Empire breaking up, with Egypt being returned to Turkey when the share-out took place. They also hoped for the return of territory on the Caucasus side, including the oil fields at Baku. Italy had not yet joined the Allies, but she had in effect thrown over the Central Powers, so that when the Allies were defeated, there might be a good chance of recovering Tripoli and the Dodecanese.

Since the *Goeben* and the *Breslau* had escaped into the Bosphorus a British squadron had been stationed off the entrance to the Dardanelles to ensure that they did not come out again. On September 21st Vice-Admiral Sackville Carden, in charge of Malta Dockyard, was relieved by Rear-Admiral Limpus and appointed in command of the blockading squadron. Although we were not yet at war with Turkey, Admiral Carden was given specific orders to 'sink the *Goeben* and the *Breslau*, no matter what flag they fly', if they attempted to escape. 'Turks have been told,' the message continued, 'that any Turkish ships which come out with them will be equally attacked by us. . . . We do not want to pick a quarrel with Turkey unless her hostile intention is clear.'

Matters soon came to a head. On October 27th Rear-Admiral Souchon took the *Goeben* and the *Breslau*, the Turkish cruiser *Hamidieh* and a division of torpedo-boats into the Black Sea and bombarded the Russian fortress of Sevastopol, sank a Russian minelayer, raided the harbour of Odessa, torpedoed a gunboat and finally caused considerable damage to oil tanks and shipping in the port of Novoros-

sisk. That put the lid on it. Turkey was in the war on the side of
the Central Powers.

'O Moslems!' announced the Sultan, 'Ye who are smitten with
happiness and are on the verge of sacrificing your life and your goods
for the cause of right and are braving perils, gather now round the
Imperial throne, obey the commands of the Almighty, who, in the
Qu'rān, promises us bliss in this world and the next. Embrace ye the
foot of the Caliph's throne and join in the *Jihād*, the Holy War. Warfare is ordained for you. Your enemies will not cease until they have
made you renegades from your religion if they can. Drive them out!
If they attack you, slay them. Such is the reward of unbelievers.'

On November 3rd, only two days after Great Britain had declared war
on Turkey, Admiral Carden led his squadron in an attack on the
forts at the entrance to the Dardanelles.

The battle-cruisers *Indefatigable* (flag) and the *Indomitable*, bombarded the batteries on the Gallipoli side by Sedd el Bahr, while two
French battleships the *Suffren* and the *Verité* took on the forts on the
Asiatic shore around Kum Kāle. The ships steamed past the forts at
a range of 13,000 yards and fired eighty shells. The Turkish gunners
replied and kept up their fire, although none of our ships ever came
within their gun range. One round from the *Indomitable* exploded a
magazine ashore. No other worthwhile damage was done. When the
run was over, ships returned to base without having received a scratch.

It has been said that this was a useless operation, which accomplished nothing except to put the Turks on their guard and to make
them strengthen their defences. That may be so, yet, three-and-a-half
months later on 19th February 1915, when Admiral Carden again
bombarded these same forts, the Gallipoli Peninsula was, as we shall
see, found still unprepared for defence and still weakly occupied.
But the point which has impressed me most is that on this first
occasion Turkish gunners fired wildly, wasting precious ammunition.
Thereafter they learnt to hold their fire until ships were within
range and to keep their heads down until their fire could be effective.
This practice was to be extended to rifle and machine-gun fire at the
landings, and our men suffered severely in consequence.

The idea of a serious attack on the Dardanelles was discussed at the
first meeting of the War Council, 25th November 1914, in the course of
discussions on measures for the defence of Egypt. Winston Churchill
suggested, with the 'hearty concurrence' of Fisher, the First Sea

Lord, a joint attack on the Gallipoli Peninsula as 'the ideal method' for defending Egypt, because a successful attack would mean control of the Dardanelles and the ability to dictate terms to Turkey. The proposal ran into a Kitchener *non possumus:* troops were not available. The immense authority and enormous prestige of this strong, silent man of awesome presence, who was at once War Secretary and virtually his own Chief of Staff, plus his well-known resentment of criticism, were such that, 'When he gave a decision,' Churchill told the Dardanelles Commissioners, 'it was invariably accepted as final. He was never, to my belief, overruled by the War Council or the Cabinet in any military matter, great or small. . . . Scarcely anyone ever ventured to argue with him in Council. . . . All-powerful, imperturbable, reserved, he dominated absolutely our counsels at this time.'[1]

At the turn of the year the Government was engaged in an inquiry into the best field of operations for the new armies, the reinforced fleets and the large quantities of *matériel* of all kinds which would be ready in the Spring of 1915.

There was an urgent need to decide between sharply conflicting strategic alternatives. On the one side were the 'Westerners', the leading generals, supported by the French Government and French High Command, who maintained that the decisive area was France, that the path of victory lay over the corpses of German soldiers and through the line of enemy entrenchments and that the withdrawal of troops for operations elsewhere might expose the Allies to crushing and possibly irretrievable defeat. This position was anathema to the 'Easterners', who, seeing no possibility of a break-through in the mud, barbed-wire and trenches of France, wanted to find an alternative theatre of war for the new armies. For them the key to victory lay in an offensive somewhere in the Near East, a campaign that would knock out Turkey and coax Italy and the Balkan Neutrals into the war on the Allied side. The discussion of alternative strategies did not relate to any specific military arguments, since the troops and munitions would not be available until the spring. Asquith, the Prime Minister, stood poised in the War Council between the two schools of thought.

The argument was decided on 2nd January 1915. Turkish pressure on the Russian armies in the Caucasus had been giving cause for serious anxiety. A telegram came from our Ambassador in St Petersburg (now Petrograd) to say that the Grand Duke Nicholas, Commander-in-Chief, had asked whether it would be possible for Great Britain to arrange a demonstration of some kind against the Turks to ease the pressure on the Russians.

1 H.M.S. *Bacchante*

2 *Bacchante* midshipmen, 1914.
From left to right: Alan Hillgarth, Tom Bashall (both wounded at Gallipoli), the author, Jack Phipps, Douglas Dixon, Stanley Lloyd Vereker, John Tennant, R. H. D. Olivier, H. A. Barclay (killed in action 1940)

4   Rear-Admiral R. E. Wemyss

3   Captain The Hon. A. D. E. H. Boyle

5   Major Aubrey Herbert, M.P.

6   Major-General W. T. Bridges, Command
First Australian Division

Lord Kitchener in his reply said that steps would be taken, although it was feared that any action which could be devised would be unlikely seriously to affect the numbers of the enemy in the Caucasus or to cause their withdrawal. This answer committed us to an operation of some kind, but it did not commit us in respect of its direction, character or scope. It was the very least that could have been said in answer to a request from a hard-pressed Ally.

The time and method of the demonstration had now to be decided. Lord Kitchener felt the only place that a demonstration might have some effect in stopping reinforcements going East (Adrianople to the Caucasus) would be the Dardanelles. He insisted that it would have to be a naval operation, since we would not be ready for anything involving large numbers of troops 'for some months'.

Apart from any assistance it might render to the Grand Duke, a successful attack on the Dardanelles would have far-reaching results. The Turkish Empire would be cut in two; a sea passage would be open to Russia, allowing munitions to be passed to her at a time when her northern ports were closed on account of ice; Russian wheat could be exported again, which would restore her exchanges; German communication with the Middle East would be severed; the defence of Egypt would be secure; and the Mesopotamian Campaign would either be rendered unnecessary or would be more speedily successful. Bulgaria would be held steady in neutrality or brought into our alliance, and all entanglements with Greece would have been averted. The Allies would in effect have surrounded the Central Powers with an iron circle.

Winston Churchill did not at first commit himself, but on the morning of January 3rd, Admiral Fisher produced, with the help of Lieutenant-Colonel Maurice Hankey, Secretary, Committee of Imperial Defence, a 'Turkey Plan'. It involved a landing in Besika Bay and depended upon the release of troops from the Western Front and the co-operation of Bulgaria and Greece who were neutral with their intentions not yet declared. Although the Plan was never even discussed by the Cabinet it was the first time a responsible admiral had mentioned the forcing of the Straits by the Navy.

'I think we had better hear what the others have to say about the Turkey Plans,' Churchill wrote in his reply to Fisher. 'I would not grudge 100,000 men, because of the great political effects in the Balkan Peninsula; but Germany is the foe . . .' Next day, January 5th, Churchill telegraphed to Vice-Admiral Carden, whose small squadron lay off the Dardanelles:

'Do you think that it is a practicable operation to force the Dardanelles by the use of ships alone? It is assumed that older battleships would be employed ... the importance of the results would justify severe loss.'

On January 5th Carden replied to the effect that he did not think the Dardanelles could be rushed, but might be forced by extended operations with a large number of ships. Next day Churchill answered, 'High authorities here concur in your opinion. Forward detailed particulars . . .'[2]

The War Council, after heated discussions, the crucial one being on January 13th when Churchill pleaded vehemently for troops, but was overruled, plus a threat by Admiral Fisher to resign, reached its final decisions on January 28th. An attempt would be made by the Navy alone to force the Dardanelles, with Constantinople as the objective. Experience could only show the effect of naval guns against the defences, fixed and mobile. An attack would first be made by a few ships against the Outer Forts. Should this preliminary attack prove successful the operations would be continued and a powerful force concentrated. If unsuccessful, attention could be diverted elsewhere and the operations broken off. A preliminary attack would do no harm and would only have the effect of a diversion.

The decision thus arrived at on 28th January 1915 marks the first great landmark in the history of the Gallipoli Campaign. In an effort to satisfy the urgent need of diplomacy, an Allied Fleet was to attempt, without the aid of a single soldier, an enterprise which in the earlier days of the War the Admiralty and War Office had regarded as a military task. The operations would be more difficult but still capable of accomplishment if the inevitable loss of ships could be accepted. This opinion, it was learnt later, was shared by the German Rear-Admiral von Usedom who, as Inspector General of Coast Artillery and Mines, knew better than anyone the strength and weakness of the fortress and the capacity of its defenders. Incidentally, Usedom was well known in Royal Naval circles as leader of the detachment of German sailors placed under command of Captain (later Earl) Jellicoe during the Boxer Rebellion in China, 1899–1900. 'Germans to the front – *Aleman asker, top beschina!*' ordered Jellicoe before he himself was severely wounded. The two navies were friends then. Now they were foes.

It is so easy to say that this purely Naval attack added enormously to the difficulties of the military attack which followed, or that we made this mistake or that; but the one certain fact is that a moment did arrive when brave decisions had to be made in order to carry the enterprise to a victorious issue and when those with whom the responsibility lay faltered. In the words of Winston Churchill seven years later, '*Not to persevere, that was the crime.*'[3]

3

Fall of the Outer Forts

The Dardanelles, the ancient Hellespont, is forty-one miles long from its mouth at Cape Helles in the Aegean Sea to the Sea of Marmara. It is two miles wide between Cape Helles and Kum Kāle, broadens to a maximum of four miles in Eren Keui Bay, eight miles from the sea, and closes again to a breadth of less than two miles at Kephez Point. In the Narrows between Chanak and Kilid Bahr the width is only three-quarters of a mile, but it extends again to an average width of four miles for the last stretch to the entrance to the Sea of Marmara, abreast Gallipoli town. Throughout its entire length it is a deep-water channel, of from twenty-five to fifty fathoms.

A current of around two to four knots flows from the Sea of Marmara down the Dardanelles into the Mediterranean. A northerly wind increases this current. A southerly wind can whip up a nasty sea. The flow is faster on the Peninsula side, where the shore is steep. On the Asian coast in the vicinity of Eren Keui Bay a counter-current, running slowly north, may be encountered where the water shallows close inshore.

In 1915 the Defences of the Dardanelles included forts, mobile howitzers, minefields and minefield batteries. There were also several powerful searchlights carefully concealed. Torpedo-tubes mounted ashore were regarded as a possibility. There were in fact two tin-pot affairs which could easily have been demolished by gunfire had they been seen.

The forts – Outer (entrance), Intermediate and Inner (Narrows) – mounted a total of about 150 heavy guns varying in calibre from 6-inch to 14-inch. Many were obsolescent, firing shell of low velocity and taking several minutes to re-load. The extreme range of the most modern guns was 15,000 yards.

Mobile howitzers were embodied in the scheme of defence to harass the bombarding ships and thus spoil the accuracy of their fire. The minefield batteries were there to concentrate on enemy minesweepers attempting to clear the minefields. In the opinion of General Liman von Sanders the minefields were the primary defence, as indeed they proved to be.

At this period of British naval architecture the old battleship stood on a far lower plane than in any previous epoch. Until the Dreadnought era, which began in 1905, the oldest was fit to be put into line with the newest. Now, however, we were left with battleships that could not be used in a fleet action but which were still actually, though not relatively, powerful instruments of war. These older ships were doomed to be scrapped in 1916 as their crews would be needed to man the great fleets and flotillas about to be completed. In the meantime, however, they were thought to prove a match for the Turkish defences, especially when supported by cruisers, by *Beagle* (860 tons) and *River* (550 tons) class destroyers and by trawlers from our fishing-fleets fitted for minesweeping.

With regard to the latter, there was a certain tough guy, Captain E. C. 'Nutty' Carver, Royal Navy, who was sent to Grimsby and other fishing ports to knock some sense of discipline into the skippers of trawlers taken over by the Admiralty for minesweeping. Later Captain Carver was sent out to Gallipoli. Some of his trawlers had come out too. One day while wending his way through strange waters a skipper heard a familiar voice letting fly in no uncertain terms. It was 'Nutty' Carver's of course. 'Five thousand . . . miles and the same b . . . d's b . . . y voice at the end of it!' the skipper is reputed to have said. No one who served with 'Nutty' Carver is likely to forget him. They don't breed 'em like that today.

In the early days of the operations it was found possible to make further important additions. H.M. ships *Agamemnon* (an appropriate name for this area), and *Lord Nelson*, milestones in the path of Dreadnought construction, joined the fleet. It was also decided that the battle cruiser *Inflexible*, fresh from the Falkland Island's battle, could be spared, and, more important still, the *Queen Elizabeth*, the first ship in the world's navies to mount 15-inch guns. These two powerful ships would be more than a match for the *Goeben* and *Breslau*. Other additions included H.M.S. *Ark Royal*, the first seaplane carrier to be built for the Royal Navy (she was designed as a tramp steamer and had a large aircraft launching platform built over her bows), H.M.S. *Manica*, balloon ship, also a merchantman, and two dummy battle-cruisers. These dummies were merchant ships cleverly disguised in Belfast to make the Germans think we had reduced the margin of our naval strength in Home Waters. The ruse worked, for we know now that the Turks reported one to Germany as the *Tiger*, and another was sunk by *U-21*. As for submarines, five 'B' class (old) and the Australian *AE2* ('E' class, modern) were also attached to the Fleet.

The French were invited to help and they sent four old battle-ships, a few submarines and some small craft.

The plan of attack drawn up by Vice-Admiral Carden was based on several main phases. The first phase was to reduce the defences at the entrance to the Straits. The next was to sweep the minefields and reduce the defences up to the Narrows. A reduction of the forts in the Narrows would then follow, and the principal minefield, which was off Kephez Point, would be swept. Finally, after silencing the forts above the Narrows, the fleet would advance into the Sea of Marmara. The whole programme was expected to take one month.

It was important to conserve ammunition, not only because there was a shortage but also for fear of wearing out ships' guns. Premature explosions did occur, as the result of firing high-explosive shells fitted with very sensitive fuses from guns long past their normal life and for which no replacements were available. The shell, instead of sliding smoothly down the bore, would tend to 'rattle' and on reaching the muzzle to tip just enough to jam slightly and so decelerate and set off the fuse. In the *Bacchante*, later on in the Campaign, our for'ard 9·2-inch gun cracked from over use and could not be fired at all during the closing stages, which was a serious matter.

In dealing with the forts, the general principle was an attack in three stages: a long-range bombardment (direct, or indirect with air-craft spotting) out of range or bearing of the enemy's guns, was followed by a bombardment at medium ranges using secondary armament and direct fire. Finally the forts would be smothered by overwhelming gunfire at point-blank range.

Importance was attached to ships not being hit in the initial stages. If they came under unexpected fire they were to withdraw and resume the long-range bombardment. The foundation of the whole plan was that battleships would only fight and manoeuvre in waters which had been thoroughly swept and were known to be clear of mines.

At nine minutes to ten on the morning of 19th February 1915 the battle began. It was the anniversary of the day on which Admiral Duckworth had rushed the Straits in 1807, a remarkable coincidence. The honour of firing the opening round went to Chief Petty Officer Davis of *Cornwallis*, Captain A. P. Davidson. Vice-Admiral Sackville Carden flew his flag in the *Inflexible*, and Rear-Admiral John de Robeck, Second-in-Command, wore his in the *Vengeance*, Captain

B. H. Smith, a recent arrival from Cape Verde. Other battleships in support included the *Albion*, Captain A. W. Heneage, from service in the Cameroons, the *Triumph*, Captain Maurice Fitzmaurice, from the China Station. Rear-Admiral Guépratte flew his flag in the *Suffren* and had in company the *Gaulois*, Captain Biard, and the *Bouvet*, Captain Rageot de la Touche.

The main forts to be destroyed were four in number, two on either side of the entrance. One stood on the cliff of Cape Helles just to the left of the shelving amphitheatre later celebrated as 'V' Beach. Another lay low down, on the right of the same beach, close in front of the medieval castle of Sedd el Bahr, where huge cannon balls of stone were to be found lying in heaps or scattered over the ground, cannon balls like those which were hurled at Duckworth's fleet more than a century before.

Upon the Asiatic side stood the fort of Kum Kāle, at the very mouth of the Strait not far from the cliff village of Yeni Shehr and separated from the plain of Troy by the river Mendere. About a mile along the coast was the fort of Orhanie. None of these four forts was heavily armed.

At first the fleet was kept under way, but it soon became apparent that moving ships could not achieve sufficient accuracy of fire, so they were ordered to anchor outside range and bearing of the enemy guns. There could be no blazing away at the forts. The fire from the ships had to be slow and deliberate, often with a single gun, the fall of shot being observed and corrected before the next round could be fired. All this took time, and it was 2 p.m. before Admiral Carden was satisfied that the forts had received enough punishment at long range. Out of the clouds of smoke and dust that enveloped the shore came no sign of life. The order to weigh anchor was given and the fleet closed the range, whereupon something happened that forebode ill for the future. Our ships were met by a brisk fire from the forts on both sides of the Dardanelles, just as if they had never been touched.

At 5.20 p.m. Vice-Admiral Carden, judging that it was too late to do any more that evening, hoisted the 'general recall'. The light to landward was failing, with our ships clearly silhouetted against the western sky. Admiral de Robeck protested, but Carden insisted, as he had every intention of returning next morning. Luck, however, was against him, for the weather broke during the night and the Allied fleet was forced to seek shelter under the lee of Tenedos, fifteen miles away. It would seem that Allah was on the side of the Turks.

The result of the day's action had clearly shown that the effect of long-range bombardment by ships on modern earthworks was apt to be slight. This lesson was repeated time after time throughout the Campaign. The big naval shells threw up stones and earth as from volcanoes and caused great alarm, but the alarm was only temporary and the effect, whether on earthworks or trenches, was disappointing. Naval guns had too flat a trajectory to produce the plunging fire, as of howitzers, which really devastates.

A contemporary Turkish report stated that a German lieutenant was lying on his stomach observing fall of shot from the earthworks above one of these forts when a 12-inch shell struck the earth below him. The shell passed through the ground and detonated some distance in rear. The officer's clothes were torn off and he was badly burnt but was soon able to return to duty. The battery remained unharmed.

This report is understandable. Ammunition supplied to a warship was for use in a sea battle. The delayed action fuse was to enable the shell to penetrate armour and burst in a ship's vitals.

Expectation of crushing the Dardanelles defences by the big guns of the *Queen Elizabeth* and of the *Inflexible* was from the outset seriously diminished.

Weather in the Aegean can be damnable between November and April. One day it will be calm and clear and mild; the next day it may be stormy with violent northerly winds bringing low cloud, rain squalls and even snow. Again after a short interval, the wind may suddenly veer to the south, heralding calmer weather and blue skies. On the whole, too, the weather during those months varies from year to year. One year the winter can be severe with heavy falls of snow. Another year snow may be seen only once or twice. I have personally made passage of the Dardanelles between November and April half a dozen times during the last few years and only on one of these occasions could it be said that the weather was perfect for long-range firings, given the equipment and the ships of 1915.

Rude Boreas often made a nuisance of himself during the Campaign, but to give him his due, he had his gentler moments.

It must have been infuriating for Vice-Admiral Carden and the officers and men of his fleet to be forced to ride out a gale for four days and nights with driving rain and heavy seas, when they were itching to get on with the battle. But for the inhabitants of Tenedos the storm was a godsend. Locals braved the elements and came off in boats to sell vegetables and olives and to take a closer look at the ships, while their womenfolk and children swarmed over the peculiar cone-shaped hill which dominates the red-roofed village. There, among the windmills, they sat and stared. Monotony was broken. They were having the time of their lives. It is an ill wind that blows nobody any good.

During these days of waiting the question of military aid again came up. There was an exchange of telegrams between Admiral Carden and the Admiralty. His Chief of Staff, Commodore Roger Keyes, urged that preparations for military operations on a large scale should be expedited to ensure that the Straits were kept open for further operations, if the first appearance of the fleet off Constantinople did not have the desired effect. After all, who could be sure that the Turks with their huge army still intact and with the Teutonic influence behind them would capitulate? And, if they stood fast, what could we do? Bombard Constantinople? No, we could not.

After spending the winter blockading the entrance to the Dardanelles Vice-Admiral Carden knew that it was out of the question to attempt landings on a large scale so early in the year, but he did tell the Admiralty that if troops were made avialable now he was prepared to make a feint in the Gulf of Xeros without disembarkation. He added that if the Fleet's progress was interrupted seriously, especially by concealed guns, military occupation of the southern part of the Gallipoli Peninsula, say up to and including the hill called Achi Baba, might become a necessity.

On February 25th the weather had moderated sufficiently to allow a renewal of the bombardment, with a view to the destruction of the forts at decisive range, and the beginning of minesweeping in a serious way. The forts were silenced by noon, and at 3 p.m. the minesweepers were ordered to advance. Incidentally, no seaplanes had put in an appearance. Bad weather had prevented them from flying since the 19th and now it was almost too calm for them to rise off the water. When eventually they did get up, they could not reach any useful height and were a target for Turkish rifle fire.

The only casualties of the day were suffered by *Agamemnon*. 'We dropped anchor too close to Fort Orhanie,' Lieutenant Godfrey Crookshank (who was killed by an elephant while on safari in 1933), recorded in his log, 'and only the turrets' crews required were kept closed up. Some men were employed painting. Suddenly three 9·4-inch shells came aboard, and we suffered three killed and seven wounded. Among the seriously wounded was Chief Yeoman of Signals Albert Arthur Bishop, a fine man with fifteen years' service. His left leg was shattered. In spite of suffering excruciating pain he managed to raise himself into a sitting position and carried on with his duties until he collapsed from loss of blood. On return to harbour he was transferred to the hospital ship *Soudan*, where his leg was amputated.

'I felt quite surprised,' said Crookshank, 'how little I seemed to worry during the battle; but it isn't swanky to say so because everyone else was the same. It was just like gun practice. All the Turkish "projs" burst on striking the water. They were evidently firing at extreme range, as the angle of descent was so steep that none of the shots "rickered".'

In spite of the weight of shell which came aboard the *Agamemnon*, the damage was surprisingly slight. This was a comfort and confirmed that projectiles fired from some of the forts were of an obsolete pattern. Secret intelligence reports of this period suggested that the money voted by the Turkish Ministry of Defence for the purchase of lyddite shell had found its way to another quarter.

On February 26th the weather had again deteriorated and little could be done. On the 27th, however, parties of seamen and marines were landed and blew up all the remaining guns in the Outer Forts.

The *Vengeance* party was the first to land. It consisted of fifty marines under Major G. M. Heriot and a demolition party under Lieutenant-Commander E. G. 'Kipper' Robinson, who, in accordance with naval practice, wore his sword in this battle – probably one of the last times anyone did. The party's instructions were to deal with Kum Kāle and push on to Orhanie to destroy the guns in that battery and also two anti aircraft guns which had been located at Achilles Tomb. (There is a legend that no bird will fly over the ground which marks the site.) They were also to complete the destruction of the bridge over the Mendere River. It was an ambitious programme but one successfully accomplished, thanks to the personal courage of Kipper Robinson and to covering fire from H.M. ships.

The *Irresistible*'s landing party under Lieutenant Francis Sandford also did well at Sedd el Bahr, and on a later date on the Asiatic side. The comparative ease with which landing parties were able to disembark was encouraging, and a feeling of optimism ran through the fleet. This optimism was expressed in no mean terms by Rear-Admiral Guépratte, who stood at the salute in a prominent position on the bridge of his flagship as he led his squadron out of the Straits, while the French bands played 'God Save the King' and 'Tipperary'. Our ships returned the compliment with 'The Marseillaise', plus three rousing cheers.

4

The Greater Struggle

News of the fall of the Outer Forts made a deep impression over the whole field of war. In Constantinople a break through by the Allied fleet was anticipated, and plans were made for the Sultan, Court and Treasury to seek refuge in the interior. Greece expressed willingness to join in the campaign and to send us an army corps, but this generous offer was vetoed by Russia, who demanded a public declaration about the future, stipulating that the question of the Straits and the capital should be settled in conformity with Russian wishes. The Turks, fearing Bulgaria might side with the Allies, detached an army to Adrianople to develop that front against possible invasion. Italy opened the negotiations which led to her declaration of war against Austria on May 23rd. Far away in Chicago wheat prices fell abruptly.

While the attention of so many countries was riveted upon the Dardanelles, with so many profound and far-reaching reactions, the progress of the naval attack unfortunately began to slow down. The weather was frequently unsuitable for long-range firing, and seaplanes proved inadequate for spotting. Mobile howitzers, which now operated in larger numbers every day from both sides of the Straits, harassed the bombarding ships incessantly. Landing parties sent ashore met with stiffer resistance, and attempts to sweep the minefields encountered much heavier Turkish fire. However, the operations were persisted in, and piecemeal reductions of the forts effected. Here are examples of some of the difficulties with which the fleet was faced.

The bombarding squadron for March 4th, for instance, passed up the Straits to a position beyond the village of Eren Keui, conspicuous upon a mountainside on the Asiatic coast, and bombarded Fort Dardanos. The fort stands upon Kephez Point, which projects from the very entrance to the Narrows. Over the top of this promontory the houses and mosques of Chanak and Kilid Bahr were plainly visible where those towns faced each other across the narrowest part of the passage. The bombardment was repeated next day and again, in stronger force, on March 6th. Some ships suffered damage, though without loss of life.

At the same time on the 6th the *Queen Elizabeth*, anchored on the outer coast well to seaward of Gaba Tepe, flung her vast shells over the Peninsula into the Chanak forts, her firing being directed by seaplane. She was strongly supported by other ships and there were hopes of putting out of action the big guns, some believed to be 14-inch, which defended the actual approaches to the Narrows.

Lieutenant Geoffrey Rylands, Navigating Officer of the *Ark Royal*, gave these details: 'A Daily Mail "Sopwith" was hoisted out. Conditions were perfect and the 'plane took off from the water without difficulty. When it had climbed to 3,000 feet it suddenly started to spiral downwards, fluttering like a fallen leaf, and fell into the sea. The destroyer *Usk* raced to the spot, lowered a boat and recovered both Pilot and Observer, who were injured. A relief aeroplane was sent up. Just as it was over the land the Pilot was shot in the leg by a rifle bullet and had to come back. A third aircraft went up at once and did some good work but unfortunately the Pilot could not climb high enough to spot the *Q.E.*'s fall of shot efficiently.'

The result of the bombardment became clear on the following day, the 7th. When Allied battleships advanced up the Straits and came within range of the forts the Turks opened fire as though nothing had happened.

While the bombardments were in progress, our minesweeping trawlers were trying to clear the minefields to allow passage of the fleet. In spite of all that has been said to the contrary, I give the crews of these unsuitable vessels high praise for their courage and endurance. The services of these North Sea fishermen, unaccustomed as they were to gunfire and to naval discipline, were often of inestimable value.

The Turks had laid not more than 400 moored mines across the Straits arranged in ten lines stretching from shore to shore. Of these 120 had been sown in November 1914, the remaining 280 between 14th and 26th February 1915. The first line of twenty-nine mines was eight miles upstream from Cape Helles and stretched from the mouth of the Soghanli Dere to Kephez Point. The last line lay above the Narrows between Kilid Bahr and Chanak. It contained fifty-three mines and was laid at the end of February.

When a battleship entered the Dardanelles she always had a picket boat in attendance supplied with a light net to throw over a mine on the surface and to tow it clear of the parent ship before sinking it. Picket boats also did splendid work 'creeping' with grapnels for the connecting wire of a line of mines which, when caught, was blown up with a submerged explosive charge. This method resulted in many mines breaking away and rising to the surface. They were then destroyed as they floated downstream towards the entrance to the Straits.

Though the work done by picket boats was important, the major task of clearing the minefields rested with the trawlers, which were handicapped by being unable to sweep against the current for lack of steam power. It was necessary, therefore, to go above a minefield, stop, pass the sweeps, turn round and come down again with the current. The mines were laid mostly at fifteen to twenty feet below the surface, which meant that in normal weather conditions it was safe for a destroyer or a minesweeping trawler to pass over them, but care was needed as these moored mines rose and fell as the current differed. An aeroplane once reported a field breaking surface in slack water above Chanak.

Our gallant fishermen did not fear the mines, but they hated the gunfire. Who didn't? Sweeping by day soon had to be abandoned in favour of sweeping by night, and that proved to be damnable, too.

On the morning of March 12th, Admiral Carden gave orders that every trawler was to have a commissioned officer in command and a warrant officer or midshipman with some naval ratings to stiffen the crew. 'Sweeping must be carried out,' he said, 'regardless of cost.'

There was no lack of volunteers for this thankless task. Here is an extract from the diary of one of them, an officer on the retired list who had been farming in Canada when war broke out – Lieutenant-Commander J. B. Waterlow, H.M.S. *Blenheim*:

'I am to lead in a trawler – to supply moral force to make them go on and on. I am to draw the fire of the batteries off the others. We have to go up in the glare of searchlights and under heavy fire of batteries and across the minefield. If hit or blown up we have to wait in the water as best we can until picked up, probably by picket boats. Captain (D) calls it a forlorn hope. We shall see. The Frenchmen are having a try tonight and we are to finish the job tomorrow night, 13–14 March. I hope to win through and expect to, for apart from all things I would like to be with the fleet when it steams up to Constantinople. . . .

'It was a relief to start. Lieutenant Pitts, R.N.R., commanded my trawler *No. 48* and it was a great comfort to have him to talk to.

'I felt like a Christmas tree, dressed in an old coat and trousers and jersey, a pair of short sea-boots because they were easy to kick off, a cork life-belt (very clumsy), a flash, a pistol and an all-over duffle coat for warmth, its pockets loaded with revolver ammunition, smoking materials, etc. The revolver was in case of having trouble with the trawler's crew, and it was such a nuisance that after a bit I ceased to keep it slung round my neck and took it off and laid it on a table. I had with me, as had each trawler, a petty officer and a signalman. The former, a stalwart R.N.R. man, turned out to be invaluable.

'As we steamed up through the entrance between Helles and Kum Kāle, the forts just knocked out, we could see the cruel searchlights, by which we had to pass, some eight miles further up. It was a relief when Commander Mellor, senior officer, minesweepers, shouted to us from his picket boat to go on at full speed – but some of the trawlers could only make about five knots over the ground against the current.

'Shortly before we passed the first searchlight, which is on the North shore, by the mouth of what we called the "Swanee River" [Soghanli Dere], came the flash of a warning gun, then another and another. Pitts said quietly: "We should soon be in it now", and I breathed a prayer. Strange, but from this point on I felt much better.

'A little later a battery on the North shore opened a desultory fire, not very alarming, and the shot not falling very close to us. Then we passed a line of buoys. Pitts told me they were Turkish range buoys and marked the beginning of the hot zone.

'After this, searchlight after searchlight began to open on both sides, and the fire became denser and was delivered from both banks. For the first time I heard shell whistling over my head. Like everybody does I ducked but got over the desire to do that in a very few minutes. I asked the skipper how he liked it, and he said he'd rather be fishing!

'By the time we got into the minefield the fire was terrific. Both banks blazed incessantly, and with the glare of the searchlights, which never left us for an instant, it was bright as day. A veritable hail of shell fell all around us. As leader I got the thick of it (Pitts had told me it would be so) and looking at Commander Mellor's picket boat close alongside me it appeared as though he was in a snow storm, but Mellor sat unperturbed on top of the cabin roof.

'It was now that the Royal Naval Reserve Petty Officer proved himself. He had been standing quietly in the wheel-house, arms folded majestically across his breast above the cork life-belt, when the two trawler-men at the wheel lost their heads and began to cringe. Lieutenant Pitts sent them below, and the old Petty Officer took over the wheel and steered absolutely unperturbed.

'A 6-inch shell hit the funnel so close to my head that scraps of paint and smuts covered me. Another shell passed through the after cabin, where two or three of the men were, going in one side and out at the other without bursting, and hit no one. The noise was deafening and made one's head ache.

'I was thankful to have something to do, little though it was, increasing and easing speed to keep the line closed up, for *No. 48* was faster than the rest. It was magnificent to look back on that little line of defenceless craft stolidly advancing through this hell with never a thought of turning back; and after all they were only manned by British fishermen stiffened by one naval officer and a rating or two. It was infuriating to have nothing with which to hit back.

'Commander Mellor now hailed us to turn and the trawlers to get out their sweeps. Then for the first time since we had entered the inferno the searchlights were off us and we were in darkness. The relief was intense.

'I looked round for the cause and found that the *Amethyst* had arrived with the destroyers and had opened fire to cover us, and the searchlights were concentrated on her. As I watched her I saw a tremendous explosion right against her side. Shortly afterwards she went away and everything was again concentrated on us. I hailed the trawlers as they swept down stream and was anxiously hailed by destroyers, appearing from God knows where, to know if I was alright. One trawler said she was in need of assistance: "One man with both legs blown off and . . ." was all I heard. I hailed a destroyer to go to her assistance, but she thought I wanted her to keep out of my way and went off at full speed. I chased him futilely but caught him by flashing light. He ordered *No. 318* alongside and took off her wounded.

'I couldn't think why the *Amethyst*, who carried a doctor, had not waited. I was to find out later. She had been hit pretty badly and was out of control. One shell entered her port side for'ard, passed through a stokers' messdeck where men were sleeping and churned them up into small pieces. It was an 8-inch shell from one of the forts. . . .

'When the sweeping was over I wondered if I ought to go back to the others getting in their sweeps, instead of waiting for them just in front and stopped. But my job was to lead them down, and I felt satisfied that stopping still under fire was more than going back.'

Lieutenant-Commander Waterlow explains later in his diary that the result of the night's work proved to be very disappointing. Only one pair of trawlers had swept successfully; the others had had their winches and sweeps damaged by gunfire and were unable to do anything effective.

Mr Henry Morgenthau, American Ambassador to Turkey, had this to say about the effect of the preliminary naval bombardments on the forts of the Dardanelles. So much has been written on the subject that it is difficult to decide who was telling the truth. He at least gave his own impressions from personal experience and was a reliable eye-witness.

'On March 16th, I visited Fort Hamidieh on the Asiatic side,' he wrote. 'My first impression was that I was in Germany. The officers were practically all from the *Goeben* and the *Breslau* and everywhere Germans were strengthening emplacements. Here German, **not** Turkish, was the language heard on every side.

'Feeling myself so completely in Germany, I asked the Commandant, Colonel Wehrle, why there were so few Turks, to which he replied, smiling, "You won't ask me that question this afternoon."

'The siting of Hamidieh seemed ideal. It stands right on the water's edge and consisted of ten guns, every one completely sweeping the Dardanelles. Walking upon the parapet, I had a clear view down the Straits, Kum Kāle, at the entrance on the Asiatic shore standing out conspicuously. No warship could enter the Dardanelles unobserved from where I was standing, yet the fort itself was not particularly impressive to my unprofessional eye. The parapet and traverses were merely mounds of earth erected as far back as 1837 by their French constructors. I had been told that the Germans had completely modernised the Dardanelles defences. I could see with my own eyes that this was not true. The guns of Fort Hamadieh were thirty years old – Krupp model of 1885, with an extreme range of about nine miles, while the range of the old battleships opposing them was about ten miles. The guns of the more modern ships, the *Queen Elizabeth, Inflexible, Lord Nelson* and *Agamemnon* were capable of firing at even greater ranges, which gave the British fleet a great advantage.

'The Turkish fortifications did not contain an unlimited supply of ammunition. At the time European and American papers were printing stories of train-loads of shells and modern guns coming by way of Rumania from Germany to the Dardanelles. These reports were pure fiction.

'Getting into a car we now sped along the military road to Fort Dardanos, by Kephez Point. It was as completely Turkish as Hamidieh was German. The guns were more modern – Krupp model 1905. Here also was a new battery consisting of naval guns from the secondary armament of German and Turkish warships lying in the Bosphorus.

'A few days back the Allied fleet had entered Eren Keui Bay and subjected Dardanos to a terrific bombardment, the evidences of which I saw on every hand. The strange thing was that despite all this punishment the batteries themselves remained intact. Not a single gun, my guides told me, had been destroyed. General Djevad Pasha, the Turkish Commander-in-Chief, a man of culture and of pleasing personality, met us and took us to his Headquarters.

'The Turkish officers were very proud of the fight this Dardanos fort had put up against the Allied fleet. They led me to the guns which had done particularly good service and patted them affectionately. For my benefit Djevad Pasha called out Lieutenant Hassan, the Turkish officer who had defended this position. He was a little fellow with jet-black hair, black eyes, extremely modest and almost shrinking in the presence of the great General. Djevad Pasha patted Hassan on both cheeks, while another Turkish officer stroked his hair; one would have thought that he was a faithful dog who had just performed some meritorious service.

'"It is men like you of whom great heroes are made," said the General. He asked Hassan to describe the attack and the way it had been met. The embarrassed lieutenant quietly told his story, but he was moved almost to tears by the appreciation of his chief.

'"There is a great future for you in the Army," said the General, as we parted from this hero. Poor Hassan's future came two days later, on March 18th. One of the shells struck his dugout which caved in, killing the boy. Yet his behaviour on the day I visited his battery showed that he regarded the praise as sufficient compensation for all that he had suffered or all that he might suffer.

'South of Eren Keui on the hills bordering the road, the Germans had introduced an innovation. They had found several Krupp howitzers left over from the Bulgarian War and had installed them on concrete foundations. Each battery had four or five of these emplacements, so that, as I approached them, I found several substantial bases that apparently had no guns. I was mystified further at the sight of a herd of buffaloes hauling one of these howitzers from one emplacement to another. This was part of the plan of defence. As soon as the dropping of shells indicated that the howitzer had been located by the fleet, it would be hauled by the team of buffaloes to a new location.

'"We have even a better trick than that," remarked one of the officers, as he showed me a dummy gun made from an elongated section of a sewer pipe. The real howitzer was mounted behind a hillock out of sight of the fleet and the two were connected by telephone. Both fired simultaneously, the howitzer live shell, the dummy a powder charge. I noticed that the area round the dummy was pock-marked with shell-holes, while the howitzer had been undetected.

'We now crossed over by steamer to Kilid Bahr on the Gallipoli side of the Narrows. Here again damage appeared slight although there were shell holes everywhere. . . .

'When on our party's return to Constantinople I could hear the chant of the leader of a band of Turkish soldiers calling to Allah the All Powerful, the Compassionate, the Merciful, to give them strength to resist the invader, I realised the full implication of the German Colonel Wehrle's remark of the wisdom of not putting Turkish and German soldiers together because of their religious differences.'[1]

The political results of the fall of the Outer Forts had been encouraging but progress of the naval attack on the Intermediate defences was too slow. The fact that the enemy, having the free run of the Peninsula as well as the Asiatic coast, could plant and conceal his moveable howitzers and batteries where he pleased made it increasingly evident that military occupation of the Peninsula was an increasing necessity. Now, except for the unsettled weather conditions, was the moment when a permanent landing would be of the highest service, and on March 10th Churchill evidently realised the need for troops acutely. But it was only on that very day that Lord Kitchener finally decided to allow the 29th Division to start from England, and it did not actually sail until the 16th. Kitchener refused to allow a landing (the weather was unsuitable anyhow) until this Regular Division of the British Army had arrived.

Accordingly Churchill strongly urged Admiral Carden to press forward the naval attack with the utmost vigour. In a telegram on March 11th he said: 'Your original instructions laid stress on caution and deliberate methods, and we approve highly the skill and patience with which you have advanced hitherto without loss. The results to be gained are, however, great enough to justify loss of ships and men if success cannot be obtained without. . . .'

To this message Vice-Admiral Carden replied that the stage for vigorous action had now been reached but that, 'when the fleet entered the Sea of Marmara military operations on a large scale should be opened at once, so as to secure communications'.[2]

On March 15th Churchill telegraphed again. He said that though no time was to be lost, there should be no undue haste. Carden replied that he proposed to begin vigorous operations but did not intend to rush the passage before the channel was clear of mines. This answer was telegraphed on March 16th and on the same day the Admiral was forced to resign his command because of serious ill-health. His condition had been giving cause for anxiety. He worried too much and was off his food. I have already mentioned that he was pulled out of a back-water job, that of Admiral Superintendent, Malta, to take up a sea command for which he was not qualified. Poor chap, I do not condemn him for breaking down, I blame the man who put him there.

Two flag officers on the spot were available to relieve him: Rear-Admiral John de Robeck his second-in-command, who knew the ropes, and Rear-Admiral Rosslyn ('Rosy') Wemyss, S.N.O. Mudros. Of the two Wemyss was the senior, but the appointment went to de Robeck who was made an acting vice-admiral. Wemyss, with a loyalty in keeping with the best traditions of the Royal Navy, agreed willingly to serve under him although he welcomed responsibility himself.

Admiral de Robeck was five years younger than his predecessor, Carden, but two years older than Wemyss. He was of course fully acquainted with the plans and expressed his approval of them. Although urged by Winston Churchill to act on his own initiative and not to hesitate to state objections, his motive in carrying on with the pre-arranged scheme appeared to have been based not so much on his confidence in its success as on a fear that withdrawal would injure our prestige in the Near East, and secondarily on his wish to do his best with a plan which he regarded in the light of an order. If the ships got through, he, like many others, expected a revolution or other political changes in Turkey. Should these reactions fail to happen he appreciated that transports and store ships would not be able to pass through the Straits or the fleet to remain in the Marmara for more than a fortnight or three weeks and that it would have to run the gauntlet coming down again. In his telegram accepting the command he made no mention of these considerations but only quoted the obvious: that success depended upon clearing the mine-fields after silencing the forts and batteries. Indeed he had little time for any considerations. For the very next day after he received his command he undertook, on March 18th, the main attempt to force the Dardanelles.

5

March 18th

The plan, with which Admiral de Robeck was in agreement, was to silence, simultaneously, the forts of the Narrows, the mobile howitzers and the minefield batteries. Ten battleships were assigned to the attack, six to the reserve. The action was to be opened at long range (14,000 yards) by the four most powerful ships, the *Queen Elizabeth* (de Robeck's flagship), *Inflexible, Lord Nelson* and *Agamemnon,* known as Line A.

When the forts had been partially subdued, Line B, consisting of the four ships of the French Squadron, *Suffren* (flag), *Bouvet, Charlemagne* and *Gaulois,* was to pass through the intervals of the first line and engage the forts at decisive range.

The *Triumph* and *Prince George* were to concentrate on the mobile howitzers and minefield batteries. Cruisers and destroyers had their own vital parts to play. Six further battleships, *Vengeance, Irresistible, Albion, Ocean, Swiftsure* and *Majestic,* were held in reserve for specific tasks.

As soon as the forts were dominated and the mobile howitzers and minefield batteries subdued, the minesweepers were to clear a 900-yard channel, covered by the *Cornwallis* and *Canopus.* Sweeping was to be continued throughout the night while the rest of the fleet withdrew.

The next morning, March 19th, when the channel was swept, the fleet would advance and, after battering the forts in the Narrows at point-blank range, enter the Sea of Marmara.

Such was the well-thought-out plan.

Dawn of March 18th came up with a warm southerly breeze and a cloudless sky 'in all the jewelled serenity for which the Aegean is famous at its best'.[1] At an early hour the minesweepers, British and French, could report that during the night they had seen all clear to within 8,000 yards of the forts of the Narrows. No mines had been found. Although the sun rose at 6.09 a.m. Admiral de Robeck knew from experience that visibility for engaging the forts would not be favourable for aircraft spotting until a later hour, which was a disadvantage since time was precious.

At 10.30 the battleships entered the Straits, attended by their armed picket boats and preceded by the destroyers *Colne* and *Chelmer*, who were towing a light mine-seeking sweep, a new innovation. No mines were located.

At 11.30 the *Queen Elizabeth* opened fire, and soon the whole of Line A was in action. It was considered unwise for ships to anchor. They kept station by stemming the current. The Turks had pulled down all windmills, minarets and other prominent marks which might aid our gunlayers and spotting aircraft. All ships soon came under fire from mobile howitzers and light artillery but for the moment were still out of range of the forts. Our shooting appeared to be accurate, and several hits were observed. At 11.50 there was a heavy explosion in one of the Chanak forts.

A few minutes after midday the French squadron advanced through the bombarding line, and, gallantly led by Admiral Guépratte, began to engage at close range. All forts now replied vigorously, and the firing from both sides became tremendous.

By 1.30 the fire of the forts had slackened. By 1.45 it had practically ceased. The French squadron, which so far had borne the brunt, was recalled, and the battleships of the reserve moved forward to take their places. The general impression was that the forts had been dominated. The minesweepers were ordered to advance.

Some ships in the Allied fleet had suffered damage, but casualties were few. For example, a battery of four 6-inch howitzers had concentrated on *Agamemnon*, and at 12.45 had found the range, with the result that she was hit a dozen times, five times on the armour without injury but seven times above it. To avoid further damage, Captain Fyler skilfully turned his ship through thirty-two points, a complete circle, and then returned to his station. In the engagement one of her 9·2 guns and a couple of 12-pdrs had been put out of action.

The *Inflexible*, the outermost ship of Line A on the Asiatic side, had been receiving the main attention of the Eren Keui howitzers. At 12.20 a shell struck her foremast and started a fire on the bridge. Within the next ten minutes she was hit three more times and her picket boat was sunk alongside. A chance shot from a field gun hit a signal yard and wiped out most of the crew of the spotting top. Also a 14-inch shell from one of the forts had fallen alongside and burst on impact with the water, causing a leak. Almost simultaneously a 9·4-inch shell made a jagged hole in the ship's side. Captain Richard Phillimore, undeterred, fought on.

The French battleship *Gaulois*, Captain Biard, had sustained a shell hole forward below the water-line which had caused a serious

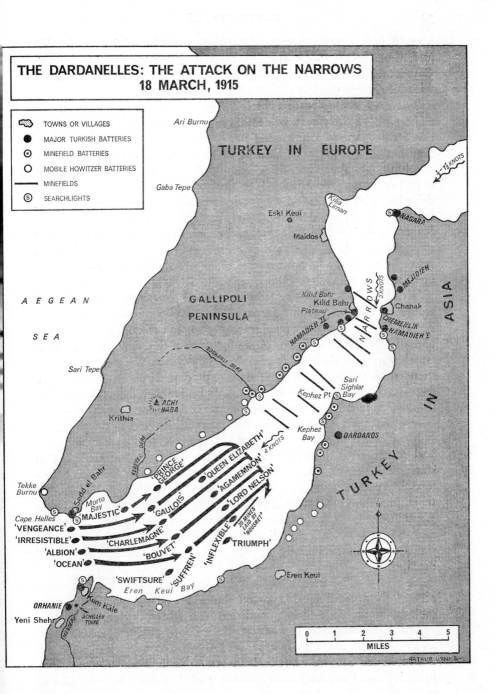

THE DARDANELLES: THE ATTACK ON THE NARROWS
18 MARCH, 1915

TOWNS OR VILLAGES
MAJOR TURKISH BATTERIES
MINEFIELD BATTERIES
MOBILE HOWITZER BATTERIES
MINEFIELDS
SEARCHLIGHTS

Ari Burnu

TURKEY IN EUROPE

Gaba Tepe

Eski Keui

Maidos

Kilia Liman

NAGARA

4-7½ KNOTS

A E G E A N

GALLIPOLI

MEJIDIEH

PENINSULA

Kilid Bahr
Kilid Bahr
Plateau

N
A
R
R
O
W
S

Chanak

3 KNOTS

S E A

CHEMENLIK

HAMADIEH II

HAMADIEH I

Sari Tepe

SURHAVLI DERE

Sari
Sighlar
Bay

I
N

ACHI
BABA

Kephez Pt

Krithia

Kephez
Bay

DARDANOS

KEREVES DERE

4 KNOTS

A S I A

'PRINCE
GEORGE'

'QUEEN ELIZABETH'

'AGAMEMNON'

4 KNOTS

Tekke
Burnu

Sedd el Bahr

'GAULOIS'

'LORD NELSON'

T U R K E Y

Morto
Bay

MAJESTIC

Cape Helles

'VENGEANCE'

20 MINES
LAID BY
'NOUSRET'

'IRRESISTIBLE'

'CHARLEMAGNE'

'INFLEXIBLE'

'TRIUMPH'

'ALBION'

'BOUVET'

'OCEAN'

'SWIFTSURE'

'SUFFREN'

N

Eren Keui

Eren Keui Bay

ORHANIE

Kum Kale

Yeni Shehr

ACHILLES
TOMB

MENDERE

0   1   2   3   4   5
MILES

—ARTHUR BANKS—

leak. A few of her young *matelots*, frightened, jumped over the side and were lucky to be rescued by the destroyer *Jed*, Lieutenant-Commander G. F. A. Mulock. The *Suffren* had also been struck, but without serious damage.

Then came the first disaster.

At 1.54, as the *Bouvet* was following her flagship the *Suffren* out of the Straits, an explosion fired her magazine. She heeled over and vanished beneath the surface in three minutes, her propellers still revolving. As she capsized, a few survivors were seen to scamper over her bottom and jump into the sea. Then up went her bows, dripping with water, and she made her final plunge, carrying 639 of her ship's company down with her, including her Captain, Valentin Rageot de la Touche. The cries of the men dragged down with her, or struggling in the water as they were swept down stream, sounded over the Straits. Only thirty-five were saved. Her destruction was attributed to a heavy shell.

'I did not think the fire from concealed howitzers and field guns would ever be a deciding factor. I was wrong,' wrote Commodore Keyes. 'The *fear* of their fire [among crews of the minesweepers] was actually the deciding factor of the fortunes of that day. Two pairs of trawlers got out their sweeps immediately ahead of Line A and commenced to sweep up stream; they exploded three mines [but, unfortunately, this vital information was not reported to the Admiral until the next day]. A little later they turned and ran out of the Straits. The other pair left earlier in the proceedings without sweeping.'[2]

Most of the naval officers and ratings lent to the minesweepers had returned to their ships since they were needed at their action stations. An exception was made in the case of Lieut Francis Sandford, Torpedo Lieutenant of the *Irresistible*, as battleships had landed their torpedoes before the bombardment. Commodore Keyes said in *Naval Memoirs*: 'I saw him on the morning of March 19th, almost in rags, with clothes and skin discoloured by the fumes of high explosive shell, and was immensely impressed by his gallant, light-hearted bearing.'

At 4.11 the *Inflexible*, which all day had been firing from the vicinity of Eren Keui Bay, reported that she had struck a mine. She took a serious list, and her condition was evidently dangerous.

Three minutes later it was seen that the *Irresistible* had also listed and was apparently unable to move. Later the *Ocean* was also stricken.

The appearance of mines – if they were in fact mines – in waters in which the Fleet had been operating all day and which, in spite of the proved limitations of the minesweepers, it was confidently believed were free from them, was profoundly disconcerting. Perhaps they were torpedoes fired from some concealed station on shore? Perhaps they were floating mines thrown overboard in the Narrows and only now carried down by the current? In any case it was obvious that some alarming cause was active in the area where the ships were working. In the face of this uncertainty Admiral de Robeck broke off the action, and at 5.50 p.m. (sunset 6.09, complete darkness 7.40) gave orders for a general retirement. The fleet withdrew to Tenedos. The minesweepers returned to their anchorage. There would be no sweeping that night. Admiral de Robeck was not prepared to expose battleships which would be required to cover the sweepers until more was known of the mysterious agency which had struck such deadly blows. Attention was now concentrated on trying to save the wounded ships.

At about 4 p.m. on March 18th the *Gaulois*, down by the head, had come out of the Straits surrounded by destroyers and steaming very slowly. One destroyer went alongside to take off men not needed to help to keep the ship afloat. *Cornwallis* and *Canopus* called away their boats to stand by. Deeper and deeper the *Gaulois* sank; slower and slower she steamed. Her stern had now lifted, and her bows had sunk down till the flukes of her anchors were submerged.

Accompanied by the flagship *Suffren*, also damaged, and by *Cornwallis*, the *Gaulois* was eventually beached on Rabbit Island. A bulkhead gave way as the ship came to rest, and her anchors were found to be jammed. The *Cornwallis* sent over her sheet anchor (an extra anchor carried by a battleship for an emergency) and laid it out ahead of the *Gaulois*, whose ship's company brought the wire hawser to their for'ard capstan. There was no steam, so they hove in by hand in the old style, until the wire was sufficiently taut to keep her bows firmly aground. Men of the *Gaulois* laid out their own kedge anchor aft, to prevent the ship from swinging broadside on to the shore.

French ships in those days did not carry skilled divers so Captain Davidson offered to send over his team complete with carpenter's crew and some engineers, an offer which was gratefully accepted. Between them they managed to fix a patch over the hole and to pump out a great weight of water. The *Gaulois* was saved.

Admiral Guépratte was not slow to recognise the value of these services. He made a personal visit to the *Cornwallis* where he was received with smiles, as he was very popular, and with the usual formalities.

'*Bonjour, Admiral*,' said Captain Davidson in his best French. '*Je suis content d'avoir l'honneur de vous recevoir à bord du "Cornwallis"*'.

'*Merci, Capitaine, de votre accueil*,' Guépratte replied. '*Je suis heureux*

*non seulement de vous connaître personnellement mais je tiens à remercier de
vive voix vos scaphandriers qui ont rendu de si grands services en nous aidant à
rementtre le "Gaulois" à flot. C'etait un bon travail. Je voudrais leur serrer
la main à chacun en les remerciant.'*

    *'Rien de plus simple, Admiral. J'aurai le plus grand plaisir à les faire
paraitre devant vous sans délai.'*

    The team of divers, engineers and 'chippy-chaps' (carpenters) duly
fell in on the quarter-deck and to everyone's delight the French
Admiral shook hands with each man in turn.

    'A fine upright and polite gentleman with long white whiskers,'
one of the men said of him afterwards.

    'When the shock of the explosion of the moored mine was felt,'
wrote Captain Phillimore of *Inflexible*, 'the electric light failed and
most of the emergency oil lamps were extinguished. Men stationed
in "A" magazine and shell room were thrown off their feet. The fore
turret was felt to lift bodily. All communications failed and orders
to the engine room had to be conveyed by messenger. No man left
the torpedo flat alive, but a stoker who was standing on the armoured
grating ten feet down was carried safely by the rush of water on to
the deck above.

    'Speed of the ship was increased to twelve knots and the trim cor-
rected by flooding the provision room, but the ship remained down
by the bow six feet. Casualties amounted to three officers and thirty
men killed, and thirteen wounded.'

    Lieutenant (E) Brian Sebastian had been sent forward by the
Engineer Commander to find out the extent of the damage, as soon
as the ship was struck. 'We reckoned,' he wrote, 'that we had about
3,000 tons of water in the ship. Unfortunately, besides the torpedo
crews, there were about a dozen Malta Dockyard workmen on
board who had been carrying out some alteration. They lost their
lives, too. There was a hole 20 × 30 feet on the starboard side of the
submerged flat and the adjacent compartments were flooded.

    'I returned to the engine-room through the mess-deck, which had
been hit by a shell, and encountered the first-aid party carrying a
sailor who had a large chunk knocked off his backside. As I passed,
one of his mates was saying, "Poor old 'Nobby', he won't enjoy
sitting on his mess stool now!"'

    The Captain's Clerk, Crichton Laborde, was at his action station
in the lower conning tower recording events. He and the bearded
old Chief Quartermaster, who had an enormous chest and huge
hands and was known as 'the Bear', scaled the vertical ladder to

safety with some others. On arrival on deck the Chief Q.M. swore
and then hurried back down the ladder. A few minutes later he was
up again, dripping wet but smiling. He had a bottle of beer in his
hand.

Lieutenant Robert Sinclair R.M.L.I., in charge of one of the
turrets, had been told to clear the turret of his men and to fall them
in on the quarter-deck with swimming collars on. 'Eventually,' he
wrote, 'when all but the left gunlayer and the turret sweeper were
out – and how long they took! – I shared with these two stalwarts
the contents of my thermos flask, not very strong whisky and water,
with mutual good healths of course. All the wooden mess-tables and
stools were brought up on deck. We were certainly undefeated. We
had a very good ship's company who had been together over two
years.

'We had a civilian on board, who had been fitting a gyro compass
– a new toy. He had finished his work that very morning, and it was
promptly destroyed by the fire on the bridge. I can see him now
wandering about the ship, no doubt thinking that this was not in the
contract!'

Sinclair now went up on to the bridge to report to the Captain
that all the confidential books were under water in the lower conning
tower and could not be reached except by a diver. 'I found him,'
Sinclair wrote, 'full of good cheer. He said to me, "We are not going
to sink!" He, alone, was not wearing a swimming collar. We made
for Tenedos and anchored under the lee of the island.'

Failure to wear a swimming collar revealed a mentality peculiar to
officers of the First World War. A military man would go 'over the
top' with a walking stick. A naval officer would leave off his life-
jacket *pour encourager les autres*. In World War II the wearing of life-
jackets at sea was compulsory, but I know of two captains, contem-
poraries of mine, who lost their valuable lives when their ships were
sunk because they would not follow the new rule.

On April 6th, the *Inflexible*, with temporary repairs completed, left
Mudros for Malta under her own steam but escorted by the *Canopus*.
While on passage the wind rose, endangering the safety of the ship
and making it necessary for *Canopus* to tow her stern first until Malta
was reached. Then the tow was slipped, and the *Inflexible* turned
round under her own steam.

At 7 p.m., April 10th, just as it was getting dark, the former flagship
of the Mediterranean Fleet entered the Grand Harbour bows first,
assisted by tugs. The Maltese gave the ship a tremendous welcome,
flocking down to the water's edge in their hundreds, clapping, cheering, and shouting '*Viva l'Inglisi!*' '*Viva Navy!*' while *dghaisas*, the local

rowboats, swarmed round the wounded warrior. But what stirred the hearts of the onlookers most was the sight of the ship's company, fallen in on the upper deck, strictly at attention, steady, resolute, unshaken. The band was playing *Heart of Oak*.

As soon as the *Inflexible* was in dockyard hands for major repairs, Captain Phillimore left the ship and returned to Gallipoli to become a Beachmaster. Promoted to flag rank after the Evacuation, he was appointed Rear-Admiral, Battle Cruiser Force, stationed at Rosyth. One evening the *Inflexible* had a ship's company concert, and of course he was invited. Lieutenant Robert Sinclair R.M.L.I. was still in the ship. He remembered the occasion well: 'To get into his seat Admiral Phillimore had to face the assembled ship's company, many of whom had served with him. As soon as he appeared the men rose to their feet and roared a welcome. If he did not know already he must have realised then what we thought of him. . . . At the end of the show the Postman, who was on the stage, called out: "Three cheers for our good old Captain"; and again they gave him a standing ovation. I have never before or since seen such a genuine expression of affection. He was very much moved and left the ship without coming into the Wardroom.'

Among the ship's company of the *Ocean*, in charge of a 12-inch magazine, was a petty officer named George Morgan, Royal Fleet Reserve, born in 1872. I quote from his journal, which was rescued by one of his daughters, Edith, after a blitz on Gloucester in World War II. Morgan takes us on board his ship during the early hours of March 18th. The *Ocean*, you will remember, did not go into action until the afternoon, as she was one of the reserve.

'We were all on deck to watch the boys steam by, waving and cheering as the fleet gathered speed and headed its way to business. As we listen to the last strains of "Come cheer up my lads" and "Britons never shall be slaves", the proud feelings that possessed us can hardly be described; mixed with the thoughts of England, home and beauty, of apprehension of the coming struggle, and then the vision of seeing ourselves off Constantinople by Sunday morning, I don't think there was fear written on any face.

'We had not long to wait for the concert to start. "There they go," said "Spud" Murphy to "Spike" Sullivan as we saw a volume of smoke and fire from the shore; but there was no answer from us yet. "There they go again," said "Tubby" Turner to "Nobby" Clarke, "Why my sister could shoot better than that!"

'Then our patience was rewarded. We returned fire. Salvo after salvo from the fleet made us dance with delight. "Oh! look at that beauty," and "lovely!" and all sorts of similar remarks. We were like youngsters on Guy Fawkes days.

'All through the forenoon those not on duty could watch. At 11.30 we went to dinner so that we should be ready by 12.00 noon. I've heard tales that our boys, before going into Action, were given "Dutch Courage" or "rum". This is an insult. I state here that any bombardment or action that I have taken part in, ashore or afloat, the rum ration (mark the word "ration", which was part of our dinner) has never been served until *after* the fighting.

'When dinner was over the anchor was weighed, and we were soon on our way to battle. Just before the bugle sounded "Action", we saw a tremendous column of smoke and fire rise from one of the French battleships. We afterwards learned that what we saw was the explosion aboard the *Bouvet*.

'We soon began to pay our respects to the forts ashore as fast as we could send up ammunition. No thoughts of anything but charges and shells.

'"What the Dickens was that?" said one to me as a monster shell must have struck the armour plating. "Oh! someone's false teeth have fallen in the shell room," said another. Working in the magazine was like being in a tank with a party outside with different size hammers belting away. Now and then the ship would heel over, trembling, the thump of the propellers going hard, now soft. The news came down that we were doing good work. At about 4.15 p.m. we heard that the *Irresistible* was mined and sinking near the shore.'

Shortly after this news had been passed down by voice-pipe to Petty Officer Morgan, he was ordered to close up his magazine and to come on deck with his crew 'to prepare to take a ship in tow'.

'We approached the damaged *Irresistible*. She was a pitiful sight with dead lying on her decks. As she was sinking it was decided to leave her to her fate. We transferred by boat [5.50 p.m.] the Captain and the towing party who had volunteered to remain on board. [Actually *Irresistible* did not sink for another seven hours.]

'We then went into action again, and as soon as I went below to the magazine I had orders to send up full charges and to prepare for a warm time. Shortly afterwards I was about to hand out a charge for the loading tray, when bang!! The force of the blow lifted me off the floor with the charge in my arms. We didn't need to ask what it was.

'The order came, "Close magazines and shell rooms". The men all went up the trunk from my magazine, but it was my duty to see all ventilators fastened and water-tight in case they wanted to flood the magazine to avoid an explosion. It only took a few minutes but it seemed such a time to me, but at last it was finished.

'There was only one way to get out and that was through the shell-room escape hatch. To my joy it was open. I was soon through and closed it behind me. But my troubles were not over. Supposing the other hatch above me was closed? Anyone seeing it open in passing would close it. I lost no time. Just as I reached the ladder I heard someone raising the catch to let it down. I yelled, and whoever it was didn't stop to argue. I was soon through and was closing it after me when the Boatswain came over and asked me if there was anyone else below, and if the magazines and shell rooms were shut. After telling him I was the last and that they were closed he said, "That's good", and away he went.

'I hurried up to the Officer of the Watch on the bridge and reported "Magazine Closed", and was told to get aboard the destroyer as orders had been given to abandon ship.

'While standing right aft on the Q.D. close by the name-plate, watching the men sliding down the ship's side and some jumping over to catch hold of the torpedo-boat's rigging and falling in a heap on her deck, I decided to wait and watch my chance, or take a dive and swim round. Whilst waiting, someone running past bumped against my left shoulder and put an end to my star gazing. I disappeared "looping the loop" in grand style between the ship's side and the T.B.D. hitting my shoulder. Then I experienced another shock. I felt something rubbing against me and saw it was the T.B.D. getting near and I should be squashed between her and our own ship's side. I yelled out and one chap in the torpedo-boat lay on the deck while another caught hold of his legs as he leaned outboard and grabbed me and pulled me aboard just in time.

'But the excitement was not quite over. The shore batteries could see that we were helpless and not able to retaliate. I passed a remark to Tom Cox, who had broken both ankles when he had jumped, that if we did not shift soon we should have a shell into us. But the captain of our T.B.D. [Commander Claude Seymour] was watching, and with a "full speed astern" off we went and a shell just missed our bows.

'If ever I had a joy-ride, I had one then. I shall never forget it if I live to be a hundred. It was the hottest time you could wish for.

'There were about one hundred and fifty aboard as our destroyer was steaming away. I was on board the *Colne*, and the other two who took off our ship's company were the *Jed* and the *Chelmer*. She took us to the *Agamemnon*, whose crew ranged themselves along the anti-torpedo net shelf to help us aboard. They gave us cocoa. The wounded were taken to Sick Quarters. As I was soaked through to the skin I was lent two blankets to roll up in. I was also given a post-card to send home. I wrote to my wife:

> '"Dear Flo, you will see by the above address
> I have had a change of ships. All's well,
> George."'

'Giving it to the steward I went outside and lay on the deck to try and catch some sleep. But this I found impossible as I trembled all over. I suppose this was reaction.'[3]

After the war it was ascertained that in the early and squally dawn of March 8th, ten days before the great battle, while our night patrol of destroyers was withdrawing from the Straits, the little Turkish steamer *Nousret* had laid a line of twenty mines just above Eren Keui Bay, running up and down stream, i.e. at right angles to the other lines of mines. It is probable that the three mines, believed to be strays, exploded by our sweepers on March 18th and not reported until the next day, were in fact part of this new field.

To suggest, as some authors have done, including Churchill in *The World Crisis, 1915*, that the *Ocean* struck her mine when going to the assistance of the *Irresistible* is not true. Captain Hayes-Sadler of the *Ocean* made no attempt to do so although pressed by Commodore Keyes (on board the *Wear*) in the name of the Admiral. That aside, it seems to me that some of the destroyers and trawlers should have had a go in spite of the shell fire. To tow a wounded ship out of action has always been a proud tradition of the Royal Navy: After Trafalgar the *Polyphemus* took the *Victory* in tow, the *Euryalus* the *Royal Sovereign*. Already in this war the *Hogue* had picked up the *Arethusa* after the Battle of Heligoland Bight; the *Lion* had been taken in tow by the *Indomitable* after Dogger Bank, and so on. In World War II there were many instances: the stricken *Kelly*, Captain Lord Louis Mountbatten, was under tow for ninety-one hours and saved, after being torpedoed by a German E-boat in the North Sea on 10th May 1940 – a classic example. And to strengthen my argument I must allow myself to say with pride, that when I was in command of the fifth *Euryalus* we took the wounded battleship *Warspite* in tow, on 16th September 1942, in the Messina Strait at

11 p.m., after she had been severely damaged by a radio-controlled missile during the Salerno landings. Our tow parted – but at least we tried. The *Ocean* is believed to have sunk at about 10.30 p.m. but the *Irresistible* not until midnight.

Much provoked by his inability to persuade Captain Hayes-Sadler of the *Ocean* to take the stricken *Irresistible* in tow, Commodore Keyes returned at full speed in the destroyer *Wear* to the *Queen Elizabeth*, which was lying just outside the entrance to the Dardanelles. He did not mince his words but told Admiral de Robeck just what he thought of the *Ocean*'s failure. He proposed now that he should go back at once, and if there were no chance of getting the *Irresistible* into the current by some means he would torpedo her. Anything was better than allowing her to fall into enemy hands. If he found the *Ocean* still afloat, he could see no reason why he should not tow her out also and ground her in shoal water off Tenedos or Rabbit Island. He suggested that a battleship should stand by and trawlers assist.

Extraordinary though it may seem – it certainly does to me – Admiral de Robeck appeared to have been quite undismayed by the news. His chief concern was that Keyes should get something to eat before he set off again, and that, to save any fuss with the Admiralty later on, he would give Keyes written authority to torpedo the two battleships should necessity arise, so that he, the Admiral, and not Keyes, would 'carry the can'.

But when Keyes re-entered the Dardanelles he searched but there were no signs of either the *Irresistible* or the *Ocean*. 'Except for the searchlights,' Keyes wrote, 'there seemed to be no signs of life, and I had a most indelible impression that we were in the presence of a beaten foe. It only remained for us to organise a proper sweeping force.

'It was with a feeling of confidence for the future that I went into my Admiral's cabin [at about 2 a.m.] to tell him that the *Ocean* and *Irresistible* were safely at the bottom in deep water and our anxiety was at an end.

'I was distressed to find him very unhappy. He told me he felt sure that he would be superseded the next day. I told him there could be no question of that. The First Lord would not be discouraged by our check, and I knew that he would rely on us to see the matter through, which we would do in the course of the next few days. . . . We discussed the situation far into the night. The exhilarating atmosphere of the lower reaches of the Dardanelles must have drifted down to Tenedos, for when the 19th broke the Admiral had become full of confident hope and determination to overcome all opposition.'[4]

The great attempt to force the Narrows with the Fleet had ended on its first day in what could only be regarded as a defeat. Of the sixteen battleships engaged three had been sunk and three more, including the only battle-cruiser, had been put out of action for a long time. The main cause of the trouble was, of course, the line of fresh mines laid by the *Nousret*. It was impossible at this stage properly to assess the damage done to the forts.

On March 20th Admiral de Robeck telegraphed to the Admiralty: 'Plan for re-organising minesweeping progressing. . . . It is hoped to be in a position to commence operations in three or four days.'

The Admiralty had regarded his report only as the result of the first day's fighting. Until it was known what damage had been done to the forts it was impossible to say that another attempt would be decisive. Political reasons for carrying on were of course very strong. Our losses would be made good.

But the fates now stepped in. On March 19th, the day following the great battle, the weather broke. Day after day it blew strong north-easterly gales, with a visibility so low that firing was out of the question. No offensive action was possible until the storms abated.

What were the reactions in Constantinople to the March 18th *débâcle*? Although the police went round ordering householders to display flags in honour of the occasion, neither the Germans nor the Turks were yet persuaded that they had really won a victory. Baron von Wangenheim, the German Ambassador, was convinced that the Allied Fleet would return, and the high tension in the capital lasted for several days. In the opinion of the American Ambassador, Henry Morgenthau, the purely naval attack was justified and he expected it to be renewed. His judgement was based on the political situation which existed in Turkey at that time. He declared that there was no stable government and that the authority of the Political Committee was exceedingly tenuous. 'As a matter of fact,' concluded Morgenthau, 'the whole Ottoman Empire, on that 18th March 1915, when the Allied Fleet broke off the attack, was on the brink of dissolution. All over Turkey ambitious chieftains had arisen, expecting the fall, and were looking for the opportunity to seize their share in the inheritance. The best elements among the Turks, far from opposing the arrival of the Allied Fleet, would have welcomed it.'

A week later the famous Field-Marshal Count von der Goltz, aged seventy-four, arrived in Constantinople. He had come to present to His Majesty a medal from the Kaiser and was taking back a similar mark of consideration from the Sultan to the Kaiser, besides an Imperial present of 10,000 Turkish cigarettes. The aspect of the action on March 18th which seemed to have struck von der Goltz and his colleagues most was England's complete frankness in publishing her losses.

'In this announcement,' wrote Morgenthau, 'I merely saw a manifestation of the usual British desire to make public the worst – the policy which we Americans also believe to be the best in war-time. But no such obvious explanation could satisfy those wise and solemn Teutons.

'No, England has some deep purpose in telling the truth so un-blushingly; what could it be?

'"*Es ist ausserordentlich* – it is extraordinary!" said von der Goltz.

'"*Es ist unerhört* – it is unheard of!" declared the equally astonished Ambassador Wangenheim.'[5]

7   H.M.S. *Agamemnon* leaving Malta for the Dardanelles, 1915

8   Commander C. R. Samson, R.N.A.S.

9　On board *Triad*.
From left to right: Commodore Roger Keyes, Vice-Admiral John de Robeck,
General Sir Ian Hamilton, Major-General W. P. Braithwaite

10　Port Mudros, Lemnos

6

No Going Back

'*He felt that if the Fleet could not get through the Straits unaided the Army ought to see the business through. The effect of a defeat in the Orient would be very serious. There could be no going back.*'
Lord Kitchener to the War Council
24th February 1915[1]

'On 11th March 1915,' wrote Sir Ian Hamilton, 'I was absorbed in the command of the Striking Force of three armies of Territorials quartered in an irregular circle round London. On the next morning, the 12th, Lord Kitchener sent for me. I entered the room. He was writing. After a moment he looked up and said, "We are sending a military force to support the Fleet now at the Dardanelles and you are to have command."

'When the King of Denmark sent Hamlet to England he commanded him to make himself scarce "with fiery quickness". Thus it was with King Kitchener and Hamilton. Within twenty-four hours I must hand over a command three times larger than the British Expeditionary Force; receive my instructions; select a staff; get the hang of the Dardanelles and of the nature and whereabouts of my new force and bundle off. Equally serious was the fact that there was no time to get my staff together. I had to start without any of my administrative officers, whether for supply, medicine or discipline. They were not destined to join me for more than three weeks, and until they came I and my small group of General Staff officers had to undertake their work, including matters so remote from our experience as unloading and reloading ships and making arrangements for the wounded.

'My troops were to be Australians and New Zealanders under Birdwood, a friend, strength say about 30,000; the 29th Division strength, say 19,000, under Hunter-Weston (a slashing man of action – an acute theorist); the Royal Naval Division, 11,000 strong (an excellent type of officer and man under a solid Commander – Paris);

a French contingent, say about a division, under the chivalrous d'Amade. Say a grand total of about 80,000, probably panning out at some 50,000 rifles in the firing line. Of these the 29th Division are extras – *division de luxe* – to be returned the moment they can be spared.

'K. went on: "You may just as well realise at once that G.H.Q. in France do not agree. They think they have only to drive the Germans back fifty miles nearer to their base to win the war. The thing is absurd but French, plus France, are a strong combine and they are fighting tooth and nail for the 29th Division. It must be clearly understood that all things ear-marked for the East are looked on by powerful interests both at home and in France as having been stolen from the West. . . . Half that number of men will do you handsomely – the Turks are busy elsewhere. I hope you will not have to land at all; if you *do* have to land, why then the powerful fleet at your back will be the prime factor in your choice of time and place. . . ."'

General Sir James Wolfe Murray, the Chief of the Imperial General Staff, was then called in, also General Sir Archibald Murray, Inspector of Home Forces, and Major-General Walter Braithwaite, Sir Ian's Chief of Staff designate. This apparently was the first occasion either of the Murrays had heard of the project. Both seemed quite taken aback and said nothing.

'Next morning, the 13th,' Sir Ian continued, 'I handed over the Central Force Command and at 10.30 went in with Braithwaite to say good-bye. K. was standing by his desk splashing about with his pen at three different drafts of instructions. When I asked the crucial question, the enemy's strength, K. thought I had better be prepared for 40,000. How many guns? No one knows. Who was in command? Djevad Pasha, "it is believed." "Is our force to have the usual ten per cent margin of reserves to fill casualties?" "No!" "Up-to-date aeroplanes, pilots and observers?" "*Not one!*" . . . And so on, and so on.

'My instructions on a half-sheet of paper were vague. They were headed "Constantinople Expeditionary Force". I begged him to alter this to avert Fate's evil eye. He consented to: "Mediterranean Expeditionary Force". The main points were that the Army was not to land unless the ships failed to force their own way through; that no serious attack was to take place until the whole of my force was on the spot; that once we had landed there was to be no return until the object had been gained.

'So I said goodbye to old K. as casually as if we were to meet at dinner. Actually my heart went out to my old Chief. He was giving me the best thing in his gift, and I hated to leave him amongst people who were frightened of him. But there was no saying a word, he did not even wish me luck, and I did not expect him to, but he did say, rather unexpectedly, *after* I had said goodbye and just as I was taking up my cap from the table, "If the Fleet gets through, Constantinople will fall of itself and you will have won, not a battle but the war." '[2]

'I feel it my duty also to represent the strong feeling we have at the Admiralty,' Churchill had written to Lord K. on March 4th, 'that there should be placed at the head of this army so variously composed, a general officer of high rank and reputation, who has held important commands in war. I heard yesterday with very great pleasure you mention the name of Sir Ian Hamilton as the officer you had designated for the main command in this theatre. Certainly no choice could be more agreeable to the Admiralty and to the Navy, but I would venture to press upon you the desirability of this officer being on the spot as soon as possible, in order that he may concert with the Admiral the really critical and decisive operations which may be required at the very outset. I wish to make it clear that the naval operations in the Dardanelles cannot be delayed for troop movements, as we must get into the Marmara as soon as possible. . . .'[3]

'At 5 o'clock that afternoon we left Charing Cross for Dover,' Sir Ian continued. 'My staff still bear the bewildered look of men who have hurriedly been snatched from desks. . . . An hour ago one or two of them put on uniform for the first time – leggings awry, spurs upside down, belts over shoulder straps! I haven't a notion of who they all are.

'As the train rumbled out I missed the thrill of the step that counts. Two bad omens upset me. The first was when dating a letter just before leaving home I realised, suddenly, that it was Friday, the 13th. Jean [his wife], who was bending over me, noticed the little shock and quickly said, "The 13th is always a lucky day for you." But it was no use; the *Penseroso* [melancholy] began to prevail over the *Allegro* [liveliness]; and then, to put a topper on it, I kissed her through her veil! A gesture which, in her turn, she said was unlucky.'

Sir Ian and his staff embarked in H.M.S. *Foresight* at Dover, crossed the Channel in a fog and took the train from Calais to

Marseilles where they joined the light cruiser *Phaeton*, Captain J. E. Cameron, for onward passage to the Dardanelles. Corfu, Sir Ian's birthplace (16th January 1863), was passed during the night of March 16th, which revived thoughts of a brave mother he never knew.

'Exquisite air; sea like a carpet of blue velvet outspread for Aphrodite,' he wrote next morning on entering the Aegean Sea. At noon they passed a cruiser taking Admiral Carden invalided to Malta. 'One week ago the thunder of his guns shook the firm foundations of the world. Now a sheer bulk lies poor old Carden. *Vanitas vanitatum*.'[4] Mudros was reached at 3 p.m. on March 17th, after a record journey.

As was to be expected, in so much agitation, all sorts of things had been overlooked. Although Sir Ian must have known the story of Admiral Duckworth's passage and retreat through the Dardanelles in 1807, not pleasant reading, what he did not know was that in 1906 the General Staff had drawn up a considered memorandum upon the question of forcing the Dardanelles. But those who then comprised the General Staff were now in France, and no one at the War Office knew of the existence of this document. Not until 1916, long after the last of our troops had quitted the Gallipoli Peninsula, did Sir Ian Hamilton even hear of it.

This memorandum contains some very pertinent questions. It was prepared at the time of a difference of opinion with Turkey over the frontier of Sinai. The whole project had been considered by a combined naval and military conference and turned down as impossible. In 1908 the General Staff considered the subject again and rather went back on their former judgement. They thought the thing was possible, but only if it were a complete surprise. In 1911 they again reviewed the situation and confirmed other previous opinion, saying that 'owing to the impossibility of effecting a surprise, an attempt to embark an army on the Gallipoli Peninsula would be too hazardous to be recommended'.

Of course this does not mean that the project was turned down for all time and under all circumstances. In 1915 circumstances had changed considerably. Naval guns had increased in range and power very much more rapidly than land guns, certainly than the guns in the Gallipoli forts. What stopped the ships on 18th March 1915 was the mines, as we have seen, plus the fact that the lighter guns, firing from concealed positions, though innocuous to armoured ships, effectively prevented the minesweepers from doing their work.

It is hard to say to what extent a study of these documents would have influenced Sir Ian's actions but their value to him would have been incalculable.

At 3 p.m. on March 17th, the light cruiser *Phaeton*, with Sir Ian Hamilton and General Staff on board, entered Mudros harbour and took up an anchor berth close to the *Queen Elizabeth*. Anchors and cables were hardly secured before the Admiral's barge called to take Sir Ian over to the flagship for a meeting. Sir Ian had arrived on the scene just in time to witness the very next day from the bridge of the *Phaeton*, as we shall see, the closing stages of the momentous naval battle for the Narrows.

'De Robeck greeted me in the friendliest fashion,' Sir Ian wrote. 'He is a fine-looking man with great charm of manner.' After introductions all sat down round the table in the Admiral's dining cabin, and the meeting opened.

For his part the Admiral stressed that he would prefer to force a passage on his own and that he was sure he could do it. Sir Ian in turn said that he was 'a waiting man' and that it was 'the Admiral's innings for so long as he could keep his wicket up'. The Admiral then asked to see Sir Ian's instructions, and Braithwaite read them out. When he stopped, Commodore Roger Keyes inquired, 'Is that all?' When Braithwaite confessed that it was, everyone looked a little blank. Asked what he meant to do, Sir Ian replied that he proposed to get ready for a landing because 'whether the Fleet forces the passage and disembarks us on the Bosphorus, or whether we have to "go for" the Peninsula, the *band-o-bast* [arrangement] could be made to suit either case'.[5]

When these introductory talks were over Sir Ian was shown round the *Q.E.* by the Flag Captain G. P. W. Hope. By this time it was nearly 7 p.m., so he stayed to dine with the Admiral, whom he found a delightful host. There followed an early night for everyone in preparation for the morrow, the action of March 18th. The *Phaeton* was not required to take part. Instead she would take Sir Ian and his Staff, General d'Amade, Major-General Paris and Brigadier-General E. G. Sinclair-Maclagan, commanding the 3rd (Australia) Infantry Brigade, on a reconnoitre.

Leaving harbour during the early hours of the morning, the *Phaeton* set course for the Gulf of Xeros, then turned and ran down the coast.

At 4 p.m. precisely, the *Phaeton* rounded Cape Helles and stood off the approaches to the Straits. The battle was then in full swing.

'Whizz – flop – bang,' Sir Ian wrote, '– what an ass I am to be here. If we keep on we are in for a visit to Davy Jones's locker.'

The wounded *Inflexible* withdrawing with 'a whole bevy of destroyers crowded round,' made a deep impression. 'In the sight of all those men standing still, silent, orderly in their ranks, facing the imminence of death, I got my answer to the hasty moralisings about war. . . . Ten thousand years of peace would fail to produce a spectacle of so great a virtue.'

On return to Mudros Sir Ian and his staff were transferred from the *Phaeton* to the Headquarters Transport *Franconia*, and then, as you already know, the weather broke and the fleet had to ride out a gale which lasted several days.

'From what I saw with my own eyes,' Sir Ian telegraphed to Lord Kitchener on the 19th, 'I am being most reluctantly driven to the conclusion that the Straits are not likely to be forced by battleships as at one time seemed probable. The Army's part will be more than mere landings of parties to destroy Forts, it must be a deliberate and progressive military operation carried out at full strength so as to open a passage for the Navy.'

Lord K.'s immediate reply was straight, strong and to the point: 'You know my view that the Dardanelles passage must be forced, and that if large military operations on the Gallipoli Peninsula by your troops are necessary to clear the way, those operations must be undertaken, after careful consideration of the local defences, and must be carried through.'

Vice-Admiral de Robeck had come out of the action of March 18th with the apparent intention of resuming the attack as soon as the weather had moderated. To Rear-Admiral Wemyss, S.N.O. Mudros, he had signalled at once: 'We have had a disastrous day owing either to floating mines or torpedoes from shore tubes . . . and we had much the best of the forts.'

Next day he wrote to Sir Ian Hamilton (who did not receive the letter until March 21st), 'Our men were splendid, and thank heaven our loss of life was quite small. . . . It was sad to lose ships, and my heart aches when one thinks of it; one must do what one is told and take risks or otherwise we cannot win. We are all getting ready for another "go" and are not the least beaten or downhearted. . . .'

On March 20th Sir Ian signalled Admiral de Robeck: 'From every point of view I consider change of military base to Alexandria and

Port Said advisable. I can bring you military help from there quickly and in better shape than from here where there are no facilities. . . .'

To which the Admiral replied: 'As a military measure I concur with your proposal to make Egypt the headquarters, but submit political result of withdrawal of troops from Mudros at the moment requires the greatest consideration. . . . I suggest their departure be delayed until our attack is renewed in a few days time. . . .'

At Mudros 10 a.m. March 22nd, a Council of War took place on board the *Queen Elizabeth*, Principal Flag and General Officers attending.

'Before ever we went aboard,' wrote Sir Ian, 'Braithwaite [Chief of Staff], Birdwood [Commander Anzacs] and I had agreed that, whatever we landsmen might think, we must leave the seamen to settle their own job, saying nothing for or against land operations or amphibious operations until the sailors themselves turned to us and said they had abandoned the idea of forcing the passage alone. But the moment we sat down de Robeck told us he was now quite clear he could not get through without the help of all my troops.

'So there was no discussion. At once we turned our faces to the land scheme.'[6]

What happened to make Admiral de Robeck change his mind, after saying only three days before that he was 'getting ready for another go'?

'My belief,' wrote Lieutenant John Godfrey, 'is that Admiral de Robeck's mind was never altered; that after the battle of March 18th he was over-persuaded by Commodore Keyes, his Chief of Staff, and by his Staff Officer, Operations, to send the telegram saying he was going on with the assault, and that afterwards, on further consideration, his mind reverted to his real and original conviction that the attack should be broken off. These two officers never wavered, but they could not carry de Robeck with them.'[7]

And now for the official view: 'When Admiral de Robeck was faced with the alternative of landing an army to occupy Gallipoli and keep our communications open, or of embarking on what he regarded as a hazardous enterprise, with a doubtful issue – doubtful since success was dependent on the collapse of the Turkish opposition after his arrival in the Marmara – how could he, having the responsibility, decide otherwise than he did?'[8]

We were now committed to a land attack on the Gallipoli Peninsula, but the force then at the disposal of Sir Ian Hamilton bore no direct relation to the numbers needed for that operation. No real attempt

had been made to work out a reasoned estimate of what force would
be needed. Sir Ian was just given what troops could be spared and
told to carry on. True, Admirals Carden and de Robeck had only
been given ships that were not wanted for the Grand Fleet, but then
the initial attempt to force the Straits was looked on more or less as
an experiment – a demonstration – a diversion. That had been the
original idea. But Lord Kitchener had told Sir Ian that once begun
this affair must be carried through.

The logical conclusion is that Lord Kitchener should have got,
before he ever allowed the land operation to begin, a definite estimate of what force was required, and that Sir Ian was the man to
make that estimate – although never, until after the landings, did
he complain to Lord K. of a shortage of numbers. However, Sir Ian
was always a bit of an optimist, and it is probable that he and Kitchener were inclined to underestimate the fighting value of the Turk.
There was some justification for this, in that the Turk had not shown
up very well so far, either in the Great War – in his attack on the
Suez Canal in particular – or in the previous Balkan wars. There is
also this consideration, that the larger the force sent to Sir Ian, the
longer it would take to collect, and so the longer the time the Turk
would have to strengthen his defences. As it was, there had been
considerable controversy at home about releasing the 29th Division
(Regular Army). Their allocation would be an admission that the
Dardanelles venture was passing definitely from the category of a
diversion and a side issue to that of a major operation. A decision,
however, had been reached on March 10th. Shortly after this date the
29th Division had sailed for the Aegean.

It is easy now for belated prudence to maintain that under the
circumstances Sir Ian should have abandoned the idea of a military
operation, secured, if he could, the acquiescence of the Navy in
defeat, counter-ordered the assembling troops, and returned to
London. Prudence could have said much in favour of such a retirement.

Small preparation had been made; the strongest part of the striking force (29th Division) was still distant; the number of the enemy,
though roughly estimated at 40,000 on the Peninsula and 30,000 in
reserve beyond Bulair, was really unknown; ever since the appearance of the Fleet, Turks had been heard, from the clink of their
spades and shovels, digging like beavers every night at the possible
points of our attack; and it had been proved that the cross-fire of
naval guns could not dislodge them even from the toe of the Peninsula. All these objections could have been urged at the time by
generals to whom, as to the German Commanders of the Turkish

defence, a landing appeared impossible. But if anyone believed that a high-spirited officer with a wealth of battle experience second to none, was likely to consider a retirement to be his duty just when he had received a command which he regarded as the surest means of terminating the war, that anyone erred in his judgement of mankind.

So, in the face of all objections, the preparations for an assault upon the Peninsula began. The troops were sent down to Egypt for training, re-sorting and re-packing in transports, ready to fight immediately on return to Mudros.

Preparations for landing an army under fire require an intense degree of organisation; above all, at least some highly trained troops are required. None at all were available until the arrival of the 29th Division. Sir Ian Hamilton pronounced that whatever the risks of delay they were less than an unorganised attack with inexperienced troops.

I need not go into the thousand and one things that had to be done or procured, before the necessary forces could be ready for landing. On March 25th Sir Ian Hamilton followed the transports to Egypt and remained there until April 8th. His Administrative Staff joined him on April 1st. He did wonders, but it was not until a full five weeks had elapsed after the naval attack on the Narrows had been broken off that the troops were assembled in Mudros and its vicinity and the weather proved to be suitable for a Combined Operation.

The really decisive factor in determining exactly when to start the landing operations was the weather. Whatever the size of the force landed, its seaborne lines of communication had to be kept open. Any Aegean fisherman could have told the planners that gales from S.W. and N.E., mist, rain and heavy seas would persist, as in fact they did, until the end of April. This seemed obvious to those who knew the Aegean, but less so to the High Command, and it is not sufficiently emphasised in histories of the Campaign.

7

The Army Assembles

'*I do not hold check on March 18th decisive but having
met General Hamilton ... I now consider a combined
operation essential to obtain great results and object of
Campaign ... To attack Narrows now with Fleet
would be a mistake as it would jeopardise the execution
of a better and bigger scheme.*'
Vice-Admiral de Robeck to Admiralty,
26th March 1915

The vague instructions given to Sir Ian Hamilton by Lord Kitchener
before his departure reveal the hesitation with which the Gallipoli
Campaign was regarded, not only by Kitchener himself but by
generals both at home and in France. Sir Ian's appointed task was
one of the most difficult that could have been given to a general,
yet Sir Ian was well qualified for it. Except that he had never yet
held supreme command in any major campaign, his experience in
military affairs was unsurpassed, and his courage and determination
were exceptional. Incidentally he was twice recommended for the
'Victoria Cross'. When selecting him for the Gallipoli command
Lord K. was unquestionably guided by his character, plus his wide
experience and his knowledge of Colonial, Indian and French
troops.

The fortunate presence in Egypt of the Australian and New Zealand
Divisions – or A.N.Z.A.C.S. as they came to be known later on, when
formed into a Corps under Lieutenant-General Sir William Birdwood – was due to Kitchener's constant apprehension of Turkish
attacks on the Suez Canal and on Egypt itself, where it was natural
to imagine that a nationalist and religious (Muslim) movement
might well bring Arabs over to the enemy's side. The Sultan of
Turkey, as we have seen, was calling for a *Jihād*, a Holy War against
the Infidel, and Lord K. naturally had Egypt much on his mind,

having been Sirdar or Military Commander-in-Chief there, as well as H.B.M.'s Agent and Consul-General in Cairo from 1911 until recalled in 1914 for the war.

These Dominion troops had reached Egypt on 3rd December 1914, encamping at points near Cairo. The Australian Division, under Major-General W. T. Bridges, was at Mena by the Pyramids, and the mixed N.Z. and Australian Division under Major-General Sir Alexander Godley was at Heliopolis. We, in the *Bacchante*, had exchanged greetings with companies of these troops stationed on the banks of the Suez Canal. A finer set of men could hardly be found in any country.

The Anzacs came from every shade of society and had grown up accustomed to natural equality. At first they found military discipline irksome and almost superfluous. They could be relied on to face death with equanimity but not to salute an officer, and their language was often unrestrained in the presence of superiors. The officers came mostly from the towns, the other ranks from the out-back. They enjoyed life but did not fear death, and while the going was good they were determined to enjoy themselves. They poured into Cairo upon any animal or conveyance which could move and the beautiful city became a scene of frequent turmoil. Their sons in World War II who fought with the Army of the Nile, also strolled the streets of Cairo oblivious of senior officers. They would drive, according to their custom, ten-up in shabby taxis and victorias (cabs) while they surveyed sardonically the town their fathers had stormed before them. The 'Gippos' of the 1940s regarded them with equal respect born, as of old, of apprehension rather than affection.

When his inspections of the Anzacs were over, Sir Ian reviewed Artillery, Engineers and Cavalry, winding up with the Supply and Transport columns. Three days later he inspected the Royal Naval Division at Port Said.

The foundation of the Royal Naval Division had been laid before the war, as it was appreciated that on mobilisation there must be a number of seamen, stokers and marines for whom no sea jobs would be available. Two brigades of seamen and one of marines were formed into a Naval Brigade. Many of the men had set their hearts on serving afloat, and it was with much disappointment but still with loyalty that they devoted themselves to the work of a soldier. Naval parlance was used on every possible occasion. To leave their camps, in which the White Ensign flew and bells recorded the passage of time, men requested 'leave to go ashore'; when they returned, they 'came aboard'; and, when they did not, they were reported as 'adrift'. Men were 'rated' and 'disrated', and for sergeants and corporals they had petty officers and leading seamen. Anchors were stencilled on their gun limbers and emblazoned on their company flags, and their regimental badges were the crests of the admirals whose names the various battalions bore. When ill or wounded they attended the 'sick bay'; field kitchens were the 'galley'; the King's health was drunk sitting in the wardroom, when an officer wanted salt at a meal he would ask his neighbour to 'give it a fair wind'. Many of the men and some of the officers requested 'leave to grow' and paraded creditable beards in the faces of a clean-chinned Army.

'From Dunkirk to Belgrade,' wrote Winston Churchill, 'from Antwerp to Gallipoli, from the Somme to Ancre in 1916, through every bloody battle they marched and suffered. By 1918 the great majority of the officers and men of the original companies were dead. Long may the record of their achievements be preserved, and long may their memory be respected by those for whom they fought.'[1]

On April 5th Sir Ian Hamilton went to French headquarters at Alexandria and inspected the French contingent under General d'Amade. There were infantry of the line in grey, Zouaves in blue and red, Senegalese in dark blue and the Foreign Legion in blue-grey. The cavalry rode Arabs and barbs, mostly white stallions. They wore pale blue tunics and bright scarlet breeches. Sir Ian was impressed by their appearance and their behaviour.

The 29th Division, commanded by Major-General A. G. Hunter-Weston, was the last regular division of the British Army as yet uncommitted to battle. It was reviewed at Nuneaton by H.M. King George V on March 12th and sailed for Egypt four days later. The division had been embarked in twenty-two ships without any proper allocation. All ammunition, for instance, was in one ship, the transport was in another and the machine-guns were at the bottom of the hold. Before these first-line troops could go into battle they must be berthed alongside at Alexandria and Port Said for re-sorting and re-packing.

Malta was reached on March 23rd, and here – as far as the 1st Lancashire Fusiliers were concerned – 'the kindness and warmth with which they had been received in Nuneaton reacted on the officers engaged in censoring the mail home. It was found necessary to restrict letters to one sweetheart and one mother'.[2]

Some authors have taken exception to the fact that in Malta officers found time to visit the opera to hear a performance of 'Faust' by an Italian Opera Company. Why not, for heaven's sake? The transports were busy coaling, and a convoy in those days could not with safety clear the Grand Harbour after dark.

The 29th Division began to arrive in Egypt on March 28th. While sorting out cargoes went on, many of the troops were encamped at Mex outside Alexandria. There, on April 6th, Sir Ian reviewed them, the mounted troops first. 'What a contrast between these solid look-ing men on their weight-carrying horses and our wiry little Allies on their barbs and Arabs,' he wrote. 'The Royal Horse Artillery were superb.'

Sir Ian was accompanied by General Sir John Maxwell, C-in-C, Forces in Egypt, which was good sense, as he (Sir Ian) particularly wanted Cox's Indian Brigade for Gallipoli – and he got them. 'The arrangement whereby I have to sponge on Maxwell for men if I want them is detestable,' he wrote. 'He (Maxwell) expects, so he says, a big attack on the Canal at any moment. Old campaigners versed in the Egyptian war-lore tell me that the drying up of the wells must put a lid on any move across the desert until the winter rains; and, apart from this, how in the name of the beard of their own false prophet can the Turks attack Egypt whilst we are at the gates of Constantinople?'[3]

After reviewing the Cavalry (who had to leave their horses behind in Egypt), Sir Ian inspected the 86th Infantry Brigade (2nd Royal Fus., 1st Lancashire Fus.; 1st Royal Munster Fus.; 1st Royal Dublin Fus.) under Brigadier-General Hare. The 87th (2nd South Wales Borderers; 1st Kings Own Scottish Borderers; 1st Royal Inniskilling Fus.; 1st Border Regt) under Brigadier-General Marshall; and the 88th Brigade under Brigadier-General Napier, consisting of the 4th Worcester Regt; 2nd Hampshire Regt; 1st Essex Regt; and the 5th Royal Scots (Territorials).

His inspection of the Indian Brigade, under Major-General Sir Herbert Cox, at Kantara, must have given Sir Ian great pleasure. 'No one can understand what it means to an old soldier who began fighting in the Afghan War, to be in touch once again with Sikhs and Gurkhas, those splendid knight-errants of India,' he wrote. 'When I addressed the parade in Hindustani the words seemed to drop down from Heaven on to my tongue.'[4]

Besides these and other fighting regiments since equally renowned, there was the Assyrian Jewish Refugee Mule Corps (better known as

the Zion Mule Corps) organised at short notice out of Jewish
refugees from Syria and Palestine, chiefly Russian subjects who had
sought safety in Egypt. Colonel J. H. Patterson had been commissioned to select a body of about 500, with 750 transport mules.
Orders were given partly in Hebrew and partly in English. The
men were armed with rifles taken from the Turks during the battle
of the Suez Canal in February. The regimental badge was the
Shield of David. Probably this was the first purely Jewish fighting
corps that went into action since Jerusalem fell to the Roman armies
under Titus in A D 70.

Sir Ian sailed from Alexandria on April 8th in S.S. *Arcadian*, headquarters ship, and reached Mudros two days later. The three weeks
originally fixed for the reorganisation of the Force had elapsed and it
was not ready. The bulk of the Australian Division was in harbour,
but only the first transports of the mixed Australian and N.Z. Division and of the 29th Division. It was still uncertain when the French
would be ready to sail from Alexandria. If necessary, Sir Ian was
prepared to go ahead without them. The Royal Naval Division left
Port Said on April 12th for Skyros, seventy miles south of Lemnos.
Trebuki, its port, was also to be the point of assembly for the French,
since the political objections to using the well-placed and far more
convenient island of Mytilene (now Lesbos), as at first intended,
had proved insuperable. In the event the French just made Trebuki
on time.

Transports proceeded from Egypt in small groups or singly. They
were unescorted. No U-boats had arrived, and the only likelihood
of attack was from two or three torpedo-boats that had been reported
by aircraft in the Gulf of Smyrna.

On April 16th the *Manitou*, one of the last of the 29th Division transports, carrying 20 officers, 626 men and 615 horses, mostly 147th
Brigade, Royal Field Artillery, had just passed Skyros on passage
to Mudros when she sighted a torpedo-boat making for her. Thinking she was a British boat that wanted to communicate, the transport
stopped, but in fact she was the Turkish *Demir Hisar*, commanded by
Lieutenant-Commander Freiherr von Fircks, Imperial German
Navy, who had with him a German lieutenant and some German
petty officers to stiffen the Turkish crew. He closed the *Manitou* and
ordered the ship to be abandoned in three minutes. There was no
possibility of resistance because, although the *Manitou* carried
guns and rifles, all ammunition was at the bottom of the hold.
As there were only enough boats for one third of the men on

board, the Captain protested against the shortage of time allowed to abandon ship, and the German commander extended it by ten minutes.

Meanwhile the men, who were actually engaged in boat drill when the T.B. turned up, went to 'panic stations'. They started to lower boats without orders, some so heavily overloaded that the davits carried away, while others, after being lowered inefficiently, capsized. In the midst of this confusion the enemy fired two torpedoes. By a miracle both missed. Thinking discretion the better part of valour, the German captain now withdrew at full speed but was intercepted and chased by the destroyers *Kennet, Jed* and *Wear* from Skyros, who had picked up the *Manitou's* S.O.S. Seeing no escape, von Fircks ran his torpedo-boat ashore, where she became a wreck. Captain and crew were interned by the Greeks for the duration of the war. They had deserved a better fate.

This was the only serious incident during the concentration of a vast fleet.

We in the *Bacchante*, in company with our sister ship the *Euryalus*, had arrived, fresh from the Canal Zone on April 12th, to find Port Mudros overflowing with shipping. The island of Lemnos, lying some sixty miles south of the Peninsula, had been yielded by Turkey to Greece at the end of the Balkan Wars of 1912–13. Its use had been granted to the Allies by the Greek government under Venizelos. The harbour itself is vast, measuring some two by three miles across with good holding ground in five to seven fathoms. Two small islands divide the outer from the inner harbour forming three comparatively narrow passages which were to prove a godsend from the defence point of view when U-boats came along.

Near the harbour mouth, just beyond the headland on the port hand and a mile or so inshore, are four hills – Yam, Yrroc, Eb and Denmad, which were named during a survey begun in secret in 1893 by H.M.S. *Fearless*, continued in 1899 by the battleship *Hood* (now upside down in the southern entrance to Portland Harbour) and completed in 1901 by H.M.S. *Irresistible* (sunk in the Dardanelles by a Turkish mine, as we have seen, on 18th March 1915).

The officer largely responsible for these surveys, Lieutenant Hughes C. 'Tubby' Lockyer, Royal Navy, was now a post captain in command of the battleship *Implacable* at anchor in Mudros. Lockyer had his own reasons for giving these four hills such unusual names, which still appear in the latest edition of the Admiralty chart. Captain Alvin Coote Corry, R.N., had made young Lockyer's surveying party

work round the clock, Sundays included. When challenged on the
unusual names he had chosen for the hills, Lockyer explained, with
his tongue in his cheek, that they were from the Greek, and Corry
was satisfied; but it had not occurred to him to read the names
backwards before giving his approval.

As a base Mudros had its disadvantages. Southerly gales, such as
spring up very quickly in the changeable seasons, blow straight
through the harbour mouth, making boat-work impossible. There
are no docks or wharves, no buildings which could be made use of as
barracks. All supplies, including most of the water, had to be brought
from Alexandria or Port Said, 500 miles away.

Mudros itself, the town from which the port is named, consists of
a small collection of wretched, red-roofed houses dominated by a
large white church. It is mostly inhabited, even to this day, by
Levantines who scrape a living from petty commerce. Our *Bacchante*
alone could have bought up its wealth of goats, fish and olives in a
few weeks. The port is ringed with bare hills and looks like some vast
crater of an extinct volcano flooded by the sea. In summer the low
hills are scorched to a pale brown, and, for an Aegean island, the
country possesses little beauty or interest apart from the hot springs
for which it was consecrated to the god of fire.

Rear-Admiral 'Rosy' Wemyss, S.N.O. Mudros, had reported to
the Admiralty, on his arrival in early February, that the official attitude of the senior Greek official, a captain in the Greek Navy, was
one of complete ignorance of all that was going on in the port. Privately the Greek captain told the Admiral, with whom he was soon
to establish very friendly relations, that neither he nor the inhabitants
would offer any resistance, passive or active, to any step that the
Admiral might consider it necessary to take. He proved to be as good
as his word.

During the few days that remained before the landings, we midshipmen hardly got ashore except for a picnic and a bathe. Midshipman Hugh R. Tate, with others from the gunroom of the *Implacable*,
did ride out on donkeys with made-up saddles and found the going
hard. While drawing to the side of the road to allow a funeral procession to pass, they saw the pallise, caught by a gust of wind expose
the body of an old woman completely naked. Poor thing. I suppose
someone in her family needed her clothes. No trees on the island
meant no wood for a coffin.

A few days after our arrival Major Aubrey Herbert turned up.
After we landed him at Port Said on our return from Alexandretta at
the end of February, he had made his way to Cairo to join the New
Zealand Division as Interpreter and Intelligence Officer.

'The golden sunlight and tranquillity of Egypt were tragic in contrast to what was coming,' he was to write later. 'Every Intelligence Officer was a Cassandra with an attentive audience. In every discussion there was, as far as I saw, unanimity between military, naval and political officers, who all wished the landing to take place at Alexandretta, and deplored (not to use a stronger word) the project of the Dardanelles, which the Turks had been given ample time to fortify.

'The heat increased and the English officers' wives who had come to Egypt to be with their husbands, were receiving a taste of the ferocious *Khamsin* that affected their complexions. This wind had the advantage of killing insects with its heat. Then came the locusts making a shadow against the sun and a carpet on the ground. "Oc" Asquith, Patrick Shaw-Stewart, Charles Lister and Rupert Brooke had come out to Egypt in the Royal Naval Division, and we lunched and dined and went to the Pyramids by moonlight.'[5]

While he was stationed in Cairo, Aubrey Herbert wanted to buy from a friend a beautiful white arab pony that had won most of the races in Cairo, but General Godley said, 'No! – you aren't the Duke of Marlborough; you can't have that white pony unless he's dyed, and even that would wash off in any rainstorm'. So Aubrey Herbert had to abandon the idea, but with little reluctance as he found that the pony pulled furiously and would certainly lead any advance or retreat by miles. Instead, he had been ashore in Mudros, with a couple of others, to buy donkeys who were to carry their kits. With help from the Mayor they had secured six, plus a little one for £1 as a mascot. They had a great deal of trouble getting them on board their transport, the German prize-ship *Lutzow*. To the annoyance of all ranks the ship was 'dry' – thanks to a puritanical New Zealand Government. 'It was even dryer than we expected,' said Aubrey Herbert. 'The troops have to wash and shave in salt water!'

As an Assault Group Commander for the D-day landings in Normandy on 6th June 1944, I was allowed the best part of six months' intensive training with the Army. For the Gallipoli landings we had just a few days together in which to complete all our arrangements.

Thank goodness Douglas Dixon, who was in charge of our steam pinnace, and I, who had the picket boat, were to land Anzacs from our tows, as they appeared to be natural seamen and were very handy in boats, as indeed were men of the 29th Division. In contrast the Senegalese were as awkward as gollywogs, but they had kind hearts. During practice periods they would reward their boat

midshipmen with oranges and a kindly smile. On one occasion, however, I did even better. A British major gave me half a crown for
taking him off to a transport, which was just enough to buy a bottle
of beer for each member of our crew of eight.

It would have been disastrous to our morale if we midshipmen had
been deprived of our part in the landings because we were so young.
After all it was in the boats that midshipmen belonged, from the early
morning beef boat to the last nightly liberty boat. To have been kept
back would have meant a complete loss of face and of heart. We
were, in a manner of speaking, just as expendable as anyone else. The
Royal Navy of our generation produced some of the finest ship-
handlers in the world, thanks to early training in boats: 'Catch 'em
young and treat 'em rough' was not a bad idea, as history had proved
often enough before us. Captain B. H. Smith of the *Vengeance* was the
only battleship captain who would not allow his midshipmen to take
part in the Original Landings. He must have hurt their pride a lot.
It was also quite a wrong decision in itself.

Sailors in those days of wooden decks used to go around bare-
footed. It was said that a sailor put his boots on before turning into
his hammock, while a soldier would take his off before dossing down.
Be that as it may, the naval custom of bare feet proved to my advantage. During my early days in charge of the *Bacchante*'s picket boat,
Petty Officer William Main, the coxswain, used to place a bare foot
over my boot (no one wore shoes), and by pressing down with his
toes would signal to me when the moment had arrived for orders to
be passed to the engine-room. Two rings on the bell meant 'go
ahead', four rings 'slow', one 'stop!', three 'go astern'. A perfect
arrival alongside the *Bacchante*, with the stern-sheets of the picket boat
nicely placed against the lower platform of the accommodation
ladder, would bring a word of praise from the Officer of the Watch
on the quarter-deck.

'Thanks awfully, Main,' I would whisper, looking up at his smiling
face.

'It's a pleasure, Mr Bush,' he would reply, and in this way we
became life-long friends.

Picket boat duties used to take me to other warships, and it was a
custom of the Service, if you had to wait, that your boat was ordered
to 'lay off', and not to stop alongside the gangway. But the midshipman was invariably invited on board by the midshipman of
the watch to wait in the gunroom, the midshipmen's mess.

One of the first ships I visited in Mudros was the *Lord Nelson*,
where the 'snotties' were all from our term, the Blake's, at Dartmouth. Though it was only 11 a.m. the occasion was celebrated by

my being invited to have a drink. I am a son of the Vicarage, as were many of our generation in the Navy, and my father kept no liquor in the house so I was at a loss for a reply. We were only allowed beer in the *Bacchante*, and I wanted to appear sophisticated.

'A glass of port?'

It was quite a time before the laughter died down.

On April 17th Rupert Brooke disembarked on Skyros from the *Grantully Castle* with his men of the Royal Naval Division. In legend, Skyros is the island where Achilles was hidden by his mother among the daughters of Lycomedes; and hence by sight of arms and sound of trumpet Odysseus lured him away to join the expeditionary force against Troy. Here was murdered Theseus whose ghost in full armour led the van at Marathon. There is a rare breed of indigenous pony which has been bred on the island since the days of Homer at least. Arthur 'Oc' Asquith described the island to his sister Violet before anything had happened.

'This island is more mountainous than Lemnos and more sparsely inhabited. It is like one great rock-garden of white and pinkish-white marble, with small red poppies and every sort of wild flower; in gorges ilex, dwarf holly and occasional groups of olives; and everywhere the smell of thyme (or is it sage? or wild mint?). Our men kill adders and have fun with big tortoises. The water near the shore, where the bottom is white marble, is more beautifully green and blue than I have ever seen anywhere.'

Rupert Brooke seemed quite well till Tuesday, the 20th. On Wednesday he stayed in bed with pains in his back and head, and a swelling on his lip; but no anxiety was felt till the evening, when he had a temperature of 103. 'Next morning he was much worse; the swelling had increased, and a consultation was held. The diagnosis was acute blood-poisoning, and all hope was given up. It was decided to move him to the French hospital ship *Duguay-Truin* which happened to be in harbour. When he was told this, his one anxiety was lest he should have difficulty in rejoining his battalion. They reassured him, and he seemed to be content. Soon afterwards he became comatose; there does not seem to have been any moment when he can have realised that he was dying. He passed away at 4.46 p.m. on Friday April 23rd, the day of Shakespeare and St George, 'with the sun shining all round his cabin, and the cool sea breeze blowing through the door and the shaded windows. No one could have wished a quieter or a calmer end'.[6]

Rupert Brooke's body was carried ashore the same evening in a picket boat commanded by Midshipman R. K. 'Bertie' Dickson, H.M.S. *Canopus*. The burial took place after dark in an olive-grove where he had sat with his friends on Tuesday, 'one of the loveliest places on this earth'. The funeral service was said by the Rev. Bernard Failes. Next morning, early, the *Grantully Castle* sailed for the Gallipoli Peninsula.

A few years ago I asked John Masefield, Poet Laureate, if he would tell me about Rupert Brooke, whom he used to know so well. 'The beauty of Rupert Brooke was that of youth,' he told me. 'He had every grace, every charm of mind, colour, make and movement, save those of maturity and the power that gives it. He seemed youth incarnate and (very softly) certain not long to endure. For wonder, loveliness and dearness he stands utterly alone in my memory of men.'

The influence of this young poet on his death, aged twenty-eight, over people in high places borders on the supernatural. Note the wording of Winston Churchill's *letter* to *The Times*, 26th April 1915: 'A voice had become audible, a note had been struck, more true, more thrilling, more able to do justice to the nobility of our youth in arms engaged in this present war, than any other . . . The voice has been swiftly stilled.'

We now come to the crucial question, should the Allied Fleet have renewed the bombardment in spite of the set-back on March 18th and persisted in the attempt to enter the Sea of Marmara while waiting for the Army to assemble and for the settled weather essential to combined operations? My answer is definitely Yes. Except in the case of the *Bouvet*, where 639 officers and men were lost, casualties in the Fleet had been negligible. The sunken ships were expendable and were speedily replaced. Most important of all, by April 3rd a flotilla of destroyers had been fitted for minesweeping and had proved that they had sufficient horse-power to sweep against the stream. Nor was it in accordance with the traditions of the Royal Navy to accept defeat so readily. Whether the appearance of an Allied fleet off Constantinople would have resulted in Turkish capitulation, or whether the fleet would have had to return empty-handed, suffering further punishment as did Admiral Duckworth's squadron, is a political question which I am not qualified to answer. But as the prize was so great, it was surely a risk worth taking.

Winston Churchill was all for going ahead. It was Admiral 'Jackie' Fisher, the First Sea Lord (whose heart was never in the project) who stopped Churchill from sending this telegram to Admiral de Robeck urging him to continue the naval operations, after Churchill had received 'with consternation' the Admiral's signal of March 26th which I have chosen as the heading to this chapter:

> 'In view of the dangers of delay through submarine attack and of heavy cost of Army operation, and possibility that it will fail or be only partly effective in opening the Straits, and that the danger of mines will not be relieved by it, we consider that you should make all preparations to renew the attack begun on the 18th at the first favourable opportunity ... The entry into the Marmara of a Fleet strong enough to beat the Turkish Fleet would produce decisive results on the whole situation, and you need not be anxious about your subsequent line of communications. We know the forts are short of ammunition and supply of mines is limited. We do not think the time has yet come to give up the plan of forcing the Dardanelles by a purely Naval Operation.'

If this message had been sent and acted upon courageously, who can doubt that the result would have been favourable?

When Winston Churchill was questioned on this matter before the Dardanelles Commission in 1917, he said:

'I proposed that we should direct the Admiral to renew the naval attack, according to his previous intention. The First Sea Lord, however, did not agree; nor did Sir Arthur Wilson; nor did Sir Henry Jackson. Lord Fisher took the line that hitherto he had been willing to carry the enterprise forward, because it was supported and recommended by the Commander on the spot. But now that Admiral de Robeck and Sir Ian Hamilton had decided upon a joint operation, we were bound to accept their view. I do not at all blame Lord Fisher for this decision. The arguments were very strong indeed. But so were the arguments against it. Both the Prime Minister and Mr Balfour, with whom I discussed the matter, were inclined to my view, but as our professional advisers and the Admiral on the spot were against it, it was impossible to go further, and I bowed to their decision. But with regret and anxiety.'[7]

So we were committed.

8

They Went Like Kings

Sir Ian Hamilton had first reached the Aegean on the eve of the
naval attack of March 18th, as we have seen, and had witnessed its
closing stages from the bridge of the *Phaeton*. He had never before
sighted the Peninsula, and on inspection his 'first fears as to the out-
works of the fortress were strengthened'.

'The head of the Gulf of Xeros', he noted, 'is marshland and unsuitable for landing.

'The Bulair neck is only three and a half miles wide. By merely
looking at the map this looks like the obvious point to go for, as it
would cut the communications of all the troops on the Peninsula by
land and sea. But I found it heavily defended by a net-work of
trenches which my staff calculated must have taken a thousand men
a month's hard work. The glitter of barbed-wire could be seen
through our field glasses. The worst feature of the ground was that
the only landing place on that rock-bound coast was one small
indentation where even on a calm day with no enemy it would
have been an undertaking to get a brigade ashore. The water is
shallow. Ships would have to lie a long way out and therefore it
would take much longer to get troops ashore. The resources of the
Navy are judged not to be sufficient to maintain a large army so far
from its base at Mudros. Also from a military point of view the
troops landed at Bulair would be in the precarious position of having
to face two fronts. Our occupation of the Isthmus would not imme-

diately affect the position of the Narrows. Further, the presence of a German–Turkish fleet in the Sea of Marmara would prove a great danger.

'Between Bulair and Suvla there is no opening.

'In Suvla Bay and its neighbourhood a splendid well-sheltered beach seems to offer all that is desired – the most extensive beach on the whole Peninsula, but it is badly overlooked by an amphitheatre of hills rising to 600 feet; long range guns from the Sari Bair Ridge (the highest peak is 971 feet) would sweep it from end to end. Situated at the widest part of the Peninsula, it is too remote from the essential zone, Achi Baba (700 feet) and the Narrows, to have any affect upon it. Moreover, to try and land in Suvla Bay and march across the open to the Straits, two Divisions will be needed just to hold our communications. These are not available.

'The strip of coast on either side of Gabe Tepe half-way down the Peninsula, is a landing place well suited to obtaining a quick decision, as a broad depression, interrupted only by one gentle rise, leads straight to Maidos [now Eceabat] four and a half miles away. Further north of Gaba Tepe the country is very ugly, very steep, cut up by ravines and covered with thick scrub. Its one advantage is that its very steepness would make it fairly immune to artillery fire. Between Gaba Tepe and Cape Helles the cliffs are from 100 to 300 feet high but here and there they might be climbed.

'The Cape Helles end of the Peninsula gives access to Achi Baba (700 feet), the capture of which as an observation post is a key to operations between ships and troops. Cape Helles in addition has the great advantage that it lends itself to support by gunfire of the Fleet more than any other possible landing place.'[1]

When Sir Ian made these observations it would seem he had not fully appreciated that although the tip of the Peninsula from Cape Helles to Achi Baba has the appearance from the sea of being a gradual slope, it is spoon-shaped and thus, to a large extent, is protected by its rim, on the coastline, from direct naval fire, a serious matter with aircraft spotting in its infancy.

In June 1971 a party of Gallipoli veterans climbed Achi Baba, from where the view was found to be disappointing. Major E. H. W. Banner (late R.A.M.C.) and Captain E. F. Wettern (late R.E., R.N.D.) wrote: 'From the summit of Achi Baba the ground to the north-east continues quite a long way reasonably flat before there is a drop into Soghanli Dere. This river valley includes the Krithia Road. There is no view into this valley from the top of Achi Baba. At the other side of the valley is the beginning of the Kilid Bahr

Plateau, which, being about the same height as Achi Baba, prevents any view of the Straits. Had we captured Achi Baba, it would have denied the position to the Turks, to our great advantage, but further advance would have been necessary before the forts could be over-looked.'

Sir Ian and his staff reached Mudros from Egypt at 7 a.m. on April 10th. After an early breakfast he went over to the *Queen Elizabeth* to unfold his plan. 'Last time the Admiral made the running,' he wrote. 'Now it was my turn, for I had to unfold my scheme and go through it point by point with the sailors.'

After everyone had settled down round the table in the Admiral's dining cabin, Sir Ian was invited to open the meeting. As a start he read out the appreciations received from Birdwood (Anzacs) and from Hunter-Weston (29th Division).

General Birdwood was inclined towards a landing on the Asiatic side. 'For preference somewhere south of Tenedos, the attractive part being that the Turks must withdraw most of their mobile artillery from the Peninsula to meet us, which will give the navy just the opportunity they require for minesweeping and so force the Narrows forthwith.'

In General Hunter-Weston's view, land operations at this stage must be directed entirely towards assisting the fleet and no operations should be commenced unless it was clear that their result would be to enable our warships to have use of the Straits.

'The fleet cannot force a passage through the Dardanelles without army help because of the improvement of the defences, the mobile howitzer, and the mine,' he said. 'The Turkish Army have received ample warning. Under German direction they have made several lines of entrenchments and machine-gun posts covering landing places. Supplies and reinforcements reach them from the Asiatic side and from the Sea of Marmara; they are not dependent on the Isthmus of Bulair, although its passage by troops and supplies at night cannot be denied by guns of the fleet. The only landing places worth serious consideration are those near Suvla Bay and near Cape Helles.' Of the two he advised Helles, because 'the Fleet can also surround this end of the Peninsula and bring a concentrated fire on any Turks.

'The prizes of success are very great,' he concluded. 'It is the most helpful method of finishing the war. No loss would be too heavy and no risks too great if thereby success would be attended. But there is not in the present circumstances a reasonable chance of success. The return of the Expedition when it has gone so far will cause discontent, much talk and some laughter, and it will confirm Rumania and Greece in the wisdom of their neutrality.

'It will be a heavy blow to all us soldiers, to attempt a landing and to fail to secure a passage through the Dardanelles. It would be a disaster to the Empire. . . .

'It is advisable to continue our preparations – to train our troops for landing so as to be able to take advantage of any opportunity for successful action that might occur. But I would repeat that no action should be taken unless there is a reasonable probability of success.'

There was a pause here for reflection and discussion while King George V, Queen Mary and the great Queen Elizabeth I looked down out of their picture-frames behind the Admiral's chair. It was painfully obvious to everyone sitting round that table (the same table at which Admiral Sir David Beatty was to accept the surrender of the German Fleet in 1918), that there was little enthusiasm to be found among the subordinate army commanders. So what should Sir Ian do? Call the whole thing off – or at least postpone the assault for a while? No, certainly not! He was made of sterner stuff. In any case de Robeck, Wemyss and Keyes spurned any thought of further delay and of hanging about hoping for something to turn up. Sea power would be a great help. Sir Ian's troops must take a good run at the Peninsula and jump plumb on – both feet together. Prudence was quite out of place.

'I would like to land my whole force in one,' said Sir Ian. 'Like a hammer-stroke of Thor, as close as possible to my objective, the Kilid Bahr Plateau, but because of a lack of small craft the thing just cannot be done; the beach space is too cramped. Having, therefore, to disperse, the best thing to do is to disperse thoroughly.

'I propose that the 29th Division and the Royal Marine Brigade, under Hunter-Weston, disembark at five simultaneous landing places at the southern end of the Peninsula, with Achi Baba as the first objective, which it is hoped to capture before night-fall. This is to be done with the help of the Navy's guns only. Then our own artillery will be landed in time to cover the attack on the Kilid Bahr Plateau next day.

'The Australian and New Zealand Army Corps under General Birdwood will disembark just north of Gaba Tepe opposite Maidos to try to seize the high back-bone of the Peninsula and to cut the

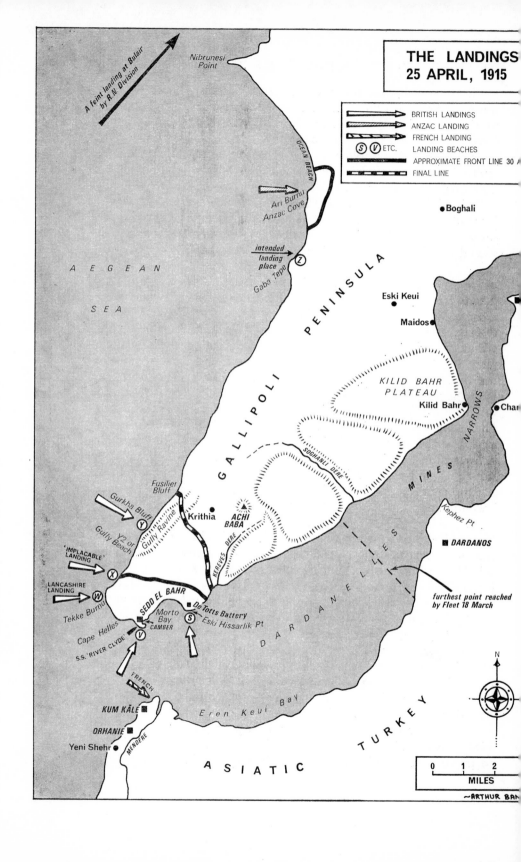

THE LANDINGS
25 APRIL, 1915

BRITISH LANDINGS
ANZAC LANDING
FRENCH LANDING
Ⓢ Ⓥ ETC.   LANDING BEACHES
APPROXIMATE FRONT LINE 30 A
FINAL LINE

A feint landing at Bulair
by R.N. Division

Nibrunesi
Point

OCEAN BEACH

Ari Burnu
Anzac Cove

● Boghali

intended
landing
place   Ⓩ

Gaba Tepe

A E G E A N

S E A

● Eski Keui

Maidos ●

G A L L I P O L I   P E N I N S U L A

KILID BAHR
PLATEAU

Kilid Bahr ●   ● Char

SOGHANLI DERE

N A R R O W S

Fusilier
Bluff

Gurkha Bluff

Y2 or
Gully Beach

Krithia ●

ACHI
BABA

M I N E S

Kephez Pt

Ⓨ

Gully Ravine

KEREVES DERE

'IMPLACABLE'
LANDING   Ⓧ

▣ DARDANOS

LANCASHIRE
LANDING   Ⓦ

Tekke Burnu

SEDD EL BAHR

Morto
Bay
CAMBER

DeTotts Battery
Ⓢ   Eski Hissarlik Pt

furthest point reached
by Fleet 18 March

Cape Helles   Ⓥ

S.S. 'RIVER CLYDE'

D A R D A N E L L E S

FRENCH

KUM KALE ▣

Eren Keui Bay

ORHANIE ▣

Yeni Shehr ●

MENDERE

T U R K E Y

N

A S I A T I C

0   1   2
MILES

~ARTHUR BAN

line of retreat of the enemy. I hope that both these attacks will become related in the event of either making substantial progress. In any case landing here is bound to interfere with movements of Turkish reinforcements towards the toe of the Peninsula.

'While these two real attacks are taking place there will be two deceptions. Transports containing the Royal Naval Division will appear off the Bulair lines and pretend to disembark, holding up Turkish Reserves. The French will land a brigade at Kum Kāle on the Asiatic shore so as, first, to draw the fire of the enemy big guns away from our troops on the southern end of the Peninsula; secondly to prevent Turkish troops being shipped across the Narrows.

'To coincide with the landings, Admiral Ebergard, in command of the Russian Black Sea Fleet, will bombard Turkish positions to check the flow of reinforcements to Gallipoli. (They were to play their part, but their attack may be regarded as a pretty feeble contribution to operations which had initially been opened on their account.)

'It is my intention,' concluded Sir Ian, 'that the feint off Bulair shall start at midnight; the Anzac landing before dawn – a surprise; and that the Covering Force of the 29th Division landing on the five beaches at the southern end of the Peninsula, and the French diversion, shall make their attacks at first light, after a naval bombardment. . . .'[2]

The conference lasted three hours and ended in an atmosphere of confidence and good will.

'Sir Ian and de R. seem to hit it off very well – the essential,' Captain W. W. Godfrey, R.M.L.I., Staff Officer, Operations, noted in his diary that evening. 'Braithwaite seems an excellent fellow and gets on A1 with Keyes. They seem to be great friends. The scheme ought not to fail for want of co-operation in high places.'

'Such was Sir Ian's plan,' wrote Brigadier-General Steuart Hare, 'and I've never yet heard anyone suggest a better one.'[3] That opinion may well have been shared among 'high-ups' in both services; but as a matter of interest I include the views of two junior officers who were not quite so convinced.

'We were instructed to show on the chart of the Peninsula all places where landing is deemed difficult or impossible owing either to defensive measures by the Turks or to the unsatisfactory character of the beach including exposure to bad weather,' Lieutenant Geoffrey Rylands, Navigating Officer of the seaplane carrier H.M.S.

Ark Royal recorded (April 1915). 'This information was forwarded to the Planning Staff through the usual channels, but when we received Operation Orders we were amazed to find that the Army had decided to land at nearly all the places which we had reported as being either difficult or impossible.'

'It is hard to say how one feels in the matter,' Lieutenant Crookshank of the *Agamemnon* wrote in his diary April 23rd, 'but personally I can only explain it by saying one looks forward to the coming event as one does to a really good theatre, or to a shoot. At the same time we all wonder how it will come off. Will there be much opposition and many killed at the landings? We fear so. But there is one thing some of us mere sea ignoramuses cannot understand – why do they decide to effect the landing on exposed beaches, covered with entanglements and open to enfilading fire from two directions, when there are nice steep cliffs quite easily climbed just to the side of the beaches and affording nearly complete protection?'

The Turks and the Germans knew, better than we did, the few, mostly narrow, landing places available to our men. 'The British gave me four full weeks before their great landing,' wrote Liman von Sanders, 'the time was just sufficient to complete the essential arrangements.'[4]

The Reverend Stephen Fowler, who served at Gallipoli in H.M. Hospital Ship *Gloucester Castle*, has fortunately kept a copy of a memorandum issued to our troops prior to the landings from which the following is an extract. It is no wonder some of our men expected a walk-over:

> 'The Turk is of very little use and has very small power of initiative when deprived of his officers and N.C.O.s. Every effort should therefore be made to shoot down his leaders.
>
> 'He is very adverse to night operations, in fact Turks as a rule do not in ordinary times of peace sleep without a light burning.
>
> 'The tactical principles followed in the Turkish Army are entirely German. The infantry are well and quietly trained but slow in movement and moderate shots. They are of little use in scouting and reconnoitring work. The cavalry is the least efficient of the Turkish arms. The artillery is the best trained and approximates very nearly to the ordinary Continental standard. . . .'

In contrast, Colonel Hans Kannengiesser, who served with the Turkish Fifth Army throughout the Campaign, offered his opinion: 'The Turkish soldier was the Anatolian and Thracian, slightly educated, brave, trustworthy, content with little. It never entered his mind to dispute authority of those above him and followed his leader in attack with no thought of his own safety. Being a fatalist he regarded life as a stepping-stone to a better one.

'On occasions when Turkish troops failed the cause could generally be attributed to their leader. The loyalty of the *Asker*, and his recognition of authority was an advantage to the good leader but a handicap to the bad. The Turkish soldier at Gallipoli did not lack intellect (the Oriental is seldom stupid, he is cunning), but he lacked education and training which was the fault of the ruling classes. He needed a reliable officer to lean on, an iron hand to guide him. In addition, the Turk has a special regard for the protection of his dignity (in other words, he hates losing face). It is uncivil to say "No". It is customary to say "Yes". But that does not at all imply that things will be done! Unpleasant matters are not reported to a superior for fear of angering him. A promise is merely a form of politeness.'[5]

Even the weather seemed to prove that Sir Ian had been wise to delay until the arrival of the 29th Division, for there were hardly two fine days together in the first fortnight of April. Provisionally the day for the assault had been fixed for April 23rd, St George's Day, but on April 21st it was blowing half a gale and the attack was postponed for twenty-four hours and then for a further twenty-four. The weather as usual was having the final say.

On the morning of the 23rd, the sky cleared and work could begin, The wind fell away, the sea became still and singularly blue. In fact it turned out to be a beautiful day.

The signal that the landings would take place on April 25th, a Sunday, was made 'general' by Admiral de Robeck. (It is a curious coincidence that some of the hardest fought battles in British history have been on a Sunday – Blenheim, Waterloo, Inkerman, and now Gallipoli.)

Messages of goodwill came pouring in.

'You are constantly in His Majesty's thoughts and prayers' – H.M. King George V.

'I am confident that your troops will clear the way for the Fleet to advance to Constantinople' – Lord Kitchener.

'May heaven's light be our guide and God give us victory' – Admiral de Robeck.

'Soldiers of France and the King, before us lies an adventure unprecedented in modern war. The whole world will be watching your progress. Let us prove ourselves worthy of the great feat of arms entrusted to us' – Sir Ian Hamilton.

Junior commanders, too, played their part. A clarion call also came from Brigadier-General Steuart Hare to his 86th Infantry Brigade, Covering Force of the southern landings: 'FUSILIERS! – Our Brigade is to have the honour to be the first to land and to cover the disembarkment of the rest of the Division. Our task will be no easy one. Let us carry it through in a way worthy of the traditions of the distinguished regiments of which the Fusilier Brigade is composed, in such a way that the men of Albuera and Minden, of Delhi and Lucknow may hail us as their equals in valour and military achievement, and that future historians may say of us as Napier said of the Fusilier Brigade at Albuera: "Nothing could stop that astonishing infantry".'

John Masefield, with the Red Cross in Mudros and an eye-witness to the departure scene, described in faultless prose how the ships, 'moved out of harbour in the lovely day, and felt again the heave of the sea. Their feeling that they had done with life and were going out to something new welled up in those battalions: they cheered and cheered till the harbour rang with cheering. As each ship crammed with soldiers drew near the battleships, the men swung their caps and cheered again, and the sailors answered, and the noise of cheering swelled, and the men in the ships not yet moving joined in, and the men ashore, till all the life in the harbour was giving thanks that it could go to death rejoicing. All was beautiful in that gladness of men about to die, but the moving thing was the greatness of their generous hearts. As they passed the French ships, the memory of old quarrels healed, and the sense of what sacred France had done and endured in this great war . . . they cheered the French ships more, even, than their own.'[6]

I too witnessed this moving scene from the bridge of the *Bacchante*. One transport I particularly noticed had displayed an enormous canvas screen, and on it was painted in bold lettering – 'To Constantinople and the Harem', with an arrow pointing to the bows. How confident we all were in those days.

Sir Ian Hamilton and Staff joined Admiral de Robeck in the *Queen Elizabeth* during the early afternoon of the 24th and sailed for Tenedos. The fleet flagship was under way again at 4 a.m. the following morning, Sunday April 25th, to witness the battle of the beaches.

The last mail which closed on board the *Q.E.* carried letters to anxious wives, sweethearts, families and friends and included one from Sir Ian to his beloved Jean. Nothing could be more natural when he picked up his pen that he should turn his thoughts to their parting on Charing Cross station, Friday March 13th, when the train rumbled out and he 'missed the thrill of the step that counts'.

'H.M.S. *Queen Elizabeth*, 24th April 1915
'I do wish so much I could see you for a moment and give you a nicer kiss than the one I snatched through your veil at my departure ... goodbye. Ian.'

This letter was followed up by words recorded later in *Gallipoli Diary* (a memoir in diary form) which again revealed some of his sacred thoughts.

'Almighty God, Watchman of the Milky Way, Shepherd of the Golden Stars, have mercy upon us ... Thy Will be done. *En avant* – at all costs – *en avant!*' ...

and a few paragraphs later: 'I hope I may sleep tonight. I think so. If not my wakefulness will wish the clock's hand forward not back.'

Finally, how does a diminutive midshipman behave who is shortly to experience his baptism of fire? I think I was too young to have much imagination. After we had got under way and I had come down off the bridge, I joined Douglas Dixon on the boat-deck to make final arrangements with our boat's crews. The hands – the ship's company – were to be called before midnight so we planned to pipe down at 6 p.m.

Our two hammocks were slung on the aft-deck with those of the other midshipmen. When I had shifted into pyjamas, I placed my monkey-jacket and shoes in case of an emergency on the pipes which ran along the deck-head above my hammock and then turned in. I should have included my life-belt, but nothing would have induced me to do so. Indeed I had deliberately left it down in the chest flat with the rest of my clothes. Dowsing the glim and wriggling down between the blankets, I turned over on my side and put my hands together. I felt scared for the first time.

9

Anzac Day

*'In one day, April 25th 1915, Australia attained
nationhood by the heroism of her noble sons.'*
Lieutenant Phillip F. E. Schuler, 1889–1917
Australia in Arms, 1916

About twelve miles northward from Cape Helles along the coast the
headland of Gaba Tepe suddenly projects. It is no great height – just
under 100 feet – but deep water, covering rocks, washes the feet of
the steep, rugged cliffs. From there nearly the whole coast, both north
and south, could be enfiladed. Immediately to the north the shore
falls into an open, gently sloping valley crossed by the track to Eski
Keui, in the centre of the Peninsula, and thence on to Maidos and
the Narrows.

Except at Bulair this is the shortest way across, under five miles
in a straight line. But on the right of it stands the threatening plateau
of Kilid Bahr and on the left the height of Sari Bair, riven by a
hundred gullies and ravines.

Sir Ian Hamilton's Operation Orders required the Anzacs to land
between Gaba Tepe and a point known as Fisherman's Hut, about
three miles further north. A Covering Force would disembark first to
seize and hold the lower slopes of the Sari Bair Ridge. The main body
of the Corps, following up, was to leave the Covering Force to hold
this position guarding the northern flank, push past south and seize
the inland spur of Hill 971, especially Mal Tepe, the conical hill near
the further end of the spur, which is only one and a half miles from
Kilia Liman on the Dardanelles. 'In gaining such a position,'
the Orders said, 'the Army Corps will threaten, and perhaps
cut, the line of retreat of the Turkish forces on the Kilid Bair
Plateau.'

In contrast to the landings of the 29th Division, which were to
take place in the Cape Helles area in daylight, preceded by a naval
bombardment, the key to the landing of the A. and N.Z. Army
Corps was to be surprise. The assault would take place before dawn

11   L'Entente Cordiale. French troops in a transport

12   General Gouraud (*standing*) and General Bailloud in the ruined old fort at
Sedd el Bahr

13 Rear-Admiral Thur
squadron on passage to
Anzac landing. H.M. Ships *C
(leading)*, *Triumph, Prince of W
Bacchante* and *London*

14 H.M.S. *Triumph* with anti-torpedo nets out; *Bacchante* in the distance

on a wide front without artillery preparation. It was important that once ashore the troops should have plenty of room to manoeuvre.

Subject to these general instructions the selection of the beach and the detailed planning of the landing were left to General Birdwood, Rear-Admiral Thursby and their staffs. They were handicapped by a lack of even fairly trustworthy maps, when compared with those found afterwards on the bodies of Turkish and German officers. Admiralty charts had also not been corrected for many years. Nevertheless an outline plan was soon ready, and on April 13th Admiral Thursby invited General Birdwood with his senior military officers to join him in the *Queen*. The ship sailed after dark and set course for the Gulf of Xeros. When daylight came the visitors were served with naval oilskins to conceal their khaki uniforms. The *Queen* turned south and followed the coast from the Lines of Bulair to Cape Helles. Turkish suspicion does not seem to have been aroused by the sight of an unusual number of sailors with moustaches, their eyes glued to field-glasses. Of course the main purpose of this reconnaissance was to observe the beach lying immediately north of Gaba Tepe. It was known from earlier reports from our aircraft, that a large camp of Turkish troops lay in the low and apparently easy passage across the Peninsula from this point (confirmed during a reconnaissance by our own ship the *Bacchante*, with the balloon ship *Manica* on April 19th), but nothing could be seen from the sea. The grey ruins of Gaba Tepe guard-house stood deserted in the sun. There was no sign of any new trenches near the shore, but across the dark, almost perpendicular sides of Kilid Bahr Plateau itself, there were fresh seams of white.

Colonel Sinclair MacLagan's 3rd Australian Infantry Brigade had been selected as Covering Force. Standing on the bridge of the *Queen* the Colonel kept his field-glasses trained on Gaba Tepe, on his prospective right flank. The barbed-wire entanglements were clearly visible inland though none were apparent in the water.

'If that place is strongly held with guns it will be almost impregnable to my fellows,' he commented.

MacLagan was deeply impressed with the difficulties. The north beach, the one selected, was exposed to guns hidden on Gaba Tepe, in an olive-grove a little further inland and on Kilid Bahr Plateau itself. Having got through the barbed-wire, to get over the gradual slope beyond would mean advancing up an unsheltered valley in the face of entrenched machine-guns.

Major-General W. T. Bridges, commanding the 1st Australian Division, thought Sinclair MacLagan pessimistic. To other officers who were making notes of what they saw, the difficulties also did not appear so great. 'The beach selected seems excellent,' wrote one. 'Coast seems suitable for landing,' noted another.

On return to Mudros the naval and military staffs got down to detailed planning. The landing was officially called Z Beach; but was always known as 'Anzac', by which name history knows it today.

The Covering Force of 1,500 was to be carried to the point of disembarkation in three battleships, the *Queen* (flag), *Prince of Wales* and *London*. It would be landed in twelve tows of boats covering a frontage of about a mile. The rest of the 3rd Infantry Brigade was to follow in destroyers and be landed by the returning tows. As soon as the bridge-head was secure, the rest of the Australian and New Zealand Army Corps was to arrive in transports at scheduled intervals and unload, as soon as possible, guns, ammunition, stores (including water), horses, mules, donkeys and all the impedimenta of battle. Attached to the Anzacs were the 7th Brigade of Indian Mounted Artillery, consisting of the 21st (Kohat) and the 26th (Jacob's) Mountain Batteries, each possessing six 10-pdrs, and the Ceylon Planters Rifle Corps of 150 young Englishmen who had joined in Colombo.

A midshipman in a picket boat or steam pinnace was to be in charge of each tow. There was also to be a commissioned naval officer in five of the tows.

Lieutenant-Commander J. B. Waterlow, whose experiences minesweeping in the Dardanelles a few days before the Naval Action of March 18th I have already recorded, was embarked in the *Queen*'s picket boat, No. 1 tow on the extreme right. It was his responsibility to put the Anzac Covering Force down in the right place at the right time.

The Senior Naval Officer in charge was Commander C. C. Dix in the *Majestic*'s picket boat on the left wing, No. 12 tow.

'*Queen*'s boats (No. 1 tow) will land on the beach one mile north of Gaba Tepe,' Admiral Thursby stated in his orders. Then, when at sea, he amended the distance to 800 yards, by signal, timed 7.05 p.m. The reason for this last minute change is not known. Naval signal logs of World War I were destroyed between the wars by order of the Admiralty, a dreadful mistake. Picket boat compasses were notoriously inaccurate and Admiral Thursby was expecting too much. Picket boats were not capable of making such a delicate adjustment in their land-fall.

Soon after leaving harbour with his squadron Admiral Thursby, in his flagship the *Queen*, with General Birdwood and Anzac Corps

Staffs embarked, detached the *Triumph* as 'marking ship'. She was to anchor at 11 p.m. on April 24th in a position five miles west of the selected landing place. At midnight a light would be shown to seaward to guide the rest of the squadron to the spot. There boats would be lowered and the Covering Force embarked.

The squadron steamed slowly ahead in formation. The night was bright and clear and there was a brilliant moon eleven days old due to set at 2.56 a.m. bearing west. The time between moonset and dawn (4.05) was uncomfortably short. Had the landing taken place on April 23rd, as originally planned, with moonset earlier, conditions would have been more favourable.

At 1 a.m. the *Triumph* was sighted and soon afterwards the ships were stopped (they did not anchor for fear of making a noise), and boats hoisted out. While this was being done the troops were given a hot meal.

Let me live again my experiences as midshipman of the *Bacchante*'s picket boat:

'It is now 11.30 p.m. and the gunroom is full of midshipmen but surprisingly quiet. We are all completely dressed. I am supping from a bowl of cocoa and munching ship's biscuits. There is other food on the table but I am not hungry.

'From my pocket I pull out the orders and start studying them all over again. "Cap covers are not to be worn," I read. "Tows are to be 150 yards apart. No lights to be shown. There's to be no smoking. When approaching the beach, boat-hooks are to be used for sounding, and directly the water shoals picket boats are to cast off their tows, boats astern sheering off to port." And so on. But there is no time to finish as I am wanted. "Midshipman of the picket boat," someone shouts at the gunroom door.

'Our squadron has stopped. Boats are hoisted out and taken in tow. We go over to the *Prince of Wales* to fill up with troops. Extra ladders have been rigged to speed embarkation and the job is soon over. The *Queen* and the *London* have finished too. The sea is like glass.

'To begin with the whole squadron leads us towards the land. Destroyers have joined up full of troops, and our transports are somewhere near, too.

'The shore is now about two miles away. The moon has set, and it is one of the darkest nights I can remember. The ships have left to take up their stations, and we are alone: twelve picket boats with their tows steaming in line abreast, spearhead of the invasion.

'It is not easy to keep station in the pitch dark nor to prevent tell-tale sparks from coming out of the funnels. The line concertinas sometimes and then opens out again. The order "tows are to be 150 yards apart", to give the soldiers the broad frontage they need for forming up, is proving impossible to carry out. I, for one, close in for fear of losing touch. Other tows are doing the same, reducing the frontage by one third, a serious matter.

'Leading Seaman Worsley and Able Seaman Bice, our two bow-men, are keeping a good look-out. It has gone 4 a.m. and the sky ahead seems to be getting lighter and the stars less distinct. Yes, dawn is breaking.

'In a moment or two, Worsley comes aft to report he can see land. I go for'ard with him. Yes, there is land there all right.

'My heart beats faster. I look to starboard and then to port. Bow waves all along the line are bright with phosphorescence. I hope this won't give us away. The men have already tossed their oars without waiting to be told. It's 4.20 now. Soon it will be all over.

'The next few minutes drag. Then Worsley indicates that he can touch bottom with his boat-hook. We stop engines. Stoker Petty Officer "Bogey" Knight takes a peep out of his engine-room hatch to see what is happening. Our heavily laden boats carry their way better than we do and forge ahead, as Able Seaman Neish and Hodgson, our two stern-sheet men, let go aft. Our launch, the heaviest of them all, comes right up alongside for a moment. One of her soldiers holds out a watch for me to send home to his mother, but it is too late to help him. Our engines are going astern, and we are out of reach.

'Oars, muffled to prevent any noise, are being lowered carefully without making a splash. The men are starting to row. Some of the soldiers are helping with the oars, others are adjusting their equipment, tightening their chin-stays, slinging their rifles. I take all this in at a glance, but what stirs my imagination most is the look on the men's faces.

'A bugle call from on shore gives the alarm. We've been seen! 'Very' lights are set off and star-shell, too. The enemy opens fire and down comes a rain of bullets. It is just dark enough to see the flashes of the rifles and machine-guns and light enough to recognise Turks moving about on shore. The time is 4.30 a.m.

'There is no cover for our soldiers, and several are wounded before the shore is reached. I see some of them fall back into the crowded boats as they stand up to jump out. Thank goodness, there are only a few more yards to go.

'The moment their boat grounds, they leap out. In some cases further out than they imagine, and they have to wade ashore up to their waists in water. A few unlucky ones are completely out of their depth, and their heavy equipment is carrying them under. But the majority are reaching the shore in safety, and I have a glimpse of them lying flat on the sand behind their packs and firing, then rising with a cheer and charging up the beach . . .'

Midshipman Eric Longley-Cook in charge of the *Prince of Wales'* picket boat, No. 5 tow, gave me his experiences when it was all over. 'Go for'ard and get both bowmen up out of the fore peak and tell them to feel for the bottom with their boat-hooks,' he told his coxswain, Leading Seaman Albert Balsom, when the boats were nearing the shore. Balsom had served with Captain Scott in the Antarctic and was a fabulously strong, brave man.

'Why only one?' Longley-Cook asked a minute or two later.

'I couldn't get the other able seaman up, Sir, he's too frightened to move,' Balsom replied; and while they were speaking a rifle bullet entered the compartment and struck the A.B. in the spine, killing him instantly.

A few minutes later an Australian officer in one of the boats started to issue some order, whereupon he was interrupted by Longley-Cook who, in a clear authoritative voice with a polished English accent (so I was told by an Australian who was there) said to the officer: 'I beg your pardon, Sir, I am in charge of this tow.' The officer subsided into silence immediately and the troops in his boat were heard to mutter 'Good on yer, kid!'

'At this moment,' wrote the Australian historian, 'the twelve tows were very close together, running into the foot of Ari Burnu knoll, which juts out in a small cape. The boats of the 9th Battalion (ex *Queen*) and the 10th (ex *Prince of Wales*), striking the point of this, were the first to reach the land. The 11th Battalion (ex *London*) went past the north of it before arriving at the beach.

'The cutters and merchant ships' lifeboats ran in till the water shoaled to two or three feet. The launches and pinnaces grounded in deeper water, whereupon the men tumbled over the bows or sides, often falling on the slippery stones, so it was hard to say who was hit and who was not. Most were up to their thighs in water; some who dropped off near the stern of the larger boats, were immersed to their chests. Others, barely noticed in the rush, slipped into water too deep for them. The heavy kit which a man carried would sink him like a stone. Some were grabbed by a comrade; one was hung up by his kit on a rowlock until noticed. A few were certainly drowned.

'Bullets were striking sparks out of the shingle as the first boat-load reached the shore. Three of the boats near the point had become so locked together that only those on the outside could use their oars.

'In many cases the men had been told that they would have to run across ten or fifteen yards of sand, line a low cliff four or five feet high, drop their packs and form up, and then rush across 200 yards of open to the first hill.

'They raced across the sand and flung themselves down as instructed, in the shelter of the sandy bank where the hillside ended and the beach began. A machine-gun was barking from some fold north of the knoll. . . .

'In the tows of the 11th Battalion, which were to the north of the point and had still 200 yards of water to cross before they touched the beach, bullet after bullet was splintering the boats or thudding into their crowded freight. Every now and then a man slid to the bottom of the boat with a sharp moan or gurgling cry. One seaman was handing Captain Butler his satchel out of the boat, when he fell back shot through the head.

'Many were fixing bayonets as they ran across the shingle; in other cases officers or sergeants, as they and their men lay down, gave orders to strip packs, load magazines, close the cut-off, pull back safety catches. No shots were to be fired till daylight.

'The men were ashore and mostly alive, but the place was clearly the wrong one.

'Anyone who depended upon a set plan for the next move was completely bewildered. It had been hoped that the halt under the sandy bank would be long enough to allow the companies to land, form and carry out an organised attack across the open against the first ridge.

'But there was no open.

'Fierce rifle fire swept over them. They had been landed in the dark on a different coast and were lying in little parties out of sight of most of their comrades, their clothes heavy with water and their rifles choked with sand. But every authority, from Sir Ian Hamilton and General Birdwood down, had dinned into the troops: "You must go forward. You are the Covering Force. You must get on whatever the opposition".'[1]

Obedient to the letter, some did not even charge their magazines or wait to throw off their packs. They just went into the scrub and up the steepening slopes. Private H. V. Howe, 11th Battalion, from No. 9 tow next to mine No. 8, was one of them. Here is his story.

'Half-way up we came to a trench from which we could see the garrison running and in which there were still half a dozen Turks with their hands up. I jumped into the trench on top of one and cut the waist band off his pants, taking his belt away. I took some raisins and dried apricots out of his pockets – the others with me did much the same. We set off up the hill with the rest of the Company. They must have been the first Turkish prisoners taken in the Campaign.

'As we topped the rise, later known as Plugge's Plateau [pronounced Pluggy. Named after Lieutenant-Colonel A. Plugge, commanding the Auckland Bn, the N.Z. Brigade], we came under heavy fire. One of my platoon was killed beside me; a few yards further on Captain Annear from another company was killed, and as we crossed the plateau quite a number went down, but it did not stop the advance which went straight across the plateau down the valley on the other side, where we re-formed under Major Brockman. He led us along the valley until we were well up the slope of Battleship Hill. Then the Turks drove us back. That piece of ground was never regained.'

In the meantime the destroyers with the 'follow up' troops had approached, at about 4.45 a.m. We in the *Bacchante*'s picket boat, had picked up our launch first. Her casualties were very distressing, but unfortunately there was nothing we could do to help them. One Australian I saw was wounded in the wrist and was clutching his arm in a desperate endeavour to check the flow of blood. Another was sitting in the bottom of the boat with a bullet sticking out of his cheek. More wounded were there, but I could not see them properly. Our picket boat had received a direct hit from a shell which had not exploded; otherwise I might not be here. Able Seaman Hodgson lay in the stern-sheets, dead. Apart from that, all was well. As we rounded the stern of the nearest destroyer, I saw that they were having casualties, too. Some wounded were being carried along the upper deck. As we turned to recover our other two boats, I saw fresh troops clambering down into our launch. There was no time to take out the wounded, so they, poor chaps, had to make another trip in shore, in fact several more before anyone could attend to them.

Each destroyer had a few Merchant Navy lifeboats in tow, empty except for a couple of seamen as crew. One captain, too eager to get his Australians ashore quickly, started to send them down into a boat while his destroyer was still going ahead. After seven men had been embarked, the boat began to yaw out of control. She was swamped and the soldiers ditched. But accidents like this one were few. Captains of destroyers handled their craft with the greatest skill, as was to be expected.

When the *Colne* came in, Commander Seymour picked up a mega-phone and passed the word down the line that the destroyers were too far to the north, but there was no response. Colonel Sinclair MacLagan was on the bridge with him and must have known at once that his Covering Force had been put down in the wrong place. Had the destroyers moved further south, we in the picket boats and steam pinnaces, after recovering our tows, would have followed them without having to be told. But instead the destroyers disembarked their troops on a beach already congested and in most cases even further north than we had done. One saving grace, however, was that the men were now landed in their proper order, which was more than we had been able to do. I should like to think that failure to act upon Commander Seymour's advice was due more to a lack of efficient communication than to a lack of initiative.

'General Buller', fox terrier mascot of the 9th Battalion was smuggled ashore from the *Colne*. He 'fought' on the Peninsula for three months until wounded. He bit the battalion doctor who was bandaging his wound and was later evacuated to Egypt where he went A.W.L. (absent without leave) and was never seen again.

The *Ribble*, Lieutenant-Commander R. W. Wilkinson (the northernmost destroyer), *Usk*, Lieutenant-Commander W. G. C. Maxwell, and *Chelmer*, Lieutenant-Commander Hugh T. England, attempted a landing on the broad and open beach beside Fisher-man's Hut, standing almost in front of the perpendicular and strangely shaped cliff afterwards called the 'Sphinx'. Here they suffered serious losses. This beach, afterwards known as Ocean Beach, gradually broadens out until it merges into the open marshy plain which extends to Suvla and the Salt Lake. The Turks were ready here to oppose a landing. For days afterwards we could see stranded boats left full of dead.

Mention of the Sphinx reminds me of a Turkish sniper shot in his perch below the crest. His foot got caught as he fell over the cliff face and there he hung head down. Soaked by rain, burnt black by the sun, we in the *Bacchante*'s picket boat watched – as the days passed – his body slowly disintegrate. First an arm went, then a leg, then his head. Horrified, we could not keep our eyes off him.

Lance-Corporal T. S. Louch, 11th Battalion, had landed on this beach from the *Chelmer*. 'It was just light enough for us to see the outline of the land,' he wrote. 'A flare went up on our right, and a machine-gun manned by two Turks opened fire. Our boat was almost to their direct front. They had fired one or two short bursts, when a picket boat with a 3-pdr Hotchkiss gun mounted forward came in and silenced them.

'Our boat grounded under fire from the direction of the Sphinx. We leapt out in water up to our waists. Crerar was killed as we reached the shore. As instructed, we shed our packs, lay down and awaited orders. Colonel Johnston, who had come in another boat, flopped down beside me and I asked him what we were to do. He said that we had landed in the wrong place, and there was no organisation.

'A bullet spattered into the sand just clear of our noses; so, hugging our box of ammunition, my mate and I climbed the hill in front. Half-way up we stopped for breath in a sandy washaway. We then pushed on to the top where there were some tents and a wounded Turk.

'Directed by an officer to the ridge on the other side of Shrapnel Gully, we slid down the sheer sandy slope on our backsides, still clutching our box of ammunition, crossed the floor of Shrapnel Gully and with difficulty climbed the ridge. We were soaking wet and enfiladed by fire from our left, though we could see no enemy, but thereafter during the day reinforcements from the 3rd Bn planted themselves in among us.

'When it got dark and we could stand up to wield picks and shovels, we took off our breeches and puttees to dry, and dug a trench from which to repel the counter-attack we felt sure would come.

'In the early part of the evening there was some movement in front and voices said, "Indian troops: don't shoot". There was a Mountain Battery somewhere behind us, but we were suspicious; so Charlie Thompson who had soldiered in India and knew some of the language, went forward to investigate, and shortly afterwards we heard a shot. When he did not come back others went to look for him, and found he had been killed.'[2]

While the Anzacs were breasting those rough and all but sheer hills in little bunches and as single individuals, luck went over to the side of the Turks.

Hard by Maidos was the 19th Division commanded by Mustafa Kemal Bey. As his good star had decreed, he had ordered his best regiment to parade at daybreak that very morning. The regiment was to fall in complete with war kit: ammunition pouches filled, water bottles filled, iron rations, etc. After inspection the regiment was to carry out a manoeuvre practice by scaling the heights of Sari Bair from the Dardanelles side.

When the firing at the landing of the Anzacs was first heard, the

Turkish Commander, Essad Pasha, made up his mind that it was a mere feint and that the real danger was at Helles. He therefore sent an order to Mustafa Kemal to send only one battalion from his division.

Had that order been obeyed the Anzacs would in all human probability have had time to reorganise as well as to entrench themselves on the heights.

But he did not obey it. Instead he ordered the whole regiment to carry out the manoeuvre practice as arranged and fell in the rest of his force to back it up.

The prompt advance of these first Turkish troops, moving with cohesion and supported by a full division and its artillery, was too much for the scattered and exhausted groups of Anzacs who by degrees were rounded up and forced back into an irregular semi-circle on the hills overhanging the landing place, a semi-circle which, curiously enough corresponded exactly to the pencil line drawn upon Sir Ian Hamilton's map by Major-General Braithwaite when the latter was pointing out what was the irreducible minimum which must at all costs be made good.

When General Birdwood landed in the afternoon with his divisional generals, he found the beach a scene of confusion. Men, animals, stores and ammunition had been dumped on the sand as the Navy brought them in. Fatigue parties were weighed down with rations, water-cans and cartridges, in readiness for the arduous climb up to the firing line. But it was the sight of the wounded, some on stretchers, some sitting, others standing around crowding the top of the beach to get shelter from the intermittent Turkish barrage, which was the most distressing.

The one hospital ship allocated to the Anzac landing had sailed at 8.30 a.m. for Alexandria, filled to capacity. Worse still, some of the transports detailed to be fitted as hospital carriers had not yet been cleared of their troops and stores, and in a few cases their medical officers and equipment had not arrived.

On this small crowded beach, soon to be named Anzac Cove, Colonel N. R. Howse, Assistant Director of Medical Service to the Corps, had hurriedly erected a dressing station, yet the wounded, however heroic, suffered a great deal. The most serious cases were being evacuated in service boats, which interfered with the steady flow of reinforcements. Troops and stores were being disembarked over one side of a transport while wounded were being hoisted in on the other.

After touring the beach and talking to some of the wounded, General Birdwood was led up the hillside by Brigadier-General H. B. Walker, commanding the N.Z. Infantry Brigade. On Plugge's Plateau they paused to reconnoitre, but the scrub was so thick that they could see little and judge nothing. Walker believed that his men on Walker's Ridge were isolated and that the Turks were between them and the Australians, as indeed was the case by nightfall. Walker was not the man to affect an optimism he did not fee. Birdwood, however, returned to the *Queen* at 5 p.m. without serious misgiving, leaving General Bridges in command of the whole Australian and New Zealand Force ashore. Until the position was thoroughly established the flagship was the best place for him to direct landing operations and to co-ordinate the gunfire of the Fleet. That crowded beach was certainly no place for a corps commander.

By 8 p.m. it was dark and raining. The wind had freshened. At 9 p.m. General Bridges made a signal to General Birdwood in the *Queen*. It was marked urgent.

'General Godley and I consider that you should come ashore at once.'

Birdwood, after making arrangements for the early landing of such infantry as were still in the transports, went ashore to confer with them. Admiral Thursby saw him over the side, keeping on board Brigadier-Generals R. A. Carruthers, D.A.Q.M.G., and Cunliffe Owen, Artillery Officer, to serve as a link between ship and shore during the Corps Commander's absence.

Two hours later, about 11 p.m., Captain Vyvyan, the Naval Beachmaster, brought off a letter from General Birdwood which recommended immediate evacuation of all troops ashore.

Admiral Thursby was taken aback, but a moment's consideration convinced him that to try and re-embark under the conditions which then prevailed would be disastrous, so, taking the two brigadier-generals with him, he set off for the shore to explain to General Birdwood the impossibility of complying with his request. In the meantime we in the *Bacchante*'s picket boat with others, had been told to pick up any boats we could find and to prepare for an evacuation. Instinctively we knew that if such a drastic step became necessary only a few would get away.

At this moment the *Queen Elizabeth*, with both Commanders-in-Chief on board, loomed out of the darkness. Admiral Thursby's boat was turned round, and in a matter of minutes he was alongside. Accompanied by the two brigadiers, he was shown into Admiral de Robeck's day cabin, where Sir Ian Hamilton joined them. Birdwood's message was handed to Sir Ian and he read it aloud:

'Both my Divisional Generals and Brigadiers have represented to me that they fear their men are thoroughly demoralised by shrapnel fire to which they have been subjected all day after exhaustion and gallant work in the morning. Numbers have dribbled back from firing line and cannot be collected in this difficult country. ... If troops are subjected to shell fire again tomorrow morning there is likely to be a fiasco as I have no fresh troops with which to replace those in the firing line. I know my representation is most serious but if we are to re-embark it must be at once. (Sgd) BIRDWOOD.'

Sir Ian, horrified, asked the two brigadiers some questions about the tactical position, but neither seemed able to add any detail of importance. So he turned to Thursby.

'Admiral, what do you think?'

'It will take the best part of three days to get that crowd off the beaches.'

'And where are the Turks?'

'On top of 'em!'

'Well then, Admiral, what do you think?'

'I think they will stick it out if only it is put to them they must.'

Without another word, all keeping silence, Sir Ian wrote to Birdwood as follows:

'Your news is indeed serious. But there is nothing for it but to dig yourselves right in and stick it out. It would take at least two days to re-embark you as Admiral Thursby will explain to you. Meanwhile, the Australian submarine has got up through the Narrows and has torpedoed a gunboat at Chanak. Hunter-Weston, despite his heavy losses, will be advancing tomorrow which should divert pressure from you. Make a personal appeal to your men and Godley's to make a supreme effort to hold their ground.

(Sgd) IAN HAMILTON.

'P.S. You have got through the difficult business, now you only have to dig, dig, dig, until you are safe. IAN H.'

'We were soon down in my boat with Sir Ian's letter and making for the shore,' Admiral Thursby wrote, 'the position of which could only be made out by the flashes of the rifles which formed an irregular line against the background of the hills. We stood on until we could see the white surf of the breakers and hear their noise as they crashed on the beach.

'It was impossible to land in the steam boat, but just then we sighted a dinghy rowed by two seamen who had landed some officers and were returning to their ship. They were just as unconcerned as if they had come off from a late trip in peace time although bullets, coming over our fighting line, were dropping all around. We climbed into the boat and after several attempts and getting very wet we reached the shore.

'The beach was crowded with men. Some, exhausted, had just thrown themselves down and slept like logs. Some were getting food and drink for the first time for many hours; others were being collected to form organised units to reinforce the fighting line which was only a few hundred yards distant.

'I found General Birdwood with his two divisional generals. He was cheerful but not very hopeful. I gave him Sir Ian's letter and told him the state of affairs down south and impressed on him the necessity of holding on at all costs. After staying with him a short time, I returned to my ship, arriving at 4 a.m. With the rising of the sun the wind died away, and it turned out to be a glorious day.'[3]

While these discussions had been going on in what frame of mind were the subjects of all this anxiety? Were the men aware that evacuation was on the cards? Was the position really as serious as some of the commanders thought?

It seems certain that the troops in the front line were unaware that evacuation had been contemplated; and that the words 'thoroughly demoralised' used in General Birdwood's letter could not be truthfully applied to them. If the commanders had known the Australian and New Zealand soldier as well as they came afterwards to know him, their anxiety would have been less.

It is not clear whether Birdwood's two divisional generals had recently visited the firing line to find out for themselves the true state of affairs, or whether they were relying on reports they received. Had the three brigade commanders – Colonels Sinclair MacLagan (3rd Australia – the Covering Force); McCay (2nd Victoria), and McLaurin (1st N.S.W.) known what was to be discussed, it is inconceivable they would not have hurried down to divisional headquarters, only ten minutes away.

It appears that Generals Bridges and Godley, with the support of Lieutenant-Colonel White, Bridges' Chief of Staff, had made up their minds on evacuation before calling General Birdwood ashore at nine o'clock that night. It is also clear that Brigadier General Walker, commanding the N.Z. Infantry Brigade, was dead against evacuation from the outset.

And now for my own little world, the *Bacchante*'s picket boat.

'It is daylight again,' I wrote, 'and we are concentrating on landing water and ammunition, troops and stores, and evacuating wounded. Then it is darkness again. Another day has gone. We are just beginning to wonder how much longer our boat's crew can keep going. Some of us can hardly keep our eyes open from lack of sleep.

'It is 10 p.m., but we need not worry any more about our fatigue. We have our three boats in tow and are steaming back to the ship. We can see her ahead of us.

'I am lucky. Lieutenant Tom Phillips (lost in the *Prince of Wales* when Commander-in-Chief, Far East, on 10th December 1941) has lent me his cabin, on the upper deck by the Quartermaster's lobby. As I go to it, I notice the time: midnight. We have been on our legs for seventy-two hours. No wonder we feel tired. My gear has been put out for me and some hot water, too, but I'm too weary to wash. . . .

'I wake up to find it is still dark, and it takes me a minute to remember where I am. I hear voices, so get down off my bunk and go over to the cabin door to investigate. "Quartermaster! – quartermaster! What is the time, please?" The talking stops, and a sailor appears, smiling. "It's close on midnight, Mr Bush," he says.

'Is it my appearance, I wonder, which amuses him? I must look a sight. No, of course it isn't. I see what's happened. I've slept the clock round.'

It is beyond my understanding why the Army High Commands, both British and Australian, took pains to shield the Royal Navy from its responsibility for putting the Anzacs down in the wrong place, thus jeopardising the success of the whole operation, and why responsible flag officers and the Official Naval Historian should have been so reluctant to admit the Navy's error.

Sir Ian Hamilton lightly dismissed the subject.

General Birdwood in his *Private Diary* confined himself to the statement that 'boats missed their landing in the dark and inclined about two miles north getting us under very difficult country there.'[4]

The Australian Official Historian, C. E. W. Bean, although apparently reluctant to nail the blame openly on the Royal Navy, did say that 'the swing of the tows bore disastrous consequences and upset every carefully laid plan for the battle'.

Rear-Admiral Thursby, who was in naval charge, wrote these words in his report of April 28th to Admiral de Robeck, words which were later repeated by Admiral Wemyss: 'The landing had taken place practically as arranged, our right flank being only a few hundred yards to the north of its assigned position. This proved afterwards to be an advantage, as it was found impossible to advance from the open beach, and our troops had to close in in order to get protection of the high ground.'[5]

This was a truly remarkable statement, when the error exceeded a mile, and when the majority of the troops never had a chance to advance from any open beach!

Finally, Sir Julian Corbett, the Official Naval Historian, blamed not the Navy but an imaginary current.

Here are my comments, which may help to establish what really did cause this fatal mistake.

The current off the Aegean coast of the Peninsula is influenced by the wind. Its general direction at a point say four miles off Gaba Tepe is north-north-west one and a half knots. A fresh north-easterly wind could cause the set to reverse to south-west two knots.

On the morning of the landing there was no wind, and the sea was like glass. The northerly flow was therefore unlikely to have exceeded its normal strength of one and a half knots. The tows could only have been carried north a quarter of a mile, from the moment when they parted company from the battleships, 3.40 a.m., to touch down at 4.43 (approx.).

The *Triumph*, you will remember, was sent ahead by Admiral Thursby after the squadron had sailed from Mudros, to act as 'marking ship'. We have no record of her point of departure, in other words, her position at her last 'fix' before she shaped course for the rendezvous. If it was obtained after dark, which is probable, it could be just a matter of luck if the *Triumph* anchored within say 500 yards of the rendezvous in any direction. No boat message reporting her estimated position on anchoring – as required by Admiral Thursby – appears to have reached the *Queen*. The *Triumph* was sunk a month later and carried her records down with her.

The *Triumph* provided two power boats for the landing: a picket boat – Midshipman John Metcalf, No. 2 tow of troops from the *Queen*; and a steam pinnace, No. 11 tow, Midshipman Fred Garner, with soldiers from the *London*. These two young officers were told that the *Queen*'s picket boat, No. 1 tow, would have a commissioned officer on board who would act as 'guide' of the flotilla and would know where to go. Metcalf told his own story.

'On reaching the rendezvous our two power boats were hoisted out, and we lay off waiting for the battleships to arrive. When they showed up, we went over to our parent ships, picked up our tows and took up our appointed stations for the run in. The big ships were moving very slowly ahead. I kept No. 1 tow in sight.

'Before long an officer with a megaphone on the bridge of the *Queen* hailed me: "Go ahead, picket boat"! I immediately ordered an increase of revolutions and "stand by for full speed". I kept my eyes on No. 1 tow, the guide boat, ready to keep station on her as she forged ahead.

'A minute or two later an angry shout was addressed to me from the bridge of the *Queen*: "Picket boat, will you go ahead!" It sounded as though I was being accused of cowardice. I ordered "full speed ahead!" and away we went.

'I soon lost sight of the *Queen* and of her No. 1 tow, though I could still see No. 3 tow off my port beam and presumed that all the other tows were in line abreast to port of her.

'At the first light of dawn I realised we were heading for the beach just north of Gaba Tepe [the correct one], which I knew to be well fortified as we in the *Triumph* had often been close to it and, from my action station in the spotting top, I had seen the headland time and time again. My immediate thoughts were that we were too far south. The troops and the boats would be lost by a murderous enfilading fire as we passed, so I hauled away from it to the north-ward as much as I dared, without crossing the bows of No. 3 tow. A few minutes later when the other tows to port had conformed, it appeared to me that we were still going too near Gaba Tepe, and again I altered course away from it. Eventually we landed south of Ari Burnu, with No. 3 tow only a few yards away on my port side.'

Commander C. C. Dix, the Senior Naval Officer in charge, was in the *Majestic*'s picket boat, No. 12 tow, on the left wing.

'When three quarter of the way ashore,' he wrote later, 'the right wing was seen to be steering across the bows of the centre, who were conforming to the movement, thus crowding the left away to port. By this time some of us were aware that we were some way to port of our objective, and so, in order to save as much ground as possible the left wing went on at full speed and held their course.

'"*London* tows veer more to starboard!" I ordered and repeated sharply. Only Nos. 11 and 12 tows complied. The twelve tows finished up in a cluster around Ari Burnu.'

'Tell the Colonel,' Dix was heard to shout in the eerie silence that preceded the touch-down, 'that the damn fools have landed us a mile too far to the north!'[6]

Lieutenant-Commander J. B. Waterlow, as already explained, was the officer responsible for putting down the Covering Force in the right place at the right time. He was in the *Queen*'s 1st picket boat, Midshipman Aubrey Mansergh, No. 1 tow, right wing. Here are some extracts from Waterlow's diary.

'General Birdwood and his staff joined the *Queen* this evening, April 23rd. The soldiers are very quiet and confident. They expect big losses and are prepared for them. They say the men in the Covering Force want to show what Australia can do. Fine fellows – I envy them their *sang froid*. ... General Birdwood inspires the utmost confidence, and the headquarters staff do the same. I'm glad that the Flag Commander Lambart who knows the beaches, is coming to lend a helpful hand. ...

'We started off on the starboard bow of the *Queen* trying to make Gaba Tepe. It was now so dark we could see but little, but Lambart assured me we were right, and it did seem as if a prominent headland such as I had been given to understand Gaba Tepe was, loomed ahead of us, so we went gaily on. As we approached the shore it became clear that there was a very prominent headland to northward of us and we began to vacillate. Our faith in our course was also shaken by the fact that all the other boats were steering more to the northward. At last I altered course to the northward also steering for the high land we could clearly see.

'We had to assume that the *Queen* was in her correct billet, and working on that assumption this prominent headland could not be Gaba Tepe. So my uncertainty increased – but still the boats steered to the northward. At last I altered course and went down the line astern trying to draw them to the southward with me. This failed and I was now convinced that my prominent headland was not Gaba Tepe. It was too high, and also on the summit there was not visible the ruined guard-house which surmounts it.

'I then tried to urge the boats to the northward where a good beach was visible – then again to the southward, but efforts in every direction failed. The dawn began to glow. Our prominent headland loomed larger and larger against the pale saffron light. [This was] the one place on the whole coast on which we would have decided not to land. However ... in despair I dashed straight at the frowning cliffs.'

Waterlow remained with the Anzac Beach Party until he was promoted to Commander on June 30th, and appointed to the cruiser

Black Prince with the Grand Fleet. His ship was sunk at the Battle of Jutland a year later, with the loss of all hands.

It would seem that Midshipman Metcalf's two alterations of course to the northward during the run in, were largely responsible for the Anzacs being put down in the wrong place. One of these alterations is noted in my picket-boat diary (No. 8 tow) recorded at the time: '4.20 a.m. land sighted, flotilla altered course two points [twenty-two and a half degrees] to port'.

Apart from the possibility that the 'marking ship' *Triumph* could have been a little out of station, it would appear that the battleships must also accept some proportion of the blame: 'When daylight came', Captain R. N. Bax of the *Prince of Wales* wrote in his private log, 'we found we had anchored one mile too far to the north.'

Lieutenant Tom Phillips had suggested that one of our submarines should lie off Gaba Tepe and surface after dark showing a white light to seaward; but the idea was turned down.

On D-Day, Normandy, 6th June 1944, it was my duty, as a naval assault group commander at the spear-head of the invasion, to put the 8th British Infantry Brigade, Assault Brigade of the 3rd Division Covering Force, ashore at the right time and in the right place. To avoid the possibility of an error in navigation as had occurred at Anzac, we had a midget submarine waiting for us off the beach at Ouistram. We steered for her ultra-violet ray light and made a perfect landing. It was a remarkable coincidence that Lieutenant Tom Phillips was with us at the time to see his father's splendid idea brought into action.

In 1964 the Turkish newspaper *Jumhuriyet* published a series of articles on the Gallipoli Campaign. The issue of March 21st contained the following statement.

> 'The making of the landing a mile further north than was intended is attributed by foreign sources to a strong current. According to Ali Su of Gelibolu, however, the explanation is as follows:
>
> '"When the sun rose on April 24th, we saw a buoy almost immediately opposite Gaba Tepe. Since we realised that the buoy had been intentionally dropped by the English, we asked permission from our section commander to move it. For the Gaba Tepe sector, which was exactly opposite the buoy, was the most suitable place on the Penin-

sula for a landing, and was the nearest point to the ridges overlooking the Straits. Three or four of our good swimmers pulled the buoy out of the sea, and, loading it on a mule, took it to a far less suitable point about a mile to the north, and replaced it in the sea. And in fact the English, who had not discovered our trick, landed the following day at Ari Burnu, instead of at Gaba Tepe."'

Samuel Pepys, when telling Charles II in 1664 some of the stories told him by the Captain of H.M.S. *Defyance*, mentioned fish that flew. The King replied, 'From the very nature of their calling no class of our subjects can have so wide a knowledge of seas and lands as the officers and men of our Loyal Maritime Regiment. Henceforward 'ere ever we cast doubts upon a tale that lacks likelihood we will first tell it to the Marines'.

I suggest Ali Su of Gelibolu should do the same.

IO

V Beach – *River Clyde*

'*No, damnable as this V Beach business seems, the motto is, never say die. Should the fates so decree, the whole of my brave army may disappear during the night more dreadfully than that of Sennacherib; so be it, assuredly they will never surrender.*'
Sir Ian Hamilton,
Gallipoli Diary (Ms)

The most important of the southern landings was at V Beach near the ruined fort of Sedd el Bahr. It comprises a strip some 10 yards wide and 350 yards long, backed for almost the whole of its length by an escarpment about 4 feet high, which drops nearly sheer to the beach. Behind it is a concave grassy slope, rising, at first very gradually, to the cliff edge between Sedd el Bahr village and Cape Helles. The Turks had tied the horns of this slope together with a web of wire entanglement so rusted to sand colour by the spray that it was only discernible at close range. It was a thick brand of barbed-wire, almost too tough for cutters, which stretched in places under the sea as well as on land. There was also a fence of the same beastly stuff at right angles to the coast-line to isolate V Beach from W, so that success at one point would be confined to narrow limits.

Such a death-trap was not to be dealt with by ordinary means, and a device from ancient times, the Horse of Troy, was used to reduce its worst dangers.

Two thousand men from the 1st Royal Dublin Fusiliers (their regimental nickname was 'Neill's Blue Caps' or 'Old Toughs'. The regiment was disbanded in 1923 after 279 years of military efficiency, faithful service and glorious traditions, coupled with intense *esprit de corps*), the 1st Royal Munster Fusiliers, a wing of the 2nd Hampshire Regiment, the West Riding Field Company of Royal Engineers and part of the Anson Battalion, Royal Naval Division, were to be packed in the hold of an old collier, the *River Clyde*, and carried to within a few yards of the shore. It was planned to bridge the intervening water-space with a motor hopper, the *Argyle*, backed up if necessary by dumb lighters.

The arrangements for disembarking were perfectly straightforward. Four sallyports had been cut, two on each side, at lower deck level, where the men would be waiting. The sallyports opened on to a gangway, three planks wide, which led forward to the bows where there was a hinged extension to lower on to the *Argyle*, which had a brow, or gangway, of her own to connect with the shore. The original intention was to have a lighter in tow on each bow of the *River Clyde*, then, when she grounded, they would hit the beach first, but the problems of towing proved to be too great. The *Argyle* instead was to be towed from a gantry on the port side, with a lighter inboard of her. A second lighter was to be towed from the starboard side and others, plus some boats, from aft.

The first echelon was to disembark, not from the *River Clyde*, but from six tows of boats. This Covering Force consisted of 500 men from the 1st Royal Dublin Fusiliers, commanded by Lieutenant-Colonel R. A. Rooth, with fifty men from the Anson Battalion, R.N.D., as Naval Beach Party. They were scheduled to touch down at 5.30 a.m., after half an hour's bombardment by H.M.S. *Albion*. The men from the *River Clyde* were to follow up at 6.30 a.m. At least that was the plan.

At the start there was a delay of half an hour, because it took much longer than had been foreseen to load the tows from the fast sweepers *Clacton* and *Newmarket* (Railway Packets ex-Great Eastern Railway). Progress was further slowed by the current down the Dardanelles, which could have been foreseen, and, perhaps most annoying of all, by the trawlers carrying the South Wales Borderers to S Beach–Morto Bay, which got in the way.

Commander Edward Unwin, Royal Navy, in command of the *River Clyde*, was in a quandary. Should he hold his course and beach his ship in advance of the Covering Force or should he wait for them to go in first as planned? Waiting posed a problem, because, if he slowed down and lost steerage way, the motor hopper *Argyle* and the dumb lighters he had in tow might get snarled up. Worse still, if he tried to take the headway off his ship by going astern, tow-ropes would foul his screw. The *River Clyde* was carrying human freight, not coal, and her propeller and rudder were half out of the water.

Military officers on the bridge implored Commander Unwin to stick to the original timing which gave him only one choice, to put his helm over.

'Hard to starboard!'

Commander Unwin took the *River Clyde* safely across the bows of one vessel, narrowly cleared the stern of another, then found two destroyers of the newly-formed minesweeping flotilla in his path. He steered between them; and only just in time did one slip her sweep-wire to avoid fouling the *River Clyde*'s screw.

It was now nearly 6.30 a.m., and the six tows with the Covering Force were coming up. Rather than hazard his ship again by repeating the manoeuvre, Commander Unwin decided to go in. Setting a course slightly different from his original approach, he ordered his engine-room telegraph put to Full Speed Ahead and made for the eastern extremity of the beach. These delays caused the *River Clyde* and the Covering Force in the boats to touch down at almost the same time, i.e. 6.50 a.m.

Sunrise that morning was at 5.08 a.m., and soon after it had risen above the land it was on an approximate bearing of N 75 E, thus shining straight into the eyes of every gunlayer on board *Albion*. The rising sun also put the shore in shadow, and a soft haze veiled the scene. Accurate spotting of fall of shot was found to be impossible.

The *Albion*, a mile to seaward, had opened fire at 5.04, and for the best part of an hour the hills, the valley between the hills, plus Cape Helles as well as all points commanding the beach, were searched. But it was blind work. By 5.30, the hour for which the landing of the tows was timed, the smother of smoke and mist ashore was so thick that *Albion* had to cease fire; then, as the tows were not approaching, she began again, expending a total, before touch-down, of twelve 12-inch, nine hundred 6-inch and more than a thousand rounds of 12-pdr.

As the six tows of boats of the Covering Force approached, three to starboard and three to port of the *River Clyde*, a single shot was heard. Whether a prearranged signal or not, it was the immediate prelude to a shattering blast of Turkish small arms and automatic-gun fire, soon to become a continuous roar. The placid water off the beach was hissing with bullets. The carnage and damage inflicted were appalling. In the leading boats most of the seamen and the soldiers were killed or wounded. Some boats were so riddled with bullets that they sank. The survivors tried to gain the beach in water frequently too deep for wading, and of these some were killed, some wounded, while many others were drowned by the weight of their equipment. In a few minutes nearly every man was a casualty. A lot of the boats could be seen drifting about helplessly, some broadside on with a few men in the water taking cover behind them; in others not a man was untouched; in one boat only two were still alive. Some boats disappeared entirely. Major Fetherstonhaugh, second in command, was mortally wounded before his boat reached the shore. Lieutenant-Colonel Rooth was shot dead at the edge of the water. 'The effect of the news could be read plainly on the faces of all ranks. They had such faith in him as their C.O. and would have followed him to the ends of the earth.'[1]

Those boats which still had some members of their crew unhurt did their best to return to the sweepers for a fresh load. One petty officer succeeded in completing the journey by making part of his crew lie in the bottom of the boat while he, with others, swam, shoving the boat ahead of them. The next flight to be landed had in many cases to climb in on top of dead comrades. Even then there was no flinching.

While this holocaust was going on, one tow was in luck. Commander Neston W. Diggle, in charge of No. 1 tow, entered the Camber, a boat harbour well to starboard of the *River Clyde*, on what was found to be dead ground. His two platoons of Dublins disembarked with only slight loss. Climbing the cliff in front of them, they advanced in short rushes as far as the windmills near the eastern corner of Sedd el Bahr village. Here, later, they were overwhelmed by a crowd of snipers. They lost all their officers, some N.C.O.s and eighty-six men. A few survivors did get back to the Camber, while others tried to join the rest of their company which was due to land from the *River Clyde*.

In the meantime, in spite of their losses, a few men were still getting ashore from what remained of the boats of the other tows, and Commander Diggle, after clearing his No. 1 tow, filled up with fresh troops and went to join them. But it was not long before he was in trouble. On the first run-in a bullet shattered his knee, and Midshipman Monier-Williams was badly wounded. Midshipman Hayden Forbes escaped injury but lost most of his crew. His boat was towed to safety in a waterlogged condition. Among the wounded was a soldier with a little brown dog who sat quietly beside his master.

Midshipman Arthur Hardiman was mortally wounded and taken on board the *Albion* to die. 'He was in great pain, unconscious but delirious and tossing and groaning in a terrible way, but nothing could be done. The Fleet Surgeon went to the Chaplain, a ripping fellow called de Jersey [sometime Vicar of New Romney, Kent], and said that he must leave the boy in his hands. De J. felt rather helpless as the 'snotty' was quite unconscious of his surroundings. However, he put his hands on the boy's head and gave him Benediction. Immediately the poor chap fell back calmly and peacefully into a sort of sleep and seemed to suffer no more pain.'[2] He died quietly later on.

It was sad that the two platoons in No. 1 tow had fared so badly after an almost unopposed landing in the Camber. Much had been expected from this flank attack. Could not Commander Diggle have told someone of the existence of this comparatively safe landing place so that another wave of troops could be sent in there instead of on to V Beach, where they were slaughtered almost to a man? Perhaps he did. But nothing was done.

The survivors of No. 1 tow who withdrew to the Camber were brought off to safety in two separate parties. The first was led by Lieutenant F. H. Sandford, with Midshipman Lennox Boswell, who had been doing good work in lost *Irresistible*'s picket boat, helping the destroyers with their minesweeping. Later in the day Midshipman Geoffrey Norman brought off the rest. 'On the way off to the *Queen Elizabeth*,' Norman wrote, 'I received a good deal of back-chat from one of the soldiers in the stern of our boat, who merely sat tight with a pipe in his mouth. I was a bit curt with him as he would give orders and make no effort to move. When we got to the ship we helped out all the others, and at last he said, "Come on, give us a hand," and for the first time I saw that one of his legs was almost completely shot away. That night I went to the sick bay to find out how he was getting on and was told that he had insisted on the others being dealt with before him. His first words on getting over his anaesthetic were to ask for his pipe, the stem of which he had already practically chewed away.'

While the murderous fire was being directed at five tows of boats carrying the Dublins, the *River Clyde* had beached, but rather further out than planned because the beach was more shelving than had been expected. On the run in she had suffered a few hits from guns sited on the Asiatic shore but no casualties. The moment she touched bottom her bows lifted, as would be expected, then with a grinding noise she came to rest. Some of the 2,000 men in the hold were thrown off balance, but, as they had been warned to face outboard, feet apart, no one actually fell down.

Hurrying over to the port wing of the bridge to watch the *Argyle* ride ahead, Commander Unwin was horrified to see she was held up alongside because the tow rope had been secured with a jamming hitch. 'Cut!' shouted Unwin, and Midshipman George Drewry, R.N.R., raised an axe. Able Seaman G. McK. Samson, R.N.R., took in the slack, and the *Argyle* was freed in a matter of seconds. But, now as she rode ahead, she took a sheer to port and grounded broadside on to the beach, leaving the gap unbridged between ship and shore. Thus the well-considered plan had miscarried.

It is hard to establish exactly what did happen on board *Argyle*, but one thing is certain. Those members of the Greek crew who were on deck ran down below when the first shot was fired, and, worse still, the Greeks in the engine-room reversed their engines when the *River Clyde* grounded instead of going full speed ahead as ordered. How easy it is to be wise after an event, but it does seem madness to have manned the *Argyle*, on whom the success of the operation so largely depended, with Greeks who were not even in the war. It seems likely, also, that, when the *River Clyde* grounded, with six feet of water under her bow, she acted like a groyne, causing the northerly flow of water across her bows to increase, which encouraged the hopper to swing round broadside on when her bow touched bottom. The naval planners could have foreseen this possibility and arranged for *Argyle* to be towed in on *River Clyde*'s starboard side, from which position she should have swung across the bow, instead of away from her parent ship.

Midshipman Drewry and Able Seaman Samson immediately abandoned the stranded *Argyle* and made their way, wading and swimming, to the leading lighter to help the crew place it in position against the *River Clyde*'s bow. Commander Unwin, with no thought other than the success of the operation, left his bridge, jumped on to the lighter and, with the assistance of a naval party, attached it to a second lighter. Then, wading in shallow water, he hauled both lighters in the direction of the rocky ledge to starboard of the *River Clyde*. Finding nothing on the rocks to secure a line from the leading lighter, Commander Unwin took a couple of turns round his body and crouched down with only his head and shoulders above water. Able Seaman William C. Williams (whom Unwin had instructed at the commencement of the operation never to leave his side) stood up in the water, adding his weight to the rope. With a bridge from ship to shore now established, Commander Unwin waved and shouted for the landing to start. The time was then 7.05 a.m.

'It was the Munsters who charged first with a sprig of shamrock in their caps; then came the Dublins and the Hampshires. Dying on the lighters, on the rocks, on the beach, they cried on the Mother of God. . . .'[3]

Commander Unwin was determined not to give up. Lieutenant J. A. V. Morse had arrived with Midshipman Wilfrid Malleson in a picket boat belonging to *Cornwallis*, towing a launch decked-in with planks laid across the thwarts. Midshipmen M. C. H. Lloyd and H. E. C. Weblin, with Able Seaman Leach, had joined from the landing of the Covering Force. Sub-Lieutenant Tisdall, R.N.V.R., from the Anson Battalion R.N.D., with some of his men from the *River Clyde*, was bearing a hand. At first all seemed to have charmed lives as they worked steadily under murderous fire to restore communication with the shore, the midshipmen mostly swimming to and fro with lines to the lighters and boats, then helping to haul them into position. Midshipman Drewry received a scalp wound, but after first aid he went back to work. Midshipman Lloyd was grazed by a bullet. Carrying on regardless, he was hit again, this time in the lung, but happily he survived. Able Seaman Samson was seriously wounded. Commander Unwin, not a young man, at one time collapsed from sheer exhaustion. After a short rest in his cabin, he went over the side again, contrary to the advice of Surgeon Burrowes Kelly, R.N., and continued to direct operations till the gap was bridged at about 9.00 a.m. (Commander Unwin, Sub-Lieutenant Tisdall, Midshipmen Malleson and Drewry and Able Seamen Samson and Williams were subsequently awarded the V.C. for valour.)

Lieutenant-Colonel Tizard, commanding the Munsters, now ordered his third company to advance. They emerged via the starboard sally ports to get some protection from the ship's side. But the moment they appeared in the open they were exposed to incessant fire. Very few reached the shore unharmed. Orders were now given that for the time being no more attempts to get ashore should be made.

Many anxious eyes had been peering out over the bulwarks of the *River Clyde*, and among them were those of the Rev. Father William Joseph Finn, Roman Catholic Chaplain of the Dublins. The sight of so many of his boys lying dead or dying was too much for him, so, regardless of all risk, he plunged down the gangway and made for the shore. On the way his wrist was shattered by a bullet, but he went on, though lead was spattering all round him like hailstones, and administered consolation to the wounded and dying who were so thickly strewn around.

'For a time he seemed to have some form of Divine protection, for he went from one man to another through shot and shell without receiving any further injury, until at last a bullet struck him near the

hip. On seeing this, some of his Dublins rushed out from the protection of the sandbank and brought him into shelter. When, however, he had recovered a little, nothing would induce him to stay
in safety while his poor boys were being done to death in the open,
so out he crawled again to administer comfort.'[4] He had to hold up
his right arm with his left hand while uttering the words of Abso-
lution, '. . . *deinde ego te absolvo a peccatis tuis in nomine Patris et Filii et
Spiritus Sancti . . . Amen.*'

Finally, hearing groans from a wounded man near the water's
edge, he tried to crawl to him, although he was in great pain and
almost totally disabled. While he was doing so, this truly heroic
chaplain was killed by what one can only call a merciful bullet.

Father Finn had landed originally in Colonel Rooth's boat. They
share the same grave in V Beach cemetery.

The men never forgot Father Finn and never tired of speaking of
him. I think they felt his death more than anything that happened
in that terrible landing. They kept his helmet as a keepsake for a
long time afterwards and carried it with them wherever they went.

General Hunter-Weston had, at 8.30 a.m., issued orders for the main
body of the 88th Brigade, under Brigadier-General H. E. Napier, to
wait off V Beach in the *Clacton*, until the boats which had landed the
Covering Force had returned, when they were to be taken over to
the *River Clyde* and put ashore there. Because of the almost complete
destruction of the tows, as we have seen, there were only sufficient
seaworthy boats available, when their dead and wounded had been
removed, to accommodate the Brigadier-General and his staff, fifty
Hampshires and two platoons of the Worcesters. Napier duly
arrived and on seeing the lighters, boats and gangways choked with
men but not appreciating that they were dead, he sprang on board
the grounded *Argyle* to lead them ashore. A warning voice from the
River Clyde shouted 'You can't possibly land, Sir!', to which Napier
shouted back, 'I'll have a damn good try!' At once there was a
renewed burst of Turkish fire. Would the General and his Brigade-
Major J. H. D. Costeker, ever get under the lee of the hopper and
jump into the sheltering water? No! Side by side they sat down by the
engine-room casing. For a moment it looked as if they had found
cover; then their legs slipped out and they rolled over.

Thus died the one man who by his rank, his nerve and his knowledge would have been of priceless value to the troops in the southern
area. His body was never found.

Soon after Lieutenant-Colonel Carrington Smith had decided that

there should be no more attempts to land from the *River Clyde*, a
message arrived from General Hunter-Weston, Commander, 29th
Division on board the *Euryalus* off W Beach, requiring troops on V
to move to the left to make contact with the Lancashire Fusiliers on
W Beach. Although such a short distance away, the General was in
complete ignorance of the situation at V Beach and of the impossibility of his order being obeyed. The message did, however, make
Carrington Smith feel that he ought to have another try to get more
troops ashore. The arrival of the *Queen Elizabeth* to renew the bombardment, with both commanders-in-chief on board, helped him to
decide, and at about 11.30 a.m. he detached one of the two companies of his own battalion, the 2nd Hampshires. Gallantly led by
Captain C. L. Boxall they set off on their perilous journey. Very
few survived. Captain Boxall was among the dead. No further
attempt was made till after dark.

Credit for the hold up on V Beach must go to the Turkish Sergeant
Yahya of Ezine and his sixty-three brave soldiers, all of whom were
eventually killed. Although some 350 yards from the *River Clyde*, his
enfilade fire was as we have seen, devastating. With very few excep-
tions, only those of our men who found shelter behind the western
horn of the crescent shaped bank on the beach, escaped injury or
death. The Turks raised a memorial to Yahya and his men in 1962,
on the site of his defensive position. He had defended V Beach with
one 27 mm battery (pom-pom) and with rifle fire, the sound of which
was at the time confused with that of machine-guns, which were
not brought in until later.

'Thereafter the wounded cried out all day . . .' Josiah Wedgwood
wrote to Winston Churchill. 'It was horrible . . . . If the "River
Clyde" had not been on that beach with our 11 Maxims on board,
not one of the 400 still living on the shore could have survived.

'That night we landed the rest of the Munsters & the Hampshires (some 1,000 in all). The losses then were small. For 3 hours I
stood on the end of the spit of what had been rock in 2 feet of water
helping the heavily laden men to jump ashore on to submerged
dead bodies & trying to persuade the wounded over whom they had
to walk that we should soon get them aboard. This is what went
on monotonously: "Give me your rifle"; "& your shovel"; "your
left hand"; "jump wide"; "it's all right, only kits"; "keep clear of
that man's legs, can't you!" And all the time the gangway along one
boat worked to & fro on wounded men; & wounded men were
brought to the end of the spit and could not be got aboard because
the other stream was more important and never ending; & there
they slowly sank and died. . . .'[5]

'Every man who landed that night,' Wedgwood recorded in his book, 'jumped on to the backs of dead men, the most horrible accompaniment in the world. It was then that I first learnt the shout of "Allah", for the Turks charged. All night long the battle raged. On shore everyone was firing at they knew not what. Our men went up the hill through the Turks, and the Turks came down through ours. Over and past each other they went, sometimes not seeing, sometimes glad to pass in the darkness.'[6]

Lieutenant-Colonel C. M. H. ('Dick') Doughty-Wylie, Royal Welch Fusiliers, was a G.H.Q. man. He had obtained permission from Sir Ian Hamilton to join the *River Clyde*, in preference to Admiral Cecil Thursby's flagship, the *Queen*, at the Anzac landing. He possessed a most intimate knowledge of the Turks and their country and had been attached to the Turkish Army during the Balkan Wars, where he was wounded. His many decorations included the Turkish Order of Medjidieh.

During the day of April 25th he was to be found everywhere, assisting the wounded and doing the work on board the *River Clyde* of officers who had fallen. On the death of Brigadier-General Napier, Lieutenant-Colonel Carrington Smith of the Hampshires assumed military command. When he was killed on the bridge while looking through his field-glasses, Lieutenant-Colonel Tizard of the Munsters took over. When he went ashore no senior Infantry officer remained. Doughty-Wylie landed after dark and walked among the weary men to cheer them up and to keep their spirits from sinking. He sent men to cut the wire ready for the morning.

At about 11 p.m. he returned on board and drank a cup of tea. 'I had a chat of about a quarter of an hour with him,' wrote Surgeon Peter Burrowes Kelly, 'and he seemed depressed about the whole affair. Several times he remarked that something must be done. He then went ashore again. With the assistance of Lieutenant-Colonel W. de L. Williams, Hampshire Regiment, and Captain G. W. Walford, Brigade Major 29th Divisional Artillery, both G.H.Q. staff, he rallied the gallant survivors. It was an action showing not only conspicuous gallantry but rare qualities which enabled him to pull together somewhat shaken troops, troops to whom he was unknown, and to get them to take on and make a success of something which they and their officers had thought impossible. After clearing the village and castle, armed only with light cane, he led the attack on the old fort at Hill 141, the final objective. The Turkish defenders fled. Doughty-Wylie was shot through the head at the moment of victory while his men were cheering. His last request was said to have been that someone bring to the notice of the authorities the gallant Commander Unwin and the boy Drewry.'

Lieutenant-Colonel Williams, who had been fully occupied elsewhere, came up at 4 p.m. to find Doughty-Wylie stretched out.

'The interment had to be done hurriedly,' he wrote to Captain Pollen, Sir Ian Hamilton's Military Secretary. 'I had to re-organise the line and think of further advance or digging in. I removed his watch, money and a few other personal things to send home to his wife. We buried him as he lay and I said the Lord's Prayer over his grave and bad him "Goodbye". That night, when things had quietened down, I asked Commander Unwin to have a temporary cross put up to mark the grave.'[7]

Hill 141 was afterwards named 'Doughty-Wylie Redoubt'. It was the irony of fate that he should be killed by the Turks for whom he had done so much in the past. Captain Walford, who had accompanied him from the *River Clyde*, fell just outside the castle of Sedd el Bahr, at the bottom of the village. Both Doughty-Wylie and Walford were awarded the V.C. posthumously.

II

S Beach – Morto Bay

*'Sedd el Bahr was supposed to be the softest landing of
the lot, as it was the best harbour and seemed to lie
specially at the mercy of the big guns of the Fleet. Would
that we had left it severely alone and had landed a big
force at Morto Bay.'*
Sir Ian Hamilton
Gallipoli Diary, 1920

H.M.S. *Cornwallis*, Captain A. P. Davidson, had been ordered to act
first as a parent ship for the S Beach landing, then to move over in
support of the *Albion* off V Beach. The Morto Bay landing, though
expected to be very difficult, had a special importance – security of
the right flank of the main attack. It had been rejected as being too
badly exposed to fire from guns on the Asiatic coast to be used for
the main landing.

Three companies of the 2nd South Wales Borderers, one of the
best battalions in the 29th Division, had been detailed for the attempt,
but there had been no opportunity of exercising the men in boat-
work. Four trawlers, each towing six Merchant Navy lifeboats, were
to take them in, and, as it would be impossible for fully equipped
soldiers to row these unhandy boats against the strong current
coming down the Dardanelles, the trawlers were to carry on until
they ran ashore. Even so, there might be quite a distance for the
lifeboats to cover under oars. Two seamen to each boat were all
that could be spared. No destroyers, no steamboats, no naval boats
of any kind were available for this landing.

The night before the attack Captain Davidson had received a
signal from Admiral Wemyss to the effect that, when he had taken in
the troops, he was not to come out of the Straits immediately, to
his bombarding station off V Beach, but was to stay and support the
South Wales Borderers until they had landed. He interpreted this
new order, as will be seen, in a sense far beyond what appears to
have been meant.

The plan was as follows. The first company of the S.W.B.s was to land just inside Eski Hissarlik Point, the precipitous headland which marks the eastern end of Morto Bay, and endeavour to seize the old De Tott's Battery which crowns it. Further in the bay a well-wooded slope falls gently from a lower ridge to a good beach. It was known to be entrenched, but here the other two companies were to disembark and rush the defences. Thus, while the right flank of the troops would be well protected by the sea, the left was in the air.

Captain Davidson, together with Colonel H. G. Casson, commanding the South Wales Borderers, decided to improve on the plan. In addition to providing a coxswain and bowman for each boat, Captain Davidson would land the marine detachment in ship's boats to form a flanking party, also twenty-five seamen as a beach party to help drag in the boats and to disembark the ammunition quickly. It was a good idea.

During the night of April 24/25th, at a rendezvous outside the Straits, the troops were transferred from the *Cornwallis* to the trawlers, and about daybreak, when well inside, they were quickly moved from the trawlers to the lifeboats. While the trawlers laboured on against the current for the two or three miles that remained, the *Cornwallis* kept station to conceal them, firing on the beach and the adjacent hills as she proceeded. As soon, however, as the light made, the Asiatic howitzer batteries detected them and began showering shrapnel, but there were no casualties before the trawlers entered the bay, which had previously been swept for mines by Captain Heneage and his destroyers under cover of the *Agamemnon's* guns.

The special covering ships, the *Lord Nelson* and the *Vengeance*, had taken up their station at 5 a.m., and since then had been assiduously searching their fire areas, especially the hill above De Tott's battery.

Owing to the congestion of shipping at the entrance to the Straits and to the strength of the current, it was not until 7.30 a.m. that the trawlers with their tows passed the *Lord Nelson*. As they went in, both she and *Cornwallis* swept the whole shore with their guns. It was not long now before the trawlers took ground some 400 yards out. Although still under distant howitzer fire, not a shot came from the immediate objective, nor could any enemy be seen, as the boats, in excellent order, pulled for the landing place. When, however, the first company on the right took to the water up to their waists, a heavy rifle fire was opened on them, but, undeterred, they formed up and made for the cliff. By 7.50 a.m. nearly all were ashore. Meanwhile the other two companies, after wading in, fixed bayonets and rushed a trench they found right in front of them, and by the time

15 Looking north from Gaba Tepe showing the beach where the original landing of the Anzacs was intended. Anzac Cove is beyond Hell Spit, the first headland

16 Ari Burnu and Anzac Cove on the day of the landing

17 The tragedy at V Beach is illustrated in this photograph taken from the fo'c'sle of the *River Clyde*. The bow of the stranded *Argyle* appears on the left. A dumb lighter brought forward to take its place is chock-a-block with dead and wounded, mostly Munsters and Hampshires. Ashore survivors of the Royal Dublin Fusiliers have found shelter under the lip of a sand bank. A few Dublins from the Camber landing approach from the right. The enfilade fire from the Turkish defenders is coming from the left, not from the old fort and the village of Sedd el Bahr

18 S.S. *River Clyde* on V Beach. Ships sunk to form a breakwater (*Mulberry*) can be seen in the background

the *Cornwallis*'s seamen and marines arrived the first company of the South Wales Borderers was half-way up to De Totts.

With the naval party was Captain Davidson himself. He had been rowed ashore in his own six-oared galley. In order the better to carry out his orders to support the landing he had decided to anchor his ship and come ashore with his men. With him was Colonel Casson and his adjutant.

While the sailors ran to draw up the boats and to help their crews to clear them, the marines were in time to assist in capturing the second trench. As soon as the sailors' work was done, they joined the fighting line and, being unencumbered with equipment, were able to bear a hand in the capture of a third trench.

Everything, indeed, had gone with such speed that by 8.30 a.m. De Tott's battery and the ridge above the slope were won and the positions secured with comparatively little loss.

Although the *Lord Nelson* had signalled to Admiral Wemyss in the *Euryalus* off W Beach – the Lancashire Landing – that the South Wales Borderers were already on the top of Eski Hissarlik, above De Tott's Battery, the *Cornwallis* had not come away to provide extra covering fire at V Beach. *Queen Elizabeth* signalled *Cornwallis* to take up her appointed station. Unknown then to both Admiral de Robeck and to Admiral Wemyss, Captain Davidson was too occupied on shore to obey at once. Again and again the signal was repeated with increasing emphasis, but it was not till 10 a.m., when the Asiatic guns ceased to be troublesome, the troops seemed firmly established and the wounded, about fifty in number had been taken off, that Captain Davidson obeyed the order.

'I can well remember,' wrote Lieutenant John Godfrey, who was then Navigating Officer of the *Euryalus*, 'the exasperation on the bridge caused by the *Cornwallis*'s failure to do what she was told and Wemyss's anger when it was subsequently discovered that her captain was ashore taking personal command of a platoon of sailors.

'I do not know what happened at the post mortem. Captain Davidson had shown considerable initiative in exploiting this soft spot by landing marines and bluejackets and going ashore himself to command them, and it will remain a matter for conjecture if the extra fire power of the *Cornwallis* would have made all that difference at V Beach.'[1]

'Ardent but misguided zeal,' Commodore Keyes called it in his *Memoirs*, but he need not have been quite so snooty because during the Boxer Rising in 1900 he did much the same thing himself. (Handing over the command of his destroyer lying in Tientsin to his First Lieutenant, he joined an army column which was setting off to relieve the British Legation in Peking and was one of the first to enter the city after climbing a thirty-foot wall with a Union Jack in his teeth. The adventure nearly cost him his ship.)

On 21st June 1936, Unwin of the *River Clyde* wrote to Lockyer of the *Implacable*: '. . . Isn't the whole of Gallipoli one mighty might have been? V Beach would have been easier for me had Davidson in the *Cornwallis* carried out his orders and after sending in his parties come round to V Beach . . . he could have saved 100s of lives, but he chose to leave his ship and go for a joy-ride on the Beach, where twenty-five Turks were awaiting his *Battalion*. He ought to have been court-martialled.'

And these are Captain Davidson's own views: 'It was a very great relief to General Hunter-Weston that his right flank was secure, especially in view of the failure of the centre, at V Beach, to make good a landing; although it will always be a matter of judgement whether the order to support the Borderers was not carried out in too wide a sense. And it was the fortune of war that when the *Cornwallis* was recalled unavoidable delay took place, which, quite rightly from the naval point of view, was inexcusable.

'No naval artillery support could have adequately secured the landing at V Beach and so, though no naval recognition was given to the *Cornwallis* for making good the landing of the Borderers, the fact remains that those on the spot knew, and the responsible generals knew, that without our efforts the landing at De Tott's battery in all probability would have failed, just as much as the one at V Beach failed.

'Given better information and more flexible organisation the landing might have been switched from V to Morto Bay. But this could only have been done by an order from Rear-Admiral Wemyss and General Hunter-Weston and they were both on board the *Euryalus* too far away to see what was going on on the right flank, and preoccupied with events that were taking place under their eyes at W Beach Lancashire Landing.

'If the Admiral and General had been in a smaller and more mobile ship they could have seen for themselves what was happening in Morto Bay and perhaps stopped pumping troops into V Beach where the hold up was complete, with the *River Clyde* experiment a failure. . . .'[2]

'Next day the recriminations came pouring in,' wrote Lieutenant Harry Minchin, Gunnery Officer of the *Cornwallis*. 'This was the only time I ever took part in a real live bayonet charge. Why wasn't the *Cornwallis* off V Beach and why was I ashore instead of on board in charge of our guns? Admiral "Rosy" Wemyss came on board to investigate. A more charming man you couldn't find anywhere, and he took my side and defended me valiantly. So no further action was taken except that my name was removed from the list for the D.S.C., and that didn't worry me; I'd seen so many potential V.C.s knocked over.'

A few days later the Admiral returned to the *Cornwallis* on a morale-boosting visit. The lower deck had been cleared and all available officers and ratings mustered on the quarter-deck. The bugler sounded the alert, the quartermasters 'piped the side'. All was deathly silence, suddenly broken by the Admiral himself, who tossed his monocle into the air in front of the whole ship's company and caught it in his eye. The spell was broken. All hands laughed their sides out and there was much hand-clapping. After the visit was over it was a delight to watch the sailors trying to emulate the great man's feat with their identity discs.

12

W Beach – Lancashire Landing

'*So strong, in fact, were the defences of W Beach that the Turks may well have considered them impregnable, and it is my firm conviction that no finer feat of arms has ever been achieved, by the British soldier – or any other soldier – than the storming of these trenches on the morning of 25 April.*'
Sir Ian Hamilton
Despatches, 20th May 1915

W Beach is a strip of powdery sand lying between the two headlands of Tekke Burnu and Cape Helles. Here a gully has been cut by a short watercourse, which is usually dry. The gentle curve of the actual beach is rather more than a quarter of a mile long. Its broadest part, where the gully emerges, is about forty yards deep. On both flanks the ground rises sharply, but in the centre a number of sand dunes provide a more gradual approach to the ridge behind.

The whole length of the beach was protected by barbed-wire entanglement and there was more of this unpleasant obstacle hidden in the shallows. A number of machine guns were tucked away into holes in the cliffs, to be immune from naval gunfire. The high ground overlooking the beach was deeply entrenched. Access to V Beach in the south, and to the more distant X Beach in the north, was closed by more barbed wire running down into the sea itself.

'My problem, as Navigating Officer of the *Euryalus*,' wrote Lieutenant John Godfrey, 'was to lead the tows of boats and small craft in the right direction during the night and to deliver them accurately off W Beach one hour before dawn. We weighed anchor off Tenedos on the evening of April 24th, and I became conscious of the loom of the land ahead about 3 a.m. . . . As we were approaching Cape Tekke, I was soon able to get a rough fix by bearings of the right and left extremities of the land at Sedd el Bahr and the cliffs to the west of Achi Baba.

'It was a still, dark night, and final adjustments of course and speed were made that enabled us to reach our stopping point about 1,500 yards from the land with reasonable accuracy and well up to time. The dip in the hills over W Beach, which I had noted during reconnaissance on April 15th, was visible well before dawn.'[1]

It was through the keyhole of this beach that the 1st Battalion XX The Lancashire Fusiliers, under the command of Major Bishop, were to open the way to a successful issue on the southern end of the Peninsula.

The three companies of the regiment were embarked in the *Euryalus*, Headquarters of Major-General Hunter-Weston, commanding the 29th Division, and flying the flag of Rear-Admiral Wemyss. All hands were called at 3.30 a.m. The soldiers were guests of the sailors at breakfast. When the meal was finished, it was time to go. There were twenty-four boats to fill – naval cutters and merchant ships' lifeboats, organised in six tows, four boats to a tow. It was slow work. Each soldier was burdened with equipment weighing seventy pounds, which included three days' rations and two hundred rounds of ammunition.

'Everyone was in high spirits,' wrote Major B. Smyth. 'They laughed, chatted and chaffed each other as they passed down over the ship's side into the boats. To check so much levity the First Lieutenant administered a mild rebuke – "This is a serious business, men!"'[2]

Embarkation was completed at 4.30 a.m. 'See you in Constantinople,' General Hunter-Weston called out from the bridge as the boats began to form up in line abreast and started for the shore. An interval of fifty to one hundred yards was kept between each tow so that the whole frontage of the beach would be covered. The *Euryalus* followed slowly but remained some way out, as she expected to be shelled. The tows were now joined by a tow from the *Implacable* carrying Brigadier-General Steuart Hare, Commander 86th Infantry Brigade, and his Brigade-Major Captain T. H. C. Frankland as well as one company of the Lancashire Fusiliers under Captain Tallents and also Brigadier-General Roper, Royal Engineers. Last but not least was Captain Richard Phillimore, R.N., late of the damaged *Inflexible* and now Beachmaster.

It was misty and hard to see from the boats what the beach was like or even where it was exactly. The land ahead was a silhouette against the first light of the rising sun. There was no sign of life on shore. No one spoke in the boats.

'Silently they sat,' wrote Major A. K. Williamson, 'Every moment taut with the uncertainty of the future, yet more firmly resolved to quit themselves like men of their ancient regiment. Through the minds of many there seemed to flash the lessons of the barrack squares, all that they had heard of the deeds of their forbears from that day of Minden down to the Great War: that Minden Day when every recruit had seen the colours and drums paraded with roses that commemorated this great deed of his regiment. And now it was to be their turn.'[3]

At 5.15 the bombardment began, with the *Swiftsure* supporting the *Euryalus*. Spirits soared with the sound of the heavy gunfire and the screech of the shells passing overhead.

Sunrise was at 5.22 a.m., and when it appeared above the land it shone straight into the eyes not only of the tows approaching the beach but also those of the naval gunners in the bombarding ships.

Just before 6 a.m., when the tows were about fifty yards from the shore, *Euryalus* and *Swiftsure* lifted their point of aim from the beach to the higher ground behind and the order to slip was given. Grabbing their oars, the men raced for the shore, each boat hoping to be the first to touch down. But the Turks held their fire until the barbed wire fouled oars and keels.

Crack! The coxswain of a cutter fell over dead, followed by the stroke oar and then by two more. That was enough. 'Stand by to go overboard everybody!' came the order, none too easy to carry out when burdened with heavy equipment.

Pioneers had been specially armed with axes and wire cutters to deal with this kind of emergency, and so, somehow, the boats scraped through far enough for the men to get out with water only up to their armpits. Soon the sea was dotted with figures struggling towards the beach. 'Thou'st given me a bloody job!' exclaimed one private to his officer. Streaming with blood, the brave fellow went on, tearing at the accursed wire with only his bayonet until he fell under the hail of bullets.

Gallantly led by their officers, the Lancashire Fusiliers hurled themselves ashore. Many were hit in the sea, and many who gained the beach were mown down immediately. Eye witnesses, anxiously watching, asked each other, 'What are they resting for?' But they were dead.

Rifles, having been denuded, by order, of their rifle covers, were soaked and useless, but the men pressed on, intent on one thing, to close with the bayonet. At the top of the beach they flung themselves down before the barbed-wire entanglements which had hardly been touched by the naval gunfire. There the wire caught them and held them, and there they were shot to pieces.

Others, warned by their fate, crawled out of the sea on hands and knees, and by the Grace of God the Turks with machine-guns in tunnels in the cliffs could not depress their line of fire below a point a few feet above the water's edge. Lying flat under the stream of bullets some men succeeded in burrowing with their hands in the soft sand and wriggling under the wire. Many wire-cutters, clogged with sand and sea water, would not function. A few men had to get through the wire over the bodies of their fallen comrades.

Regardless of the Turkish fire some men solemnly sat down, rummaged in their packs for a tooth brush and set to to clear their rifles of sand. Compasses, field-glasses and watches also needed attention.

An officer spied a gap and shouted to his men to follow him. Major Bishop waved his cap to those towards the centre to make them move over to their left. Major Pearson shouted impatiently to some others to follow, not realising that they were dead. Then fortune began to smile on the attack.

Brigadier-General Hare, coming in with the tow from the *Implacable*, saw that the water was calm enough to land on the rocks to the north of the beach. In a moment a handful of Fusiliers had effected a lodgment on the cliff and so found themselves above the beach. Although the naval bombardment had been generally ineffective, it had done some good here. The heavy shell bursting on the cliff-side had cut steps up which the men clambered, taking the Turks in flank.

At the same time enough men had forced their way to the sand dunes beyond the beach, where a fierce struggle took place. Gradually the superb determination of the Lancashire men told. The old regimental spirit kept them moving until a line had been gained which covered the actual beach from any but stray shots.

Meanwhile, as one of the attendant destroyers was closing the shore, a rifle bullet passed through both cheeks of the coxswain at the steering wheel, taking out two of his teeth. The bullet then sailed on and killed a signalman standing in a corner of the bridge.

Order now began to evolve, and the attack proceeded more according to plan, but the Turk was stubborn and took further toll before he was driven back. His deep trenches had been untouched by gunfire, and one small party of Turks, emerging late, 'captured' an officer and four men who were trying to get in touch with the Royal Fusiliers landed on the left, on X Beach. However, when these enemies found themselves behind our line, they in turn cheerfully surrendered to their prisoners.

The time was now 9.30 a.m., and the supports were being landed, but they were late. The naval beach personnel had been instructed that evacuation of the wounded was to be carried out only by the medical boats provided and that tows engaged in landing fighting troops were on no account to be delayed for casualties. But the boats' crews could not bear to leave the soldiers lying around on the beach, so in many cases they took them to *Euryalus*, whose upper deck soon resembled a casualty clearing station. The comfort of the wounded was not enhanced by the frequent firing of the ship's guns, but they were none the less grateful to the sailors for bringing them away, and vastly preferred the *Euryalus*'s upper deck to the beach.

'Meanwhile,' wrote Brigadier-General Hare, 'I thought I would try and work round to meet the Royal Fusiliers who had landed on X Beach and bring them up to make a flank attack on the Turks who were opposing the Lancashire Fusiliers. The latter had made a certain amount of progress (it was wonderful that they had made any), but I did not think that they could possibly get far unsupported. I started with Frankland, my Brigade-Major, and two signallers and we were just above the top of the cliff not far from Cape Tekke when we found ourselves within about 100 yards of a trench full of Turks. We dropped down over the top of the cliff as they opened fire. Suddenly I received a blow on my calf and had to sit down. Frankland and the signallers put on three field dressings without stopping the bleeding. If the Turks had had the enterprise to come out of their trench to look for us they could have bagged the lot. I told Frankland and the signallers to carry on with what they were doing and started back to the beach to look for a stretcher.'[4]

Two stretcher bearers turned up and put iodine into Brigadier-General Hare's wound and tied him up again. He was then carried down to the beach where he found Captain Phillimore and his Beach Party hard at work. A lot of bullets were flying around but they were not under direct fire. Hare was lifted on board the *Euryalus*'s picket boat, Midshipman H. M. Wilson, and taken off to the ship where his wound was properly dressed.

Frankland and Mynors Farmar (who became Brigade-Major on Frankland's death), met on the beach. The former wanted to get going on the right to establish the Lancashire Fusiliers on Hill 138. Some forty or fifty men were given the order. They were a little dazed after their landing experience but came on well.

'We reached the lighthouse', Farmar wrote, 'and pushed on until hung up by a maze of barbed wire. Fortunately there was almost dead ground against the wire for a strip. The Signal Section were established under cover of the lighthouse and they got communciation with the Royal Fusiliers, the *Euryalus* and the *River Clyde*. Frankland left me and went to the ridge on the right to see if there was any way on from there. At about 8.45 a.m. he stood up in order to see, and was shot through the heart, neck and head. We buried him two days afterwards.'[5] (Frankland had been captured with Winston Churchill in the armoured train ambushed by the Boers, Pretoria, 20th November 1899. 'I noticed particularly a young officer who with a happy confident smile on his face was endeavouring to rally his men', wrote Churchill[6]).

In the meantime the Essex Regiment and the Worcester Regiment had disembarked and joined the Lancashire Fusiliers in the assault.

An attempt was then made to relieve the bad situation at V Beach – *River Clyde* – by advancing along the top of the headland. Lancashire and Royal Fusiliers came over in small parties to assist the Worcesters.

The distance to V Beach was barely half a mile, and, if it could have been covered, the enemy must have abandoned their V Beach trenches. Wire cutters came out. Through binoculars the men could be seen snipping away under a hellish fire as if they were pruning a vineyard. But the rows of heavy interlaced wire proved too thick. The troops, now thoroughly exhausted by the long day's fighting under a hot sun and some rain, had to rest on their laurels for a spell. The bravest of the brave had to abandon the attempt and pause in the trenches along the summit of the cliffs now deserted by the enemy.

When night fell, the British position in front of W Beach was consolidated. Practically every man had to be thrown into the trenches to hold this line, and the only available reserves on this part of the front were the 2nd London Field Co. R.E. and a platoon of the Anson Battalion, R.N.D., which had been landed as a beach working party.

An inspiring sight as the afternoon closed in was the magnificent shire horses dragging the 6-inch howitzers up the steep sandy slope at the back of the beach.

During the night several strong and determined counter-attacks were made by the Turks. At about 1 a.m. on the 26th the noise of the battle seemed to reach a climax. It sounded as if our men were being pushed back, so General Hunter-Weston, on board the *Euryalus*, was called. He listened for a moment, but his trained ear told him that there had been no appreciable movement and he turned over and went to sleep again. When day broke it was confirmed that the front line had not moved.

The counter-attack had lasted from midnight till 4 a.m., when all work on the beach had to be stopped to enable beach parties to carry ammunition to the trenches. By 4.30 a.m. normal work on the beach could be resumed. Casualties on both sides were not heavy but Turkish losses were always difficult to assess as they carried away their dead whenever possible.

'On the Lancashire Landing front the firing had died down, and we proceeded to lick our wounds and count the cost,' wrote Major R. R. Willis, V.C. 'Of 25 officers and 932 men we had only 16 officers and 300 men left. But these 300 were full of spirit and even cheery in spite of all. "We won't need to talk of Minden no more, Sir," said one man with a twisted grin.'[7]

'It is impossible to exalt too highly the service rendered by the 1st Battalion Lancashire Fusiliers in the storming of the beach,' Vice-Admiral de Robeck recorded in his Dispatch. 'The dash and gallantry displayed was superb.'

Sixty-three out of the eighty naval ratings manning the cutters and lifeboats were killed or wounded, but not one boat failed to return to the minesweepers for a second load.

In the presence of so much heroism the normal method of selection for awards failed. The battalion was therefore allocated six Victoria Crosses and ordered to choose the recipients. 'Six V.C.s before breakfast has been the regiment's proud boast': Captain Richard Willis; Sergeant Alfred Richards; Private William Keneally; Captain (temp. Major) Cuthbert Bromley (later drowned); Sergeant Frank E. Stubbs (later died of wounds); and Corporal John Grimshaw.

Eighteen V.C.s awarded for valour were gained in the Great War by Lancashire Fusiliers, more than any other regiment in the British Army. The motto of the regiment is appropriate: '*Omnia Audax* – Daring in All Things'.

'The dead and wounded lay everywhere on the strip of sand, and the sea for fifty yards out was streaked with blood,' wrote the Rev. H. C. Foster, Chaplain to the Anson Battalion, R.N.D. 'From man to man I went ministering to their needs as best I could. The great cry was "Water!"

'A man wants to see his priest before he is dead. A few words whispered in a severely wounded man's ear are magical in effect. An ineffable change appears over the face, death has now no horrors for him and he passes into the great hereafter content and uncomplaining, at peace with all the world and fit to meet his Maker.'[8]

Private Wilkinson, A Company, Lancashire Fusiliers, was carrying a little extra weight when he landed with the first flight of boats. He had picked up a puppy – 'Rags' – a sheep-dog of doubtful parentage, while in Alexandria. He smuggled it on board the troopship and had it with him in the *Euryalus*. Rags is remembered as being quite a character and popular with the ship's company. When Wilkinson got down into his boat he had Rags with him hidden in his knapsack. Within a few minutes of landing Wilkinson was killed. Rags was later taken over to V Beach, River Clyde, where he scampered about, cadging food from soldiers and sailors. He loved to swim out and bark at splashes from shell falling into the sea. Midshipman Hayden Forbes of the *Cornwallis*'s picket boat befriended the dog, and when the Provost Marshal spoke of having it 'put down' Rags was welcomed on board the *Cornwallis* as ship's pet. Forbes took Rags with him to his next ship the *Aster*, which struck a mine off the coast of Malta. Both dog and master were saved.

When Forbes went to Buckingham Palace to receive his D.S.C. from the hand of H.M. King George V, 'Rags' of course went with him, wearing the ribbon of the General Service Medal attached to his collar.

'Rags' died of old age in Malta on 23rd October 1926, where Lieutenant-Commander Forbes was serving with the Fleet Air Arm. There is a tablet to the dog's memory in the garden of the Villa Gezira, Sliema, which is now a Mess for the staff of Queen Alexandra's Royal Naval Nursing Service.

Forbes was killed in a flying accident seven months later and is also buried in Malta not far from his dog.

Major-General Sir Steuart Hare never fully recovered from his wound. He died on 25th October 1952; and shortly afterwards this letter reached his family.

> 1299 Rochdale Road,
> Blackley, Manchester.
> Nov. 1st 1952.

Dear Sir or Madam,
    It is with the Deepest Regret I heard of the death of General Hare. Please accept my condolences in your Sad Bereavement.

As I read his Obituary in *The Times*, 27th October, my mind went back 37½ years. I happened to be in the same boat that left the *Implacable*. I will admit right now although I was an old soldier with 12 years service, I had never been in action before. The General had seen quite a lot of active service and his encouraging words to each one of us in his boat was gratifying.

As you know the first few hours on the beach after we landed was no picnic. One thing that happened that day I shall always have imprinted on my mind as long as I live.

The General had made up his mind to get in touch with the Royal Fusiliers. I got an urgent order to search on our left flank, as the news had come through that he had been wounded.

No one knew where he was, so off I went with another stretcher bearer. I found him near the water's edge in a semi-conscious condition with a severe leg wound, and what with loss of blood I thought he would die before I could do anything for him. He must have been a real tough man to get over his wound.

Not until I read of his Death in the Paper last week did I ever realise he was alive. Honestly I thought he had died.

I am 65 years old and a pensioner of the Manchester City Police, so forgive me taking this privilege of writing to you. I have only written in good Faith.

Yours very truly,

H. BROWN.

13

X Beach – *Implacable* Landing

'*The splendid manner in which our Captain handled his ship makes me feel about ten feet high to serve under him.*'
Stoker Petty Officer Chas. R. Cook, R.N.
H.M.S. *Implacable*

If you could scramble round the foot of Tekke Burnu for something more than half a mile along the rocks till the cliff face westward towards the Aegean and the Gulf of Xeros was reached, you would find another but smaller natural amphitheatre. The cliff here is – and was – 100 feet high, but not too steep, with a soft, indeed crumbling surface. This was X Beach, referred to in history as *Implacable* Landing. It had been well prepared for defence, and only a brilliant feat of seamanship, combined with the gallantry of the 2nd Royal Fusiliers, commanded by Lieutenant-Colonel H. E. B. Newenham, turned a near impossibility into a success.

H.M.S. *Implacable*, Captain 'Tubby' Lockyer, had anchored under the lee of Tenedos during the evening of April 24th, where 750 cheerful Royal Fusiliers were embarked. These men were nearly all cockneys, from the East End of London. They were smaller men than the Lancashire Fusiliers and not so muscular, but very tough, and they never stopped talking and joking, which might be rather trying in peace-time, but was an asset on an occasion like this.

At 9 p.m. the four picket boats, with their tows of four boats each, made fast astern, and the *Implacable* got under way. 'The boats were uncomfortable and the prospects gloomy,' Midshipman Hugh Tate recorded in his log. 'In fact we were numb with cold.'

At 3.45 a.m. Captain Lockyer reached his pre-arranged position on the correct bearing of X Beach, distance three miles. The boats were called alongside, and while the troops embarked the boats' crews were given fannies of ship's cocoa to warm them up. A fanny is a tea-urn. The cocoa made out of large blocks of chocolate is, alas, a beverage of the past. Each man would have drunk his share in turn, no doubt grunting with satisfaction as the hot thick beverage penetrated his vitals. When all were aboard the tows shoved off and took up their stations, two to port and two to starboard of their parent ship.

Boat midshipmen wore their dirks. Midshipman A. W. 'Nobby' Clarke was one of them. He rightly claimed this as the last occasion on which dirks were carried into battle and has presented his to the National Maritime Museum to mark the occasion.

While the boats were forming up the *Implacable*'s starboard anchor was lowered 'under foot' and cable veered to one and a half shackles or seventy-five feet, then stopped to the riding bits with a hemp lashing. Another short length of cable was then ranged, i.e. flaked down on deck ready for running, so that when the anchor touched bottom the strain on the cable would part the stopper and the ship would be brought up very close to the shore. The parting of the hemp stopper was to be the signal for Captain Lockyer to ring down to the engine-room for full speed astern. This plan worked admirably.

Captain Lockyer's ingenuity did not stop there. His plan for covering the landing by ship's gunfire was unique. This is what he did: At 5.30, just after sunrise, he steered for the beach at slow speed while one of his 6-inch guns fired continually with fixed sight set at 1,800 yards. As soon as the first round (actually the eighth to be fired) hit the beach rapid fire by all guns was ordered, and the foreshore was drenched with bursting shell. The 6-inch gun sights were raised as the boats went in, but the *Implacable* continued to fire her 12-pdr Q.F. guns on to the shore just above the beach while the troops were actually disembarking. As many of the seamen were away in the boats, the guns were mostly served by marines, stokers and bandsmen, and very well they did it. During the bombardment the ship was riding to her anchor with only thirty-nine feet under her stern. As she was drawing twenty-nine feet her screws were mighty close to the 'putty'.

Naturally, at such close range, the ship drew heavy rifle and machine-gun fire upon herself and consequently away from the troops who were landing. Lockyer had prepared for such an eventuality. Before sailing for the Dardanelles the bridge of the *Implacable* had been converted into a citadel by Portsmouth dockyard. Admiral Sir Hedworth Meux had approved of the alterations but at first refused to supply sand for the 800 sandbags ordered, adding a witty remark in his signal to the effect – 'Why take coals to Newcastle?'

But when Captain Lockyer, who was a friend of the Admiral, asked permission to pay for the sand, adding 'I am the person who is going to be shot at,' the C.-in-C. relented. Owing to Lockyer's foresight, the *Implacable*'s bridge personnel suffered no casualties although almost continuously under small arms and shrapnel fire.

'The blast of the guns of the *Implacable* over our heads as we went in was most unpleasant,' continued Midshipman Tate, 'as were the bullets which were coming down all round like little wasps. I was on the extreme left and found a sandy patch and got right in – third boat ashore. Nearly all the rest had the misfortune to run on an uncharted reef about twenty yards out, and the troops had to jump overboard and wade. As we touched land one of our shells hit the cliff just overhead and filled our boat with earth. I thought we had been mined. We then pulled out to the trawlers, which could get in closer than the ship, and embarked more troops. On my third trip I went aground on the point, and we formed rather a tempting target for some Turks in a trench whom we could see quite plainly. We were hit by bullets several times but no one was hurt. I eased off my revolver in their direction but didn't do much damage beyond nearly falling overboard! Finally we floated again and landed boat-load after boat-load.'

So close to the shore had Captain Lockyer anchored his ship that when she opened fire on the cliff with all her guns the Turks in the rifle pits were simply stunned. As a result, the first half of the battalion was able to climb the cliff face with very slight loss, though at the top it found itself faced by a Turkish trench and a half-battery of guns. The soldiers sent a signal, and 'Mother' forthwith knocked out the guns. The trench was then carried by the bayonet.

Securing his left with one company and the front with part of another, and leaving one company to bring up ammunition and water, Lieutenant-Colonel Newenham proceeded to effect communication with the Lancashire Fusiliers at W Beach on his right flank. This was accomplished by a violent bayonet attack up the height on the top of Tekke Burnu. In this attack the whole battalion was engaged.

In spite of heavy loss, the summit was taken about noon, and the Royal Fusiliers joined the W Beach troops in the forlorn hope of relieving V Beach, *River Clyde*.

In the meantime the centre above *Implacable* Beach was seriously threatened, while Colonel Newenham was wounded; and the situation was only saved by the arrival of the 1st Borderers and 1st Inniskilling Fusiliers of 87 Brigade, whose Brigadier-General J. W. R. Marshall had also been wounded.

'While the landing was in progress,' wrote Midshipman Desmond Thompson, 'a small shell came clean through the upper deck of *Implacable* into the Paymaster's cabin without bursting; but it did bowl over and break up the "safe" which was full of gold coins. When the Carpenter's Crew assembled to view the damage they found the Marine sentry on his hands and knees stuffing sovereigns and half-sovereigns into his pockets "to save them from rolling overboard, Sir!"'

After the landing beaches had more or less settled down Captain Lockyer found that he had four men missing, deserters from the Beach Party, and the word was passed round. 'A few days later a boat came alongside and they arrived on board, dressed in a mixed uniform of Royal Fusiliers and Lancashire Fusiliers,' he wrote in his diary. 'On being brought before me as defaulters they all had broad grins, and on being asked why they had left the beach, their reply was, "We couldn't help it, Sir – we had to – but", said one, "we had the hell of a time." They had been in the front line a week. So all I could do was to congratulate them on being alive!'[1]

It is worth recording that Captain Lockyer was at first admonished by Admiral de Robeck for disobeying orders by continuing to bombard the foreshore while the boats were actually grounding. But when it came out that only the close gun support from *Implacable* had made it possible for the Royal Fusiliers to disembark with hardly a casualty, the Admiral's attitude changed. Lockyer was congratulated on his initiative and later suitably rewarded.

Captain Lockyer received many tributes, but the one that appealed to me most was in a letter from A. W. 'Nobby' Clarke, one of his boat midshipmen, written years later when Clarke was a Commander.

'I remember the first hour of joining the *Implacable* and the nervousness we all felt. You passed us and said a cheery word which made us all, I think, feel at once that the Captain was after all a human being as well as that unapproachable person with four stripes.

'My most vivid recollections, of course, were at the first landing and the impression the ship made on my boat-load as she steamed with us right at our elbow, so to speak. Apart from the material effect of the gunfire, I cannot forget the moral support it gave to those of us who felt hopelessly exposed and naked in the open boats. My little contingent went ashore completely confident and without a nervous thought as a result of your personal support.

'You were generally on the quarter deck when we returned between trips, to ask us how many Turks we'd killed – not that we had, but it gave us confidence to try and do things we hardly knew how to do.

'I have never had the fortune to meet you again since we paid off, yet I shall never forget those days 1914–1916 and the interest and care you showed in your Young Gentlemen, nor shall I forget that the *Implacable* was put on the map for ever by *you*.'[2]

14

Y Beach and Deception

Rather less than a mile up the coast from X Beach, the *Implacable* Landing, there is a wide opening in the cliffs known at that time as Y2 and later as Gully Beach. By the shore one could reach it by climbing over rocks, but there was no actual path. On the summit it was easy to reach by tracks from the high ground at Cape Helles and Tekke Burnu, but these tracks, like the rest of the interior of the Peninsula, were hidden from the sea by the slope of the ground from the edge towards the centre in the same manner as the ground between V Beach and Achi Baba, which proved so much to our disadvantage.

The opening in the cliff at Y2 is caused in part by a short gully dropping from the summit almost directly to the beach but primarily by a long, deeper gully coming down from the direction of Krithia and running for some three miles almost parallel with the sea, from which its existence is concealed. Owing to our lack of trustworthy maps, the inner course of this gully was unknown, but it came to be called Gully Ravine. In it the Turks had massed large forces of infantry, deeply entrenched and supported by machine-guns and pom-poms.

Formidable though it was, it could hardly be stronger than V or W, but Sir Ian Hamilton had no desire, mainly for want of men, to storm yet another point at which the enemy would naturally expect an attack. So he planned instead to mount an assault at a place two miles further north, about 7,000 yards from Tekke Burnu. It was intended to serve the same purpose as S Beach on our extreme right, in protecting the flank. Its value was indeed obvious. To the end of the Campaign it was known as Y Beach. It is so small, and the cleft or dry waterfall which forms it is so steep and narrow, that the Turks had neglected the position because they thought it unassailable.

The 1st Kings Own Scottish Borderers and one company of the South Wales Borderers had been detailed for this attack, but on account of its importance and because the landing would be beyond reinforcement from X Beach, Sir Ian had added the Plymouth (Marine) Battalion, Royal Naval Division.

The battleship *Goliath* and the cruisers *Sapphire* and *Amethyst* were the conducting ships, and at first light the troops were put ashore by trawlers with four tows of boats. It turned out that the men had to disembark in deep water, owing to reefs, but they reached the shore without opposition and at once climbed the precipitous watercourse and the cliffs on both sides of it. *Goliath* now shelled the summit, perhaps unfortunately, for the party's presence was thus disclosed. Nevertheless, except for the appearance of a few Turkish snipers there was no opposition and the whole of the assault force was ashore by 7.15 a.m. without a single casualty. Surprise was complete.

The soldiers had landed first, under Lieutenant-Colonel A. S. Koe (K.O.S.B.). The Plymouth Marines, commanded by Lieutenant-Colonel G. E. Matthews, followed up. While the men were employed digging far-extended trenches along the summit (the Marine Battalion on the left, the K.O.S.B. in the centre, the S.W.B. on the right), the two colonels argued over their relative seniorities.

No enemy was in sight, though Turkish snipers soon set to work, their fire becoming more searching as the day wore on. Yet no organised attack was ordered. It was not considered feasible to carry out the orders to make contact with X Beach, because communication was effectively prevented by the powerful Turkish force at Y2.

During the afternoon the sniping developed into assault. At twilight repeated assaults increased in violence. Under the rising moon, line after line of Turks advanced, at some points reaching our trenches before they were cut down. Sir Ian Hamilton mentioned a pony led right through the trenches with a machine gun on its back, and an eye-witness saw a German officer killed by a blow from a shovel, as, with grenade in hand, he called upon the trench to surrender.

Throughout the night the conflict continued, the Turks charging repeatedly with great courage, our men driving them back with the bayonet, when the rifles became foul and choked with dirt. Casualties, which included Lieutenant-Colonel Koe, mortally wounded, were serious. In spite of the heroism displayed and the service rendered by holding up a larger Turkish force for twenty-four critical hours, the effort at Y Beach had in fact failed, a failure that was serious.

Evacuation was ordered – but by whom? It seems that no one knows. . . .

The *Queen Elizabeth*, Admiral de Robeck's flagship and Sir Ian Hamilton's headquarters, had been off Anzac during the night of the 25th–26th. It was then that he wrote his 'Dig! Dig!' message to General Birdwood which put a stop to wild thoughts of evacuation.

In the meanwhile the flagship's wireless room had intercepted, at 8.30 a.m., a mysterious message from Lieutenant-Colonel Matthews to the ships staioned by Y Beach to the effect that he was holding the ridge till the wounded had been embarked. Seeing that this had been the easiest landing of all, the signal was difficult to understand. The disquieting inference was that the beach which had been so cleverly seized and was so vital to the overall plan was being abandoned. Its evacuation would mean the failure of the hoped-for envelopment. It was a situation which needed Sir Ian's immediate attention. Shortly after 9 the Q.E. started for the spot.

The truth was that at daybreak Lieutenant-Colonel Matthews, now in undisputed command, had signalled that 'without fresh ammunition and reinforcements he could not hold on', but the message had not got through to General Hunter-Weston, the 29th Division Commander in the *Euryalus*, still off W Beach, the Lancashire Landing.

In the desperate fighting during the night the Turks had been so roughly handled that they were no less exhausted than our own men. With daylight the *Goliath* and the other supporting ships had renewed the bombardment, which had made the Turks retire, apparently into the Gully. Advantage was taken of the respite which followed to call for ships' boats to take off the wounded, and the result appears to have been a serious misunderstanding. It seems that the right wing (the S.W.B.s) believed an order to re-embark had been given. They began to leave the trenches and to make their way down the cliff. The centre (K.O.S.B.s) followed.

Well as the troops had responded throughout, it was only too clear at this point that the comparatively raw men of the Plymouth Battalion, R.N.D., had been shaken by their hard night's work and were in no condition to meet another attack in force, and it was now (8.30 a.m.) that Lieutenant-Colonel Matthews sent out the signal which was picked up by the Q.E. off Anzac. Matthews followed it with another message to General Hunter-Weston saying that unless he received reinforcements he could not maintain his hold on the ridge and would have to retire to the beach under cover of the ships' guns. This, he said, was approved, but whether the idea was to re-embark at once or merely to take cover and wait for reinforcement is not clear. What he did was to organise from the King's Own Scottish Borderers and the South Wales Borderers, who were still perfectly steady, a rearguard to cover the withdrawal, while at his request the ships stood by to open fire on the coast the moment he gave the signal that his men were off it.

Such was the situation when, a little after 9.30, the *Queen Elizabeth* arrived. The wounded were being passed to the *Goliath* and her cruisers; a trickle of troops could be seen coming down the cliff to the clusters of men and boats on the beach; but no precise information could be obtained of what it all meant.

'We steamed south to Y Beach where we got into signalling touch with an officer of the K.O.S.B.s,' Sir Ian Hamilton wrote. 'His men were being badly cut up and tried to direct our fire on to the main force of the enemy, only two hundred yards beyond him, so he said. Numbers of our fellows are being re-embarked, so, clearly, they believe themselves, or are believed to be, unable to hold on, and Hunter-Weston must have issued orders for a withdrawal. He should not have done so without my direct, personal authorisation. The men are coming off steadily enough, and there is nothing of a stampede about the movement. Indeed, there is no occasion for it. ... The failure of the K.O.S.B.s and Plymouths is a drop of poison in my cup. Thereby the bright idea of cutting the enemy's line has been extinguished. Many feared the party would be unable to land, or that, having landed, they would be unable to scramble up the cliffs. I went strong in hope for both attempts and I have proved right. But I never thought – nor did anyone else – that once they had made good they would not have been able at least to dig in and hold on. The most vexatious part is that now I might have sent another battalion and a couple of guns to help them; and it is too late.'[1]

I have always held Admiral John Godfrey, the famous Director of Naval Intelligence of World War II, in great esteem. At Gallipoli, as navigating officer of the *Euryalus*, he was in a good position to judge the causes of the calamity at Y Beach. Under the heading 'The Chain of Command' in his *Memoirs*, he has hit the nail right on the head.

'Naval tradition tempts the senior officer to override, in emergency, the powers delegated to a junior and to limit the initiative of the subordinate. The expression "the Senior Officer is always right" may sound ridiculous, and of course, is a satirical over-statement. Nevertheless it contains an element of truth which anyone can check who cares to examine the court martial returns into the wrecking or hazarding of a ship for the last half century.

'I have known of no court martial that has looked kindly on a captain who tried, in his defence, to unload the blame on to a subordinate. Right or wrong, the captain takes the blame and accepts the praise when, by the collective effort of good officers and ship's company, a ship acquits herself well.

'In an Army, the chain of command down, and up, seemed to

me, as I watched the divisional general and his staff at work on the bridge of the *Euryalus*, to be fragile and at times almost impalpable.

'Something was going radically wrong just round the corner, at V, S and Y Beaches. We couldn't see what was happening. My instinct, following the naval tradition, would have been to go and look, either in the *Euryalus* or, better still, in some small craft, and if necessary, intervene. But this would have been contrary to military ethics, and so we continued to pour troops into V Beach where the resistance was strongest and failed to exploit the soft spots at Y and S. . . .

'General Hunter-Weston, the divisional commander, afloat in the *Euryalus*, lost control of the battle through lack of mobility and adherence to the military doctrine of non-intervention.'[2]

Still further up the coast, at the head of the Gulf of Xeros, the Royal Naval Division (less the Plymouth Bn detailed for Y Beach) had been engaged upon a clever piece of deception, to persuade the enemy that a further landing was about to take place, either north of the Bulair Lines or on the opposite coast.

Accompanied by the battleship *Canopus*, Captain Heathcote Grant (S.N.O.), the light cruisers *Dartmouth* and *Doris*, plus destroyers and trawlers, the division had left Trebuki Bay, Skyros, early on the 24th. They reached their rendezvous, five miles W.S.W. from Xeros Island, under cover of darkness.

A very brave act was now performed by Lieutenant-Commander Bernard Freyberg of the 'Hood' Battalion. Painted brown and thickly oiled, he was lowered into the water from a destroyer and swam ashore with a raft carrying flares. Landing on the beach at midnight, he crawled 400 yards up to a trench and there heard talking, which proved that the trenches were occupied. Returning to the beach unnoticed, he lit three lots of flares a quarter of a mile apart along the shore in the direction of Bulair. Two destroyers at once opened fire, and the Turks fired back. Freyberg then swam out and was picked up an hour later none the worse for his experience.

At about 4.30 a.m., just as it was getting light, the covering ships opened fire at points along the shore, trawlers got out their sweeps and all the transports, now at anchor well outside the range of shore batteries, made a show of hoisting out boats, etc., as if a landing were about to take place.

The Turks did not reply to the bombardment, nor could the *Canopus* which now stood in, see any sign of the enemy. Not even when the destroyer *Kennet*, with military officers on board, made a close reconnaissance of the whole of Xeros Bay were any troops seen. Only once did she draw the fire of a small gun, and a seaplane which had been sent up reported the lines apparently deserted. At the time it seemed that the feint was having little or no effect in relieving pressure at the real landing places, but we now know that it did all that the Commander-in-Chief had hoped from it.

Another deceptive feint, on a much larger scale, was made by the French Division upon the Asiatic entrance to the Straits. The object was partly to hold a Turkish force and partly to check the fire from the Asiatic side upon S Beach – Morto Bay and V Beach – *River Clyde* landings. For this purpose General d'Amade selected the 6th Regiment, Lieutenant-Colonel Nogues, of mixed Senegalese and Lyons men, of the Brigade Coloniale, supported by the *Jeanne d'Arc* and the Russian cruiser *Askold*. The remainder of the French squadron was concentrated at Besika Bay, five miles further south. Landing from their own transports, the infantry captured Kum Kāle and Yeni Shehr villages after severe fighting, taking about 600 prisoners. In spite of violent counter-attacks they held on through the night. Next day, without advancing further along the coast than the Mendere River, they drew enemy fire upon themselves, thus defending both our transports and the landings at S and V.

General d'Amade had boarded the *Queen Elizabeth* off Cape Helles at 11.45 a.m. and arranged for the withdrawal of his troops at nightfall. They were transferred to the Eastern section of the Helles area, where they remained until the end of the Campaign.

The French suffered 167 killed, 459 wounded and 116 missing. They put the Turkish casualties at 2,000, apart from the 600 prisoners. The affect of this feint had not been any less successful than that of the R.N.D.

General Liman von Sanders, Commander-in-Chief, Turkish Army, summed up the situation as he saw it on the morning of Sunday, April 25th, when news of the invasion arrived.

'From 5 a.m. onwards on April 25th reports of great landings of enemy troops followed rapidly one on another. In the south, on the Asiatic side, the 11th Division reported great concentration of enemy warships and transports off the Besika Bays and a landing threatening. Somewhat further north, at Kum Kāle, outposts were already in lively combat with French troops. At the southern tip of the Gallipoli Peninsula strong British forces fought the outposts of the 9th Division for possession of the landing places. At Gaba Tepe troops were being disembarked. Near us, in the upper Gulf of Xeros, warships and transports were approaching the coasts. . . . It was evident from the white faces of the reporting officers that although a hostile landing had been fully expected its occurrence at so many places at once had surprised most of them and filled them with apprehension.

'My first feeling,' he added with some complacency for he was completely deceived as to which were the true and which the feint attacks, 'was that there was nothing to alter in our dispositions. The enemy had selected for landing those places which we ourselves had considered would be the most probable and had defended with special care. Personally I had to remain for the present at Bulair, since it was of the utmost importance that the Peninsula should be kept open at that place.' Thither he also ordered immediately the 7th Division encamped near the town of Gallipoli. All day long, in spice of the news that reached him of the desperate struggle proceeding at the other end of the Peninsula, he held this Division and the 5th intact close to the Bulair Lines. It was only in the evening that he convinced himself that the ships and transports gathered in the Bay of Xeros were intended as a feint, and even then he dared only to dispatch by water five battalions from this vital spot to the aid of his hard-pressed forces further south. Not until the morning of the 26th, twenty-four hours after the landings had begun, could he bring himself to order the remainder of the 5th and 7th Divisions to start their voyage from Bulair to Maidos, where they could not arrive before the 27th. . . . 'The removal of all the troops from the coast of the upper part of the Gulf of Xeros was a serious and responsible decision but it had to be risked in view of the great superiority of the enemy in the Southern part of the Peninsula. Had the British noted this weakness they might well have made great use of it.'[3]

15

Desperate Resistance

'I did not know, to tell you the truth, that the Turks were nearly as good as they turned out to be.'
Sir Ian Hamilton
Evidence before the Dardanelles Commission, 1917

The initial landings on Sunday, April 25th, had won a footing on the Peninsula, if no more. At least it had settled the German brag published shortly before the landings that 'if the aggressors are fools enough to enter our mouth we only have to close it'. It was clear to everyone now that the enemy had been given, to quote again the words of Liman von Sanders 'sufficient time to complete the most indispensable arrangements' and that they had taken full advantage of it. It must also be admitted that 'our troops had achieved the impossible'.

By the early afternoon of April 26th, as we have already seen, the position at the southern end of the Peninsula had improved. On the south-west side of the theatre, connection with W Beach – Lancashire Landing, was confirmed, and V Beach became a fairly safe landing place at last. The French set to at once to construct a stone pier (which was still visible in 1973) and a firm gangway of lighters between the *River Clyde* and the shore. V Beach, however, was never to be free from intermittent bombardment from Turkish guns on the Asian side.

The French sector, as V Beach and the right flank now became, was organised with characteristic thoroughness. Stores were arranged in faultless piles, and later a light railway was laid along the shore to the cliff at Cape Helles. The Old Castle served as a depôt for ammunition. Compressed forage for horses and mules was piled high to limit the effect of shell-fire, a practice later repeated on all beaches. Behind the lines the arrangement of the French equalled and sometimes surpassed ours, except when it came to sanitation. The Reverend Ernest Raymond, a chaplain at Gallipoli, found 'the slope, from the beach upward, as alive with French and Senegalese as a cloven ant-hill is alive with ants. The stores of the whole French Army seemed accumulated in the neighbourhood. There was an atmosphere of French excitability, very different from the stillness of the British Zone. Stepping from the British Zone into the French was like turning suddenly from the quiet Rotten Row into the bustle of the Boulevard des Italiens. It was *prenez-garde* and *attention-là! dépêchez-vous* and *pardon, m'sieu*, and *sacré nom de Dieu!* before we got through all these hearty busybodies and drew near the hull of the *Clyde*.'[1]

Here are a few little stories written at the time which may help you recapture the atmosphere that our gallant Ally created on and off shore.

Shortly after the French troops had started landing, Captain C. M. Staveley, Royal Navy Beachmaster (it had been his privilege as a young lieutenant to hoist the Union Jack at the Requiem for General Gordon in Khartoum, 1898, in the presence of the Sirdar, General Kitchener), was approached by one of their officers. Among the animals due to arrive that night was a valuable horse belonging to his general, who was particularly anxious that every care should be taken getting it ashore. 'The horse can be easily recognised,' the French officer said, 'because it is well-bred Arab with a long tail.'

Staveley in reply explained that in the darkness and bustle of disembarkation it was not going to be easy to identify this particular beast, but that he would do his best to oblige. Whereupon he warned the French beach party, composed mostly of hard-bitten Breton fishermen, – real *de sacrés bourlinguers* or old salts, to keep their weather-eyes open for the long-tailed *cheval*.

Next morning, while Staveley was resting after working all night, he was woken by an altercation outside his dug-out where he found an irate French staff officer demanding his blood. The General's horse had been delivered safely, but its appearance was ruined.

A moment or two later the French general turned up in person. '*Espèce de connard*,' he yelled at Staveley, '*j'vais t'fautre au block*. You dolt, I'll clap you in irons!' So Staveley very tactfully suggested that they should go down to the pier together and find out exactly what had happened.

The French general mellowed somewhat on the walk to the beach and chatted amiably, till suddenly he rushed ahead.

Sitting on the gunwale of the grounded motor-hopper *Argyle*, fishing quietly among all the turmoil, were a couple of old Bretons.

'*Bande de Salopards!*' the General shouted, literally banging their heads together and holding up a fishing line. '*La voilà, la queue de mon cheval!*'

Between adjacent French and British battalions friendly communication was frequent, and by simple barter the tedious ration of apricot jam was often exchanged for the French ration of a light red wine, though these articles of barter were received with scornful hilarity by both sides.

'Engine-room Artificer T. Stevens was sent to the *River Clyde* with a working party from the *Cornwallis* on April 26th to mend a steam-pipe which had been fractured by a shell from a tiresome Turkish gun, later known as Asiatic Annie. The job took a few days, and during that time he and his party had ample opportunity to further the *entente*.

'One day a weary Frenchman arrived on the scene, covered with dirt, with a tin in his hand.

'"What cheer, Froggy! Had a rough time?"

'The Frenchman stood holding up his tin, which had liquid in it, and asking for *sucre*.

'"What does he want, Ginger? Tea, I suppose. Here yah, mate; have a wet of this."

'"*Sucre!*" said the Frenchman slowly – "*Sucre!*"

'"Garn! it's bread he wants – no, he don't. Hanged if I know how to suit him."

'I gave him some of my sugar, and the weary face smiled gravely.

'"*Merci, monsieur, merci.*"

'"Why, of course it was sugar he wanted all the time."

'The men all laughed together.

'By then many of the Frenchies had fallen asleep on the coals. I wondered what they would dream about – home or battles?'[2]

Commander Gerald Charles Dickens of the Destroyer *Harpy*, a grandson of the writer, had occasion to visit Admiral Wemyss in the *Euryalus* off W Beach, when a very voluble French officer arrived with a list of commodities his people wanted ashore, a list which included thirty trench periscopes and a lot of medical stores. When told to get the stuff from one of his own ships he replied, '*On voit bien que vous ne connaissez pas les officiers français – on s'fera ceinture!*'

However much the French officer was sure that he would not get anything from his own people, there was certainly one item which he

asked for that he would be unlikely to find anywhere except in one
of H.M. ships, viz a trench periscope. The Royal Navy used to turn
them out by the hundred. Lieutenant Tom Phillips, our Navigating
Officer in the *Bacchante*, made some in his chart-house. Fascinated, I
used to watch him at it.

On April 27th, two days after the landings, the whole line at Cape
Helles was able to advance without opposition to cover all the
landing beaches except Y, which had so unfortunately been abandoned. The strong Turkish position at the mouth of Gully Ravine
was found deserted. The Turks had withdrawn further up the ravine,
their flanks being now exposed to an advance of the Royal Fusiliers
from X Beach – *Implacable* landing. The western end of our line was
accordingly fixed at Gully Beach and then extended for about three
miles to the right across the Peninsula to Eski Hissarlik, Morto
Bay.

The rest of the 29th Division, strengthened by the Royal Naval
Division and the French, were all ashore by the evening. They had
been sadly deprived of sleep since the Saturday before, and their numbers were reduced by heavy losses, especially in officers. Nevertheless
Sir Ian resolved to press on, the following day, while the Turks were
still disorganised. This operation was afterwards known as the
First Battle of Krithia.

Only general instructions could be given, as the situation ahead
could not be gauged, but it was necessary to take risks to reap advantage from the success already achieved. It was particularly important that enough ground should be gained to give more security
when landing stores and guns.

The 87th Brigade, whose Commander, Major-General Marshall,
had been slightly wounded on the day of the landing, yet was now
temporarily commanding the three brigades, led from the left or
coastal flank. The 88th Brigade, whose Brigadier-General, Napier,
had been killed abreast the *River Clyde*, was on the right under command of Colonel C. E. Cayley. The 86th Brigade, which had
also lost its Brigadier-General, Hare, wounded at the Lancashire
Landing, was kept in reserve. The objective was a spur lying
north-east of Krithia, and its capture involved the capture of that
village.

On April 28th, in spite of extreme weariness and the prolonged
shock of battle, the relics of the immortal 29th Division advanced
sturdily against increasing opposition, but, alas, by midday all progress was halted.

The French started well and under a barrage of '75s' advanced about half a mile with great gallantry, taking trench after trench. Then shrapnel compelled them to take cover, and presently they began to drift back in twos and threes until the whole right flank was thick with Frenchmen running in all directions, apparently quite disorganised. Eventually, however, they reached some sort of cover and rallied. There followed a pause, devoted to violent altercation, and then out they were again with bayonets fixed, charging up the slope with great courage and almost reaching their former line.

Whereas the French had gone forward to the sounds of drums and bugles, many of them, in their blue tunics and red trousers (uniforms unchanged since the Franco-Prussian War) providing a painfully clear target against the dun-coloured earth, it was barely possible to see what was happening on the left where the British regiments' khaki made them relatively inconspicuous. Their tactics were of necessity slower than the French as they had to advance over very jagged country. It was also noticeable that the French expended far more ammunition.

In the afternoon the Turks counter-attacked with the bayonet, and the French line was forced to withdraw a little, which exposed the Worcesters to heavy losses on the right. A new line had rapidly to be secured, from a point a short way up the coast from Tekke Burnu (W Beach), to a point about a mile further up the Strait from De Totts Battery (S Beach).

Here the line rested, and the next two days were spent in strengthening it and sorting out the confused battalions. Fortunately the Turks made no further counter-attack before May 1st. Barbed wire was brought up to construct obstacles, reserves of ammunition were assembled and the Allied position was generally improved.

When the Brigade-Major, 86th Brigade, went to arrange the consolidation of the position held by the 1st Royal Dublin Fusiliers he found only one officer left, Lieutenant Desmond O'Hara, who had risen to every occasion with the greatest coolness and competence, from commanding a platoon at the landing from the *River Clyde* to command a company the next day and, after the 28th, a battalion. Unfortunately he was mortally wounded at Suvla in August.

Colonel H. G. Casson was now appointed to command the Fusilier Brigade (86th). He established his H.Q. under shelter of the walls of a ruined stone farmhouse, later known as Fig Tree Farm.

The Royal Munster Fusiliers and the Royal Dublin Fusiliers were temporarily amalgamated into one unit, the 'Dubsters', under Major Hutchinson.

On April 30th a roll call was made. Out of a normal strength of 104 officers and some 4,000 men, there mustered:

	Officers	Other ranks
2nd Royal Fus.	12	481
1st Lancashire Fus.	11	399
1st R. Munster Fus.	12	596
1st Dublin Fus.	1 (O'Hara)	374
	36	1,850

On the morning of the 29th, to encourage his worn out troops, Sir Ian issued the following Order of the Day:

'I rely on all officers and men to stand firm and steadfastly to resist the attempts of the enemy to drive us back from our present position which has been so gallantly won. . . . It behoves us all, French and British, to stand fast, hold what we have gained, wear down the enemy and thus prepare for a decisive victory';

and that evening in the privacy of his cabin he found time to pen a few lines to his wife:

'*Queen Elizabeth* – 29:4:15.
    'Just two words to say I am fit and facing with what courage I can the various alarmist and despondent tendencies of some of my Commanders. They are more alarming than the enemy who is really a very stout and terrifying fellow when you see him in a long line running at you in a heavy jog trot way with fixed bayonets gleaming in the sun. However, we've come here to stay – in so far as my fixed determination can make it so, – whether alive or dead is another question. . . . Good night . . .'.

On April 29th Sir Ian had visited the front lines at Helles and at Anzac with some of his staff. At Helles he found General Hunter-Weston in his newly established headquarters, which was no more than a few holes burrowed into a hillock. Here he learnt that some of the men were shaken by the loss of so many officers and by the heavy losses of other ranks as well as by sheer physical exhaustion. Not the spirit but the flesh had failed them. 'With a fresh division on the ground,' Hunter-Weston told him, 'nothing would have prevented us from taking several thousand prisoners. Our advance has been half heroic, half lamentable. The men were so beat that if they tripped and fell they lay like dead things. The enemy are almost in a worse plight.'

When the visit was over, Sir Ian re-embarked in the destroyer *Colne* and sailed for Anzac Cove. Here he was met by General Birdwood and Admiral Thursby, also Generals Bridges and Godley.

'From the trenches that ran along the coast a hot fire was being kept up,' Sir Ian wrote, 'and swarms of bullets sang through the air. Yet, when we arrived there were full 500 men fooling about stark naked on the water's edge or swimming, shouting and enjoying themselves as it might be at Margate. Not a sign to show that they possessed the things called nerves.'[3]

Next day Sir Ian visited the position at Helles again, and on May 1st the French lines. There he found the trenches in the firing line inadequate compared with ours. Bullets were coming through the joints of the badly built sandbag revetment. '*Un peu de repos, après, vous verrez, mon général,*' was a comment which seemed to reflect the mentality of the French at this stage. Yet the celebrated '75s' were already in action, and from that time onwards the French gunners, never being stinted of shells, were the envy as well as the admiration of our artillery.

The Commander-in-Chief had much of the regimental officer's disposition in him and felt restless and unsatisfied unless he were himself in the front line. Throughout the campaign, whenever his presence was not essential at G.H.Q. he might well be found walking about the trenches. General Braithwaite, his C.O.S., and others concerned had frequent difficulty in averting a death that would have elated the enemy. Birdwood behaved in just the same way.

On May 1st, the 29th Indian Infantry Brigade, under Major-General Sir Herbert Cox, began to arrive from Egypt and to disembark on V Beach. They had hardly taken up their position as reserve, with some battalions of the R.N.D., when, in the darkness before a waning moon had risen, the Turks began a furious attack on the British and French front. For this attack 16,000 were employed, with 2,000 in reserve. It was evident that the best troops were used. They came on in three solid lines, all crawling on hands and knees till the word was given. The front was allowed no cartridges, but bayonets only.

Their first charge aimed at the centre of the 86th Brigade, already so much shaken by loss of men and officers. Here they forced a gap, very dangerous had not the 5th Royal Scots at once filled it. This battalion of the 88th Brigade, under Lieutenant-Colonel J. D. R. Wilson, was the only Territorial unit at this time in the 29th Division.

It was anxious to prove itself worthy of that unequalled corps, and now it did prove itself. Facing to their right flank, the men charged with the bayonet, the Essex Regiment supporting them.

When the Turkish masses were checked close to the British line, Germans could be heard cursing and also the sound of blows as they tried to urge on the Turks.

A counter-attack was ordered, but our men were worn out and no progress was made. However, at dawn the sight was more hopeful. The countryside was alive with the enemy withdrawing, the French artillery and our own encouraging them with shrapnel and warships joining in with indirect fire.

Sir Ian had watched the battle from the bridge of the *Arcadian* to which he had shifted his G.H.Q. from the *Queen Elizabeth*. The sounds of British cheers and the Turkish shouts of Allah! Allah! were carried to him across the water. 'To hear the battle cries, and be tied to this *Arcadian*,' he wrote, 'what torture! I tried to think of some possible source of help I had overlooked and could not. How bitterly Hunter-Weston and I regretted the War Office policy whereby we were deprived of our ten per cent margin to replace casualties, a margin allowed by regulation and carried out in every other theatre. Just think of it. Today each battalion of the 29th Division would have been joined by 2 new officers and 100 fresh men. The fillip given would have been far, far greater than that which the mere numbers would seem to imply.'[4]

Quiet now reigned on the Peninsula. Literally dead quiet. The Turks were out with Red Crescent flags burying their piles of dead. There had been some difference of opinion as to whether this should be allowed, but Sir Ian decided that the Turks should be left alone, not only from humanitarian but also from sanitary reasons. Both sides suffered heavy casualties, and our people were similarly employed. The French, finding the ground too hard, or perhaps the task too great, slung some bodies over the cliffs into the swift-flowing Dardanelles. They were clearly seen by observers in H.M. ships: '*Un, deux, trois – lâchez* – one, two, three, leggo!' – so it is said.

Before Turkish reinforcements could consolidate a new position across the southern slopes of Achi Baba and convert it into an impenetrable maze of trench and wire, it was imperative for Sir Ian to continue striking at their front. Only thus could the pressure upon the beaches be relieved, the continuous danger from dropping shells reduced and the Turks hampered in their schemes for driving us into the sea.

19 Mustapha Kemal Bey (*centre*) and above him (X) Major Kemal Ohri, the Plenipotentiary at the Anzac armistice

20 Captain Sam Butler leading Major Kemal Ohri out of Anzac Cove

21 The summit of Chunuk Bair is in the centre, just visible in the background. Table Top is on the left and Rhododendron Ridge leading to the apex on the right horizon.

22 Watson's Pier, Anzac, where Commander Cater was killed and Petty Officer Morgan seriously wounded

The Army's losses to date were officially reckoned as:

	Killed	Wounded	Missing
Officers	177	412	13
Men	1,990	7,807	3,580

These figures, which include the Anzac front, give a total casualty list of 13,979. The 29th Division had suffered particularly heavily and in addition to reinforcement by General Cox's 29th Indian Brigade already mentioned and the newly arrived Lancashire Fusilier Brigade (Territorials) from Egypt, Sir Ian had brought down from Anzac for the new battle the 2nd (Victoria) Australian Infantry Brigade and the New Zealand Infantry Brigade. They were formed into a composite division under Major-General Paris, with the Drake and Plymouth Battalions, R.N.D. Two other battalions of the R.N.D. (Howe and Hood), were sent to reinforce the division on the right.

This fresh attempt to push forward, known as the Second Battle of Krithia, began on May 6th and lasted three days. Sir Ian could count 33,000 rifles, of which only 5,000 were British and Irish regulars. Of the rest there were 8,000 French troops (of these at least 5,000 were natives), the 5th and 6th Battalions of Territorials from Egypt, both excellent, and the Royal Naval Division, finely tempered though only partially trained, whose heavy losses to date were due more to devotion and courage than to a lack of experience.

There was a serious shortage of shell which made the Commander-in-Chief think it would be good policy to 'make use of the half hour before dawn to close the enemy and then fight it out on his own ground'. This, however, did not appeal to Hunter-Weston, who considered that the heavy casualties suffered by regimental officers ruled out the possibility of a night attack. He felt that our best chance of success lay in a daylight assault after a preliminary bombardment, and he got his way.

The attack opened at 11.30 a.m., after half an hour's bombardment which was all that we could run to. Sir Ian remained on board the *Arcadian*, getting messages till 2 p.m., and then went ashore to see Hunter-Weston and d'Amade.

There were furious semi-detached fights by battalions and brigades throughout the day. The reinforcements who had only just arrived were thrown straight into battle. Their gallantry was superb, but their losses were devastating. They had neither clear objective nor adequate support and were launched in lines, 'into the blue'. Each line consisted of men about a yard apart. Their officers led the way or followed close behind. An officer was no more able to give orders than a private soldier. In most cases the noise was so great and smoke was so thick that he could not even see what was happening.

As the front line withered, it was followed by a second at a pre-arranged distance, until it, too, was decimated, and finally the only reserve left was itself the front line.

'The Indian Brigade was holding a line of trenches on the extreme left, and the Anzacs had been ordered to attack through them,' wrote Lieutenant Reggie Savory, 14th (K.G.O.) Sikhs. 'This meant jumping over our trenches; no mean feat for men in full fighting-order. They came along in great heart, while we covered their advance by shooting at the enemy in front. Then they swept up to us, jumped our trench and surged on. At once a murderous fire broke out. There was not much that we could see, as by then we were sitting in the bottom of our trench, unable to shoot. Up came the second line; over our trench they jumped. One of them landed short and fell in among us. As he did so, a packet of "smutty postcards" cascaded from one of his pockets. He had been slightly wounded. We patched him up; collected his postcards; put them in his breast pocket; buttoned it up and sent him back to the aid-post. As he left he thanked us warmly, but not so much for our skill at first aid as for our generosity in returning his cards. His battle was over. As for his comrades who had gone ahead so valiantly, they faded away under a murderous fire; and before long the few survivors came trickling back. Once more we were in the front line. That night we sent our patrols and brought in some of the wounded.

'It had been another wasted effort; another frontal assault by strange troops, in long uncontrollable lines, against an unrecon-noitred position, and with an invisible objective.'[5]

The Turks were driven back about 200 or 300 yards, but none of their main trenches or redoubts were captured. The Hood Battalion, R.N.D., received a bad knock. The Prime Minister's son, Arthur 'Oc' Asquith, Rupert Brooke's friend, and Lieutenant-Commander Josiah Wedgwood M.P., who had done so well with his machine-guns in the bows of the *River Clyde* during the V Beach landing, were among the wounded.

At 4.30 p.m. Hunter-Weston acknowledged failure and ordered his troops to dig in. After dark on the 6th the Turks launched a counter-attack on the French with the bayonet, but the French held. When daylight came, the Allies renewed their attack after a short and violent bombardment, but only a little ground was gained.

Though well aware of loss and exhaustion, Sir Ian resolved to make one more call upon his troops for the following day. A new

French division which had long been promised was at last arriving. General Bailloud was in command, a bald-headed veteran of sixty-eight.

At 10.15 on May 8th the customary bombardment from sea and land began, to be received with the customary silence. At 10.30 the infantry moved, and at once the roar of rifles and machine-guns arose from the Turkish trenches while shrapnel began to burst overhead.

The 87th Brigade tried hard to push forward but could barely advance 100 yards, the South Wales Borderers losing heavily. The New Zealanders managed to advance by short rushes for nearly 300 yards, when, exposed to machine-guns on both flanks, they were forced to dig in. Shortly before, General Paris, R.N.D., commanding the composite division, ordered the Australians, commanded by Brigadier-General J. W. McCay, to advance on the New Zealanders' right. 'Though heavily laden with packs, shovels, picks and entrenching tools, and exposed to intense fire, they pressed on, rush after rush, their Brigadier directing and encouraging them by waving his stick. They advanced more than 800 yards and came within half a mile of the eastern approaches to Krithia itself. Seldom has so reckless and irresistible an advance been recorded.'[6]

The French, though late, also went forward gallantly, drums beating, bugles blowing, as in a Napoleonic battle. Their white troops in good order fought their way about 300 yards further on, capturing a redoubt. But a gap was left. The Naval Brigade was delayed in filling it, and in the falling darkness the whole line, exhausted and reduced, had barely enough life left in them to dig trenches for the night. In the centre we had made good 600 yards and on the flanks 300 to 400 yards. That night the Turks delivered several counter-attacks, which in every case was repulsed with heavy loss.

'We are on our last legs,' wrote Sir Ian. 'The beautiful battalions of the 25 April are wasted skeletons now; shadows of what they had been. In some sense I am disappointed. In another sense matters might have been very much worse. The enemy, who have had to give up so much ground, must at least be dispirited too.

'After killing and wounding God knows how many thousand Turks we are now today [9th May] fighting as many of them on the Peninsula as Lord Kitchener thought there were on both sides of the Straits on starting. They are stronger now on Gallipoli than they were when we first landed. "Our troops have done all that flesh and blood could do against semi-permanent works", I have told him, and they are not able to carry them. "More men," I have said, "will be needed to do so". K. will hate me for this but there is no way out of it.'[7]

In spite of the heavy counter-attack against the French in the night of May 9/10th, comparative quiet now reigned over the Helles front. This pause in the fighting gave Hunter-Weston the chance to withdraw the 29th Division from the front-line where they had served since April 25th.

The relics of those immortal battalions began to come back on the 11th for such rest as was possible with the beaches still under shell-fire. That night and the next day it rained heavily, but the exhausted men sank down into mud or even pools of water, indifferent to everything except sleep.

Sir Ian Hamilton came ashore on the morning of the 12th and saw some of the Essex, Hants, Lancashire Fusiliers and the 5th Royal Scots. He spent the forenoon chatting with officers and men who were caked with mud, haggard from lack of sleep and often pale as the dead. Many were slightly wounded, their clothes blood-stained, their eyes blood-shot. Later in the day he watched a battalion of the R.N.D. march in. They, too, had come to the end of their tether. The faces of some of the officers and men wore a crushed, finished look. It seemed that no one was even capable of raising a smile.

'An hour or two of rest, Sir, will make all the difference,' the Colonel had said. But the Commander-in-Chief knew that this was optimistic. 'Those men had nerves,' Sir Ian noted. 'No one fights better than they do, for a good long spell but they are not invincible like the Old Army. How can they be?'[8]

On board the *Queen Elizabeth*, Admiral de Robeck had convened a series of meetings to discuss the Navy's future role. Grieved beyond measure at the cruel losses that the Army had sustained, out of all proportion to anything expected, the forward school, led by Commodore Keyes, was convinced that the quelling of the forts, the sweeping of the minefields and ultimately the forcing of the Straits were practical propositions and that the Naval attack, broken off after the action of March 18th, should be re-opened. All these pressures and the spectacle of the Army's torment had their effect upon the Admiral, who finally resolved to send a telegram to the Admiralty. This message, as you will see from the following extracts, does not exactly 'recommend' that the Fleet should return to their attack upon the forts and minefields but indicates his willingness to comply if ordered to do so. The telegram bears the imprint of several hands and of opposite opinions.

'*Vice-Admiral de Robeck to Admiralty*

10 May 1915.

'. . . General Hamilton informs me that the Army is checked. . . . The help which the Navy has been able to give the Army in its advance has not been as great as was anticipated. . . .

'From the vigour of the enemy's resistance it is improbable that the passage of the Fleet into the Marmara will be decisive and therefore it is equally possible that the Straits will be closed behind the Fleet. This will be of slight importance if the resistance of the enemy could be overcome in time to prevent the enforced withdrawal of the Fleet owing to lack of supplies. . . .

'The temper of the Turkish Army in the Peninsula indicates that the forcing of the Dardanelles and subsequent appearance of the Fleet off Constantinople will not, of itself, prove decisive.'

Any detailed description of the discussions which went on in Admiralty on receipt of this signal is outside the scope of this book. Admiral 'Jackie' Fisher, First Sea Lord (whose days in office were numbered) put his foot down firmly: 'I cannot, under any circumstances,' he wrote in a memorandum, 'be a party to any order to Admiral de Robeck to make an attempt to pass the Dardanelles until the shores have been effectively occupied. . . .'

But Churchill was more realistic: 'You will never receive from me,' he replied, 'any proposition to "rush" the Dardanelles. . . . Surely here is a combination and a situation which requires from us every conceivable exertion and contrivance which we can think of. I beg you to lend your whole aid and good will, and ultimately then success is certain.'

But, alas, Churchill did not get his way.

'We think the moment for an independent naval attempt to force the Narrows has passed and will not arise again under present conditions,' Churchill replied on May 13th to de Robeck's message of the 10th. 'The Army is landed; large reinforcements are being sent and there can be no doubt that with time and patience the Kilid Bahr plateau will be taken. Your role is therefore to support the Army in its costly but sure advance and reserve your strength to deal with the situation which will arise later when the Army has succeeded, with your aid, in its task.'[9]

Thus it will be seen that never after March 21st were the Admiralty and the Naval Commander-in-Chief able to come to a simultaneous resolve to attack. On March 21st all were united. Thereafter, as you will see, when one was hot, the other was cold.

On May 21st de Robeck brought to Sir Ian the first news of the deliberate overthrow by Asquith, the Prime Minister, of his own Cabinet and his attempt to promote the national cause by a large coalition Ministry, together with the shattering news that Churchill, who could be counted upon to promote the interests of the campaign as his own particular brain-child, had left the Admiralty in Mr Balfour's charge, retiring to the Duchy of Lancaster. Just before his resignation Churchill's trusted adviser and 'opponent', Lord Fisher, had himself resigned. His place as First Sea Lord was taken by Admiral Sir Heny Jackson.

Sir Ian confided to his wife:

'20:5:15.
I am beset with nightmares dreadful enough to turn grey the head of *un homme serieux*; but that you know I am not; never was, and never will be as long as a spark of life exists within my poor old carcass.

'A *Reuter* has just come through bearing news of these Cabinet changes. Winston's leaving the Admiralty is an awful blow to us here . . . these mad dogs don't know where they are going. . . . However, I only have to fight, fight, fight. Do make a point of being extraordinarily nice to Winston and his wife and don't get huffy because a young thing like Clemmie is casual. . . .

'I am *so* interested and pleased about what you are doing for our masses of wounded . . . casualties are mounting up to heights absolutely terrific. For the *whole* Turkish Army is coming at us in relays, and we have to keep on wiping out fresh troops from Constantinople, Syria, Adrianople, with our poor old remnants who have been at it now for a month. . . .'

And ten days later:

'30:5:15. Somewhere on this terrestrial.
No one is going to help us but ourselves and all the power of Turkey is concentrating against us – Still: are we downhearted? No!!!'

16

Loss of *Goliath*

'*Last night a Turkish torpedo-boat sneaked down the
Straits and torpedoed the 'Goliath' – David and his sling
on the grand scale. The enemy deserve decorations, con-
found them!*'
Sir Ian Hamilton
Gallipoli Diary

It was customary every night to send two battleships into the entrance
to the Dardanelles to guard the Army's right flank. On the night of
May 12/13th *Goliath* and *Cornwallis* were detailed for this duty. The
Goliath anchored in Morto Bay, the *Cornwallis* to seaward of her. A
protecting patrol of two destroyers, *Beagle* and *Bulldog*, was stationed
above De Tott's battery. Two more, *Wolverine* and *Scorpion*, were on
guard on the Asiatic side in Eren Keui Bay. The *Pincher* was in mid
channel. All five destroyers remained under way.

The night was still and dark. There was no moon. About midnight
a fog began to roll down the Asiatic shore and spread across the
Straits.

On board the *Cornwallis*, lying in her berth astern of the *Goliath*,
the normal duties of a flanking ship were being carried out. A proportion of the ship's company was at night defence stations. A
searchlight was switched on at intervals and trained on to the Turkish
trenches which led down to the sea. Sometimes a call for gun
support came from the shore.

The Officer of the Watch of *Cornwallis* had been relieved at 1 a.m.
and left the bridge at 1.12. When winding his watch in his cabin he
noticed the time was 1.17 and almost immediately felt – rather than
heard – three distinct bumps on the ship's side, so faint, however,
that he thought it was only the engines being turned a revolution or
two, which is the practice when a ship is at immediate notice for
steam. A moment later the alarm was sounded, followed by the pipe:

'Starboard Watch fall in!'

'Away all boats!'

It was soon evident that *Goliath* was in trouble, but only when the cries of men in the water came out of the darkness was it realised that she had been torpedoed and was sinking. Black smoke rose, and above the continuous rattle of small arms fire from the trenches, one could just hear the noise of escaping steam. Then bits of wreckage began to drift by, clearly visible in the rays of searchlights, with men clinging to them. There were also men swimming. Unfortunately the current was too strong for anyone to reach the *Cornwallis* before being swept past her. The nearest only got within two hundred yards. Many were taken out to sea. But her boats did well to rescue fifty-six.

It was indeed David and his sling. But who was this David? And what of his sling? The explanation came within the hour. A German wireless message, time of origin 1.45 a.m., addressed to the Naval Commander, Dardanelles, was broadcast in plain language and repeated several times:

'*MGV AM für Flotte ein Englisches Schiff in der Morto Bucht durch drei Torpedo Treffer versenkt – Firle.* – Sank an English ship in Morto Bay by three torpedoes – Firle.'

An acknowledgement was received by Firle (and also intercepted) at 10.15 a.m. '*Gut gemacht, Muavenet* – Well done, *Mauvenet*.'

The messages quoted were taken from the W/T log of the *Scorpion*, Lieutenant-Commander Andrew B. Cunningham. Most H.M. ships kept a listening watch on enemy wireless frequencies which was known as Procedure 'Y'. Much valuable intelligence was obtained in this way.

Lieutenant-Commander Rudolph Firle, Imperial German Navy, had planned and carried out a brilliant attack with Teutonic thoroughness. He told his own story:

'On 10th May 1915, on return to the Bosphorus from patrol, I was handed a letter from the Commander of the Fortress of the Dardanelles, Admiral von Usedom. The letter explained that the English battleships stationed on the flank of the Turkish line [in Morto Bay] were causing havoc, and might soon result in the English rolling up this part of the line. I was to consider a night attack with torpedoes. He explained that the channel selected for passage through the minefields would be marked for me with small barrel buoys. Ideal weather conditions were essential because the buoys would submerge in the slightest lop, or if the current exceeded its normal strength. I was instructed to proceed at once to his headquarters in the Dardanelles to discuss the matter with him.

'That same evening I embarked in the German built Turkish

torpedo-boat *Muavenet-i Millet*, commanded by Lieutenant-Commander Achmed Effendi. We crossed the Sea of Marmara during the hours of darkness and at dawn, May 11th, entered the Straits.

'Admiral von Usedom, opening the discussion, said that he had in mind that I should lead a night attack, using three of the smallest Turkish torpedo-boats. These 300-ton craft had been built in France, launched in 1908, and had a designed speed of twenty-eight knots.

'"Herr Admiral", I replied, "the only advantage of employing these boats lies in the difficulty of seeing them, but if they are spotted they will be recognised at once as hostile. Their draught is only sixteen inches less than the larger 610-ton boats which have three torpedo-tubes instead of one and could in the darkness be easily mistaken for an English destroyer. Moreover, to have to manoeuvre three craft as one unit, in the very limited sea room available, might prove impossible." The Admiral agreed.

'Just before sunset I took a pinnace and crossed the minefield to a howitzer battery on the Asiatic shore at Eren Keui to get an idea of what went on in the Dardanelles at night. The Anglo-French fleet with its transports was lying off the entrance to the Straits in a sea of lights which reminded me of Kiel Harbour in the piping days of peace.

'Two English battleships were lying at anchor in Morto Bay illuminating positions on shore with their searchlights and firing intermittently.

'Lieutenant-Colonel Wehrle, the German Commander of the Eren Keui area, whose guns had played such havoc with the English and French ships on the glorious March 18th, told me about the movements of the English night patrol of destroyers. He said the only route where there would be a reasonable chance of my escaping detection was close to the European shore. All this was indeed "*Ein gefundenes Fressen*", just what the doctor ordered, as I had formerly commanded the gunboat *Otter* up the Yangtse River. Navigation in confined waters held no mysteries for me.

'Reporting again to the Admiral on my return, he told me that as weather conditions were ideal I was to attack the following night, May 12th/13th. This gave me just enough time to make all necessary arrangements.

'Everything inflammable was landed. Boats were removed. To reduce draught only half the normal supplies of coal and stores were carried. Three Schwarzkopf torpedoes were loaded in the tubes and a reserve torpedo secured on deck, all set to run 1,300 yards at a depth of 6 feet. Net cutters were not fitted, as the English battleships were not in the habit of getting their nets out after dark. Special attention was given to boilers. It was absolutely imperative that not a single spark should escape during the attack.

'Two German naval officers joined the ship, Lieutenant Andreae and Sub-Lieutenant Sebeling, the latter because of his intimate knowledge of local conditions. Several German key ratings were also embarked.

'Lieutenant-Commander Achmed Effendi and his crew were now put into the picture. All were keen on the venture except Achmed, who was scared of the mines. At dinner that night, while we were eating our white bread and cheese, he was very silent.

'At 7 p.m. we weighed anchor and set course downstream following the line of buoys. We touched bottom once without doing any damage. We watched the two English battleships enter the Straits. At 7.30 we dropped anchor in the mouth of the Soghanli Dere where I had decided to await the hour of attack.

'After another glance at the chart I told my orderly that I was going to rest. He was to call me at midnight.

'I slept well and on being awakened got some relief from the thought that the attack would soon be over.

'At 12.45 the anchor was weighed, and I set course for Morto Bay, which was only five miles away. The boat proved difficult to handle at slow speed, stern on to the current. The fact that we had landed all our surplus stores added to the problem, because now her rudder was almost out of water.

'At 1.00 a.m. a pair of enemy destroyers [*Beagle* and *Bulldog*] passed 800 yards off on the port beam proceeding slowly on an opposite course. They did not see us against the dark background. I kept as close under the land as the depth of water allowed.'

Some authorities claim that the *Muavenet* was disguised with a third funnel to make her resemble one of our River class boats. This is not true.

'At 1.10 a.m. the silhouette of two fat ships with thick masts and funnels [*Goliath* and *Cornwallis*] came in sight, clearly recognisable as battleships. I increased to full speed and headed for the nearest [the *Goliath*].

'"*Licht voraus* – light ahead!"

'I was being challenged in morse code by signal lamp, which I had expected. Not knowing the proper reply I had instructed the signalman to flash back the same signal 'O' (Otto). This he did not once but twice, and simultaneously with the third challenge I sounded the horn for a torpedo to be fired from the foremost tube. A few seconds later the second and third torpedoes also found their mark. The enemy ship heeled over to starboard immediately and was enveloped in a thick black cloud of smoke. The time was 1.17 a.m., 13th May 1915, Ascension Day.

'The third torpedo must have penetrated an ammunition chamber, for its impact was followed by a flash of fire as high as the mainmast, which immediately collapsed. Much more I could not see. The ship capsized quickly and was lost to view.

'Utter confusion followed. Turkish shore batteries opened up. Searchlights swept the waters. Soldiers ashore started a barrage of fire.

'"Hard-a-starboard!" I shouted to the helmsman, then, down the voice-pipe to the engine-room, "Full speed ahead!"

'We gathered way and closed the shore, from which we were fired at by Turkish soldiers. Of course they couldn't tell who we were.

'"What lucky devils we are!" I confided to my German colleagues on the bridge. Then, turning to Lieutenant-Commander Achmed I repeated the words slowly to make sure he understood. "*Da haben wir ja wieder mal Schwein gehabt.*" He was learning German.

'He turned to me with a smile. "We must all be good men," he said, "otherwise Allah would not have protected us in so wonderful a manner."'[1]

The *Muavenet* made a triumphant entry into the Bosphorus on the morning of Friday, May 14th, a Turkish Sunday. Every ship was dressed overall, and the band of the *Goeben* played the Turkish and German National Anthems, while her crew manned ship and cheered. After she had berthed alongside some sheep were slaughtered and their blood sprinkled over the torpedo-tubes.

Firle was awarded the Iron Cross, First Class, the Austrian Iron Cross, and the highest Turkish war decoration, the *Mschan-i Imtiaz* or Order of Privilege. His officers received the German Iron Cross, Second Class. Every officer and rating also received an engraved gold watch from the hand of the Sultan, and the sailors, in addition, a little bag of money.

The attack on the *Goliath* had been carried out as skilfully as it had been daringly conceived. No ship could survive such punishment, and so rapidly had the blows followed one upon the other that most of the officers and men had no time to reach the upper deck. Only 183 were saved out of a ship's company of over 800. The stream was strong and the water cold at 58°F. The night was very dark.

Our Blake Term of fully fledged midshipmen aged fifteen and a half got it again, but happily only three out of eight were lost. The body of one stalwart – probably T. H. L. Macleod – supported by a

Gieve's life-saving waistcoat, was picked up two days later with breath still in his body, but he could not be brought round. No one can deny that we were not tough 'babies' – 'Winston Churchill's War Babies' we were called.

Captain T. L. Shelford went down with his ship. It is not known for certain how he met his death, but some survivors believe that on leaving the bridge, after giving the order 'Abandon ship', he was crushed by a picket boat which fell on him as he was crossing the boat-deck.

I am sure that had he lived he would have accepted full blame for the loss in accordance with the best traditions of the service. The Officer of the Watch survived, but I can find no trace of his report. The proper thing for him to have done was to have opened fire on the unidentified vessel directly the incorrect reply to the *Goliath*'s challenge was made. It is possible, of course, that the Captain had given orders that no shot should be fired without his permission, and that the *Muavenet*'s torpedoes struck as he was hurrying up the ladder from his sea cabin to the bridge, which would have taken him about two minutes.

Regulations were tautened after the loss of the *Goliath* and battle-ships no longer anchored in the Straits at night, to provide a sitting target for adventurous young officers like Rudolf Firle. He died in Bremen on 2nd July 1969, aged eighty-five, a very gallant enemy.

17

Heroic Hearts

'. . . *that which we are we are;*
One equal temper of heroic hearts,
Made weak by time and fate, but strong in will
To strive, to seek, to find, and not to yield.'
Lord Tennyson, 1809–1892
Ulysses

While the British and French were strengthening their hold upon the southern end of the Peninsula, the Anzacs clung tenaciously to the rugged triangle which was to remain a thorn in the enemy's side. By April 30th the firing line had been reinforced by the 1st Light Horse Brigade (Brigadier-General H. G. Chauvel) and by four battalions of the Royal Naval Division. The arrival of the latter is described by Captain C. F. Jerram, R.M.L.I., in his Journal:

'We landed in a small cove. The Australians and New Zealanders had a most successful landing and I don't believe many other men could have done what they did. But they were individualists – especially the Australians. The New Zealanders were far better disciplined. The Australians, up to the last day of the war, were always magnificent in attack but quite hopeless after it. It was like that here at Anzac. There was a line and the first job was to find it, then send the Australians back to organise.

'Everywhere hidden in the steep moorland country were enemy snipers and wandering Australians. One day I met one of the latter when on my way back from taking a message. He was quite un-worried, cooking a billy of tea. "Boy, you look tired," he said. "Set down and have a mug of tea." It was hot, black and sweet and a life-saver, as was also the big pipe he gave me which he had collected off a dead German officer. I had lost my own when landing.'

On Sunday, May 2nd, a week after the landing, a determined effort was made by our troops to capture a knoll, known as Baby 700, on the slope of Sari Bair. The attack began in the early morning with a rapid bombardment, and right through the day Australians and New Zealanders fought with their customary self-confidence. The R.N.D. supported them well, and some trenches were captured. But the plateau had by now been carefully fortified with trenches, wire and machine-guns and the attempt failed, after it had cost 800 men.

At dawn on the same day the *Colne* and the *Usk*, with a party of New Zealanders embarked, had made a raid in Suvla Bay, surprising an observation post on Nibrunesi Point and destroying it. Most of the occupants were brought back as prisoners.

Encouraged by this, Admiral Thursby planned a similar raid to destroy another observation post which was known to exist on Gaba Tepe. From this point, as already explained, the whole coast to the north was enfiladed. Guns in the vicinity of Olive Grove were strafing Anzac Cove daily and with ever increasing accuracy, the fall of shot being spotted from there.

A small force of some 120 officers and men was put at the Admiral's disposal, and he detailed for their inshore support four destroyers, with our ship the *Bacchante* and the *Dartmouth* as attending ships.

While it was still dark, two tows provided by the *Triumph* and *Dartmouth* were taken close into the north shore of Gaba Tepe, and, at first light the boats rowed in. But surprise was not achieved. As they neared the beach they met with so heavy and sustained a fire that on landing they could only seek cover under the high bank at the top of the beach. At 6.30 a.m., under covering fire from the destroyers, the raiding party was withdrawn. They had suffered four killed and sixteen wounded. All the wounded were successfully re-embarked, except for one who could not be found. The dead were left where they fell.

Later in the day the lost wounded man was seen to be crawling on hands and knees towards the water's edge. The *Dartmouth* sent in her steamboat, with a dinghy from the *Chelmer*, both boats wearing Red Cross flags. The Turks did not object; on the contrary they helped the wounded man and, while waiting for the rescue party to land, bound up his wounds under their own Red Crescent flag.

After this casualty had been collected, some more enemy soldiers appeared from behind the scrub. Under the eyes of the Fleet they buried our dead; and when the job was over they fell into line facing the sea and solemnly presented arms.

Who could even begin to understand the mentality – the inconsistency and the nobility – of the Turkish soldier?

Three of the *Dartmouth*'s men were rated up in recognition of their good services. The two A.B.s were advanced to Leading Seamen, and the other, a signalman who had recently been disrated for misconduct, was given back his leading rate.

On May 14th, while working in his dug-out, General Birdwood had an almost miraculous escape. A bullet came through the chinks of a sandbag, and just skimmed the top of his scalp. He fell to the ground senseless and pouring blood. But, when picked up and washed he quickly came round, apparently none the worse. He even refused to rest, although later on a piece of metal was found embedded in his skull.

The very next day General Bridges, commanding the Australian Division, was mortally wounded while crossing the mouth of Shrapnel Gully where the protecting parapets had not yet been completed. He was struck in the groin by a sniper. Colonel White, his G.S.O., Major Villiers-Stuart, Intelligence Officer (who was destined to die two days later), and Lieutenant R. G. Casey (later a Governor of Bengal) were with him at the time. 'Anyhow,' he remarked, while being carried down to a picket boat which was to take him off to the hospital ship *Gascon*, 'I have commanded an Australian division for nine months.'[1] (His command was at once taken over by Major-General H. B. Walker.)

'Bridges will be a real loss,' wrote Sir Ian. 'He is a single-minded, upright, politics despising soldier. With all her magnificent rank and file Australia cannot afford to lose him. But perhaps I am too previous. I pray that he may live.'[2]

Unfortunately it was not to be. Bridges died at sea on May 18th and was buried in Alexandria. His body was later exhumed and taken to Australia for re-burial on a hill overlooking the Royal Military College at Duntroon in Canberra, of which he was founder and first commandant. Bridges was the only Australian soldier in two world wars whose body was returned for burial.

Private John Simpson, 3rd Australian Field Ambulance, is a legendary figure in the history of Anzac. Born John Simpson Kirkpatrick in the County of Durham, he dropped his family name after emigrating to Australia in early youth.

Witty, always cracking jokes, happily lazy at times, careless of dress, he soon became popular but was a handful to his sergeant.

'Simpson was the second man out of the boat from which he landed on April 25th. The chap ahead of him was killed. He carried wounded with other bearers on the first day, and then was reported missing from his unit.

'Having carried a succession of casualties down the awful slopes of Shrapnel Gully, he saw a donkey nibbling the undergrowth. It responded to the sure touch of a friendly man who loved animals. From that day they became inseparable.

'So he began work as a lone unit, and his colonel, recognising the value of his service, let him carry on.

'His daily trail was up Shrapnel Gully into Monash Gully and the deadly zone round Quinn's Post. Fearless for himself, he was always considerate for his donkey, which he would leave under cover waiting patiently.

'Simpson would then crawl through the thick scrub until he got within striking distance of a casualty. Then – a lightning dash and he had the wounded man on his back and was making for cover again. In those fierce seconds he always seemed to bear a charmed life.

'Most of his casualties were wounded in the legs so were not able to walk to the Casualty Clearing Station. He was sometimes seen to hold an unconscious man in the saddle with one arm while he guided "Jack", the donkey, with the other.

'On the return journey Simpson used to carry water up for the wounded. Frequently warned of the peril he ran, his answer was always the same "My troubles!"

'"He has hands like a woman's," said a badly wounded Australian of him when brought down to safety.

'"Glad to help you," said Simpson to another who thanked him for saving his life.

'He camped with his donkey at the Indian Mountain Battery mule lines and seemed much at home with them. "Simpson sahib *bahadur*," they called him – "Simpson the brave."'

On May 15th, as we have seen, Major-General W. T. Bridges, Commander 1st Australian Division, was mortally wounded in Shrapnel Gully. As he lay on the ground, while a medical officer tried to stop the dreadful bleeding from the wound in his groin, Simpson passed with his donkey.

'"You'll be all right, 'Dig'," he said, "but I wish they'd let me take you down on my donkey."

'It was on the morning of May 19th that Simpson made his last journey. He set off up the valley to the water guard where he usually had breakfast, but it was not ready so he went on his way. "Never mind," he called cheerily to the cook, "Get me a good dinner when I come back."'

On the way down he was shot through the heart by a machine-gun bullet at the very spot where General Bridges had been killed four days before. Death was instantaneous. He was twenty-two.

'Andy Davidson and others who were carrying from the top of the Gully had just spoken to him. "We went back," said Davidson, "covered his body and put it in a dug-out by the side of the track, then carried on with our job. At 6.30 p.m. we returned and buried him, putting a single cross over his grave with the name 'John Simpson' – nothing else."' Some say that the donkey was cared for by sepoys of the 6th Mounted Battery and taken to India after the evacuation, but according to a letter from Colonel Monash, Commander 4th Australian Infantry Brigade, 'Jack' was killed with his master.

Simpson's remains lie today in the Beach Cemetery at Anzac, which is on Hell Spit facing Brighton Beach. The personal inscription carved on the headstone marking the grave was chosen by his mother and reads, 'He gave his life that others may live'. He and his donkey are featured on stamps issued by the Australian Post Office to mark the Fiftieth Anniversary of the Gallipoli Landing. There is also a statue of 'The Man with the Donkey'.

'"Where's Simpson?" asked one of his battalion who missed him from the Gully on the day of his death.

'"At Heaven's Gate," answered the sergeant, "helping the soldiers through."'[3]

'No. 951, Private D. J. Simcock of my Battalion – the 11th,' wrote Major H. V. Howe, 'was known to his comrades as "Pinktop". His hair was pink – not red, and his face also bright pink liberally sprinkled with freckles. On leaving school he first started selling newspapers and later on got a job as cook's offsider. At this work he saved enough to set up in business for himself as a fruit and vegetable vendor from a street barrow outside Perth Railway Station, where his quick repartee made him a well-known figure during the two or three years prior to the outbreak of war.

'On enlistment "Pinktop" became a popular figure in camp. He had a good rough voice and an endless repertoire, his best turns being doggerel about the Army and its officers, not always appreciated by some of the latter.

'Prior to landing, when the troops were briefed about the possibility of under-water barbed-wire being encountered, "Pinktop" set his mind to work. Egged on by chaps in his platoon he paraded one day before the Colonel with his invention: a pair of leggings fashioned from a biscuit tin worn under the puttees. The Colonel was not impressed.

'"Pinktop" was one of those unusual characters found in every battalion who become one of the battalion's identities. Splay-footed and awkward, clumsy and untidy in dress, he was the despair of his sergeant major.

'The highest tribute Australian troops ever paid to any of their comrades was, "He is a good soldier". In a short time "Pinktop" earned that title. Among Australian troops the influence of the men upon each other was the factor which really mattered. An officer's opinion was negligible in comparison.

'"Pinktop" had landed with Captain Tulloch's company of the 11th Bn which reached within a couple of hundred yards of Battle-ship Hill, the battalion's objective, before being driven back towards the beach at 3 p.m.

'It looked then as if the wounded still lying on the beach and those still in the stranded boats would have to be abandoned.

'"I'll pick 'em up," said "Pinktop", "stick 'em in a boat and shove 'em along the beach."

'"You haven't a chance, mate, till it's dark," his friends protested. But he went all the same.

'When his body was recovered a few days later it was found to be riddled with machine-gun bullets. Under his putties he was seen to be wearing a pair of biscuit tin leggings – his invention.'

'Pinktop's' body was identified after the war. He lies now in Baby 700 Cemetery which contains some 500 graves, mostly un-knowns. Aged thirty-two, of West Leaderville, Western Australia, he was a native of Callington, South Australia. The headstone over his grave bears his name only, and date of death. I wish the tally 'Pinktop' had been added.

Now, on the Anzac front, there was to be the most violent attack that the Turks ever made there.

In spite of the loss of General Bridges and the absence for a few days of two Brigades sent to Helles, the Australian and New Zealand Army Corps had continued to strengthen their hold on this lip of the Peninsula. Meanwhile Liman von Sanders had been gathering a force of 30,000 men and of artillery believed to include at least one 11-inch gun, some 8-inch and several 4.7 inch, all well posted and efficiently concealed.

Early on May 19th, directly the moon had set, a heavy fire of guns and rifles opened from the surrounding Turkish lines, a thing that often happened at Anzac, and, following the usual pattern, the

noise, after about half an hour, died away. On this occasion, however, at 3.30 a.m. some silent figures were detected creeping close
to the centre of the Australian position. When our sentries opened
fire, masses of the enemy, in thick lines, leapt to their feet to rush
forward screaming their battle cry, 'Allah! Allah!'

The assault soon extended over the whole front. The assailants
came on so thickly that the Anzacs had only to fire point-blank to
ensure that every shot told. Many Diggers just mounted the parapet
and, sitting astride upon it, fired continuously. The conflict raged
from 3.30 until nearly 11 a.m., when the fury of battle gradually
died away. The attack had been completely repulsed at every point.
The Turks had lost some 5,000 men, of whom 3,000 dead lay in
front of the Anzac trenches. Not a yard had been yielded on any
part of the front. Our losses were less than 100 killed and about
500 wounded.

Except for a spirited counter-attack at the Nek by the New
Zealanders, no serious attempt was made by General Birdwood to
take advantage of a favourable situation until it was too late. A
further assault planned by the New Zealanders for the afternoon
was cancelled, as the Turks had by that time recovered. Except for
very occasional bursts of machine-gun and rifle fire, the whole of the
Anzac front fell silent.

On the morning of May 20th, the day following the attack, the sun
came out in full fury and the sizzling of the corpses began. By early
evening the stench was so frightful that an Australian colonel, acting
on his own initiative, hoisted a Red Cross flag. It was promptly shot
down. Then a Turk came over and apologised. Next the Turks put
up some white flags, and it is said that we shot one Red Crescent man
by mistake. Both sides had been frightened.

Lieutenant-Colonel A. Skeen from General Birdwood's headquarters now arrived and went out to talk to the Turks, who wanted
an armistice to bury their dead. Some sort of parley followed, and
while this was going on Major Aubrey Herbert was sent by General
Birdwood to the *Arcadian* in Kephalo Harbour, Imbros, to obtain
Sir Ian Hamilton's approval. The answer was 'Yes, provided "Birdie"
clearly understands that no corps commander can fix up an armistice off his own bat, and provided it is clear that we do not ask for
an armistice but grant it to them – the suppliants.'[4] Aubrey Herbert
returned with these instructions and the matter was speedily settled.
Captain Stephen (Sam) Butler, who had taken over the duties of
Head of Intelligence on the death of Villiers-Stewart, went over to
the Turks under a white flag on May 23rd with Aubrey Herbert as
Interpreter.

'On arrival at their lines we had a pow-wow,' Sam Butler wrote in his diary, 'and, as a result, I took back with me a representative – Major Kemal Ohri of Ohrida in Macedonia, a very smart "Jean Turk". I blindfolded him and led him in by the hand, more than a mile, through the sand of the seashore and how we sweated! Aubrey Herbert stayed in the Turkish lines as a hostage.'

'We had cheese and tea and coffee,' Herbert wrote, 'my host offering to eat first to show me that it was all right. He tried to impress me with their well-being, saying he hated all politicians and had sworn never to read the papers. The Turks had come sadly into the war against us, otherwise gladly. They wanted to regain the prestige that they had lost in the Balkans. "You have made a cruel mistake by us," he concluded. "The taking of those two warships – and the way in which they were taken!"'[5]

When the parley at Anzac was over Captain Sam Butler escorted Major Kemal Ohri back to the Turkish lines and collected Aubrey Herbert. The Major was brought in again next day to wait in our lines while the Armistice was in progress. On this occasion he was mounted.

'It was indescribable,' wrote Aubrey Herbert. 'One was grateful for the rain and the grey sky. A Turkish Red Crescent man came and gave me some antiseptic wool with scent on it, and this they renewed frequently. There were wounded crying in that multitude of silence. "At this spectacle even the most gentle must feel savage, and the most savage must weep," a Turkish captain said.

'The dead filled acres of ground. One saw the result of machine-gun fire very clearly; entire companies annihilated – not wounded, but killed, their heads doubled under them with the impetus of their rush and both hands clasping their bayonets.

'Half a dozen funeral services were going on all round, conducted by chaplains. I asked the Turks if they did not want an Imām for a service over their own dead, but an old Albanian pagan roared with laughter and said that their souls were all right. They could look after themselves. One huge, savage-looking Anatolian looked curses at me. Greeks came up and tried to surrender to me, but were ordered back by the Turks pretty roughly.

'Considering the number of their men we had killed they remained extraordinarily unmoved and polite. The burying had not been well done. It was sometimes impossible to do it. The Turks asked me to witness their taking the money from their dead . . . burying was finished sometime before the end. Our men and the Turks began fraternising, exchanging badges etc. I had to keep them apart. There were certain tricks on both sides.'[6]

At 4 p.m. the Turks came to Aubrey Herbert for orders. This sort of thing could not have happened anywhere else and shows that in spite of the war this remarkable man, Herbert, was still able to command their respect.

He now retired their troops and ours by walking along the line. A few minutes later he retired the Turkish white-flag men, making them shake hands with our men. Then the Australians began coming up, and said, 'Goodbye, old chap, good luck,' and 'So long, Jacko. Good luck and keep your head down'.

'*Allahaismarladik!* farewell,' called Aubrey Herbert as he turned away.

'*Ughur ola güle güle gedejekseniz güle güle gelejekseniz* – Good luck! Smiling may you go and smiling come again,' the Turks replied in chorus.

The Armistice must have come as a surprise to some Anzacs. It certainly did in the case of Corporal H. Brewer.

'On the day I and two others were at a part of the line known as the Chamber of Horrors,' he wrote. 'It was the unfinished section of what we hoped would eventually join up with Quinn's Post. There was only room for three in it, and it was quite close to the German officers' quarters in the enemy trenches.

'Taking a peep out I saw to my surprise a big German officer in his shirt sleeves advancing with a white flag. I told the others. By this time more were advancing. One of the boys in the Chamber of Horrors thought that at least this section of the enemy was surrendering. He leapt on the parapet shouting, "Good for you, matey! Are you going to quit? Come and shake hands with us." He was dragged down, and the news of the armistice soon passed along to us.

'The quietness of those few hours was almost more than we could bear after the continual firing. If a man spoke to you, you jumped at the sound of his voice. It was uncanny the way all the little singing birds came back as soon as it was quiet. The whole thing got on your nerves, and we were glad when the time came for the armistice to end.

'The Turks had the right to start off again, and I never heard anything so puny as the first shot that was fired. Then the old naval guns got to it, and we were happy again.'[7]

'When I was head of Naval Intelligence, Constantinople, 1919–1920,' Sam Butler concluded in his diary, 'I was going round the Sultan's Palace at Dolma Bagtche and in one of the state rooms saw a smart

Turkish officer in uniform. He looked at me and I looked at him, both thinking there was something familiar. After a minute or two we both realised that, once again, the man from the English lines and the man from the Turkish lines – who had met and been responsible for making the armistice at Anzac possible, in May 1915, had met again!

'Greetings were many and long, and this time in great friendship. We [now both lieutenant-colonels] saw a lot of each other. He came to a meal with us with his wife, and we went to a meal at his house. He was a charming and able man and on retirement from the Army became Agent for the German Junkers Company in Turkey.'

A naval intelligence report, dated Constantinople, 12 December 1919, attributes the following statement to a lieutenant-colonel in the Turkish Army. No name is given.

'I am the officer who came into the English lines on the Armistice at Anzac.

'When I volunteered to go the C-in-C said I might get shot, but I replied that it was worth the risk; and what did one man matter in view of our terrible losses on May 19th? and I knew the English were an honourable foe – and well indeed they treated me; but never shall I forget how hot I got on that long walk in the sand on the beach in my thick clothes and long boots with a towel round my eyes. They played a game on me and made me step over imaginary barbed wire on my way in, to give a false impression. But I told them all, when I got back, how well I had been treated . . . and the Armistice was carried out loyally by both sides.

'Yes! those were interesting days, but Turkey staked on the black and red won. Now she must pay.'

Our ship, the *Bacchante*, remained off Anzac until May 24th, and thereafter returned from time to time throughout the campaign, where she became the Diggers' best friend. Whether it was her four funnels or the accuracy of her gunfire which did the trick I do not know. Perhaps it was a bit of both.

My turn to run the picket boat came round again and again, and thanks to Petty Officer Main and our splendid crew we were able to make ourselves really useful. When the *Bacchante* went off to fulfil some other task she invariably left her picket boat behind, in which case Midshipman and crew slept in Naval Beach Party dug-outs.

The weather was getting hot, and, since we were not issued with any sort of khaki rig, we tried dipping our whites into permanganate of potash. The results were awful.

General Birdwood's A.D.C., Lieutenant B. W. Onslow, Probyn's Horse (XIth Bengal Lancers), who was killed during a beach strafe a few weeks later, came up to me with an invitation to lunch with the General. To prepare for this great event I had a bathe and got clean. Then I improved my shirt by rinsing it in sea water. I was too young to need a shave. It was natural that I should expect a party, but when I reached his dug-out and had mounted the short flight of steps I discovered I was the General's only guest.

Army commander and midshipman sitting on upturned boxes sharing a meal. . . !

Everyone, including General Birdwood, had a swim every day. Only Indian troops wore pants, it being against their religion to do otherwise.

The well-known photograph which appeared in the press at home of the Anzac Commander enjoying a swim 'during a lull in the fighting', had the effect of swelling Birdwood's parcel mail over a period of some weeks. The General was delighted, of course, when 'Postie' brought into his dug-out the first armful, and he smiled happily as he struggled with string and sealing-wax, anticipating the contents: Cigarettes perhaps? Chocolates? A cake? How exciting, aren't people kind!

But 'God forbid!' he muttered when he began to appreciate that every parcel contained a bathing costume sent in most cases by an anonymous and very shocked donor.

Whenever the beach-strafing started, Lieutenant-Commander Edward Cater, Assistant Beach Master, would blow his whistle, whereupon everyone would swim madly for the shore and run naked for shelter. The Diggers were all very fine swimmers, so the sea was cleared in no time. I only saw one man badly hit in the water the whole time I was there.

Cater was a remarkable man, as tough as old boots and as brave as a lion. A survivor of the battleship *Audacious*, mined north of Loch Swilly, Ireland, on 27th October 1914, he had come out to Gallipoli in the *Queen Elizabeth*. It was the talk among us midshipmen that he was so much of a martinet on board his ship that he had been sent ashore to be killed. This was rubbish, of course. But now at Anzac he became a legend. No one, soldier or sailor, who served there is ever likely to forget him. Heedless of back-chat from Australians, he could out-swear any of them. It was not long before Cater had them all by the short hairs, and it pleased them.

'He was a sardonic looking devil who knew exactly what he wanted done,' wrote Captain Philip Norman Walter, who was then midshipman of the *Queen*'s picket boat. 'My efforts did not always meet with Cater's approval and there were sarcastic remarks. But I thought he was grand – a form of hero worship now, alas, out of fashion. Tireless and fearless, he roamed the beach, keeping everyone up to their jobs.'

When the day arrived for Walter to return to his ship, Cater called him over, smiled and said, 'Post this letter to my wife, will you – there's a good chap?'

'I hope she got it all right,' Walter concluded, for he never saw Cater again.

Sometimes we had to bury Indian dead at sea from the *Bacchante*'s picket boat, while other midshipmen did the same from theirs. A *havildar* – a corporal – with two sepoys, would bring the body down to the pier on a stretcher. It was always tightly wrapped in an army blanket weighed with stones. An *Imām*, a bearded priest with his upper lip shaved, wearing a *chugha*, a black gown, and a turban or skull-cap, would usually come too. When all were on board, off we would go.

There is a tradition among Muhammedans, presuming the body was one, that no one shall precede the corpse, as the angels go before. Being unaware of such niceties, we must have given offence, though nothing was ever said. Our bowman had to go for'ard of the body to shove off with his boat-hook and would usually stay on the fore deck to keep out of the way.

It was a rushed affair, with the *Imām* noticeably in a hurry. Muhammed is related to have said that it is good to carry the dead quickly to the grave to cause the righteous to arrive soon at happiness, and if he be a bad man it is well to put wickedness away from one's shoulders.

When half a mile out we stopped engines. Then prayers were said by the *Imām* in Arabic from the *Qu'rān*, which were known to him by heart. 'There is no God but THE GOD (Allah), and Allah is great.' While he was reciting he would first place his hands on the lobes of his ears, then the right hand upon the left below his navel. '*Allah-ho-Akbar* – Allah is great' – and so it went on.

When the *Imām* turned his head, it was the signal that the service was over. Then, by lifting one end of the stretcher, the corpse was launched into the water.

Fascinated by the strange ritual, Petty Officer Main and I never failed to hold on to the cabin rail with one hand and to lean outboard to watch the body twist and turn until it reached the bottom. The water was very clear.

No one at Anzac will ever forget the terrible smell of rotting corpses, which was worse at night as far as we were concerned, because of the off-shore wind. Hundreds of bodies, friend and foe, lay between the trenches, frizzled by the sun and black with flies. Some Diggers tried slinging lime over the parapet to hasten decomposition, but it was an endless, hopeless task.

Our front-line trenches were barely a mile inland, which made it possible for the Turks to bring their guns out at will and to strafe attending small craft as well as enfilade the beach. Our particular enemies were 'Anafarta Annie' and 'Beachy Bill', and not a day passed without their toll of men killed and wounded while going about their tasks on the beach. The pier was an awful death trap, as will be seen.

We in the *Bacchante*'s picket boat became so accustomed to this shelling that on hearing a bang in the distance we used to cock our ears before deciding to seek shelter. If we were alongside the pier we were sometimes ordered ashore, sometimes told to lay off.

Looking back now, I can remember trying hard neither to run for cover when Lieutenant-Commander Cater blew his whistle nor to be seen to be as frightened as surely I must have been.

The *Albion* ran aground off Ari Burnu at about 4 a.m. on May 23rd, and Captain Algernon Heneage had the devil of a job to get his ship off the putty. Midshipman 'Growler' Felton (so named because his size and weight were a reminder of the carriage of those days), of our Term confirmed to me afterwards that as soon as the Turks realised the ship was ashore they brought field guns to bear on her. Two destroyers secured alongside the *Albion*, bow to stern, and went full speed ahead, but that was no good. Then the *Canopus*, commanded by Captain Heathcote Grant, took her in tow, but the wire parted. The *Albion* then fired broadside after broadside of her main armament, and at the same time her ship's company, led by their Commander 'Puggy' Stephenson, known as the 'Terror of Tobermory' in W.W. II, held heavy weights and jumped up and down together on the upper deck, trying to shake the ship off. But this was no good either. To add to their troubles, a Turkish battleship came out of her hiding-place and had a few half-hearted pots at her across the Peninsula, fortunately to no effect.

Eventually the ship came off quite suddenly at 9 a.m. She had suffered some damage and some casualties from the field guns, and the *Canopus* had been knocked about, too. The *Albion* had dummy sailors in her spotting top who were all 'killed'.

We had watched this performance from the picket boat while working off Anzac. Next day we were recalled to our ship, and *Bacchante* sailed for Kephalo, Imbros Island, to provision and coal.

One day, while anchored there, an enemy biplane came over, flying very low. Our ship's company took cover, except the Marine Detachment, who were ordered to fall in on the quarter-deck under arms. Bayonets were fixed and rifles loaded ready to open fire. Afterwards everyone was asking what the bayonets were for.

The plane dropped a couple of small bombs wide of any target, but none of the nasty little steel darts they had been using against us on and off the beaches. When she flew away we all cheered.

H.M.S. *Minerva* was patrolling the approaches to the Gulf of Smyrna in June, when Captain Warleigh received a cypher message from Admiral de Robeck to the effect that the Italian S.S. *Tripoli* now approaching those waters, was believed to be carrying a German spy, a Fräulein Linda Pastor, disguised as a hospital nurse.

When S.S. *Tripoli* showed over the horizon she was closed by the *Minerva* and ordered to stop. A boarding party was sent in the seaboat, a twelve-oared cutter.

Thanks to the co-operation of the Master of S.S. *Tripoli* Fräulein Pastor was identified and arrested.

As the sea was pretty rough, it was asking too much to expect the girl to be able to climb the vertical ladder placed against the ship's side of *Minerva*, so she was hoisted on board lashed in a chair taken from the wardroom, the officers' mess.

While a prisoner on board the *Minerva* Fräulein Pastor was accommodated in the Captain's harbour cabin. A marine sentry was placed on the cabin door with strict orders as to his duties.

When the sun was below the yard-arm on the day of her arrival, the breeze fell away and it turned out to be a lovely evening, so the wardroom gramophone was brought on to the quarter-deck where – damn silly though it may seem today – the officers danced with each other.

While swinging round to the tune of 'Valse Septembre', two of the young watchkeepers had a brain wave.

'Whether the Captain's permission was asked first, I don't know,' wrote Commander William Morley who was a midshipman in the ship. 'Anyway, on deck she came under close escort and we partnered her in turn. Lieutenant Bruce Fraser, now Admiral of the Fleet Lord Fraser of North Cape, was our gunnery officer. I wonder whether he had a dance too.'

Then, at last 'Pipe down!'

'*Gut nacht, Fräulein, Gut Nacht – Schlafen sie wohl* – sleep well!'

'Escort the young lady to her cabin, sentry.'

'Very good, Sir'. . . .

It must have been late when the Fräulein's bell rang. A new sentry had taken over the middle watch, midnight to 4 a.m. He was a younger man, rather shy, so sooner than enter the cabin alone he put his head up the quarter-deck hatchway and reported to the officer on watch there. He, too, did not relish the idea, so they both went to the Commander, who was furious at being disturbed. However, in the end, all three proceeded to the after cabin together to find out what the girl wanted.

'*Kann ich wohl einen Glas mit Wasser* – Please can I have a glass of water?!'

A few days later Fräulein Pastor was transferred to our ship, the *Bacchante*, for passage to Mudros. 'Received on board, 6.30 p.m. one female prisoner for safe custody', is the entry in the ship's log.

Both Midshipman Douglas Dixon and I were down with dysentery when she arrived, but we were allowed by the aft-deck sentry to have a peep at her in the cabin next to ours. I remember her as a nice-looking girl, aged about twenty-five and of average height, fair hair tied into a bun on the top of her head; born in Austria, so we were told. She wore plain clothes, not the uniform of a nurse. Everyone on board was very kind to Linda, but there was no dancing on the quarter-deck in our ship. Not with Captain 'Algy' Boyle in command!

Linda Pastor was eventually taken to Malta in the *Vengeance*, not to be eliminated, as some of us feared, but for onward passage to Switzerland, where I am told she remained for the duration of the war.

I have often wondered what she was doing in the Aegean. Spying for the newly arrived U-boats I suspect. She must have been a brave girl.

18

The Fatal Periscope

*'The fatal periscope had been sighted. I saw them in
full flight, transports and battleships, like dogs running
away with their tails between their legs. The sense of
abandonment was acute.'*
Compton Mackenzie, 1883–1972
Gallipoli Memories, 1929

As soon as the February bombardments of the Allied Fleet had
begun, German and Turkish authorities in Constantinople took turns
to press the German High Command in Berlin to send U-boats to the
scene of operations. Baron von Wangenheim, the German Ambassador, stated in his appeal that the 'effect upon neutrals of the
Dardanelles being forced might give the whole war a turn unfavourable to Germany.' Enver Pasha, the Turkish War Minister,
offered to purchase three submarines, with German crews if necessary. A favourable reply was soon received. Five small U-boats
would be dispatched in sections by rail for assembly in the Austrian
dockyard at Pola (now Pula, Yugoslavia). A larger submarine,
U-21, would be sailing shortly from Wilhelmshaven.

The first to arrive was *UB-8*. She was assembled quickly and,
after an adventurous voyage, reached the Dardanelles on June 2nd
unobserved by our patrols. A channel through the minefields had
been marked with small drum buoys laid close inshore as had been
done for the *Muavenet-i Millet* in her attack on the *Goliath*, May
12th–13th.

It can only be assumed that Lieutenant von Voigt, in command
of *UB-8*, had been ordered to keep his arrival in the Eastern Mediterranean a secret for, except for firing a single torpedo at an unidentified three-funnelled ship at dusk on May 30th, he had taken no
offensive action during a passage of 800 miles, which, with one stop
in the Dodecanese for fuel and a second at Smyrna for repairs, had
lasted twenty-nine days.

However, he must have had to dive frequently to avoid being

sighted. As his submerged speed is unlikely to have exceeded five knots, he probably found the voyage frustrating. The submarine of the day, British, French, German or any other nationality, operated like a whale, i.e. she had to have air. Although submersible, she was obliged to come to the surface at decent intervals to breathe. Not only did the air inboard get foul but her batteries needed recharging. When submerged she ran on electricity stored in huge batteries weighing half a ton each; when on the surface, she used her diesel engines, which relied on small quantities of crude oil plus enormous quantities of air. These diesel engines, in conjunction with dynamos, also made the electricity which charged the batteries. The *Schnorkel* of World War II, which enabled a submarine to charge her batteries while submerged, had not yet been invented.

The probability of an early appearance of German U-boats in the Aegean was much in the minds of Vice-Admiral de Robeck and his naval staff. On 13th March 1915, a week before *UB-8* had left Germany, the Admiralty signalled: 'It is anticipated that U-boats in sections will shortly be sent to a Mediterranean port by rail from Germany. Sections may be described as "machinery for civil purposes", to conceal their identity.' The British Minister in Athens was also warned. He inserted notices in Greek newspapers offering large monetary rewards for 'reports on German U-boats should they lead to their destruction'. Our secret service agent in Bizerta had reported a week or so earlier that '*telefunken* [the old spark set. *Funk* = spark] signals have been heard within fifty miles of Malta'. Another report said, 'A U-boat has been seen drawing supplies at sea from a Greek steamer, name unknown'. Finally on May 15th a reliable source said, 'An oil company in Samos [in the Dodecanese] is trying to sell a large store of oil to a Turkish subject.'

Our secret service agents in the Eastern Mediterranean even knew that Lieutenant-Commander von Mohl from the *Breslau* had been detailed to take charge of supplies for U-boats and that he had complained to his Commander-in-Chief, Admiral Wilhelm Souchon in Constantinople, that 'the only means of transporting fuel oil is by means of camels'.

The German submarine *U-21*, commanded by Lieutenant-Commander Otto Hersing, left Wilhelmshaven at 5.30 a.m. on 25th April 1915, the day of the landings. He chose the route north of the British Isles, not the Channel. At 7 p.m. on May 2nd *U-21* met S.S. *Marzala* off Cape Finisterre and was escorted to a sheltered anchorage near Arosa Bay on the west coast of Spain. After taking in twelve tons of oil fuel and some stores, she went on her way.

Soon after reaching the open sea, however, Hersing found to his horror that the fuel was of the wrong grade. It would not ignite. He reckoned it would be useless to turn back, better to press on and try to reach Cattaro (now Kotor, Yugoslavia) with the twenty-six tons of the old oil fuel he still had in his bunkers. It was a brave decision.

During the forenoon of May 6th *U-21* passed through the Straits of Gibraltar on the surface, close to the Moroccan coast. She was forced to dive when two of our torpedo-boats hove in sight. Her periscope was seen and her presence reported. She met two British steamers on May 9th and was again reported by W/T.

U-21 fell in with her enemies again on May 11th when south of Sicily. She was sighted by two French destroyers, one of which opened fire, projectiles falling close, but there was no damage. She reached Cattaro on May 13th, being escorted into harbour by an Austrian torpedo-boat. A journey of 2,100 miles had been successfully completed, the fuel remaining being 1.8 tons.

Eager to reach the scene of operations, Hersing allowed only seven days for rest and refit. At 6.30 p.m. on May 20th *U-21* sailed for the coast of Asia Minor. Normal shipping lanes were avoided. The cruiser *Askold*, the only Russian warship with the Allied Fleet, was sighted at anchor near Dedeagatch. Although a hit was considered a certainty, Hersing decided not to give his position away by wasting a torpedo on this old ship, but instead to continue his voyage in secret to the coast of Gallipoli where he might expect to find the main body of the Allied Fleet. His judgement proved correct.

The sea was flat calm with visibility maximum when Hersing turned up off Cape Helles at 7 a.m. on May 25th. He saw the *Swiftsure* riding at anchor without nets. Although she was screened by several merchant ships he was determined to attack her. Approaching at forty feet he raised his periscope with great care but was spotted immediately and fired on by destroyers. He crash-dived to eighty feet and crept away.

In the *Swiftsure*, carrying nearly all active service ratings, men highly disciplined and as keen as mustard, the whole thing seems to have been regarded as a kind of sport. People got up sweepstakes, the winner to be the first man actually to sight a periscope. Of course, the older ratings – mostly reservists – regarded the U-boat menace more seriously than their juniors did. When you are a father or a grandfather and over fifty, you do not look forward with relish to the prospect of having your ship blown up and being obliged to take a cold bath at any hour of the day or night. In spite of this, however, the Royal Fleet Reserve and the Royal Naval Reserve nobly upheld the best traditions of the service. Indeed, they were often steadier than some of the less experienced youngsters.

Leaving the Cape Helles area, Hersing took a northerly course and before long sighted the *Vengeance*. He made a good approach and at 10.7 a.m. fired a torpedo, range 1,000 yards. Again he was unlucky. Air bubbles from the approaching torpedo were sighted from the bridge and avoiding action was taken. *U-21* was engaged by gunfire but not hit.

A short while ago I was asked whether blind obedience to orders was a rule in the Royal Navy. Answering in the negative, I quoted as an example the happenings on board the *Vengeance* when *U-21* fired a torpedo at her.

Lieutenant-Commander Kenneth Macpherson, Navigating Officer, was on the bridge when Hersing made his attack. He spotted the track of the torpedo approaching and knew that running at a depth of about ten feet the torpedo would be well ahead of its air bubbles. There was no time to lose.

'Hard-a-port . . . Full speed ahead!' he ordered down the voice-pipe. The ship swung round. Being a coal-burner, smoke belched out of her funnels as the stokers got to work.

'Torpedo approaching the ship, Sir!' yelled one of the 'lookouts'. This report was heard by Captain B. H. Smith, who was in his sea cabin one deck down.

'Hard-a-starboard!' he called, as he rushed up the bridge ladder. But Macpherson knew only too well that if the helm were reversed at this stage the torpedo would strike the ship, so he ordered the quartermaster to keep the helm hard-a-port.

'Hard-a-port it is, Sir,' came back the reply, and the torpedo passed harmlessly astern.

'I consider Lieutenant-Commander Macpherson, by his promptitude of action and by his ready acceptance of responsibility in countermanding my order,' wrote Captain Smith that night to Admiral de Robeck, 'prevented the ship being struck and is deserving of great credit.'

For wilfully disobeying the lawful command of his captain, who was not so well placed as he was to judge the situation, and for his courage and initiative, Macpherson was awarded a Commander-in-Chief's Commendation.

After these two disappointments Hersing felt that he ought to stop attacking ships in daylight. 'It was too clear and too calm a day,' he wrote. But his batteries would not last if he ran away now and remained submerged until dark. Anyway he was not the man to give up while there was still a chance of success. '*Wo ein Wille da ein Weg*, where there is a will there is a way,' he told his crew, and carried on up the coast.

At about noon Hersing spotted the battleship *Triumph* off Gaba Tepe. There was a destroyer circling round her, and he had to dive deep several times to avoid being rammed. The noise of propellers passing overhead was disturbing, but he was made of the right stuff. '*Ran an den Feind*, let's go for the enemy!' he ordered, regardless of the danger.

A torpedo with a net-cutter was loaded into the forward tube and the depth setting adjusted. Excitement was intense.

'*Sehrohr ausfahren!* Periscope up!'

Six hundred yards range. Five hundred yards. Four hundred . . . 328 yards . . .

'*Los!* Fire!' The boat rose a foot or so and rocked with the force of the discharge. All hands waited with bated breath as the torpedo sped on its way. Two detonations were heard. First a low metallic blow as the explosive cutter tore a hole in the nets; then, in a matter of seconds, *U-21* was shaken by a tremendous underwater explosion. The time was 12.23 p.m.

'*Gut gemacht. Weiter so.* Well done, carry on!' from the gallant Hersing, as he ordered the helm to be put over and the boat to be taken down to maximum depth, sixty feet. *U-21* crept away to safety.

After being submerged for twenty-one hours Hersing brought his boat cautiously to the surface at 9.25 p.m. It was dark and there was nothing in sight. '*Batterien aufladen*,' he ordered. 'Re-charge the batteries!'[1]

It was the *Rohrmeister*, the petty officer in charge of the forward tube, who started to sing the song of the Imperial Navy, 'The Flag', which was to be sung four years later by sailors of the High Sea Fleet when they scuttled their ships at Scapa Flow on 21st June 1919:

> '*Stolz weht die Flagge Schwarz-Weiss-Rot*
>   Proud waves the flag Black-white-red
> *Von unsres Schiffes Mast.*
>   From our ship's mast.
> *Dem Feinde weh*
>   Woe to the enemy

23   Lieutenant-Commander Otto Hersing and crew of *U-21*

24   Lieutenant-Commander Rudolf Firle,
T.B. *Muavenet-i Millet*

25   Lieutenant von Heimburg, *UB-14*

26 Commander Nasmith, V.C. (note the pipe) and Lieutenant D'Oyly Hughes of *E11*

27 Lieutenant Wilfrid Pirie, R.N., H Submarine *H-1*, with his two officers Lieuten Clive Robinson (*right*) and Midshipman J Bethell

28 Nasmith of *E11* torpedoes the storeship *Stambul* off Constantinople

Der sie bedroht
  Who threatens it
Der diese Farben hasst!
  Who these colours hates.'

The *Triumph* was at her firing station off Gaba Tepe on May 25th, a billet vacated only the day before by our own ship, the *Bacchante*. She was under way, but her engines were stopped. Slight headway gave her nets the appearance of a dowager's long skirt. Light guns were manned, and the hands were at dinner.

At about 12.25, as the destroyer *Chelmer*, Lieutenant-Commander Hugh T. England, was rounding the battleship's bows, he saw a suspicious white wash 500 yards on the *Triumph's* starboard beam. Instantly he made a dash for it but was too late. The *Triumph* opened fire at the wash, but in a matter of seconds a shock of extraordinary violence seemed to lift the ship as she almost disappeared from view in a shower of falling water and coal. The torpedo had fairly got home as though her nets had been a spider's web. While she listed over, the *Chelmer*, by a fine display of seamanship, closed the *Triumph's* stern-walk (she could not get alongside because of the nets) and took off 465 officers and men. One officer, stripped to the buff but still wearing his uniform cap, was just about to take the plunge when *Chelmer's* bows touched the quarter-deck and he was handed across on to the destroyer's fo'c'sle to the delight of the sailors and much to his own embarrassment. There is a strong tendency when a ship sinks for the men to strike out in the water and to cover a large area, making rescue work difficult. It is of little use an officer shouting to the men to gather round him unless he can be spotted. Hence the cap. Chief and petty officers would be expected to do the same.

The *Triumph* capsized seven minutes after being struck but remained floating for nearly half an hour. When she made her final plunge the rescued men gave her a last cheer, with cries of 'Goodbye, old *Triumph*' for her requiem. Happily there were many to swell the sound of farewell. Only three officers and seventy-two men perished.

Captain Maurice Fitzmaurice was on the bridge when his ship was struck. He saw at once that there was no hope of saving her and went down on to the fo'c'sle.

'Drummer!' he roared. 'Drummer!' Out came 'Sticks', the little R.M.L.I. drummer-boy, aged fifteen, from behind the screen door. He was naked as the day he was born but he held a brightly-polished bugle in one hand, his swimming collar in the other, and wore his cap squarely on his head.

'Sir?' he said, saluting smartly.

'Sound the advance!' ordered the Captain. It was the bugle call normally used for 'hands to bathe'.

'Very good, Sir!' As the last note died away Sticks threw his bugle into the 'drink' and dived in after it.

The Captain's departure was more dignified. He just took off his jacket, slipped down the side into the sea and swam clear with a steady breast-stroke, to be picked up by a boat from the *Colne*, still wearing his eye-glass.

On leaving the China station at the outbreak of war the *Triumph* had retained her Chinese wardroom stewards, Ah Lam, Laing Po, Lai Fat, Ah Wan and Ah Kum. It must have been quite a sight to see them shinning up the net-defence booms as the ship heeled, shouting out 'Me no catchee swim!' After being catapulted into the sea as the ship capsized they were, I am happy to say, all saved.

Some weeks before, while the *Triumph* was bombarding, a flag had been seen being waved on shore abreast the ship. All boats were away at the time off Anzac beach, except the galley, which Captain Fitzmaurice sent inshore under oars to investigate. To the surprise of the boat's crew a young bugler from the South Wales Borderers appeared. He was wounded and had made his way along the shore from the landing at Y Beach. In so doing he had passed through the enemy's lines without knowing it. He was brought on board, and the surgeon had to amputate the fingers of his right hand. He was placed on the sick list to recover and had become a sort of ship's mascot. When the *Triumph* was sinking, Lieutenant Philip Kilgour, seeing that the youngster could not use his right hand, gave him his own lifebelt. He was picked up and claimed by his regiment. Kilgour, who came from Newcastle, County Down, was also saved.

Among the officers lost was a grand fellow, Engineer Commander Hilgrove Hammond, a large black-bearded chap of the old school. The moment the ship was struck he hurried down to his place of duty, the engine-room, and as he passed Midshipman Garner he said, 'I hope I shan't be left alone'. He was left, but not alone, as several of his department went down in the ship with him.

It is always nice to met an old friend. This time it is none other than Petty Officer George Morgan, late of H.M.S. *Ocean,* sunk on March 18th. He was certainly a Jonah, because he had only just joined the *Triumph* from the Anzac beach party, where he had served since the day of the landing.

'I found the *Triumph* an easier routine than the *Ocean,*' he wrote, 'but harder in other respects. We had the feeling that we survivors were not wanted, but as time went on things got better. The officers were very good and showed consideration for us as we had no change of clothing when we joined, and there was none in the ship to kit us up.

'I had just finished my dinner and thought I would like a smoke, so I went on deck. I was in the act of lighting my pipe when the Boatswain's Mate piped "Close watertight doors!" I managed to have two or three puffs before the bugle sounded "Defence Stations". So I put my pipe away and hurried to my gun on the after shelter deck. I had no sooner cleared it away for action when I saw men running aft from the fore bridge towards me, all the time looking over the side. Then "bang!" from the gun on the opposite side of the ship from mine. She was firing at the periscope of a submarine. I had hardly time to turn round before there was a tremendous explosion. The ship heeled over to port, and up went coal, wood, iron and water as high as the mast head. Then she heeled over to starboard, and this great volume of debris and water came crashing down on the decks.

'Now we realised our position, and all hands were busy throwing overboard timber, gratings, hammocks, ammunition boxes – anything that would float. There were no signs of panic or excitement. On the quarterdeck the sick and non-swimmers were able to get aboard the destroyer.

'I made my way aft and pressing my hat firmly on I took a dive over the stern and, with three others, started to swim for the shore, until we saw shrapnel bullets striking the water not far from us. One chap had the muscle of his arm shattered and was kept afloat by his chums, so we decided to keep out of range until we were rescued. My companions were the Captain of Marines, a stoker and a Chinaman.

'We were picked up eventually by a trawler's dinghy, after refusing the whaler, and when we were aboard we got out again to allow two chaps who were supporting an unconscious Australian [a guest] to get in. I remained hanging on to the rudder lanyard.

'After about half an hour in the water we were taken on board the trawler. Some hot coffee worked miracles, but I was in great trouble. My bacca and matches were wet, and as soon as I began to pick up a bit I wanted a smoke. One chap on the trawler, seeing my difficulty, went to his bunk and brought me a fill – so I had a smoke. I then took off my clothes and wrung them out and put them back on again.

'At about 5 p.m. we were at Imbros and were taken to the *Lord Nelson*, sister ship to the *Agamemnon*, the ship I boarded when picked up after the *Ocean* had been mined.

'"Dear Flo," I wrote on the post card I was given. "I have changed my ship again and am safe and well."'

'Just before sunset we went over to the transport *Saturnia* where the Captain told us he would apply to the Admiralty to let the ship's company go home.

'On May 27th we were paid £1 each. The Captain told us he had had his request granted (loud cheers!) but that he had to reinforce the Beach Parties on several beaches and that he intended to do that with survivors of the *Ocean* and the *Irresistible* . . .

'But it was no good giving way to my feelings, so I resolved to make the best of it. After asking a fellow who lived in Gloucester to tell my people how things were, I set to work to overcome my disappointment. Next day some of us were given a soldier's tunic, trousers and shirt and in the afternoon were sent ashore to Anzac beach to rejoin the Australians and New Zealanders whom we had only left ten days before.'[2]

Two days later, on May 27th, Hersing struck again.

Admiral de Robeck had decided to leave one capital ship at anchor off Cape Helles to act as bombarding ship and to give the Army confidence. She was berthed in shallow water and had some protection from small vessels stationed around her. The *Majestic* of 1890 vintage, never had a chance. If she had foundered on an even keel, her upperworks would have remained above water, but like all these old tubs she capsized almost at once. Only forty-three lives were lost. Rear-Admiral Nicholson and the War Correspondent Ashmead Bartlett were among those saved. Our soldiers lined the beaches, horror stricken. 'What is going to happen to us now?' they asked.

The *Majestic* remained upside down in full view of the shore until the November storms came, when she slipped down out of sight. While she was still visible, passing H.M. ships saluted her in respect for the dead still on board.

Hersing now moved over to the Gulf of Smyrna, where he torpedoed the dummy battle cruiser *Tiger*. He was seen to scratch his head as, through his periscope, he watched her sink, while her ship's company took to the water and floated away on 15-inch guns, turrets and pieces of the upperworks all made of wood!

'*Nun brat mir einer einen Storch, die "Tommies" haben uns anschieten!*' he called to his First Lieutenant, adding the words: '*und die Beine recht knusperig!*' 'Now someone should fry me a stork, for the "Tommies" have hoaxed us. Make the legs very crisp!'

Still not fully satisfied with his 'bag', the adventurous Hersing manoeuvred to get into position on May 29th to fire at a battleship lying at anchor in Kephalo harbour, Imbros. But good luck had deserted him. *U-21* fouled the net defence and was fortunate to escape destruction. This experience put him off making a similar attempt on ships in Mudros.

At 9.00 a.m. on June 2nd, *U-21* entered the Dardanelles. She reached Constantinople at 5 p.m. on June 5th, and received a tumultuous welcome. Since leaving Wilhelmshaven Hersing had been at sea for forty days and had done very well.

Hersing brought *U-21* down from Constantinople on July 4th and torpedoed the *Carthage* off V Beach. She had been lent to the French and had almost completed unloading much needed ammunition for their 7·5-mm guns. The *Carthage* was a sister ship of the *Waratah*, whose disappearance in July 1909, with all her passengers and crew, leaving no trace, while on passage between Durban and Cape Town en route to England from Australia, remains one of the great mysteries of the sea.

In addition to the honours which were showered on him and his crew, an Intelligence Centre established in a small bay on the west coast of the Peninsula was named *Hersingstand*, or Hersing's Post. A A fitting tribute. He died in Münster, Germany, in 1960, a hero of the Old Imperial German Navy.

In spite of these and other sinkings our measures to deal with the U-boat menace off Gallipoli were largely successful. Great netted areas proved an effective protection. Major units of the Fleet were only exposed when required for some definite object. The normal day-to-day support of the Army was provided by destroyers and light craft. In July four large monitors mounting 14-inch guns, some smaller monitors and four bulge cruisers began to arrive; and they were all on the scene by the end of the month.

These monitors had unforeseen limitations. The steering engines of the 14-inch gun class were too weak for them to operate in the currents of the Dardanelles without the help of tugs. Any attempt to try and force the Narrows with them would certainly have posed a problem. In the smaller 9·2-inch and 6-inch gun types the exhaust fumes from the funnels were apt to stifle bridge personnel, and certain deck weaknesses also became apparent. Incidentally, it may not be generally known that the bulges fitted to the larger monitors were not for protection but to reduce their draft.

The bulge cruisers were the *Theseus*, Captain A. K. Macrorie; *Endymion*, Captain A. Vyell Vyvyan (late Beachmaster, Anzac); *Edgar*, Captain D. L. Dent (late *Irresistible*); and *Grafton*, Captain H. E. Grace (son of W. G., the great cricketer). The general idea of the bulge-blisters, as they were called, was to make a torpedo explode on impact with the outer casing of the blister, thus minimising the effect on the hull itself which could be as much as twelve feet away with a steel bulkhead and a water compartment in between. Of course one effect of the bulge was to reduce the ship's normal speed, and another was to make her float higher in the water, thus offering a larger target. However, a firing platform of greater stability was a distinct advantage. After Jutland some battleships of the Grand Fleet were fitted with blisters. Our ship the *Revenge* was one of them.

Although U-boats were arriving in the Aegean in increasing numbers, the killings were really suprisingly small. Many of their commanders must have been an unenterprising lot. But not all were. Lieutenant von Heimburg, for example, commanding *UB-14*, one of the small boats assembled at Pola, entered the Dardanelles early in July for refit at Constantinople before returning to the Aegean. While lurking near his secret base in the Dodecanese on August 13th, he sank the transport to *Royal Edward* on passage from Egypt to Mudros with 31 military officers and 1,335 other ranks, mostly details for the 29th Division, on board. The Captain managed to send a message before his ship was sunk and two French trawlers and the hospital ship *Soudan* rushed to her assistance, but there were less than 500 survivors.

On September 2nd *UB-14* struck again, this time at the troop-carrier *Southland*, also on passage from Egypt to Mudros but by a different route. She carried 1,400 men, mostly from the 2nd Australian Division. This time, however, thanks to the skill and courage of her Captain and all on board, both naval and military, and to the help rendered by H.M.S. *Racoon*, Lieutenant-Commander H. N. M.

Hardy, the *Southland* was brought into Mudros and was anchored in shallow water. Her casualties were few.

On September 4th *UB-14* entered the Dardanelles, dropping anchor near the fortress of Chanak. Here von Heimburg found another job waiting for him, and a little later on yet another handed to him almost on a plate. Perhaps he was born under a lucky star, but he certainly knew how to seize his opportunities.

19

The Tattered Battalions

*'The men of the tattered battalion which fights till it
dies,
Dazed with the dust of battle, the din and the cries,
The men with the broken heads and blood running into
their eyes,
Of these shall my song be fashioned, my tale told.'*
John Masefield
A Consecration

In May there were no flies. In June they came by armies; in July by
multitudes. They came fresh from tins of putrefying food cast into
no-man's-land, from blackening bodies in the scrub or on the wire,
and from the excrement in the Turkish trenches.

These bloated flies alighted on the moisture of your lips, your eyes,
your nostrils; they dropped on each morsel of food and pursued it
into your mouth and down your throat . . .

Dysentery raged. It became universal. Everybody had it. In any
normal campaign every man of them would have been sent on a
stretcher to the base. Yet, in spite of all this, of the heat, the flies, the
stench, the disease and the frustration, yes, frustration, for being
held up, unable to get ahead, in spite of all this the Army's spirit
never faltered.

It was in these circumstances that it became important to gain
more room at Helles and by repeated assaults to push the enemy's
lines further back from the beaches. Orders were issued for another
general attack to take place on June 4th.

Early that morning Sir Ian Hamilton crossed to Helles from
Imbros with his headquarter staff and took up a position on high
ground above Cape Tekke. Here he was joined by General Gouraud,
who on May 14th had taken over from the original French commandant, General d'Amade, the latter having found the prolonged
strain too great for nerves weakened by illness.

For the forthcoming battle, known as the Third Battle of Krithia,

General Hunter-Weston's VIII Corps, consisting of the remains of the 29th Division (now under command of Major-General de Lisle, a cavalry officer from France), the Sikhs and Gurkhas of Major-General Cox's Indian Brigade, the 42nd (East Lancashire) Division (Territorials) under Major-General W. Douglas and the Royal Naval Division (Major-General Paris), occupied the left and centre of the line. The French and their Colonials of two divisions were as usual on the right.

Although U-boats were still showing themselves, Admiral de Robeck had agreed to support the attack with two battleships well covered by destroyers and indicator nets. But the ships had to keep moving, and indirect fire at unseen targets while under way was worth little beyond its moral value. Still the attack opened brilliantly.

It was a day of overpowering heat, with the usual dust-storm obscuring everything. At 8 a.m. the preparatory bombardment began afloat and ashore and was kept up till 11.20, when the order was given to fix bayonets and to show them over the parapet. This was to bring the enemy into their advanced trenches to meet the attack.

But that hour was not yet; the real bombardment had not begun. Only when the enemy trenches were full did it burst forth, to be maintained for half an hour with steadily increasing intensity.

This devastating barrage lifted at noon, and from end to end of the line the men sprang from their trenches. Bayonets were fixed crossing no-man's-land, and in spite of a stubborn resistance the effect was all that could be wished.

On the right the French, well backed by the cruiser *Latouche-Tréville*, swept into the formidable works on the Kereves Dere, which had so long held them up. On their left Anson Battalion of the R.N.D. rushed a redoubt quite in army old style, and the Howe and Hood battalions captured the trenches in front of them. The Collingwoods, which were sent in support, suffered rather heavily.

Further on the left the Manchester Brigade, with whom were the 5th Lancashire Fusiliers, did very well. In five minutes they had poured over the first-line trenches, and in half an hour they were masters of the second line, 500 yards further on. On their left again, the 29th Division, including the Indian Brigade, were able to win the first enemy line. On the extreme left, however, which was dead ground for the ships, there was unfortunately no progress.

Still all promised well. The Manchesters were lying out on the slopes of Achi Baba with nothing between them and the coveted summit, waiting only for the word to go on. But that word never came.

On the extreme right, by the Kereves Dere, the work the French had so gallantly captured proved a death-trap. They were simply blasted out of it by high explosive and under an overwhelming counter-attack were forced back to their starting-point.

The Royal Naval Division, with its right now exposed by the French retirement, was cruelly enfiladed and forced to let go its hold, leaving the Manchesters in their turn in the air. They were got away by sunset, but only at the cost of heavy casualties.

So June 4th, which had begun with so much promise and had brought us almost within reach of the vital height, ended with no gain beyond the central sections of the enemy's first line trenches. It was little enough for what it had cost in death, wounds and heroic endeavour.

In 86 Brigade the Royal Fusiliers had only 2 officers left, the former Sergeant-Major and the Quartermaster, and only 140 men out of all those who had originally come out from home. All 10 officers who had joined recently were now casualties. The 1st Lancashire Fusiliers, whose casualties had already been appalling, had a further 14 officers and 500 men, killed and wounded. The Hampshires (88th Brigade) had fared still worse, having only about 100 of their original men left and no officers at all.

The Royal Naval Division had suffered 1,170 casualties, including 40 officers. Their losses were so severe that the Benbow and Collingwood Battalions had to be disbanded, their survivors being absorbed into the remaining three battalions, the Hood, the Howe and the Anson. Denis Browne, Rupert Brooke's friend, and Bernard Freyberg's brother were numbered among the dead. 'My dearest Jack,' Churchill wrote on June 12th to his brother who was Camp Commandant, G.H.Q. Staff '. . . Poor Naval Division. Alas the slaughter has been cruel. All are gone whom I knew. It makes me wish to be with you . . . Your loving brother, W.'[1]

'By July 5th the Indian Brigade had shot its bolt,' wrote Lieutenant Reggie Savory, 14th Sikhs. 'All its four battalions had been decimated. The 14th, with little more than ninety men, had to be amalgamated with the 10th Gurkhas, who themselves had only a subaltern in command. The 5th and 6th Gurkhas, in a like state, were also combined. We were all then relieved and sent to Imbros for a rest. Twice our numbers had been reduced to less than a hundred men. Now we were no more than a band of survivors.

'We had been on the Peninsula for two months. Our men, all Sikhs, had never turned, never wavered, never complained. They had been helped in battle, by the ingrained antipathy of the Sikh for the Mussulman, but by now they had had enough. To state that their morale was high would be an over-statement, but it certainly was not low.

'Their wants were simple. Their chief request was for sarson-oil, with which to anoint their long hair and their beards, which during the past weeks had become grey and grubby with the dust and dirt of the trenches. They were non-smokers to a man, so were not worried by the shortage of the tobacco ration. A tot of rum, how-ever, they appreciated. They cooked their *chapāti* on iron sheets laid over wood fires and traded them now and again with British soldiers for a loaf of bread.

'Otherwise they kept to themselves. Their comments on their fellow-warriors were in general non-committal, except perhaps for the Senegalese troops of the French contingent, whom they referred to as *Habshi log* – wild men.

'My sepoys looked upon me as if I were one of their younger brothers,' Reggie Savory [b. 26th July 1894] concluded. 'We had been through dangers and discomforts together, and there was a feeling of community among us. One night, while trying to snatch some sleep, I was disturbed by a Sikh bending over me in the cold early dawn. It was a fleeting moment and I was soon asleep again. It was too dark to recognise him but it was an action I shall never forget. He had covered me with a blanket, probably his own.'[2]

Here is a letter written at this time by the Commander-in-Chief to his wife, Jean. It gives a hint that he had begun to realise how lack of success to date might be followed by a lack of confidence in his ability to succeed at all.

'5:6:15.
   'I was in battle all yesterday. . . . The troops did splendidly, but these Turks are so fortified and so entrenched, and they bring up so many fresh troops that we can only gain ground by continued ghastly sacrifices.
   'I suppose all these conspirators and intriguers will begin to occupy themselves with poor me before long . . .'

Further attacks on the Helles front were made throughout June and July, and both sides suffered severe casualties. Our position was strengthened, though there were no decisive gains. Two brigades of the 52nd Division had arrived, and a third was due. The 52nd was a territorial division, the 'Lowland', commanded by

Major-General H. A. Lawrence, son of the great Lord Lawrence of Indian Mutiny fame.

The Turks asked for a truce on July 10th to bury their piles of dead. They made the request – according to our Intelligence – because their men were refusing to charge over the corpses of their comrades.

'Dead Turks are better than barbed-wire,' said Sir Ian, 'and so, though on grounds of humanity as well as health, I should like the poor chaps decently buried, I find myself forced to say No.'[3]

20

No Page More Wonderful

'*Naval history of Britain contains no page more wonderful than that which describes the prowess of her
submarines at the Dardanelles. Their exploits constitute the finest example of submarine warfare in the whole
of the Great War.*'
Winston Churchill
The World Crisis, 1915

While every effort was being made to frustrate U-boat attacks, a
vigorous offensive measure was also in operation.

As early as 13th December 1914, before naval operations had begun
in earnest, Lieutenant Norman Holbrook had entered the Dardanelles in the coastal class submarine *B-11*, with orders to torpedo
anything he could get at. Holbrook dived off Cape Helles, hugged
the European shore and slowly made his way against the current.
After passing safely under five rows of moored mines he reached the
approaches to the Narrows at 10 a.m. Here he sighted a large two-
funnelled vessel painted grey and flying a Turkish ensign. He fired
a torpedo and gave the order to dive deep. As his boat dipped, he
heard the explosion and, putting up his periscope saw the vessel
settling by the stern. So far so good, but he had now to make the
return journey and to the danger of the minefield a fresh peril was
added, in that the lenses of the compass had become so badly fogged
that steering by it was no longer feasible. He was not even sure
where he was but calculated he must be in Sari Sighlar Bay, ten
miles from the entrance, which proved to be true. Several times,
caught by eddies, he bumped bottom as he ran along submerged at
full speed, but the risk of ripping open the submarine had to be
taken. It was not until half an hour had passed and he judged that the
mines must by then be behind him that he put up his periscope again.
There was now a clear horizon to be seen on his starboard hand, and
he steered for it, taking peeps from time to time to correct his course
since the compass was still unserviceable. Not till he returned to base,

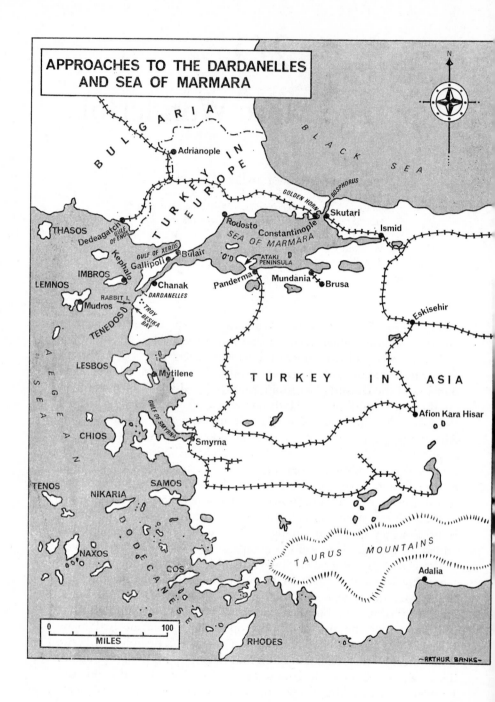

APPROACHES TO THE DARDANELLES
AND SEA OF MARMARA

N

BULGARIA

Adrianople

TURKEY IN EUROPE

BLACK SEA

GOLDEN HORN

BOSPHORUS

Skutari

THASOS

Dedeagatch
GULF OF ENOS

Rodosto

Constantinople

Ismid

SEA OF MARMARA

Kephalo
GULF OF XEROS
Gallipoli

Bulair

ATAKI PENINSULA

IMBROS

Panderma

Mundania

Brusa

LEMNOS

RABBIT I.
Mudros

Chanak
DARDANELLES

Eskisehir

TROY
BESIKA BAY

TENEDOS

TURKEY   IN   ASIA

LESBOS

Mytilene

Afion Kara Hisar

A E G E A N   S E A

GULF OF SMYRNA

CHIOS

Smyrna

TENOS

SAMOS

NIKARIA

TAURUS   MOUNTAINS

DODECANESE

NAXOS

COS

Adalia

0   100
MILES

RHODES

~ARTHUR BANKS~

after being nine hours under water, did he learn that the vessel he had torpedoed was the Turkish cruiser *Messudieh*. For this daring exploit Holbrook was awarded the V.C.

After *B-11's* successful exploit an urgent request was made for some of our latest E-class submarines, which should be capable of penetrating the 30 miles into the Sea of Marmara and of reaching the Golden Horn 110 miles further on. Unfortunately no E boats were available till April 1915. In the meanwhile the French submarine *Saphir* arrived off the Dardanelles with a new battery which her commandant declared would take her 140 miles at 5 knots without recharging. I believe he was forbidden by his Admiral to pass through the minefields without special permission, but on 15th January 1915, while diving on patrol at the entrance to the Straits, he apparently could not resist the temptation of trying to eclipse *B-11's* achievement. He did succeed in passing the Narrows but then ran aground off Nagara Point and was lost.

The honour of commanding the first British submarine to attempt the passage into the Sea of Marmara went to Lieutenant-Commander Theodore Brodie of *E-15*. He took with him Lieutenant Clarence Stanhope Palmer, R.N.V.R., late H.B.M. Vice-Consul, Chanak, who had local knowledge.

The general idea was that *E-15* would arrive submerged at day-break April 17th, off Soghanli Dere, then carry on upstream, keeping in the middle of the channel, while our aeroplanes watched her passage and created a diversion by dropping bombs.

The start was made as planned, but at 6 a.m. heavy firing was heard upstream. After an interval of time Commander C. R. Samson, R.N.A.S., returned to report *E-15* aground on Kephez Point right under the guns of Fort Dardanos. Apparently she had been caught by the current and swept into shoal water but was undamaged. With him Samson had Brodie's twin brother Charles, who was also a submariner. He had volunteered to act in support of Theodore on this daring venture.

The Turks had opened fire on her even before she was aground. One shell killed the unfortunate Theodore Brodie as he was climbing through the conning-tower hatch to assess the situation; another burst in the ammonia tank, killing six men. The rest of the crew were obliged to take to the water to avoid being asphyxiated. They were rescued by the Turks and became prisoners of war.

Although these details were not all known till long afterwards, Admiral de Robeck assumed that *E-15* was still intact and determined to destroy her, no easy task considering how close she was to Fort Dardanos. The seriousness of the situation lay not so much in the probable loss of the first E-boat to enter the Straits as in the probability that the Turks would now obtain the free gift of a submarine, which, with a German crew, might do great damage both to our prestige and to our fleet. A second anxiety was that her secret and confidential books might fall into enemy hands.

We know now that Theodore Brodie had tried to get his craft afloat by emptying her tanks and going full speed astern and that all confidential material, including charts, was effectively burned by his two officers as a matter of routine the moment *E-15* grounded.

First de Robeck sent the old submarine *B-6*, Lieutenant R. E. Birch, with instructions to blow up *E-15* by torpedo, but she had difficulty in mastering the strong current. She did fire two torpedoes, one of which struck and sank an enemy tug alongside *E-15* but without touching *E-15* herself. Aeroplanes next tried to drop bombs on the stranded submarine but were driven off by anti-aircraft fire. Then, at nightfall, two destroyers, the *Scorpion*, Lieutenant-Commander Andrew B. Cunningham, with Charles Brodie on board, and the *Grampus*, Lieutenant-Commander R. Bacchus, went up the Straits to see what they could do. While they were stopped at the entrance waiting for darkness, there was a bump-bump-bump alongside the *Scorpion*. It was a torpedo from *B-6*, fired that morning, coming back with the stream. Since it was as dangerous as a live mine, Mr W. W. Thorrowgood, Gunner (T), who feared nothing, chased it in a dinghy and removed the pistol. When it was 'safe' he towed it back to the ship, where it was hoisted on board. It was returned to *B-6* next morning 'with the compliments of H.M.S. *Scorpion*'.

When the right moment after dark had arrived for the *Scorpion* and the *Bacchus* to have a try, they were picked up immediately by searchlights cleverly handled to screen the wreck. Although they steamed some distance above *E-15*'s reported position, being heavily shelled for their trouble but not hit, they failed to locate her.

Next morning, April 18th, the intrepid Norman Holbrook, V.C., took *B-11* in to see what he could do, but as luck would have it a fog came down, reducing visibility to nil.

In the afternoon the weather cleared, and yet another plan was devised. The *Triumph* and the *Majestic* would bombard *E-15*. As they approached, however, they were received with such a volume of shell that it was not feasible to get within 12,000 yards of their target, and to fire at that range would have been just waste of ammunition.

Finally, two picket boats, one from the *Triumph* with Lieutenant-Commander E. G. 'Kipper' Robinson (in charge of the operation), Lieutenant A. Brook-Webb, R.N.R., torpedo specialist, and Midshipman J. B. Woolley; and the other from the *Majestic* with Lieutenant Claude Goodwin also a torpedo specialist, were brought to bear. Both picket boats carried two torpedoes with dropping gear.

It was a pitch-black night as they crept up under the Gallipoli shore towards the point chosen for the final dash. All went well until they reached the bend before the Narrows, when two searchlight beams shot out of the darkness to light up both boats. In a moment the sea about them was boiling with shrapnel and bursting shell, while they were blinded by the glare of the searchlights. The determined Robinson, however, led on, and he had his reward. By almost a miracle neither boat had been touched, when suddenly the careless handling of a Turkish searchlight illuminated the wreck. It was only for a moment but long enough for the *Majestic*'s boat to fire her two torpedoes. What happened to them could not be seen, but there came a loud explosion and a blinding flash inshore. Almost at the same instant a shell burst in the boat's sternsheets, and she began to sink rapidly. Fortunately the other picket boat, which had also fired her two torpedoes, though apparently without result, was able to take off the last man just as the sinking craft went under. They had done their work, and their luck stood by them. Somehow the doubly laden boat managed to get back without being hit. Only one man had been lost.

In a club in Constantinople a few days later a group of German naval officers was seen to be having a heated discussion over this incident, but, as they were dispersing, one turned back and was heard to say:

'*Man muss ihren Schneid bewundern!* – One cannot but admire their pluck!'

Much capital is made out of the loss of *E-15* in the Naval Museum, Istanbul. For instance there is a photograph of Turkish soldiers crowding on and around the conning tower to get into the picture, also an imaginative painting of British survivors surrendering, part of a 14-inch torpedo and poor Theodore Brodie's uniform cap, although it is not his cap in spite of the caption, since it belonged to an officer of the Royal Naval Reserve. The lettering R.N.R. is embodied in the cap-badge round the 'foul' anchor, under the crown. To my certain knowledge the same cap has been there twenty years.

The next submarine to make the attempt was the Australian *AE-2*, Lieutenant-Commander H. G. Stoker, Royal Navy. On April 25th, while the landings were in progress, he most gallantly and skilfully dived through and under the minefields and succeeded in entering the Sea of Marmara – the first British submarine to do so. There for five days he attacked enemy shipping, but, on April 30th, while diving to escape the attentions of the Turkish torpedo-boat the *Sultan Hisar*, his submarine got out of control. As he was alternately breaking surface and descending to a great depth, the enemy scored a hit. Stoker ordered his crew to swim for it and went below alone to open the sea cocks.

'"Hurry, Sir, she's going down!" came an anxious voice from above,' wrote Stoker. So, grabbing his dispatch-case from a shelf in the wardroom (it contained some money which was bound to be useful) he dashed up the ladder, reaching the bridge just in time. The water was about two feet from the top of the conning tower; and only a small portion of the stern was out of water. On this were clustered the last half-dozen of the crew, the remainder being already overboard.

'Curious incidents impress one at such times,' Stoker continued. 'As those last six men took to the water, the neat dive of one of the engine-room ratings will remain pictured in my mind for ever.

'Perhaps a minute passed, and then, slowly and gracefully, like the lady she was, without sound or sigh, without causing an eddy or a ripple on the water *AE-2* slid away on her last and longest dive.'[1] Captain and crew were made prisoners of war.

The currents in the entrance to the Dardanelles between Kum Kāle and Sedd el Bahr made passage for submarines very difficult. At a depth of about 60 feet strong whirlpools were encountered, which effected steering. Inside the Dardanelles, however, it was found that at a depth of 80 to 100 feet there was no current. Below that there was a counter-current.

A great deal of fresh water flows through the Bosphorus into the Sea of Marmara and is of lighter density than sea water. A submarine diving from the fresh water stratum near the surface into the heavier stratum below would be liable to lose control, much as happens when an aircraft encounters an air pocket.

Other submarines subsequently shared *AE-2*'s experiences though not her fate. On the contrary, they soon learnt to make good use of this phenomenon. When it was unsafe to stay on the surface, or too deep to sit in the bottom, by carefully adjusting their buoyancy they learnt to rest in suspension on the heavier strata which were generally found at a depth of about 60 feet.

On April 27th Lieutenant-Commander Courtney Boyle brought *E-14* into the Dardanelles at 2 a.m. His experiences were similar to those of Stoker in *AE-2*. Proceeding on the surface under cover of darkness, until he reached the first minefield, where fire from the shore batteries forced him down, he then went deep to dive under the mines, while the crew listened to the mooring wires scraping along her hull. The second minefield, just below Chanak, was even more of a trial, as progress was painfully slow against the strong current, and Boyle decided that he might well be safer passing over the mines as under them. Accordingly he came to the surface. Trimmed down so that only the top of his conning-tower was above the water, he steered through the Narrows at full speed. Inevitably he was sighted, and the batteries opened fire, but the smallness of the target and the high speed made *E-14* difficult to hit. So he got past the Narrows in safety until above Chanak he was forced to dive by a patrol of surface craft, one of which, a torpedo-boat, he sank. He was then horrified to discover that he could see nothing through his periscope. Unable to imagine the reason for this, he raised his second periscope and through it saw an elderly Turkish fisherman in a rowing-boat trying to pull the first periscope out of the water. His hand was over the top glass, shutting out the light.

In spite of losing his consort, *AE-2*, three days later, Boyle did much to dislocate the build up of reinforcements and supplies which followed our landings of April 25th. When all his torpedoes had been expended he again ran the gauntlet of forts and mines to reach the open sea on May 18th and was escorted in triumph into Mudros.

It was now the turn of our French allies to show their metal, and they were eager to do so.

On April 30th the *Bernoulli* had a try, but while attempting to operate above the Narrows she was caught in the current and swept out again. She was followed on May 1st by the *Joule*, which unfortunately fouled a mine and was lost with all hands. The *Mariotte* tried next, on July 26th, but was equally unlucky. She met an obstruction near the Chanak batteries, and in her struggle to free herself she rose unexpectedly, exposing her conning-tower. To make matters worse, there was a mine attached to her bows. Then she received damage from enemy gunfire which made further diving impossible, and her captain had no choice but to abandon ship. After wrecking the machinery and making sure that the *Mariotte* would sink, he ordered the conning-tower hatch to be opened and the boat abandoned. Officers and crew were all taken prisoner, to the great regret of their British colleagues.

It was our turn again, and the news this time was good, indeed the best ever, because Lieutenant-Commander Martin Nasmith, the greatest of them all, had arrived on the scene with *E-11*. Though fired at whenever his periscope showed, he reached the Marmara on May 19th. Proceeding to the eastern end of that sea, where patrols were less active, he seized a small sailing vessel and, trimming well down, lashed her alongside the conning-tower. It was an ingenious idea, though the ruse failed. Casting off the disguise, he went to try his luck elsewhere.

At first nothing but small game could be found in the open until, on the morning of May 24th, a small steamer hove in sight. When ordered to stop, she ignored the order. *E-11*'s gun had not yet been fitted, so Nasmith had to use a rifle, but the effect of a few rounds of ·303 was startling. The Turkish crew panicked and managed to capsize a couple of their boats while lowering them. Nasmith's men had to come to their assistance.

During the confusion a sedate figure appeared on the upper deck and introduced himself. 'Silas Q. Swing of the *Chicago Sun*,' he said, which was not strictly true as he was really Raymond Gram Swing, writer and later broadcaster of the well-known 'Letters from America' on B.B.C. radio. 'Tell that guy to stop pooping at us with his shot gun. I'm headed for Chanak, dog-gone it, to get some dope of what's happening over here.'

'Are there any military supplies on board?' he was asked.

'I don't know what the heck this vessel's carrying. I'm only here for the ride.'

The First Lieutenant, D'Oyly-Hughes, went on board to make a search. He found a 6-inch gun lashed down on deck, its mounting in the for'd hold, its ammunition aft. On deck he found cases marked Krupp, the big German armanent firm.

Mr Swing was invited to join the crew in one of the boats and for the time being to forget about Chanak. The waiting world would have to wait while they made for the shore under oars, a long pull. A demolition charge was placed in the steamer and 'Silas Q. Swing' saw his quick means of transport slide out of sight.

'Come on you guys, hit those oars and let's get the hell out of here.'

Nasmith smiled and waved a hand while *E-11* proceeded on her way.

Next day, May 25th, shortly after midday, at the fatal hour when the *Triumph* was sinking, *E-11* was off the entrance to the Bosphorus, where, to use Nasmith's own words, 'he dived into Constantinople'. Rising close to the United States guardship, he saw a large vessel lying alongside the arsenal. She was the storeship *Stambul* and on her his blow fell. The first torpedo failed to run true and came back towards the submarine. The second went straight for the target, but the result could not be seen, for *E-11* was suddenly swept aground by a cross-tide. But two explosions were heard, so that both torpedoes must have taken effect somewhere.

'As for the *E-11*, she behaved like a thing intoxicated by the wild adventure. Bouncing from shoal to shoal and spinning round with the current, she was out of control and in acute danger. Yet she survived. When, after some twenty minutes, she was calm enough to come to the surface she found herself well clear of the entrance. Nasmith headed for the centre of the Marmara, and when out of sight of land he stopped engines to call all hands on deck for prayers.

'The material result of this unprecedented exploit was not great, but the moral effect was all that could be desired. On the shore there was panic. Troops were disembarked, shops closed. For over 500 years since the Turkish flag first flew on the city walls, no foreign enemy has ever desecrated the sacred waters of the Golden Horn.'[2]

Nasmith remained in the Sea of Marmara as active and successful as ever for another eleven days, until June 7th, when failing machinery warned him that it was time to return.

He had passed the Narrows, diving deep to clear the minefield beyond, when a nasty grating sound started as if the boat was touching bottom when no bottom was near. One of his for'ard hydroplanes had fouled the mooring of a mine. With both shores bristling with guns Nasmith had no choice but to carry on with their new and evil shipmate. For an hour the nightmare continued till they were clear of the entrance. Nasmith then trimmed his vessel so that while her bows were submerged her stern was afloat. In this position he reversed his motors until, after a breathless interval, the way she had on her, combined with the rush of water from the screws, caused the mine mooring to slip free and to drop off ahead like a necklace.

Everyone on board breathed freely again.

For their exploits in the Marmara, both Nasmith, and Boyle of *E-14* received the V.C., and their crews were suitably rewarded.

On June 10th, three days after Nasmith's return in *E-11*, Lieutenant-Commander Courtney Boyle went up again in *E-14* and remained there for twenty-three days, keeping the whole sea in a state of disturbance.

E-12, Lieutenant-Commander K. M. Bruce, arrived on June 20th but was obliged to return with engine defects. *E-7*, Lieutenant-Commander A. D. Cochrane (great-grandson of the famous seaman Lord Dundonald), entered the Marmara on June 30th to take *E-20*'s place.

Cochrane's exploits against the enemy's rear communications included the bombardment of trains and of a railway viaduct. He also followed the example of Nasmith and dived into Constantinople. The strong current there swept him off course, and he grounded on a sandbank under the Leander Tower, his bows pointing directly at the Naval Arsenal. It was too good a chance to miss, and a torpedo was soon on its way. An explosion followed. *E-7* managed to slide off the sandbank without damage. That night, July 16th, *E-7* surfaced under the walls of the city and bombarded the Zeitun powder mills. The psychological effect was tremendous. It was rumoured in Constantinople that the British Navy had at last forced the Narrows and that invasion was imminent. Many of the inhabitants fled from the city into the surrounding countryside.

Early the following morning Cochrane saw something that boded no good to the British boats in the Sea of Marmara, especially as it turned out, for him. It was a destroyer towing a German submarine, the *UB-14* (Lieutenant von Heimburg), in the direction of Constantinople.

On July 21st, Cochrane was joined by Commander Courtney Boyle of *E-14*, who was making his third trip of twenty-three days. The policy of successive submarine commanders getting together was of particular value in this case. Boyle was able to tell Cochrane that a new peril was being added to the passage. The Turks were laying an anti-submarine net at Nagara.

Three days later Cochrane had to face this obstruction on his way down. Fortunately it had not been properly moored and had dragged in the strong current, so he got through all right, but lower down the Strait he fouled not one but two mine moorings, one of which swung *E-7* right round head to stream and anchored her for half an hour. Cochrane had to use full power to free his vessel, with the result that when he reached the open sea his battery was completely exhausted. *E-7* had been submerged for eleven continuous hours. The strain on the crew was severe.

Nasmith brought *E-11* up for the second time on August 5th, which meant that the two holders of the V.C. were together during the opening days of the August offensive, the attack on the Sari Bair Ridge and the Suvla Bay landings. These important military events are not described till later; and though I run the risk of jumping the gun I believe that the prowess of our submarines can be more truly appreciated if told in this chapter.

Since the arrival of our submarines in the Sea of Marmara, the practice of occasionally sending an old Turkish battleship into the Straits to harass shipping off Anzac, had been discontinued. But on the day of the Suvla landings, August 6th, the Turkish Supreme Command made an urgent appeal for battleship support to raise the morale of the troops. 'If the enemy's new offensive is crowned with success and the Dardanelles fall,' he said, 'the fate of the Turkish Navy will be sealed in any case.'

'It was not an easy decision to make,' Admiral Souchon wrote in his War Diary. 'The ships had been lying idle in the Golden Horn for weeks and no convincing reason could be given for a refusal. I therefore yielded to the Army's pressure, in spite of the danger, and ordered the *Barbaros Hayreddin*, flying the broad pennant of Commodore Arif Bey, to sail from the Bosphorus after dark on August 7th with a quantity of ammunition and machine-guns for the Fifth Army.

'After entering the Sea of Marmara it was found that the little torpedo-boat, the only one available for escort duties, was unable to keep up, so the battleship proceeded on her way without anti-submarine protection. Several officers in the battleship, particularly her Executive Officer, Lieutenant-Commander Mehmed, joked about the ship being under special protection from Allah. Others, however, were in a more serious mood, knowing that on the Gallipoli Peninsula the fate of their country was in the balance at that very hour.

'The night passed off quietly, and as dawn began to break a zig-zag course was steered. The ship had just passed Bulair when she was struck by a torpedo and capsized, carrying 253 of her crew down with her, including the Executive Officer who had taken the voyage so cheerfully.'[3]

Needless to say this was the work of Nasmith in *E-11*, and for him the achievement had a special significance. In the early days of the war, while he was operating in the Heligoland Bight, a German battleship offered him a sitting target at very close range. But *E-11*'s torpedo passed harmlessly under its target. Nasmith was so annoyed with himself that he swore he would give up tobacco till he had sunk a battleship, and he proved as good as his word. After the satisfaction of seeing the *Barbaros Hayreddin* go down, he took *E-11* into the centre of the Marmara and when a safe distance from the shore brought his boat to the surface for a breath of fresh air, to charge his batteries and for the hands to bathe.

He did not have a dip himself. He had something better to do. He stood on the bridge, watching his men at play and happily smoking his pipe.

During the forenoon of August 12th *E-11* met *E-14* at a pre-arranged rendezvous. Boyle was taking *E-14* out that night. The two submarine crews spent much of the day exchanging experiences, a very valuable procedure.

Before parting company at 8 p.m. *E-14* shot her two remaining torpedoes out, and, when they bobbed to the surface – their engines were not running – they were grabbed from *E-11*'s dinghy by Petty Officer Axworthy, second Coxswain, and guided skilfully through *E-11*'s stern tube, leaving her the richer by two torpedoes. When *E-14* parted company, *E-11* dived to sixty feet where she remained for the night in suspension with motors stopped so that everyone could get some sleep, except one hand on watch at the diving gauges.

'On August 19th', Petty Officer Axworthy wrote in his diary, 'we rose to the surface at 6.30 a.m. and chased a dhow which was carrying a lot of wood. We took some off her and next day made a raft on deck for the First Lieutenant D'Oyly-Hughes to take ashore with a gun cotton charge to blow up Ismid railway bridge. At 2 a.m. he set off, shoving the raft in front of him. When he reached the shore he found a number of men working on the bridge, repairing the damage we had done bombarding it, so he walked along to the viaduct and laid his charge against the pillars. The explosion could be heard for miles.

'We were just about to give up hope of seeing him again when we heard a whistle blow. He had already once swum nearly out to us when he saw in the darkness what he thought to be two small boats, so swam back to the shore.

'He then realised that it was *E-11*'s bow and conning-tower that he had sighted, as we were trimmed down. We hauled him aboard much to our delight and relief. At 6.30 a.m. we turned away and dived.

'At 7.30 a.m. on August 22nd,' P.O. Axworthy continued, 'we opened fire on a torpedo-boat which ran off at full speed. We then turned our attention to the armed tug, with a sailing vessel in tow full of ammunition, which the torpedo-boat had been escorting. Giving the crews time to take to their boats, we sank both with our new gun, then called the boats alongside. All twenty men from the sailing vessel were completely naked with the exception of one who was wearing a pink vest. They had discarded all their clothes because they were really Turkish officers on their way to pay Turkish and German troops on the Peninsula. They told us that they had left thousands of pounds on board – now at the bottom of the sea. We kept them as prisoners and rigged them out with some clothes. At 3 p.m. we stopped a dhow loaded with water melons (and they were very nice, thank you). We put the prisoners on board and let them go . . .'

At 3.30 a.m. on September 2nd Nasmith took *E-11* back through the Narrows. He burst through the new boom defence at Nagara without difficulty, and brought his boat to the surface by the entrance to the Straits. He was escorted from there by H.M.S. *Grampus* into Kephalo Harbour, with cheers!

Pretty fair success had crowned our submarine efforts so far, but now there was to be a reverse.

On September 5th, *E-2*, Lieutenant-Commander Stocks, set off for a prearranged rendezvous with *E-7*, which was due to arrive on her second visit, but she was not there.

What had happened was that at 7.30 a.m. the morning before Lieutenant-Commander Cochrane had reached the Nagara net and, at 100 feet, had got *E-7's* bows through when a wire fouled one of her screws. He tried to make headway with the other propeller, but the result was to bring *E-7* broadside on and in a worse tangle than ever. The struggle went on for nearly twelve hours, while the batteries ran down, the air became foul, and there were signs that the lighting would fail.

Preparations were now made to bring the trapped submarine to the surface. It was Cochrane's last hope.

First, he burnt his confidential papers and made sure that the submarine would sink if the sea cocks were opened. Then explosive charges were rigged against the warhead of a spare torpedo, which, if fired, would destroy the boat in an instant. While these preparations were going on he advised his crew to take the pickings from the larder and have a square meal.

'If we fail to rise to the surface when the tanks are blown,' he
told them, 'or if on reaching the surface the wires which have fouled
our boat prevent the conning-tower hatch being opened, I shall have
no choice but to blow up *E-7* – which will at least destroy the net
defence system. The only alternative is a long drawn out torture of
death by suffocation, and we don't want that.'

While they were munching away at their meal there was a loud
bang close to the ship's side. Lights flickered, and the boat rocked,
capsizing a teapot on the mess table. Cochrane's decision was
swift.

'Diving stations!' he ordered.

'Stand by to Surface!'

'Blow Main Ballast!'

There was a tearing sound as *E-7* rose rapidly, bringing much of
the net defence with her. Mercifully the conning-tower hatch could
be opened. The men filed out. They had only a minute or two to get
away before *E-7* made her last dive.

Cochrane had planned that his submarine would blow up on her
way to the bottom, destroying the net defence in the process, but,
when he could not persuade Turkish boats engaged in rescue work
to keep clear, he ordered John Scarfe, his First Lieutenant, not to
light the fuse but to 'Come up out of it!'

Cochrane and all his crew were saved and made prisoners of
war.

What had caused the 'bang' against the hull, which had decided
Cochrane to bring *E-7* to the surface? It was the work of Lieutenant
von Heimburg of *U15-14*, who, after torpedoing the transports
Royal Edward on August 13th and *Southland* on September 2nd, already
mentioned, had anchored off Chanak that very morning, September 4th.

Seeing that one of our submarines was obviously caught in the net
and that the Turkish torpedo-boat which had arrived on the scene
and the Turkish gunners on shore were alike powerless, unless the
submarine could be brought to the surface, he took immediate action.
'A bundle of explosives were made up on board *UB-14* and attached
to a long line. This charge was lowered from a boat by Leading
Seaman Herzig and fired.'[4] Damage was negligible, but it had the
desired effect.

UB-14 was making history, had they known it. It was not long
before the real depth charge came into service, operated by a
hydrostatic valve set to a calculated depth, the most deadly weapon
of all against submarines.

Stocks now had to carry on alone with *E-2*. He planned to repeat the exploit of *E-11* against the enemy's railway communication between Constantinople and the battle area. The point he chose was where the Adrianople line runs close to the sea. His First Lieutenant, L. V. Lyon, volunteered to go, using similar apparatus to that used by D'Oyly-Hughes of *E-11*. Lyon was an unusually powerful swimmer, and his chances of success were regarded as good.

In the early hours of September 8th, *E-2* reached the point of disembarkation. Lyon slipped quietly into the water and with a last cheerful wave of the hand made for the shore. His shipmates watched him until he disappeared in the darkness and waited anxiously for the sound of an explosion, or a single pistol shot that would tell them Lyon was in trouble. Given it, *E-2* was to open fire on the railway station.

Minutes dragged into an hour. How slowly only those who stood on the conning-tower, staring into the darkness and straining their ears for every sound, will ever realise. Another hour crawled by and then another, each one longer than the last.

Day began to dawn. With dawn came a devastating explosion – but no signal from Lyon.

It was nearly daylight. *E-2* and her loyal crew still clung to the desperate hope that Lyon would return. Lieutenant-Commander Stocks held on as long as he dared, but shortly after 7 a.m. he was forced to submerge and put to sea. An hour later saw him back again cruising on the surface. He thought that Lyon might have secured a small boat and would be drifting somewhere off shore.

Next day at dawn *E-2* came again, still hoping. But no boat was seen, nor was Lyon ever heard of again; and nothing could be learnt from the Turks after the war.

On October 2nd the first of a new class of submarine, the *H-1*, which was little more than half the tonnage of the *Es*, was taken up by Lieutenant W. B. Pirie. Of British design but with American material, she had been built in Vickers Works, Montreal, Canada, in the record time of seven months. With others of her class she had been towed across the Atlantic.

H-1 carried two other officers, Lieutenant Clive Robinson, brother of 'Kipper', and Midshipman 'Jock' Bethell, who has the distinction of being the only midshipman to have seen service in a submarine in the Sea of Marmara. He told me he was only scared once and that was on the way up the Dardanelles the first time, when, instead of crashing through the net, *H-1* grounded on a sandbank. During the noise from Turkish shells falling, the blowing and flooding of tanks, engines going full speed astern, there was a sudden loud bang. 'I nearly had a heart attack,' Jock Bethell said, 'but it was only a clumsy sailor who had chosen that moment to drop a large electric light bulb on the deck of the control room.'

'One day we sighted a tiny dhow,' Petty Officer Oscar Moth, Second Coxswain of *H-1*, recorded in his diary. 'We came to the surface very close to her. Her only occupants proved to be a bearded old Turk and a small boy about seven. The old man was in a terrible panic, and the boy cried pitifully. I had a big lump in my throat when I saw the boy crying, and we did the best we could to comfort him. Of course we let him go, and the youngster soon dried his tears. The old man called down blessings on us, and, hoisting his sail, waved his hand. We talked a good deal about this incident, for the best part of us were married and the youngster's tears had touched our hearts.

'Next day we sighted a sail. There was a fresh breeze and she was going very fast. We had to go all out on both engines to get near her. As soon as she was within range we fired a round across her bows, and she hove to. We could see that there was a good deal of panic and that she carried a whole crowd of women. We hailed her, but the women got into such a state of terror that our captain decided not to go too close for fear they might jump overboard. We did our best to quieten them and told the man at the helm that he could continue his journey. The women showered blessings on us as the dhow sailed away.'

After a successful cruise which had lasted twenty-nine days Lieutenant Pirie took *H-1* down on October 31st. It was not an easy passage. None of them were.

'The destroyer *Basilisk* arrived to escort us to Kephalo,' Petty Officer Moth continued, 'where every ship from the largest battleship to the smallest monitor gave us three (I think it must have been thirty-three) cheers.

'One of the dhows we had searched carried a number of cases of umbrellas and goloshes, and we had helped ourselves to a case or two before we sank her. It was now raining hard, so for a skylark all hands on deck, including the captain, put up umbrellas as we entered harbour. When the time came to handle the wires – we were to berth alongside the Commander-in-Chief's flagship, the yacht H.M.S. *Triad* – the umbrellas were folded by numbers and 'grounded' as in rifle drill. Admiral de Robeck came on deck and had a good laugh.'

The French submarine *Turquoise* had arrived in October with a new battery. Admiral Guépratte sent her Commandant Ravenel to Commodore Keyes for briefing. He was given all necessary information, which included co-operation with our submarines and the rendezvous he was expected to make with them. Also, of course, copies of our signal books. The date of the attempt was fixed for October 22nd.

Inspired by this message from his Admiral:

'Vous avez une tâche merveilleuse. Les yeux de toute la
France sont tournés vers vous,'

it must be assumed that Ravenel entered the Dardanelles with confidence. Anyway he took the *Turquoise* safely under the mines and through the nets and, to everyone's relief, reached the Sea of Marmara. He was followed next day by *E-20*, and was sighted by *H-1* sitting on the surface flying an enormous tricolour, but Pirie avoided making his presence known. Some British submariners were not enamoured of their French colleagues, and it seems that Pirie was one of them.

On October 30th, after only eight days on patrol, Commandant Ravenel decided he had had enough. Without informing anyone of his intentions he set off for home.

Before reaching the Nagara net on the way down the Straits, *Turquoise* grounded on a shallow patch. When shore batteries opened fire and his periscope was damaged Ravenel brought his boat to the surface, showed a white flag and surrendered.

The *Turquoise* was captured intact. Commandant and crew, according to a German report, were in such a hurry to leave that they left all the lights burning and an alarm bell ringing.

The following entry was made by Ravenel in his War Diary on the third day of his arrival in the Sea of Marmara, which goes far to explain his unsatisfactory behaviour. Obviously the fellow had no guts.

'Grand Dieu quelle perspective atroce! Nous devons rester
ici 18 jours. Comment survivre à cela? C'est epouvantable.'

The *Turquoise* was refloated next day and towed to Constantinople where, after many mishaps and bad seamanship on the part of the Turkish Navy she arrived on November 5th. Her battery was not exhausted, and her machinery was O.K. She was re-named the *Mustejab Onbashy*, 'Worthy of Acceptance', in honour of the Turkish corporal who fired the shot that made her surrender. She was enrolled into the Turkish Navy and used as a charging station for

German U-boats. The sight of her lying in the Golden Horn gave the Turks much satisfaction.

We now come to the crisis of this distressing story.

In Commandant Ravenel's cabin in the *Turquoise* the enemy found his secret papers and War Diary which he had failed to destroy. They revealed details of the rendezvous at which the *Turquoise* was to meet *E-20* on November 6th. These details were rushed to Constantinople, where *UB-14*, Lieutenant von Heimburg, was under refit. *E-20*, expecting to meet a friend, was blown to pieces by the torpedo of a foe. Here is the enemy's own story.

'*UB-14* was ready for sea in the unbelievable time of twenty-four hours. We left Constantinople at 12.10 a.m. on November 6th and proceeded on the surface at full speed. At dawn we submerged so as not to be seen and set course for the rendezvous where *E-20* was due.

'The sea was as smooth as a mirror, and when the periscope was raised for a moment at 4 p.m. I could see the conning-tower of a submarine about five miles away. Half an hour later I looked again and she was still there, which was very nice of her. At 5.10 p.m., range 550 yards, I fired a torpedo and scored a hit. My men cheered.

'Surfacing immediately, I climbed on to the conning-tower and all I could see was a large patch of oil in which a few black spots were moving, which proved to be survivors.

'I closed them and called out in English – "How do you do?"

'"All right, Sir!" one of them replied.

'There were two groups. One consisted of six and the other of three men. We approached the former first and helped them on board, then we went for the other three, who turned out to be the Captain supporting two non-swimmers. They were shivering with cold and, like all submariners, very dirty.

'I greeted the Captain in a friendly manner, and we exchanged salutes. After cautioning him to refrain from committing any hostile act, I told him that he could take his men down below where they would be given dry clothes and a hot drink.

'It was now almost dark, so I decided to return to Constantinople on the surface at full speed.

'Of course I had to tell the Captain how we had learned of his rendezvous. The information left him speechless. Later I heard him discussing the situation with his officers. They were cursing their French allies as I had hoped.'[5]

The story does not end here. On November 11th, Commander von Korff, of S.M.S. *Breslau*, had occasion to visit one of the most exclusive hotels in Constantinople, where, to his fury, he found Lieutenant-Commander Clyfford Warren and his two officer survivors comfortably seated in the restaurant having dinner.

Mr Henry Morgenthau, the American Ambassador, had persuaded Enver Pasha to give all the survivors of the *E-20* five days parole. Immediate objections were raised by von Korff, and the privilege was withdrawn. Warren with his officers and men was sent to Seraskerat prison for questioning by the Turkish Intelligence, and from there to the infamous Afium Kara Hisar (Opium Black Fort) Prisoner-of-War camp in Asia Minor.

The *Turquoise* had been captured on October 30th and the *E-20* sunk on November 6th. Commandant Ravenel's notebook also names *E-12* (returned October 25th) and *H-1* (returned October 31st), but mercifully no mention of *E-11*, Commander Nasmith, who arrived in the Marmara on November 6th, the same day as *E-20* was sunk. It must have been a 'near miss' because November 7th found *UB-14* returning to the rendezvous after disembarking the survivors of *E-20* at Constantinople; also *E-11* making for the same rendezvous unaware that *E-20* had been sunk. On passage *E-11* was attacked by a German Taube aircraft and forced to crash dive. When Nasmith failed to meet *E-20* he did not wait but carried on with his patrol. *UB-14* hung around for a couple of days and then returned to Constantinople to complete her refit.

News that the *Turquoise* had been captured intact reached Admiral de Robeck on November 7th. On the same day the Gemans announced that our *E-20* had been sunk, but at the time there did not appear to be any connection between the two losses. Later the full story reached the Admiral's ears.

'The possibility,' wrote von Heimburg, 'of the American Ambassador Morgenthau or one or other of the many enemy subjects still living in the Turkish capital giving the warning cannot be denied.'[6]

He was just about right! I have heard it suggested that the Papal bag may have carried the message to our new ally in Rome.

With the loss of *E-20*, Nasmith with *E-11* was left single-handed from his arrival on November 6th until he was joined by *E-2*, Lieutenant-Commander Stocks, on December 10th.

One of Nasmith's first jobs was to land a secret service agent he had brought up with him.

'Our friend was an Armenian who had joined at Kephalo,' wrote Petty Officer Axworthy who helped to land him. 'He came on board dressed to look like a Greek and carried a sack on his shoulder. We fixed him up with quarters in the torpedo space and left him there, but it wasn't long before he came on deck disguised as a Turkish soldier. We landed him from the dinghy on the neck of Ataki Peninsula.

'As we approached the shore we could hear voices which seemed to be kept low, so we expected a warm reception.

'We knelt in the bottom of the boat, facing for'ard, paddling without oars so as not to make any noise. Everything was so quiet, too quiet to please us. The boat beached with a crunching noise which startled us. Our friend stepped out over the bows and then remembered he had left his overcoat in the stern of the boat. I picked it up to hand to him when a large Colt revolver fell out of a pocket into the bottom of the boat, making a terrible clatter. Then we did expect the balloon to go up, but no, all was well. We waited a few minutes while he crossed the beach, then shoved off quietly and returned to *E-11*. The Captain got under way and steered out to sea as soon as the dinghy was stowed.

'At 1.30 p.m. on December 3rd we observed the Turkish torpedo-boat *Yar Hisar* proceeding westwards towards the Bosphorus. Our torpedo struck her amidships. She broke in halves, each end sinking in less than two minutes.

'We rose to the surface at once to pick up survivors. The sea was rough and cold. We managed to rescue the Captain, one other officer and forty men out of a crew of eighty-five. Fifteen of the rescued men were Germans wearing the Iron Cross which they had won while serving on board the *Goeben* in the Black Sea.

'At 5 p.m. we met a sailing vessel, went alongside and transferred the survivors to her. They were shivering with cold, so our Captain gave them each a tot of rum to warm them up before they left us.'

When *E-2*, Lieutenant-Commander Stocks, joined on December 10th, Nasmith left him to look after the western half of the Sea of Marmara while he took *E-11* to the entrance to the Bosphorus. Here he remained a menace to Turkish shipping until December 23rd, when, narrowly escaping an attempt by a U-boat to torpedo him, he returned down the Straits in safety. His cruise had lasted 47 days; his total time in the Marmara was three days short of 100; he had sunk 96 vessels of various types. Each one of these achievements was a record.

E-11 had always patrolled with the words 'In all things ready' painted on her conning-tower. No one can deny that captain, officers and crew had lived up to their motto. Today the words are on display in the Outward Bound Moray Sea School where Admiral Sir Martin Dunbar-Nasmith V.C. was a founder member of the

29　By Karakol Dagh, Suvla Bay

30　Men of Kitchener's Army preparing for battle during the August offensive.
Note the white identification badges, men on the latrines (*left*) and around a
field kitchen (*right*)

31 Simpson and his donkey

32 14th (K.G.O.) Sikhs having 'elevenses'

33 1/6th Gurkhas

Board of Governors. The bell of *E-11* is in the submarine museum, H.M.S. *Dolphin*.

Out of 12 allied submarines which made, or attempted, entry into the Sea of Marmara, 6 had perished, 4 of them with all or nearly all hands. The bag included 1 battleship, 1 destroyer, 5 gunboats, 11 transports, 44 steamers and 148 other vessels.

Although not a single non-combatant is believed to have lost his life through our operations in the Sea of Marmara, the German Ambassador, Baron von Wangenheim, and the Turkish authorities were not slow to protest against what they called 'frequent violations of the Hague conventions'. This sort of propaganda was designed to impress neutrals and contained not a word of truth.

Turkish hospital ships crossing the Sea of Marmara were known to be carrying arms and ammunition on their downward journeys, so as a matter of routine they were stopped and searched. On their return journey to Constantinople our submarines generally remained out of sight as they had no wish to alarm the wounded.

The Turks admitted using transports as hospital ships, and it was therefore lawful for us to sink them, but neither Admiral de Robeck nor General Sir Ian Hamilton was willing to embitter the conflict by exacting the extreme penalty.

Admiral Eberhard von Mantey, the Official German Naval Historian, writing in *Der Krieg zur See*, summed up the situation admirably. I will close with his words:

'The activity of hostile submarines was a constant and heavy anxiety. They dislocated very seriously the conveyance of reinforcements to the Dardanelles and caused many disagreeable losses. If communication by sea had been completely severed, the Turkish Army would have been faced with catastrophe.'

21

The New Venture

On the Peninsula and in the fleet it was rumoured that Winston Churchill was coming to Gallipoli to judge the situation for himself. In fact on July 16th he had asked Mr Asquith, the Prime Minister, for a formal letter 'expressing your wish and that of my colleagues, that I should go'. Asquith replied the same day:

'My dear Winston,
  'I believe that your visit to the Dardanelles will secure for the Cabinet valuable information & suggestions in regard both to the future of the campaign & to our policy in that theatre of the War.
  'Your object will be to survey & report upon the situation, after Conference with the Commanding Officers. You will no doubt make it clear to the General & the Admiral that your mission is not dictated by any want of confidence in them, but by a wish to get into closer touch, so far as they are concerned.
  'They both enjoy, as they have deserved, our gratitude & trust.
                                                  'Yours always,
                                          H. H. ASQUITH.'

Churchill proceeded to make the necessary arrangements. He realised that he would come under fire and might be killed, so on July 17th he wrote a letter 'to be sent to Mrs Churchill in the event of my death'.

'... I am anxious that you shd get hold of all my papers, especially those wh refer to my Admiralty administration ... There is no hurry; but some day I shd like the truth to be known. Randolph will carry on the lamp. Do not grieve for me too much. I am a spirit confident of my rights. Death is only an incident, & not the most important wh happens to us in this state of being. On the whole, especially since I met you my darling one I have been happy, & you have taught me how noble a woman's heart can be. ...'[1]

The following day he set out formally, in a letter to Asquith, his reasons for the visit. In the first place should the coming attack fail to succeed, or succeeded only partially, he wished to be able to advise the Cabinet 'with the fullest knowledge upon the new & grave situation wh will then arise', adding that he could acquire this knowledge only on the spot. Secondly, if a decisive victory is won, he would be 'at hand shd the Govt decide to send a special mission to Sofia or Athens, in order to reap to the full extent the fruits of the victory'.

While Churchill's plans went forward Kitchener was beginning to doubt the wisdom of his going unaccompanied. 'I wish you would send Hankey with him,' he wrote to Asquith on July 17th. 'I am sure it would be a wise step & very useful to me'. Asquith at once agreed to Kitchener's request. In the event Churchill did not go because of a division of opinion in the Cabinet. Lieutenant-Colonel Maurice Hankey, Secretary to the Committee of Imperial Defence, went alone.

Hankey arrived at Mudros in H.M.S. *Chatham*, Captain Drury-Lowe, on the morning of July 26th. There he transferred to a destroyer for onward passage to Imbros to report to Sir Ian Hamilton at G.H.Q.

The following letter in the Admiral's own handwriting does suggest that Hankey's visit was not altogether welcome. His age was thirty-eight compared with Churchill's forty-one, de Robeck's fifty-three and Hamilton's fifty-nine. Perhaps that had something to do with it. Yet Hankey had admitted before starting that he might be regarded as a 'government spy'.

'H.M.S. *Triad*
Wednesday.

'My dear General,
  'Re Hankey, I quite understand; Have no fear, it was never my intention to let him loose at Mudros, only to transport him! If you think it would do him good he shall come in a trawler, though it was my intention to let him come in something that goes quicker!
                              'Yours sincerely,
                              J. M. de ROBECK.'[2]

But all was well. 'A General Staff Officer has been told off to help him,' Sir Ian wrote a few days later. 'I am not going to dry nurse him. He showed me of his own free will a copy of a personal cable he had sent to Lord Kitchener in which he says, speaking of his first visit to Anzac, "Australians are superby confident and spoiling for a fight." This is true, and I feel it is good that one who has the ear of the insiders should say it. Actually I am very glad to have him. Lies are on the wing, and he, armed with the truth, will be able to knock some of them out.'[3]

A couple of days after his arrival Colonel Hankey wrote to his wife Adeline telling her about his visit to Anzac on July 28th.

'Anzac is the most extraordinary place you can possibly imagine. Approaching the shore one is within comparatively close range of the Turkish batteries and they nearly always shell the boat but never hit it . . . I had a long talk in a "dug-out" with General Birdwood, who is one of the best generals we have, and, after lunching with his Chief of Staff, I went off to visit the trenches.'

Then follows a description of the 'artificial "dug-outs" or caves in which the Australian and New Zealanders live, together with teaming swarms of flies! Through a wonderful system of communication trenches with temperature of, I suppose, over 100°F . . . These Australian trenches are the most wonderful thing in the world and far better than anything I have seen in France. The men also are wonderful, huge, strong, intelligent soldiers, devoid of nerves, full of wonderful cunning, every man thinking of nothing but how to beat the enemy. I don't believe we have anything to touch them . . . In the trenches one is absolutely safe, but the beaches are dangerous to the last degree, for sudden death stalks abroad there.'

In a letter written two days later to his wife Hankey gives an account of his impressions on landing at Cape Helles:

'We saw over the old fort of Sedd-el-Bahr which was knocked to pieces by our naval guns. Then they took me to see the French C-in-C, an old chap of 68 named Bailloud, who only got the command through the wounds or sickness of his superiors. He is a notorious pessimist, not only about the Dardanelles but about the whole war, and more than hinted that the English are not trying. I had a fearful wrangle and went for him tooth and nail in fluent but faulty French, to the great amusement of two French staff officers who were present . . . You know exactly the arguments I used and he referred to me as *"un officier tant intelligent que vous, monsieur! ! !"* We parted quite good friends, and I felt that he had not had the better of me . . .

'We did not get back [to G.H.Q. Imbros] until after 9 p.m. . . . I was very tired and thirsty and glad to get to bed. Considering I was on the bare ground except for the valise I slept very well but was woken at 5 a.m. by the loathsome flies which pollute all parts of the Gallipoli Peninsula . . .'[4]

'Admiral Wemyss came over from Mudros and saw me,' Sir Ian wrote on July 27th. 'He is . . . an interesting man and a Keyesite; i.e. he'd go right through the Straits to-morrow, – or go under . . . These rival tenets are straining the fabric of the Fleet, but, as I constantly tell our General Staff, my course is as clear to me as a pikestaff. I back the policy of the *de facto* Naval Commander-in-Chief – my own coadjutor. There is temptation to do wrong, but I resist it. What would it not be to me were the whole Fleet to attack as we land at Suvla! But obviously I cannot go out of my own element to urge the Fleet to actions, the perils of which I am incompetent to gauge.'[5]

Sir Ian was always loyal to Kitchener, though starved by him of men and munitions, and he was now loyal to de Robeck although his, Sir Ian's, wish was for a grand assault to be mounted by both the Army and Navy. On August 3rd he wrote these words in his own bold handwriting on two sheets of foolscap.

'Dined with Admiral de Robeck in "Triad". Several of his Staff are mad to have a smack at the Narrows and to make their push *through* at the very moment we make our push *across*. I know from Braithwaite these chaps would like me to urge the Admiral to play a leading part in the game instead of a waiting one.

'This *I will not do*. The Admiral has not this time said one word to me as to active co-operation . . . I mind my own business, he minds his – that's all. Were he a timid, cautious type of man I might feel justified in giving him a prod, but I never heard anyone say that of de Robeck.'[6]

Sir Ian's determination not to mention the subject of naval co-operation unless the Admiral raised the matter first, was in keeping with the attitude he had adopted at the Council of War on board the *Queen Elizabeth* at Mudros on March 22nd. It was held, you will remember, after the Allied Fleet had failed to force the Straits on March 18th: 'Before ever we went aboard,' Sir Ian wrote at the time, 'we agreed that, whatever we landsmen might think, we must leave the seamen to settle their own job, saying nothing until the sailors themselves turned to us . . .'

This holding back on the eve of battle is not in keeping with modern thinking; nor is it likely to have occurred in World War II with a Supreme Commander to adjudicate.

In early July three divisions of reinforcements began to arrive. All were formed from 'Kitchener's Army', and were without experience of active service. They comprised the 13th (Western) Division under Major-General Shaw, the 11th (Northern), Major-General Hammersley, and the 10th (Irish), Lieutenant-General Sir Bryan Mahon. They were variously disposed, some at Mytilene (Lesbos), some at Mudros and Imbros and some with the divisions at Helles to gain experience, which served them well. The infantry of two territorial divisions were also promised – the 53rd (Welsh) and the 54th (East Anglian) – but they did not arrive till August 10th and then at only half normal strength with no guns.

When it was decided to group the three new divisions into an army corps, Sir Ian Hamilton had asked Lord K. on June 15th for a Corps Commander. He suggested Byng or Rawlinson, saying in his message 'that in that position only men of good stiff constitution and nerve will be able to do any good'.

Lord Kitchener replied immediately: 'I am afraid that Sir John French [C-in-C, B.E.F., France] would not spare the services of the two generals you mention, and they are, moreover, both junior to Mahon, who commands the 10th Division which is going out to you.'

'Oh God,' Sir Ian wrote. 'This block by Mahon makes a record for seniority fetish ... There *are* only about one dozen British Service Lieutenant-Generals senior to Mahon, and, of that dozen only two are *possible* – Ewart and Stopford! There *are* no others. Ewart is a fine fellow ... But he would not, with his build and constitutional habit, last out here one fortnight ... He has never approached troops for fifteen years, although I have often implored him, as a friend, to do so. Would not Stopford be preferable to Ewart, even though he does not possess the latter's calm?'

Sir Ian sent a cable to Lord K. expressing his 'deep disappointment that Mahon should be the factor which restricts all choice', adding, 'I will do my best with what you send me.'[7]

The fatal decision was then made.

Lieutenant-General the Hon. Sir Frederick Stopford entered the Grenadier Guards in the early seventies, and saw the usual service of officers of his generation in India, West Africa and Egypt. During the South African War he was Military Secretary to General Buller and entered Ladysmith with him at the Relief. His reputation stood high as a student and teacher of military history, but he had never held high command in the field, either in peace or in war. And he retired in 1909.

Stopford reached Imbros on July 11th and was put in temporary command of VIII Corps at Cape Helles to give him experience in the kind of fighting required of his forces when in command of IX Corps, now gradually concentrating for the new venture.

The vacancy in VIII Corps had been caused by the departure on sick leave of General Hunter-Weston, who had never spared himself nor his men and had endured all their perils when in command of the immortal 29th Division and latterly of VIII Corps. Now, made haggard by the strain of too much work and too much unrequited optimism, he had fallen ill of the prevailing dysentery and had to be invalided.

'Towards the end of July,' wrote Lieutenant Geoffrey Rylands, 'I was lent to the destroyer *Arno* from the *Ark Royal*, to point out to the newly-arrived senior military officers the salient features of the landscape north from Gaba Tepe, round Suvla Point into the Gulf of Xeros.

'I suppose at the age of twenty-five most people over forty-five look old, but I was shocked at the apparent age of some of these officers and wondered how they would be able to stick the very unhealthy conditions on the Peninsula. However, the weather was perfect and it was on the whole a pleasant outing. I pointed out to them all the features which we knew so well.

'One of the generals asked me what I thought of the plan, and I said that while I was not qualified to give an opinion I did think it sounded feasible but that it would be essential to advance over the Salt Lake and the plain and secure the foothills quickly, or the Turks would get there first. Another general asked me where the Turkish trenches were and seemed surprised when I told him that there weren't any. I do not think he believed me.'

Sir Ian Hamilton's plan for the new venture had for its supreme objective the capture of Hill 971, Koja Chemen Tepe, the dominating point on the Sari Bair Ridge and then, working from there, to grip the neck of the Peninsula from Gaba Tepe to Maidos. The object, similar to that given to the Anzacs on April 25th, was to cut off the bulk of the Turkish Army from land communication with Constantinople and to gain artillery positions which would cut off sea communication with that city. Sir Ian's troops would then seize the forts of the Narrows from the rear, to allow the Allied Fleet to pass safely through the Dardanelles into the Sea of Marmara.

For this purpose separate attacks were prepared in extreme detail by the Army Staff during the month of July. There was to be a holding attack by two divisions of VIII Corps (Major-General de Lisle), at Cape Helles, to prevent the Turks from moving any troops from that sector, and, under General Birdwood's command, a great attack from Anzac on the Sari Bair Ridge by the two Australian and New Zealand Divisions reinforced by New Army troops and by Major-General Cox's 29th Indian Infantry Brigade. This Anzac attack, the main feature of the whole plan, was to be preceded by an assault on the Lone Pine Ridge to the right of the Anzac position, its object being to deceive the enemy and draw him to the right while all the time the decisive manoeuvre was to proceed out of the Anzac left.

While these battles were being fought, IX Corps, of New Army troops under General Stopford, was to land under cover of darkness in Suvla Bay and advance rapidly across the Suvla plain, giving the Turks no time to bring up reinforcements. They were then to link their right hand with the Anzac attack and help it as it progressed.

The Helles sector was held by 35,000 men; 37,000 were assigned to the Anzac attack and 25,000 to the Suvla landings. The whole British force, including reserves on the islands or approaching on the sea, amounted to 120,000 rifles, which made the forces on both sides approximately equal.

As cover to these operations Sir Ian Hamilton decided to attract Turkish attention away from the Peninsula towards the coast of Asia Minor. Troops sent to Mytilene were landed on that island every day for route marches and inspected by Sir Ian Hamilton in person, all to create the impression of an impending attack on the railway from Smyrna to Panderma, a line of supply which the operations of our submarines in the Sea of Marmara had doubled in importance.

General Liman von Sanders, commanding the Turkish Army on the Peninsula, was aware that we had received substantial reinforcements and that a general attack, together with a landing, was likely to take place early in August. He realised, as he had done before the original landings of April 25th, that the Sari Bair Ridge was a key to the Narrows, and he was again apprehensive of landings near Bulair. In addition he would have to guard the Asiatic shore. He also appreciated – and this is important – that Suvla Bay and Ejelmer Bay, seven miles further north, were possible landing places, but he did not regard disembarkation at either of these two places as sufficiently probable to warrant any special precautions.

The morning of August 6th was fine and clear at Cape Helles, with scarcely a breath of wind. The assault troops were in their assembly positions by 8 a.m. The heat was oppressive and there was little or no shade, but in spite of that everyone was in good heart. Their ranks had lately been brought up to strength with well-trained drafts from home, so that each of the three battalions was going into action with 24 officers and over 800 men. Thus encouraged the old hands of this brigade of the 29th Division, the 88th, were happily confident about the relatively small task required of them that day.

The Turks had been unusually quiet in this sector, but their silence can now be explained: they were saving ammunition for the big attack they had long been warned to expect. No hint had yet reached them that an attack at Helles was imminent, but all their preparations had been made.

Within a few seconds of the opening of the bombardment, supported by the Royal Navy, it was answered by a sustained fire from Turkish batteries. This caused numerous casualties in the crowded British trenches. Then, at 3.50 p.m. our infantry rose out of their trenches to advance. For the first few minutes all appeared to be going well, and watchers in rear were reporting that the objectives had all been taken. But the truth, first realised at Brigade headquarters but not by higher formations till many hours later, was quite different, for the strength of the Turkish defence had been gravely miscalculated. By only a few minutes after zero hour the 88th Brigade had been almost completely shattered.

Every man in the assault carried a large triangular piece of biscuit tin tied to his back. These shining triangles were intended to show the furthest points attained. Thus VIII Corps headquarters were soon able to inform divisional headquarters that they knew the Turkish front line had been captured, as their forward observation officers could see the British metal discs all along the trench. In fact those discs marked the line of the British dead.

Next day, August 7th, at 9.40 a.m. the 42nd (East Lancashire) Territorial Division, launched a second attack on a different section of the line. There was a similar artillery preparation, but the results were equally disappointing and equally costly. The northern edge of the Vineyard was captured but lost again on the 12th. A trench dug across its centre became the final British front line.

This holding attack at Cape Helles had cost the 29th Division 54 officers and 1,851 other ranks and the 42nd Division 80 officers plus 1,484 other ranks, and had not prevented – as had been hoped – the Turkish reserves moving to Sari Bair to meet the main attack from Anzac.

'The 6th Battalion, the Manchester Regiment, 42nd Division, were nicknamed the "Office boys" battalion and were outstanding in their neatness and prissiness. They had been recruited from the offices and warehouses of our northern metropolis and were valiant youngsters. In a corner of the notorious Krithia vineyard dozens of them now lay packed in neat array – caught in a murderous machine-gun cross-fire. They lay head to foot in layers. Even in death they were neat and orderly, their average age twenty or twenty-one.

'"Looks bloody queer, don't it?" said a corporal to Charles Watkins when the firing had died down.

'"What does?"

'"All them lads like that."

'"Yes, bloody shame, too – nice lads," Watkins replied.

'"No, you don't catch on, do you, mate? Wot does tha see about 'em wot's different?"

'"Well," said Watkins, rather stupidly perhaps, "you mean – being all dead – like that?"

'"Tha daft beggar – look again. Then tell me what tha sees is different; or does ta want a pair o' specs?"

'Then the penny dropped, said Watkins. They were all *properly dressed* – not like the other bodies we had come across, nor all the living ones in their usual scruff order. These dead boys were wearing neat khaki drill tunics. Even their belts and bandoliers were clean and polished.'

'"Well, I'll be—!" the corporal burst out at last. "Ah wonder who the officer wur who made 'em go into battle dressed like that."

'The corporal was right,' Watkins comments. 'Maybe one even shares the pathetic regimental pride of the officer who had decreed that these boys of his, due soon to be transferred to Higher Echelon, should go there properly and smartly turned out. I tried to put over this point of view to the corporal, but he spat with disgust.

'"Tha allus was one of them quare fellahs tha thinks round bloody corners, wasn't tha, Cobber? Come on, let's move on, before ah spews me guts up looking at them poor bastards."'[8]

The plan for the assault on Lone Pine Ridge, to the right of the Anzac position, had been carefully laid by Major-General H. B. Walker, Commander, 1st Australian Division (vice Bridges, mortally wounded). Its object was to deceive the enemy and to draw him to the right while all the time Birdwood's decisive manoeuvre was to proceed out of the Anzac left. Walker was not enamoured of the idea from the start, while the Turks, who considered their position impregnable, had every reason to be confident. Their trenches were covered with baulks of timber, and a series of deep support trenches ran back from the front line. Barbed-wire entanglements provided additional defence.

General Walker's plan of attack included the digging of underground tunnels under no-man's-land from which the first wave of assault troops could emerge, leaving only a short distance in the open before the Turkish front line.

Commencing on August 4th, a slow barrage was opened which continued for the best part of three days. The Turks had been trying to annoy the Australians by displaying placards announcing the capture of Warsaw, so when our shells started coming over they thought it was retaliation. They never guessed it was the prelude to an attack.

On the afternoon of August 6th the leading assault troops of the 1st Australian Brigade entered the tunnels, and at 5.30 p.m. precisely they emerged *en masse*. Surprise was complete.

'*Ingil izler geliyor* – the English are coming!' yelled the Turkish outposts, but little could be done before the Australians had reached the front-line trenches, where they were checked, nonplussed, by the unexpected head-cover.

Countless stories of great heroism have emerged from the fighting at Lone Pine, and indeed both sides fought with great courage. No quarter was given. The dead lay so thick that the only respect which could be paid to them was to avoid treading on their faces. A group of Australians actually reached Turkish battalion headquarters and a point named The Cup, but there they were annihilated.

When dusk fell the whole Turkish front line and two thirds of the rest of their trenches were in Australian hands. After many counter-attacks the firing died away because of exhaustion on both sides.

The casualties were truly appalling. The Australians lost over 2,000 men and the Turks nearly 7,000.

Today it takes barely ten minutes to walk over the Lone Pine position, which is dominated by the Australian war memorial. The Turks have erected a monument there too.

22

Suvla Bay

*'Our Generals are really heroes when I am on the spot to
direct them, but, when I am obliged to quit them they are
children.*
Duke of Wellington
during the Peninsular War, 1808–14

Beyond the Asmak Dere which was to form the northern limit of
General Birdwood's movement, the coast continues its north-westerly
trend to Nibrunesi Point, while, inland, the plain increases in size as
the hills diverge towards the north-east. It is a flat, open land, studded
with low trees and bushes. Nearly all the surface is waste, but small
farms, surrounded by larger trees and patches of cultivation, occur
here and there.

As one proceeds the ground becomes more and more marshy, and
in winter the region nearest the Salt Lake is waterlogged. The bush
also thickens, so much so that on a recent visit, in November 1973,
I had difficulty identifying the Salt Lake from the seaward side
because the undergrowth was so dense. But the plain can always be
crossed by sheep tracks and is nowhere actually impenetrable. Low
sandhills follow the shore.

Nibrunesi Point, which is the southern horn of Suvla Bay, has
steep cliffs on both sides but steeper on the north side, where they
fall abruptly into Suvla Bay. The distance between Ari Burnu,
of Anzac fame, and Nibrunesi Point is only three miles. The Asmak
Dere is equidistant between the two.

It seems probable that Nibrunesi Point is the end of what was once
a high ridge marked now by a series of isolated knolls, all of which
were to play an important part in the Suvla operations. First comes
Lala Baba, which rises to about 150 feet; then a larger rounded hill
like an inverted bowl some 160 feet high, known as Chocolate Hill
from its reddish-brown colour; then Green Hill; and lastly the formidable mass of Ismail Oglu Tepe, named W Hill, about 330 feet
high.

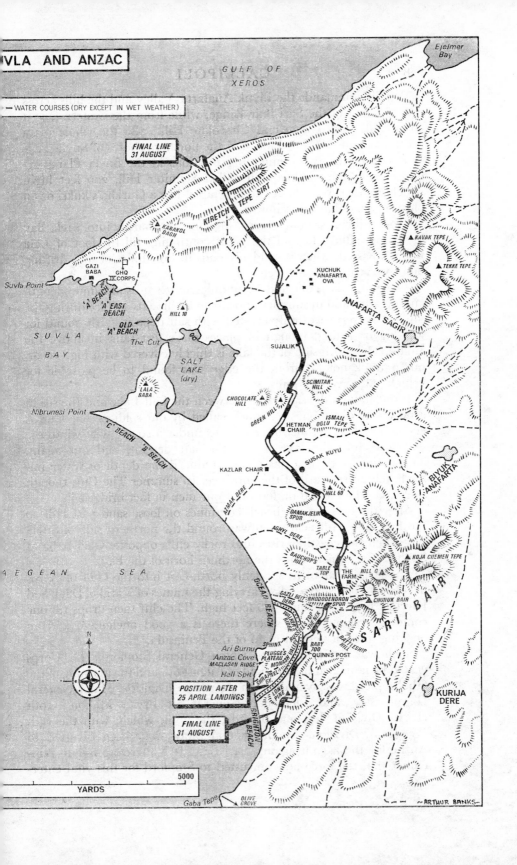

SVLA AND ANZAC

WATER COURSES (DRY EXCEPT IN WET WEATHER)

GULF OF XEROS

Ejelmer Bay

GALLIPOLI

FINAL LINE 31 AUGUST

KIRETCH TEPE SIRT

KARAKOL DAGH

ANAFARTA SAGIR

KAVAK TEPE

TEKKE TEPE

GAZI BABA

GHQ IX CORPS

Suvla Point

'A' BEACH

'A' EAST BEACH

OLD 'A' BEACH

HILL 10

The Cut

KUCHUK ANAFARTA OVA

S U V L A

BAY

SALT LAKE (dry)

SUJALIK

LALA BABA

CHOCOLATE HILL

SCIMITAR HILL

Nibrunesi Point

GREEN HILL

ISMAIL OGLU TEPE

HETMAN CHAIR

BIYUK ANAFARTA

'C' BEACH 'B' BEACH

KAZLAR CHAIR

SUSAK KUYU

HILL 60

A E G E A N   S E A

ATMAK DERE

DAMAKJELIK SPUR

AGHYL DERE

KOJA CHEMEN TEPE

BAUCHOP'S HILL

TABLE TOP

THE FARM

HILL Q

SARI BAIR

N

OCEAN BEACH

GAZLI BEIT DERE

RHODODENDRON SPUR

CHUNUK BAIR

WALDEN'S RIDGE

RUSSELL'S TOP

BATTLESHIP HILL

SPHINX

Ari Burnu

Anzac Cove

PLUGGE'S PLATEAU

BABY 700

QUINN'S POST

MACLAGAN RIDGE

MONASH GY.

SHRAPNEL GY.

Hell Spit

POSITION AFTER 25 APRIL LANDINGS

LONE PINE

BRIGHTON BEACH

FINAL LINE 31 AUGUST

KURIJA DERE

5000

YARDS

Gaba Tepe

OLIVE GROVE

~ ARTHUR BANKS ~

W Hill commands the Biyuk Anafarta Valley and the hills across it at the foot of the Sari Bair Ridge, while from the western face it commands both Green and Chocolate Hills, also the whole plain north of them, the Salt Lake and the northern shores of Suvla Bay. It is one of the two dominating positions in the Suvla Plain, the other being the rounded hill called Scimitar Hill, 200 feet high, which appears from the sea to be shaped like a Gurkha's kukri or an old-fashioned Turkish scimitar.

From Nibrunesi Point the coastline curves sharply into Suvla Bay itself, the clifflike face of the point continuing till the foot of Lala Baba is passed, when it suddenly ends in low dunes of soft, drifting sand, very tiring to the feet.

The Salt Lake is one and a half miles across at its maximum length and breadth and in summer appears to be dry. Its surface during the Suvla landings was thinly crusted with salt deposit, fairly sound for walking or riding, though in places one's feet sank in above the ankles. The south side of the lake is thickly covered with high reeds, but a track not far from the edge was found to be passable for vehicles and even for guns.

If one follows the sandy spit between the Salt Lake and the sea in a northerly direction, a channel, called by our soldiers The Cut, is encountered. Here, in winter months under a strong west wind, the sea flows into the lake, hence the salt deposit, and out again. This action of the sea has greatly reduced the depth of water immediately to seaward of the entrance. In summer The Cut, though sticky, can be crossed on foot, but our men in fact bridged it.

After the crossing the beach continues on loose sand past Hill 10 (40 feet high), till nearly halfway round the northern side of Suvla Bay when the coastline rises into rocky cliffs opposite Gazi Baba at Suvla Point, which forms the northern horn of the Bay.

The coast next turns suddenly north-east into the Gulf of Xeros in the form of a sharp ridge carrying the names of Karakol Dagh and Kiretch Tepe Sirt, some 600 feet high. The cliff then drops till one comes to Ejelmer Bay, where there is a good anchorage and an opening into the central plain of the Peninsula.

Such was the district into which General Stopford's IX Corps was to be launched on the night of August 6th and the morning of the 7th. Stopford was given the 11th (Northern) Division, Major-General Hammersley, and Lieutenant-General Sir Bryan Mahon's 10th (Irish) Division, less one brigade, the 29th, which, with the 13th (Western) Division, Major-General Shaw, had been diverted to Anzac for the assault against Sari Bair. It is therefore fair to remember that the force now entrusted to Stopford for this vital enter-

prise was an Army Corps only in name and that all the battalions,
as already explained, were New Army men who had never been in
action before.

So determined was Sir Ian to keep his Suvla plan a profound secret
that even General Stopford was not told anything about it till July
22nd. On that day, however, Sir Ian personally unfolded the plan to
him.

'Tell Sir Ian,' said General Stopford later in the day, after going
through the scheme point by point with a Staff Officer from G.H.Q.,
'that this is the plan which I have always hoped he would adopt.
It is a good plan. I am sure it will succeed, and I congratulate whoever was responsible for framing it.'

But Stopford's satisfaction with the scheme did not last long. After
discussing it with Brigadier-General H. L. Reed, V.C., his Chief
of Staff, IX Corps, whom he summoned next day from Mudros,
Stopford's early confidence began to fade.

Sir Ian had been unhappy when he heard that Reed was joining
Stopford, as Reed had been his own Chief of Staff once and he knew
his limitations. 'The combination of Stopford and Reed is not a
good one,' he had written to General Wolfe Murray, Chief of the
Imperial General Staff, when the appointment was made, but no
further action was taken. Reed was four-square, professional, brave
and dogmatic. He was lame and found getting about difficult. His
personal courage, as his memorable V.C. in South Africa demon-
strated, was beyond question, and he had what Stopford lacked –
recent experience of modern warfare. He had also been attached to
the Turkish Army during the Turko-Bulgar war and had been deeply
impressed by the courage and discipline of the Turkish infantry,
particularly in defence. He had also brought from France a hatred
of undertaking offensive operations without artillery support, and he
considered the artillery allocated to IX Corps wholly inadequate.
(Indeed it was virtually non-existent.) General Stopford was charming, intellectual and pliant; he was also conscious of his own lack of
battle experience and was eager to learn. Reed was to ride over him
rough shod.

Sir Ian Hamilton's original design had been to land the whole of
the 11th Division on the long beach just south of Nibrunesi Point,
where the shore is steep-to and the water comes in deep. A large part
of the force would be concealed by the cliffs and hills. The beach
itself – and I have seen it so often since those far-away days – is level
and wide enough for forming up. Sir Ian's outline plan also detailed

two brigades of Mahon's 10th Division to disembark on the north side of the bay near Suvla Point to occupy the sharp ridge which carries two separate names – Karakol Dagh and Kiretch Tepe Sirt.

Admiral de Robeck had already turned down an earlier suggestion that troops should land inside the bay. The only chart available was from a sketch survey made in 1878. It was considered almost certain, as I have already pointed out, that silting would have occurred to seaward of The Cut, which is the outlet of the Salt Lake. Further-more the beach there was very exposed and could provide no shelter either from weather or from enemy artillery. But eventually, though not without misgiving, the Admiral agreed to one infantry brigade being allocated to attempt a landing on a strip of beach some 600 yards long just north of The Cut. Accordingly in the final instructions to IX Corps issued on July 29th, it was laid down that one brigade of the 11th Division should land inside the Bay. The other two brigades were to land, as originally arranged, to the south of Nibrunesi Point.

'The other modifications of the memorandum were of a much more serious nature. It was decided that General Stopford must not be tied down in advance by any hard-and-fast order that such-and-such a point had got to be reached by dawn. In the final instructions, therefore, he was told that his primary object would be to secure Suvla Bay as a base for the northern zone. He was given a free hand in drawing up his plan to achieve this purpose, subject only to the Commander-in-Chief's final approval; and, though his special attention was directed to the Chocolate and W Hills, the original clear-cut order to capture these positions before dawn was whittled down to read: "If it is possible, without prejudice to the attainment of your primary objective, to gain possession of these hills at an early period of your attack, it will greatly facilitate the capture and retention of Hill 971".'[1]

I speak for myself when I say that the Suvla Bay landing seemed to go wrong from the start. As at Anzac, I was in charge of the *Bacchante*'s picket boat, and we had most of our original crew, including Petty Officer Main. Midshipman Douglas Dixon came, too, in charge of the *Europa*'s picket boat, since our steam pinnace was not considered powerful enough for the new task.

There was to be no towing of launches or cutters this time. Steel-plated motor lighters which Lord Fisher had designed in 1914 for his Baltic project (a scheme which he was never able to get fully out

of his mind) had arrived from home. They were flat bottomed, of
shallow draught, and chugged along under a single engine at a
speed of some five knots. The slightest puff of wind on the beam or
quarter was enough to drive them broadside on to a beach when they
touched down. As they were so unhandy, a picket boat was required
to hold them bows on to the shore while the troops were disembarking
over the ramp and to haul them off afterwards. Each of these K
lighters, as they were officially called (although we always referred
to them as 'beetles' because of their appearance), carried 500 men,
half on deck and half under cover below. After the Gallipoli Campaign was over, a number were taken to Malta and, astonishing
though it may seem, were used in General Wavell's attack in the
Western Desert twenty-five years later. A question of *faute de mieux*, I
suppose.

On 3rd August 1915 our picket boat sailed with several others from
Mudros to Kephalo, a matter of sixty miles. We anchored under the
lee of a dummy battleship, whose useful life of deception was over.
She had been run aground and sunk to form a breakwater. Here our
first trouble started. We were sent some spare hands from another
ship, but one picket boat with two crews embarked just does not
work. Those from the watch below get in the way and then grumble
that they are being disturbed and can't rest, while those on duty
complain that the boat is cluttered up with sleeping bodies and they
can't get at their gear. Thank goodness there was no relief midshipman.

On August 6th, after coaling and provisioning from the monitor
Raglan, we joined up with our motor lighter, *K-63*. She went alongside one of the transports, collected a load of men of Hammersley's
11th Division, and transferred them to our parent destroyer, the
Grasshopper. She then returned for a second load, which she kept on
board. We both now secured alongside the *Grasshopper* until it was
dark and time to go.

At 8.30 p.m. our group, carrying the 32nd Brigade (Brigadier-
General Haggard) and the 33rd Brigade (Brigadier-General Maxwell), got under way. It consisted of seven destroyers with troops,
each towing a motor lighter with troops and a picket boat, plus the
bulge cruisers *Endymion* and *Theseus* also packed with soldiers and
some trawlers towing horse-boats loaded with guns and mules. We
were bound for B and C Beaches south of Nibrunesi Point. Once
we were clear of the harbour a second group, consisting of three
destroyers each towing a motor lighter, followed, with Sitwell's 34
Brigade, bound for the much disputed landing place inside and at
the head of Suvla Bay.

Sir Ian Hamilton, with George Brodrick, his A.D.C., had walked down from G.H.Q. Imbros, to Kephalo Harbour to watch Hammersley's 11th Division embark. 'I spent quite a time talking to Hammersley and to no end of regimental officers and men,' he wrote. 'Hammersley has been working too hard – at least he looked it; also for the occasion rather glum. The officers and men were in good fettle and game enough to have a go, but miles removed from the state of hot enthusiasm in which the old lot started out of Mudros harbour on that April afternoon. They reflect, so it seems to me, the frame of mind of their old unenthusiastic commanders.'[2]

For a moment Sir Ian debated whether or not he should cruise round in a motor launch, saying a few encouraging words to each unit as he went by, but he dismissed the idea when he reflected that the men did not know him by sight, and that in any case, as several hours would pass before they were due on the beaches, it was too long an interval for his words to survive. 'All the same, I rather regret not having done so,' he said later on.

Sir Ian looked for Stopford and his Chief of Staff, Reed, hoping that they might have done something to enthuse their soldiers, but they were nowhere to be seen. So he returned to G.H.Q. Imbros. Nothing to do but wait . . .

Stopford had been lying on his valise spread on the floor of his tent, and Colonel Aspinall found him there. The General had slipped and sprained his knee that morning and was not feeling too well. 'I want you to tell Sir Ian Hamilton,' he said, 'that I am going to do my best and that I hope to be successful. But he must realise that if the enemy proves to be holding a strong line of continuous entrenchments I shall be unable to dislodge him till more guns are landed.' Glumly he went on to quote his Chief-of-Staff: 'All the teaching of the campaign in France,' he said, 'proves that continuous trenches cannot be attacked without the assistance of a large number of howitzers.'

It seems unbelievable that on the eve of battle a Corps Commander could 'bellyache' like this (to use Montgomery's expression of 1942) or could 'croak' in this way (if you prefer to quote Wellington in the Peninsular War). Stopford was sadly lacking in self-confidence. However he got on board the *Jonquil* with Rear-Admiral Christian and sailed at 11 p.m.

It was pitch dark during the passage. There was a moon somewhere, but it was hidden by rain clouds. A fresh wind was blowing, and the sea was choppy. Although the destroyers went dead slow, some of the tows parted and valuable time was lost as we all had to stop till fresh wires were passed. There should have been no waiting for lame ducks. It was made clear nearly thirty years later, on D-day, Normandy, that if anyone fell out of the line we had to go on without them.

When half-way over we could hear a battle raging and see gun-flashes off the starboard bow. The sortie from Anzac had begun.

At 9.30 p.m. we picked up a white light ahead. It was displayed by the destroyer *Pincher*, Lieutenant-Commander H. W. Wyld. 'I knew a lot depended on me,' he wrote in his diary, 'because if I were seen or heard I should get a warm reception from Lala Baba and so would the soldiers when they arrived. I had taken bearings in daytime to help guide me in, but when we closed now it was so dark I couldn't see a thing. However, I just managed to spot the reflection of a star shining in the Salt Lake which gave me a line on our position. We closed in to three and a half fathoms, which I thought near enough. We eased down our anchor quietly, and I eventually found we were only two degrees from our proper bearing and about 100 yards too far out, so I was rather pleased. There was not a sound ashore except from a dog barking some distance inland.'

The sea calmed down as we came under the lee of the land, I wrote in my midshipman's log. At 9.30 p.m. we saw the *Pincher*'s white light and at 9.50 the seven destroyers slipped their tows, which was a signal for all motor lighters to go full speed ahead for the beach with picket boats following. The run-in took less than ten minutes. But how different from Anzac! The landing was a complete surprise. There was no opposition and not a single casualty. A few rockets were fired, and one or two rifle shots rang out in the darkness, but that was all.

Our motor lighter had grounded rather far out, making it necessary for the men to wade in about three feet of water. They made a poor showing – no dash and a certain amount of talking. Indeed a handful, who obviously had the wind up, looked as if they were afraid to land. Petty Officer Main sang out and told them to get a move on. They went ashore after that.

It took longer to land the second wave, because some of the motor lighters had stuck. However all seven destroyers were cleared by midnight, and all soldiers from the *Endymion* and *Theseus* were ashore by 1.30 a.m., followed pretty closely by the few guns and mules. Then warships and transports started arriving, and trawlers began to lay anti-submarine nets round the anchorage. Soon after daylight we saw a horse-boat foul the boom defence, as it was called, and capsize, with the horses still tied to it by their heads. They were struggling and making the devil of a noise. The next time we passed they had all drowned, poor things. A couple of men in a dinghy were setting the bodies adrift so that the work of net laying could proceed.

Meanwhile disaster had overcome the arrangements for the landing of Brigadier-General Sitwell's 34 Brigade at the head of the bay, the one place, you will remember, where the Navy did not want to go. In the blackness of the night, with no marks to guide them, the three destroyers anchored at 10.30 p.m. south instead of north of The Cut. Ignorant of the error, the motor lighters made straight for the beach and were soon aground a long way from shore.

Very gallantly and under scattered rifle fire the heavily equipped men disembarked. There were slimy rocks to negotiate and non-swimmers to be helped. One battalion commander spent nearly two hours with water up to his chin helping his men. It was long past midnight before the three motor lighters were cleared and their troops formed up.

The leading company of the battalion that had been detailed to advance on Hill 10 found itself on the edge of the Salt Lake, with no sign of the objective. Another battalion was now ordered to march north to clear Suvla Point and Kiretch Tepe, in compliance with original orders. But the whole plan for a rapid advance had already collapsed.

'On the voyage from Imbros to Suvla in the *Jonquil* General Stopford had confided to Admiral Christian his misgivings about the whole adventure, but his spirits rose as they approached the coast. *Jonquil* anchored just inside the bay abreast Suvla Point soon after midnight. Extraordinary as it is to relate, no one was sent ashore to inquire for news, no one came out to the *Jonquil* from the beach and no message was sent to the Commander-in-Chief at G.H.Q. Imbros. The night was warm, and General Stopford had his mattress brought up on deck under the bridge where he went to sleep. At 4 a.m. Commander Unwin, beachmaster, who had been very busy throughout the night, came on board to urge Admiral Christian to have monitors open fire to hearten the troops, who were still held up in confusion on the shore.'[3]

Shortly before 5 a.m. Major-General Hammersley, commanding the 11th (Northern) Division, 'who had been ashore at B Beach since 1 a.m. and from the moment of landing had felt "rather exhausted", instructed all the remaining troops of Haggard's 32 Brigade still "sitting idle" on Lala Baba to hurry forward to the assistance of Sitwell's 34 Brigade in their advance on Hill 10. Precious time had been lost, and the Turks were now fully on the alert and in occupation of Hill 10. Eventually, however (6 a.m.) the position was turned and the deployment, which had been planned for 1.30 a.m., could begin.'[4]

Unhappily the hold-up did not end there. At break of day, while Hill 10 was being occupied, transports carrying Brigadier-General Hill and his battalions of the 10th (Irish) Division had arrived in the bay to be greeted with shrapnel fire but ready to be thrown straight into the fight. These troops had been living on board since July 11th, and throughout that period had had very little exercise. Owing to an excess of secrecy even General Hill did not know the exact nature of the operation he was about to undertake. Immediately on arrival Hill went on board the *Jonquil* to report to General Stopford.

Overnight General Stopford had intended to land the whole of the 10th Division at A Beach (henceforth referred to as Old A Beach) by The Cut, to complete the capture of Kiretch Tepe Sirt. But, from what the Navy had told him at daybreak, any further landing at Old A was out of the question and no other suitable beach had yet been found inside the bay. Stopford therefore ordered Hill to take his Battalions to C Beach, and place himself under General Hammersley's orders until the arrival of his own Divisional Commander, Sir Bryan Mahon, due to arrive from Mudros with the rest of the divisional troops.

The disadvantages of General Stopford's position on board ship had already begun to show themselves. He would have been better advised to land at once and establish his headquarters ashore, where he could control the battle, if a battle it can be called.

Major-General Hammersley's 11th Division was ashore by 8 a.m., with two mountain batteries and ships of the Royal Navy behind him. The 10th Division was disembarking. This force, rising as the day passed to 20,000 men, had only to advance three miles from their landing places to brush before them what was left of the Turkish defenders and then to occupy positions where water was plentiful and which were of decisive importance to the whole plan. Instead of doing this, all the troops that had landed either remained idle for hours or toiled along the sandy shore round the Salt Lake, a march of five miles in the heat of the day, before attacking Chocolate Hill. The evening was far advanced before by a spirited attack they made themselves masters of Chocolate Hill. The night closed with the troops very tired, their units intermingled, their water supply in confusion and only their earliest objectives attained. Over a thousand casualties had been suffered, almost all from three or four battalions.

We in the *Bacchante*'s picket boat, with our motor lighter *K-63* and three others, were the first to enter a newly found landing near Ghazi Baba which our patrols had marked with red flags and named A East Beach. The approach was rocky and the water shallow in patches.We touched bottom twice and then grounded. It was a question of all hands on deck to shove her off with boat-hooks. The four motor lighters beached and the soldiers trickled out. As there appeared to be no opposition they formed up on the foreshore and then had the shock of their lives for a whole string of mines exploded right and left of them and there were many casualties.

It was a tame job looking after the motor lighter and waiting about. We would watch the fall of shell from the ships' guns and then comment on the Army's lack of progress. The thousands of troops hanging about on the beaches worried us. When will somebody give the order to advance, we wondered.

Commander Unwin commandeered our picket boat before nightfall to use as a dispatch boat. The first thing he said to me was, 'You had better go down into the after cabin and get some rest, I'm sure you need it.' I hated being told this and would much rather have been left alone in charge of my own picket boat working until ready to drop, as I had done at Anzac.

In the meantime G.H.Q., Imbros, had been finding the absence of news insupportable. Situation reports were flowing in from Anzac and Helles but from Suvla virtually nothing. The cable ship *Levant* had sailed with the invasion fleet, paying out its cable on the passage over, and it had been expected that the first message received would announce the troops were ashore. There was a dial face in the signals tent at the Imbros end of the cable, and throughout the midnight hours headquarters staff kept a watch on it. At last, at 2 a.m., the needle moved for the first time, and a telegraphist spelt out the message: 'A little shelling at A has now ceased. All quiet at B.' There was no signature. It was in fact the signalman on board *Levant* passing a private message to his mate at the Imbros end, but it did at least serve to ease the situation. 'Now, thank God,' wrote Sir Ian, 'the deadliest of perils is past. The New Army are fairly ashore.'[5]

Throughout this new and vital day, August 7th, G.H.Q. was to exercise no influence over the course of the Suvla operation. Such inactivity can only be explained by over-confidence. Early in the morning, as we have seen, the absence of news from General Stopford caused uneasiness, but this was soon dissipated by reassuring reports from other sources. At 8 a.m. Admiral de Robeck signalled that the landing had been a complete surprise. Turkish prisoners, he reported, were saying that no fresh troops had reached the area. Major-General Hammersley, 11th Division, reported direct to G.H.Q. that the landing at B had been most successful, and that, although Brigadier-General Sitwell's 34 Brigade landing (at Old A) had been 'much hampered by a muddy foreshore', both 34 and 32 Brigades were 'now pushing inland', but he made no reference to British losses or Turkish opposition. From Anzac the news arrived that 'almost complete tranquillity' was reigning over Suvla and that Turkish guns were retiring through Anafarta Sagir. Ships returning from Suvla reported that Suvla Bay was full of shipping and that troops and stores were landing in accordance with plan.

In face of these reports, the first message from Stopford, received about midday, came as a shock. It gave the position of his troops at 7.30 a.m., showing that even Hill 10 had not been captured at that hour, and it ended with the phrase: 'As you see we have been able to advance little beyond the edge of the beach'.

'It is perhaps difficult to understand,' wrote the Military Historian, why, upon receipt of this message, which disclosed the slow progress of IX Corps, Sir Ian Hamilton did not at once proceed to Suvla.'

But no one at G.H.Q. dreamed of trouble at Suvla, and it seemed essential that Sir Ian should remain at Imbros, where alone he could keep in touch with the situation at all the three points of attack, Helles, Anzac and Suvla. It was plain that General Stopford's message had been delayed in transmission. It was also plain that the situation had greatly improved since the early morning. Before the landing Stopford's one fear had been that the Turks were in great strength and heavily entrenched. These forebodings had proved groundless. Mahon's 10th Division had apparently landed safely. No one at G.H.Q. anticipated that IX Corps would have any trouble in pushing forward to its objectives. This confidence was increased by a message from Major-General Hammersley, 11th Division, that opposition on his front was weakening.

During the afternoon, in the absence of any further news from Stopford, Major-General Braithwaite, Sir Ian's Chief of Staff, telegraphed to IX Corps: 'Chief glad to hear enemy opposition weakening and knows you will take advantage of this to push on rapidly . . .'[6]

But if the mildness of this first application of the spur can be taken as a measure of his uneasiness, it would seem that Sir Ian still believed there was no real cause for anxiety.

All the world knows now that at the time of the landing only

Major Willmer, a Bavarian officer with 1,800 Turkish Gendarmerie, stood between Stopford's Divisions and the high ground. It is a disturbing thought.

When Colonels Aspinall and Hankey accompanied by Major Jack Churchill reached Suvla Bay from Imbros a little before noon on the 8th, they were convinced by the holiday appearance of the place that the hills had at last been captured. There was no sound of firing ashore, and all round the bay were clusters of naked men bathing in the sea. In high spirits Aspinall went ashore to find IX Corps headquarters, but as no one could direct him he started to walk inland. He had not gone far when he met the C.R.E. of the 11th Division, who told him that the leading troops were only a few hundred yards ahead and that there were no signs of fresh advance. The Corps Commander, he said, was not ashore but still on board *Jonquil*. The location of corps headquarters had, however, been decided on. It was a short distance inland from A East Beach, and Lieutenant Rex Palmer, R.E. (later destined to launch 2-LO, the first London station of the B.B.C.) was at that moment superintending its erection. 'Dig deep,' Stopford had told him, 'for we shall be here a long time.'

Aspinall was then directed to 11th Division headquarters, where Major-General Hammersley explained that 'he had received no orders to move forward, that his troops were dead beat and had suffered heavy casualties. They could not advance till they had had more rest and till more guns had been landed. He hoped to move forward again next morning.'

In face of this information Aspinall hurried off to the *Jonquil* to see General Stopford. By chance on his way to the beach he met the C.R.A. of the 11th Division, who urged him 'to get a move on'. 'Nothing is being done,' said the Brigadier, 'and it looks as though nothing is going to be done.'

'Arriving on board *Jonquil*, about 3 p.m., Aspinall found General Stopford on deck. He was in excellent spirits.

'"Well, Aspinall," he said, "the men have done splendidly and have been magnificent."

'"But they have not reached the hills, sir," said Aspinall.

'"No," replied the General, "but they are ashore."''

Aspinall said he was sure Sir Ian would be disappointed that the high ground had not yet been taken and begged the General to order an immediate advance before the enemy's troops from Bulair could forestall him.

To this Stopford answered that he realised the importance of losing no time but that it was impossible to move till the men had rested and more guns were ashore. He intended to order a fresh advance next day.

In despair Aspinall went off to the flagship, the *Chatham*, where he found Vice-Admiral de Robeck and his Chief of Staff, Commodore Keyes, in equal distress at the inexplicable delay. With the Admiral's permission, he reported by wireless to G.H.Q.:

'Just been ashore, where I found all quiet. No rifle fire, no artillery fire and apparently no Turks. IX Corps resting. Feel confident that golden opportunities are being lost and look upon the situation as serious.'[7]

In the meantime the lack of news from Suvla had been preying on Sir Ian's imagination, and at 11.30 that morning, the 8th, he had ordered the destroyer *Arno*, which had been placed at his disposal, to be ready to take him to Suvla at noon. Then occurred one of those unfortunate mishaps which seem to be the work of the Devil. *Arno* had developed a defect and could not sail, so Sir Ian was obliged to wait for the arrival of the *Triad* at 4.30.

'This damned amphibious hitch,' Sir Ian called it; and Compton Mackenzie, a Captain in Royal Marine Artillery on G.H.Q. staff, gave the occasion a write-up. 'I was startled by a picture which will never fade from my memory. Sir Ian Hamilton at the mercy of the Furies was striding down the slope toward the beach at such a pace that little George Brodrick was half running to keep up with him . . . Sir Ian returned our salutes mechanically. Those tormented eyes were seeing not us but Suvla and the heights beyond, not us but the Anafarta ridge beyond, not us but the silver Narrows, not us but the cupolas and domes and minarets of Constantinople, which with every wasted moment were becoming more and more remote and nebulous and unattainable.'[8]

Sir Ian arrived at Suvla at 6 p.m. (8th). After a hurried word with Admiral de Robeck in the flagship, he boarded the *Jonquil* with Commodore Keyes and Colonel Aspinall.

Meanwhile General Stopford had been ashore for the first time. Aspinall's visit had given him an incentive. It was clear that G.H.Q. were getting impatient, and it was up to him – Stopford – to make sure that his instructions were being attended to.

On reaching 11th Division headquarters he found Hammersley

was out, but the Divisional Staff assured him that plans for the attack next day were well advanced, so he returned to the *Jonquil* in time to receive Sir Ian.

The meeting did not last long. Stopford told Sir Ian everything was going well but that the troops needed more artillery and another night's rest before renewing the attack. He intended to resume the advance next day at a time to be fixed by Hammersley.

'But tomorrow may be too late. It is imperative that we get Tekke Tepe now.'

Stopford turned to Reed, his Chief of Staff, who said that any immediate advance was out of the question. The troops needed water, and, besides, orders would have to be re-written.

'I thought to myself,' Sir Ian wrote, 'of the many, many times I had fought some objection; of the old days when I had to steel my heart and force men half dead with hunger, thirst and sleeplessness to push along. A cruel, pitiless business, but so is war itself.'[9] So Sir Ian made the suggestion that he should go ashore himself and see Major-General Hammersley and his brigadiers, so as to get a better grip of things than seemed possible on board the *Jonquil*.

Stopford agreed that it might be a good thing to go but begged to be excused. He had not been very fit; he had just returned from shore and wanted to give his leg a chance.

A moment later Sir Ian was in a picket boat heading for Lala Baba. At the same time Stopford was signalling to Hammersley:

'6.45 p.m. Commander-in-Chief wishes you to commence advance at earliest possible moment, as vital to forestall the enemy, who is bringing up reinforcements. . . .'

Hammersley, whose warning order to his brigades regarding the attack next day had just been issued, was reading this message when Sir Ian bounded up. To the Commander-in-Chief's demand for an immediate advance Hammersley replied that it would not be possible to warn the troops for an earlier move than 8 a.m. next morning. But Sir Ian was insistent. Finally Hammersley suggested that 32 Brigade (Haggard), which he believed to be more or less concentrated near Sulajik, might be fit to make the attempt. 'Then order at least one battalion of it to be on the top of the ridge by daylight,' said Sir Ian quickly. 'The presence of that one battalion on the higher ground at daylight will be invaluable to the rest of the corps when they advance tomorrow morning.'

This accordingly was decided on, and a staff officer was sent with verbal orders to 32 Brigade headquarters on Hill 10. He was to tell the Brigadier that the objective allotted to him half an hour ago had been changed and his new objective was the high ground on the Tekke Tepe ridge. The brigade was not to wait till tomorrow but to move forward during the night to ensure that at least one battalion should gain Tekke Tepe before daylight. As an afterthought, Hammersley added: 'Tell them to send the Pioneers!'

It was unfortunate – indeed disastrous – that neither the divisional nor brigade commanders knew exactly where their units were. However, a little before 4 a.m. one company – the 6th East Yorkshire Pioneers – had been collected, and Lieutenant-Colonel H. G. A. Moore, appreciating that every moment was valuable, pushed off with it, leaving word for the other three to follow. It was now more than seven hours since Sir Ian had insisted that 'at least one battalion' must be established on the crest of the ridge before daylight. Day would be breaking in less than a quarter of an hour; and at this moment two Turkish battalions were breasting the slopes on the opposite side of the ridge.

As soon as daylight came, Moore and his leading company were fired on from the direction of Anafarta, and very soon the little force became split up into scattered groups moving in single file. Turkish rifle fire increased, and, when Moore and a handful of men approached the top of the ridge, Turks were already pouring over it from the other side. The only course open to Moore was to fall back on the rest of his battalion. The race for Tekke Tepe had been lost by less than half an hour.

The Turkish attack now really began. Streams of Turks came pouring down the hill, and shrapnel fire opened on the troops in the plain. The retirement of Moore's little party was attended by heavy loss. Only the Colonel, two other officers and two men succeeded in reaching the foothills, and there they were overpowered and taken prisoner. Moore and Major Brunner were bayoneted after surrendering. The third officer, Lieutenant John Still, a Ceylon planter and hunter in civilian life was spared and lived to tell the tale:

'The rampart of hills to the east of us was black against the chill, pale sky as we moved out across the grey flats that led to the foot of Tekke Tepe, towering nearly 1,000 feet ahead of us', wrote John Still. 'As we moved on and on, up and up, men got lost in the prickly scrub oak, and it became increasingly difficult to maintain any sort of formation. The enemy's fire grew in volume as we mounted, poured into us at ever decreasing range from the right and from the front.

'In that hour my admiration for the splendid courage of the men rose to a pitch of exaltation. They were Yorkshire miners for the most part, dogged, hard men of the sturdiest breed on earth. Those who were hit stayed where they fell, and those who were whole climbed on. The only complaint heard upon that hillside was that no enemy could be seen to fire at.

'About thirty of us reached the top of the hill. And when there were about twenty left we turned and went down again. We had reached the highest point and the furthest point that British forces from Suvla Bay were destined to reach.

'A sapper major [Brunner] who walked with me said, after a long silence, "Are you married?"

'"Yes," I replied.

'"If it were not for that this would be good fun," said he.

'So we agreed that if one of us got out he should go to see the other's wife. And it fell to me to do it, for he was shot through the ankle soon after that and an hour later was bayoneted in cold blood.

'We hoped that the foot of the ravine would bring us out among our own supports, but the enemy held it. Five out of all those who had gone up got down again alive. We could do nothing but surrender.'[10]

At daybreak on the 8th Liman von Sanders, who had ridden out to watch the expected advance of his two divisions from Bulair, learnt that the main columns were still strung out on the roads and that no attack could be delivered till late in the afternoon.

The situation was bleak. Major Willmer's tired Gendarmerie could hardly be trusted to withstand a determined assault. Messages from the Anzac front reported that strong British forces were advancing on Koja Chemen Tepe, Hill 971. But the Turks were fortunate in Liman von Sanders, who was not the man to be dismayed. General Ahmed Fezi Bey's XVI Army Corps had arrived from Bulair twenty-four hours earlier than expected, but he had planned to rest his men and to counter-attack next day. This led to a confrontation strangely similar to the one taking place between General Stopford and Sir Ian. Liman von Sanders wanted XVI Corps to go forward without rest, and when General Fezi Bey demurred he had him relieved on the spot. 'That same day [August 8th],' he wrote, 'I transferred the command of all troops in the Anafarta sector to Mustapha Kemal Bey, formerly commanding the 19th Division.'[11] It seems that von Sanders was more ruthless than Sir Ian.

'We may now pause to survey the scene on this sunny August Afternoon,' later wrote Winston Churchill. 'On the one hand we have the placid, prudent English gentleman [Stopford] with his 20,000 men spread around the beaches; and on the other the skilful German [von Sanders], stamping with impatience for the arrival of his divisions, expecting with every hour to see his scanty covering forces brushed aside, while the furious Kemal animated his fanatic soldiers and hurled them forward towards the battle.'[12]

'*Size ben taaruz emretmiyorum ölmeği emrediyorum,*' Kemal had called to his troops. 'I don't order you to attack. I order you to die!'

Daylight on August 8th was fading when Sir Ian returned from Hammersley's 32nd Division headquarters, first to the flagship to put Vice-Admiral de Robeck in the picture, then to the *Triad* close by where he had decided to spend the night. He did not communicate again with Stopford, and no one else seems to have bothered to tell IX Corps headquarters in the *Jonquil* that the Commander-in-Chief had caused plans to be changed and that 32 Brigade was on the march.

Sir Ian stayed on the bridge of the *Triad* until 11 p.m. when, having heard nothing, he went below and turned in, satisfied that 32 Brigade had made good Tekke Tepe and were probably at this moment digging themselves in.

'I got up to the bridge next morning at dawn, with my glasses,' he wrote later. 'The country was so covered with scrub that it was hard to see what was going on in that uncertain light, but the enemy shrapnel-fire coming from a knoll a few hundred yards due west of Anafarta was proof that our troops were not holding the shoulder of Tekke Tepe.

'When it became light enough to distinguish troops I could see our men pushing up the western slopes of the long spur. The scrub was so thick that they had to clump together and follow my leader along what appeared to be cattle tracks up the hill. Then shrapnel got on to those fellows and drove them in. Not only did they come back, but they came like a crowd streaming away from a football match, back some of them almost to the sea. My heart had grown tough amidst the struggles of the Peninsula, but the misery of this scene well nigh broke it . . . Words are no use.'

Our losses were less than 1,000 on the 7th, but nearly 8,000 officers and men were killed or wounded on the 9th and 10th, without any decisive position being gained.

'Even in the midst of the misery of witnessing this repulse,' concluded Sir Ian. 'A misery intensified by the "too late" and "might have been" self torture, I could not keep my eyes off the Sari Bair Ridge. All the naval guns were turned on to it. What was going on there? Anyway Birdwood and Godley would be equal to whatever Fortune might have in store for them.'[13]

23

Sari Bair

*'These hills and the ground commanded by them were
the scenes of some of the noblest heroism which ever went
far to atone for the infamy of war.'*
John Masefield
Gallipoli, 1916

At Anzac on the evening of August 6th all was set for the great assault
on Sari Bair, the range of heights dominated by Hill 971, the Commander-in-Chief's supreme objective. The plan was strewn with
difficulties, but the main hope of success lay in its boldness. It was
hoped that the attacking troops would gain the crests before the
Turks could muster sufficient strength to stop them.

Major-General Godley, whose New Zealand and Australian
Division had so long occupied the northern half of the Anzac line,
was to be responsible for the capture of the heights as well as for
subsidiary attacks to assist the main operation. His force had been
increased and now amounted to 20,000 rifles.

General Godley's plan was to attack the Sari Bair ridge with two
columns. The Right Assaulting Column was to advance up Rhododendron Spur to Chunuk Bair. The Left Assaulting Column had a
dual objective. After reaching the last left-hand fork in Aghyl Dere,
half would strike across the Damakjelik Spur and Azmak Dere to
Abdul Rahman Spur and then advance on Hill 971, while the other
half would move up to Damakjelik Spur to capture Hill Q.

To prevent the Right and Left Assaulting Columns being held up
at the outset, the nearer foothills were to be cleared and piqueted by
independent detachments known as Right and Left Covering Forces.
These were to move forward soon after dark. It was hoped that the
objectives of the covering forces would be captured by 10.30 p.m.
The two Assaulting Columns were expected to reach the summit of
the main Sari Bair Ridge at least an hour before dawn.

After capturing Hill Q and Hill 971, the Left Assaulting Column
was to consolidate its position. After securing Chunuk Bair the Right

Assaulting Column was to capture Battleship Hill. A subsidiary attack on the Nek at 4.30 a.m., by detachments of the Australian Light Horse would help them to gain their objective.

Due to fear of rousing Turkish suspicions it had not been possible to make a detailed survey of all the routes to be followed, but for some weeks Major P. J. Overton and other officers of the New Zealand Mounted Rifles had carried out a number of reconnaissances of the lower foothills, and these officers were to lead the various columns.

General Godley's battle headquarters were down by Ocean Beach. Major-General F. C. Shaw, commanding the 13th (Western) Division, New Army troops, was there with him.

Soon after dark on August 6th, at much the same time as the invasion fleet was setting out for Suvla Bay, Brigadier-General A. R. Russell's Right Covering Force, some 2,000 strong, consisting of the New Zealand Mounted Rifle Brigade (dismounted, of course, and including a Maori contingent) broke camp.

Earlier in the evening the Maoris had mustered silently for a religious service conducted by their chaplain, Henare Wainohu. 'Whatever you do tonight,' he said, exhorting them in the spirit of a warrior chief cum religious leader, 'remember you have the *mana*, the honour and good name of the Maori people in your keeping. Go forward fearlessly, do your duty to the last and never turn your backs on the enemy.'[1]

It was then not long before the order to march. The Right Covering Force had to 'proceed along the beach to Fisherman's Hut, then wheel right into the Sazli Beit Dere. Crossing this, they were to continue north to assault the ridge separating the second gully, the Chailak Dere, and to hold that position. The Right Assaulting Column, also of New Zealanders under Brigadier-General F. E. Johnston, would then be able to enter these two gullies and begin their climb to Chunuk Bair.

A spur, heavily entrenched by the Turks since they wrested it from the Anzacs on May 20th, dominated the approach to these two gullies. Its early capture was essential and a clever ruse had been devised to that end. For several nights, exactly at 9 p.m., the duty destroyer on this flank (either the *Colne* or the *Chelmer*), had burnt a searchlight and bombarded the trenches. Then, after a pause of exactly ten minutes, the dose was repeated until 9.30. Consequently the enemy had learnt to stand down when the searchlight was switched on the first time and not to stand-to again until the second bombardment

34   Petty Officer George Morgan   35   Petty Officer William Main

36   'Rags' between Midshipmen Forbes (*left*)
and Last

37 Lord Kitchener on Russell's Top, Anzac, looking beyond Ocean Beach and
Nibrunesi Point towards Suvla Bay

38 General Birdwood outside his dug-out at
Anzac

39 General Sir Ian Hamilton and Colonel Ce
Allanson on a visit to the author's ship, H.M.
Devonshire, Monte Carlo, 24 March 1939

was over. On the night of the assault, the New Zealanders were able to creep forward in the pitch darkness outside the rays of the search-light and immediately it was switched off, at 9.30, to get in among the enemy with the bayonet. For the loss of only 6 killed and 15 wounded the New Zealanders killed 100 Turks and took 70 prisoners. By 11 p.m. this important position was securely in New Zealand hands.

'It was the Maoris' first battle with the bayonet, and they had gone forward in a mood of savage determination and delight. They went grimly for those Turks and burst into a tremendous *haka* – dance – when they had cleared the trenches.

'"*Ka mate, ka mate – ka ora, ka ora!*" they yelled. "You shall die, you shall die!" Then forward again in silence to the next objective.'[2]

Meanwhile the Wellington Rifles of Russell's Right Covering Force had captured Destroyer Hill, to follow that up with the stiff climb of a crag known as Table Top, a position of the type classified as 'impracticable for infantry'. Nevertheless the cliffs were scaled with bayonet and bomb, and the plateau was carried by midnight.

The detachment which had entered the Chailak Dere was held up by a strong barricade laced with barbed wire, and it took an hour or so for the New Zealand sappers to hack their way through.

Bauchop's Hill was captured by the Otago and Canterbury Regiments at 1 a.m.; but, sad to relate, Lieutenant-Colonel Bauchop, while shouting 'Come on, Boys! Charge!' was mortally wounded. The hill had been named after him several days before the assault, in recognition of his reconnaissance.

Now for news of the Right Assaulting Column. Its task was to enter the Sazli Beit Dere and the Chailak Dere in the wake of its Covering Force and then to begin the arduous climb to Chunuk Bair. Although the column had left Anzac nearly an hour later than planned, good progress was made up the Chailak Dere, and Table Top had been reached by 1 a.m. At one point during the advance Johnston's men heard the sound of piling arms, followed by cheering and hand-clapping. Some Turks, by-passed earlier in the dark, were determined to surrender and did not want there to be any mistake about their intentions.

The moon had now risen, making progress more rapid, but it was getting late, and, by the time the Right Assaulting Column had gathered on the lower slopes of Rhododendron Ridge, Chunuk Bair showed deep purple against the rising sun. As the light increased shrapnel began to spit and shower overhead, combined with cross-fire from Battleship Hill and from a position on the left of Chunuk Bair itself.

The men were very tired. They had accomplished a night march of great difficulty, exposed to continuous perils and surprises. At 8 a.m. a point known as the Apex was reached. Here a depression afforded some cover from the guns, so the Right Assaulting Column entrenched.

The order to halt came from their commander, Brigadier-General Johnston, but it should never have been given. It was contrary to General Birdwood's strict instructions that every unit was to press forward regardless of all difficulties. Johnston's fatal mistake was evident when the attack was delivered a few hours later. Although supported by the fire of all available guns including those of the ships, it made no progress, and we now know, from the evidence of a German officer, that the only Turkish troops on Chunuk Bair at 7 a.m. that morning had been a Turkish battery of two mountain guns with an escort of twenty riflemen, who were asleep . . .

The Left Covering Force, commanded by Brigadier-General J. H. de B. Travers of 40 Brigade, 13th Division, New Army, started from Anzac at 9.30 p.m. They marched along Ocean Beach and, as soon as the Chailak Dere was cleared, continued to the Aghyl Dere, ignoring enfilade fire from the hill to the right, which was not yet captured. Led by the 4th South Wales Borderers and supported by the 5th Wiltshires, they rushed every trench which they encountered and assaulted Damakjelik Spur with the bayonet. By 1.30 a.m. they had occupied the whole hill. The surprise was complete. Turkish officers were even caught in their pyjamas. The New Army had won its spurs. The Left Assaulting Column would now be able to follow into the Aghyl Dere unmolested.

The Left Assaulting Column was under the command of Major-General Cox, who had arrived at Anzac only five days previously. With a total strength of 5,000 rifles, it comprised the 4th Australian Brigade (Brigadier-General J. Monash), Sikhs, Gurkhas and the 21st (Kohat) Mountain Battery of Cox's own 29 Indian Brigade, plus a company of New Zealand Engineers.

Its allotted task was more intricate and confusing and more than twice as long as that given to Johnston's Right Assaulting Column. Only a small fraction of the ground had been reconnoitred.

The whole column, headed by the 4th Australian Brigade, was to march north to the broad plain of the Aghyl Dere, led by Major Overton, detached from the New Zealand Mounted Rifles and

already mentioned, who had risked his life so often during reconnaissance. Alas this gallant officer was to be killed by a sniper at
daylight.

Working up the valley of the Aghyl Dere for three quarters of a
mile, with its left flank protected by the two New Army battalions
already established on the Damakjelik Spur, the two leading
(Australian) battalions were to push out left-handed to form a line
of piquets as far as the Abdul Rahman Spur. The rest of the column
would then strike north-east up the last main tributary of the Aghyl
Dere. At the head of this gully two battalions of Gurkhas would be
sent uphill to attack Hill Q, while the two remaining Australian
battalions, with the 1/6th Gurkhas and 14th Sikhs, were to continue
north-eastward into Azmak Dere and then to Abdul Rahman Spur.
There they would form up and prepare for the final advance on
Hill 971.

It was calculated that the forming-up phase on Abdul Rahman
Spur would be reached about 2 a.m. and that this would give plenty
of margin for the summit of the ridge to be captured an hour later.
The first streak of dawn would come about 4 a.m. But these cal-
culations, though they allowed three and a half hours for an advance
of only three miles, were too optimistic. Apart from the chances of
opposition, they made an insufficient allowance for the checks and
delays inseparable from a night march through very difficult country
culminating in a steep rugged hill not previously reconnoitred.

After proceeding some distance up the Aghyl Dere the Australians
ran into strong opposition. Advancing slowly they found themselves
passing the emplacements of two guns which had long troubled
Anzac, those nicknamed the Anafartas or Anafarta Annie. But the
guns themselves had been hurriedly removed.

It was not till dawn that the brigade reached the ridge above the
upper reaches of the Azmak Dere. There General Monash received the
order to concentrate and attack the towering height of Koja Chemen
Tepe, with the 14th (K.G.O.) Sikhs in support. The enemy in front,
however, was now strong and fully aroused, whereas our troops were
exhausted. No immediate advance was possible, and the ridge
overlooking the Azmak Dere was hurriedly entrenched.

Meanwhile the 1/5th, 2/10th and 1/6th Gurkhas had clambered
up the steep course of the Aghyl Dere's southern (right) fork till they
reached a position facing the Farm. Their right thus came into
touch with the New Zealanders on Rhododendron Ridge, while
their centre and left stood ready to climb the steep front of the main
range and assault Hill Q.

By about 9 a.m. on August 7th, the whole Anzac Force was thus extended in a broken and irregular line from the upper slopes of Rhododendron Ridge, past the front of the Farm, down the southern fork of the Aghyl Dere, along the northern fork across the rugged ground above the Azmak Dere. The right flank rested on Anzac. The left flank was guarded by Damakjelik Spur and by the division now landed at Suvla, whose co-operation was anticipated with eagerness.

Except for Johnston's grave mistake in ordering his Right Assaulting Column to entrench at the foot of Chunuk Bair instead of advancing, all movements had been carried out as designed. But the Turks could now be seen swarming over the summits which should have been in British hands by dawn.

'The troops had performed a feat which is without parallel,' General Birdwood was to say in his report. But this was not sufficient.

In the belief that Chunuk Bair would be occupied by the Right Assaulting Column before dawn, General Birdwood had planned to complete the capture of the summit of the main ridge with the help of two converging attacks on the Nek and Baby 700 at 4.30 a.m. These two points form a bridge between Russell's Top and Sari Bair.

When the hour fixed for these two attacks drew near both Generals Godley and Birdwood were told that the Left Assaulting Column was still in Aghyl Dere and that only a proportion of the Right Assaulting Column had reached the western shoulder of Rhododendron Spur. But it was also known that neither column had encountered much opposition, and General Birdwood was persuaded that Johnston's New Zealanders might at any moment be pushing forward to the summit of Chunuk Bair. The go-ahead was therefore given.

The storming of the Nek and Baby 700 had been entrusted to the 8th (Victorian) and the 10th (West Australian) regiments of the 3rd Light Horse Brigade (Brigadier-General F. G. Hughes), which was raised as part of the first A.I.F. in August 1914. The 10th was well known because it was manned by the sons of farmers and pastoralists. In the first rush to enlist, these young men provided their own horses and saddles. Similarly the men of the 8th came from all over Victoria.

Two parties were selected for the charge from each of the two regiments, 600 men in all. They filed into the Russell's Top trenches just before daylight on Saturday August 7th, all in shirts and shorts with sleeves rolled up but carrying water-bottles and packs. Each man had 200 rounds of ammunition, though the orders were to trust to the bayonet.

At 4 a.m. the bombardment by artillery and by warships began. Unfortunately only a little of this could reach the first Turkish trenches, although those behind it were severely battered and the garrison as a whole was put under heavy strain.

So far all was to schedule, but seven minutes before zero hour the bombardment virtually ceased, due perhaps to faulty synchronisation of watches. At all events the Turks had seven precious minutes to prepare for the attack they knew was coming. They manned their trenches, massing two-deep so that two rifles could fire from a space occupied by one man. They flexed their fingers on the triggers of the machine guns and waited.

'The Commander of the 8th Light Horse was Lieutenant-Colonel A. H. White, a prominent Melbourne businessman. He chose, gallantly, to lead the first line of his regiment, and he it was who gave the fatal order to "Go!" Followed by a crowded line of men he leapt from the trench, went ten paces and died.

'His men met a fantastic fire from rifles and machine-guns. A great many did not even get out of the trench. They were killed or wounded the moment their heads appeared. In thirty seconds the line was gone.

'It was clear in such a torrent of bullets that the fate which had overtaken the first wave must surely overtake the second. Yet within two minutes out that second line went. It had to be waved forward because no spoken order could be heard above the thunderous roar of rifles and machine-guns.

'With 300 of their enemies quite easily disposed of, the Turks now brought to bear two field guns which made even more deadly the task of the men of the 10th Regiment, West Australians, whose turn it now was.

'From a trench crowded with wounded Victorians, a trench from which they had watched a merciless annihilation, they leapt and charged. . . .

'When the sound of battle died away 472 out of a total of 600 had become casualties. No ground was gained.

'The Nek remains in Australian military history as an instance where incredibly brave young men gave their lives in attacking an incredible position under incredible orders.'[3]

By early morning on August 7th, as we have seen, neither of the two Assaulting Columns had reached its objective, and the dawn attacks had ended in failure. 'Despite the care of General Birdwood's preliminary concentration,' wrote the Military Historian; 'despite the important surprise which had been effected; and despite the capture of the Turkish northern outposts in the opening moves of the battle, the scheme for gaining the crest of the main ridge of Sari Bair had definitely failed. The goal might still be reached, but Turkish reinforcements were hurrying to the threatened points; and it was plain to the officers of both assaulting columns that their best chance had gone. . . .'[4]

'In his orders issued overnight Brigadier-General Johnston, commanding the Right Assaulting Column who had so unwisely given the order to halt at the Apex instead of pushing on, arranged to assault Chunuk Bair before dawn on August 8th with the Wellington Battalion in the centre, the 7th Gloucesters on the left and the 8th Welch on the right. The Auckland Mounted Rifles [dismounted] and the Maori contingent were to follow in support, and the Otago Battalion was to hold the Apex position. Zero hour was fixed for 3.30 a.m.

'The enemy showed no activity during the night, and all was quiet when, shortly after 3 a.m. the troops began to form up. The advance was late in starting, and dawn was just appearing when the leading platoons of the Wellingtons headed for the main ridge.

'After the previous day's experience it was looked upon as certain that the advance would be very costly, and every moment a storm of fire was expected from the frowning ridge above. But to the general surprise the troops went on unchecked. Not a shot was fired as the dreadful hill was breasted, and the top was gained without a blow. The Turkish infantry had gone.

'Two companies of the Wellington Battalion (Lieutenant-Colonel W. G. Malone) started to dig in on the crest. The men were in high spirits. Away on the right the growing daylight was showing up the paths and tracks in rear of the enemy's lines at Anzac, now at last outflanked. Straight to their front were the shining waters of the Narrows, the goal of the expedition.

'But the triumph was short-lived. It was only at Chunuk Bair that the Turkish garrison, influenced by some unexpected panic, had abandoned their new line. Battleship Hill on the right, and Hill Q on the left, were still occupied, and, as soon as it was light enough for these troops to realise what had happened, a fierce fire was opened from both flanks on the crest of Chunuk Bair. The 7th Gloucesters suffered very heavily.

'In a few minutes the situation had changed. Major-General Cox's columns, in a brave attempt on Hill Q and Hill 971, found

themselves outflanked on the left by Turks owing to the failure of the
Suvla landing. They had no choice but to hew their way back to
their starting point after losing 1,000 officers and men, leaving the
Turkish garrisons at these points free to devote their whole attention
to the recovery of Chunuk Bair.

'Fighting grimly, the two Wellington companies on top of the
ridge maintained their exposed positions till nearly every man was
killed. The few survivors were at last overwhelmed, and soon after
9 a.m. the enemy tried to close with the main line but the remnants
of the 8th Gloucesters and 8th Welch continued to hold their own.

'For the rest of the afternoon incessant fighting continued. The
Maoris joined up with some of Cox's troops. The Auckland Mounted
Rifles, dashing forward a little later, suffered so heavily that they
only reached the Pinnacle. At 2 p.m., however, in answer to an
urgent call for help, they made another effort and eventually managed to reach the Wellington Battalion's line.

'It was only by frequent counter-charges that the New Zealand
troops could keep the Turks from lining the crest of the ridge immediately above them, and in one of these sallies the gallant Colonel
Malone was killed. But his splendid leadership had won the day
for his troops. The Turkish attack began to flag and finally died
away.

'Of the Wellington Battalion only two officers and forty-seven men
remained unwounded. The 8th Welch had lost 17 officers and 400
men; the 7th Gloucesters had lost 350 men, and every one of its
officers and sergeants had been either wounded or killed.'[5]

Sir Ian Hamilton in his Dispatch, where he refers to the 7th
Gloucestershire, wrote: 'By midday on the 8th the battalion consisted of small groups of men commanded by junior non-commis-
sioned officers or privates. Chapter and verse may be quoted for the
view that the rank and file of an army cannot long endure unless
given confidence by the example of good officers. Yet here is one
instance where a battalion of the New Army fought right on, from
midday till sunset, without any officers.'

For the renewed attack next morning, August 9th, a third assaulting
column was organised out of the battalions from the 10th and 13th
Divisions of the New Army, in reserve. Brigadier-General A. H.
Baldwin (38th Brigade) was given a strong mixed force of five
battalions and ordered to assemble in the evening of August 8th in
the Chailak Dere. Advancing from that point through the night,
he was to follow up Rhododendron Ridge and, co-operating with

Brigadier-General Johnston's Right Assaulting Column, was to move in successive lines to the summit, and thence left towards Hill Q. This was to form the main attack of the day.

Baldwin sent the Loyal North Lancashires in advance, and followed with the remaining four battalions. The track was by this time well trodden, and every precaution was taken to keep clear of wounded and 'empties' coming down. Guides for the column were also provided.

Progress was slow, the night pitch dark, the ascent rough and, towards the end, very steep. The column lost its way and found itself at 5.15 a.m., an hour after daylight, down in a deep hollow of the Farm on the left of the ridge, which it should have climbed to the Apex.

At this moment, when Baldwin's support was badly needed, one of the epics of the Gallipoli campaign was being enacted upon the summit far above them.

During the night of August 8th/9th Major Cecil Allanson, commanding the 1/6th Gurkha Rifles, was dug-in not far from the crest of Hill Q. He had been ordered to get on to the top starting at 5.15 a.m., after a naval bombardment from 4.45 to 5.15. All troops in the vicinity were to co-operate. Baldwin's Brigade 'would come up on his right for certain'. At least so he was told.

As it happened Major Allanson had already acted on his own initiative. He had been down to the battalions nearest him, the 9th Warwicks, the 6th South Lancashires and the North Staffords, to get their support. 'The South Lancashires gave me two companies and the Warwicks one,' he wrote in his diary. 'The entire three regiments should, in my opinion, have pushed up and joined me.'

By this time the enemy had discovered that Allanson was immediately below but the Royal Navy greatly helped him by keeping a searchlight trained on the hill to discourage the Turks from attacking.

Allanson spent the night in Battalion headquarters (a rough dug-out or fox-hole, some 300 yards from the summit) with Captain Edward Selby Phipson, I.M.S.

'Allanson was wearing a bright red cloth patch on the back of his uniform to make him easily recognisable from the rear,' Phipson said in his diary. 'It reminded me of the Crusaders, and indeed there was a good deal of the Crusader in Allanson.'

At 4.30 a.m. (9th) Allanson telephoned Lieutenant Le Marchand, senior officer of the detachments of Warwicks and South Lancashires, giving him his plans for the attack. 'Right, Major, everything is quite clear,' he replied. Whereupon they synchronised their watches.

Company commanders were inclined to regard the plan as hopeless, and the cliff too stiff to climb and asked if the 1/6th Gurkhas would lead. 'No!' Allanson had replied, 'We must all go up together.'

'I put the three companies into the trenches among my men,' Allanson continued, 'and said that the moment they saw me go forward everyone was to start.' He then commented on the artillery preparation, saying how the trenches were being torn to pieces by the naval bombardment. 'The accuracy was marvellous as we were only just below.'

The bombardment was due to stop at 5.15 but at 5.18 it had not stopped, which made Allanson wonder whether his watch was wrong. Then at 5.20 came silence. He waited three minutes to be certain, in spite of the risk; then off they dashed. A most perfect advance and a wonderful sight, the Gurkhas shouting their war cry '*Aiyo Gurkhāli*, the Gurkhas have come!'

'At the top we met the Turks,' Allanson continued. 'Le Marchand was down, a bayonet through the heart. I got one through the leg; and then for about ten minutes we fought hand to hand. We bit and fisted and used rifles and pistols as clubs. And then the Turks turned and fled, and I felt a very proud man; the key of the Peninsula was ours, and our losses had not been so very great for such a result. Below I saw the Straits, motors and wheeled transport on the roads leading to Achi Baba.'

Looking back and seeing that he was not being supported, Allanson felt that he could help best by going after the Turks, which he did.

'We had only got about 100 yards down,' he said, 'when suddenly our Navy put shells into us, and all was terrible confusion; we were obviously mistaken for Turks. The place was a mass of blood and limbs and screams. We all flew back to the summit and to our old position just below.'

'The blast of the shells was so tremendous,' wrote Surgeon Phipson, that although protected by the ridge I was blown backwards, head over heels out of our fox-hole – but was not hurt. Allanson stayed a little while on the ridge, gazing, as he said, on the "Promised Land"; but he soon saw that the attack had failed and that the Turks were massing for a counter-attack. He limped back very dejected and in considerable pain. I attended to his wound. I shall never forget the sight of the casualties, dead and wounded after the naval shelling. They looked as if they had been sprayed with canary-yellow colour-wash.'

'We were counter-attacked by large bodies of Turks,' Allanson wrote, 'but they never got within fifteen yards. Every man remained glued to his trenches. How I admired them and how I blessed them. It all wanted courage after four nights without sleep, only two days' meagre rations and one water bottle each.'

Late that afternoon (9th), Allanson was ordered down by Brigade H.Q. and told that before leaving he was to hand over his command to Captain Geoffrey Tomes, 53rd Sikhs, who had been sent up for the purpose. But Tomes had hardly been there an hour before he was shot through the heart.

'When Phipson told Allanson of Tomes's death, he thought for a minute and then said: "Well, Phippy, there is no one left to hand over to but you."' Then, assisted by two stretcher-bearers and limping painfully Allanson started his weary descent down to the field dressing station far below.

Left to himself and feeling rather lonely, Phipson's first thought was to remove his Red Cross Brassard and put it in his haversack, as he could no longer claim the protection (if any) of the Geneva Convention. Then, after a discussion with Gambirsing Pun, the Subadar Major, he decided to try and find some troops in reserve to give support.

Phipson sought out what appeared to be the nearest troops, a unit of Kitchener's Army. They were 'comfortably disposed in a small open glade, surrounded by trees, about half-way down the main nullah, and were having a hearty meal from steaming field-kettles emitting a savory aroma.'

'I explained our situation to the C.O. He was a man of heavy build and uncompromising manner, who, in answer to my earnest request for reinforcements, firmly and rather indignantly refused, saying that he could not think of disturbing his "lads" who "had not had a square meal since breakfast that morning".'

Seeing that that argument would be fruitless, Phipson returned empty-handed to his Bn H.Q. and tried his luck with written messages to troops on his flanks but drew a blank. 'They had either retired, or expected to retire, or themselves needed reinforcements.'

That night, August 9th/10th, Phipson and the gallant survivors of the 1/6th Gurkhas were harassed by constant sniping apparently from their flanks, but mercifully the Turks never approached nearer than about thirty yards. Next morning orders came from Brigade headquarters to 'retire on to the next position held by our troops'.

'The operation was carried out wonderfully well. The men were worn out, suffering from want of sleep, hunger and thirst, but not one man broke from a walk. That evening saw them 1,000 feet down, back within half a mile of the sea, digging themselves in, in spite of their fatigue, in the continuous line it had now been decided to hold.

The regiment had lost very heavily. All its British officers except Surgeon Phipson were casualties, as well as 60 per cent of the Gurkha officers and 52 per cent of the rank and file.

'*Kāphar hunu bhanda marnu rāmo chha*' – the Gurkhas had said: 'It is better to die than to be a coward.'

After the evacuation of Gallipoli, Colonel Cecil Allanson served on Haig's staff in France; was at Versailles for the peace-making; and with the Russian Expedition under General Ironside. Finally he commanded a brigade in Waziristan, 1920–2. After leaving the Army, he joined the Consular Service and was among the last to leave Monaco after the Germans entered France in World War II.

H.M.S. *Devonshire*, in which ship I was serving, visited Monte Carlo on 24th March 1939, when to my surprise and delight both Sir Ian Hamilton and Colonel Allanson, the Consul-General, paid our ship a visit. On shore, that afternoon, Allanson and I discussed Hill Q and all that it had meant to him and to us midshipmen of the *Bacchante*. He was astonished to learn that on that fatal day, 9th August 1915, three days before my sixteenth birthday, I had been taken up to the trenches below Chunuk Bair and saw through a trench periscope heaps of casualties – friend and foe – lying on the slopes. Such is the impressionable nature of a boy of that age that the memory of the scene had remained imprinted on my mind. Among the dead I remembered one man in particular. He was smiling. . . .

The Company of the 9th Warwicks was commanded by Captain Bill Slim (later Field-Marshal the Viscount Slim of Burma), who was among the wounded. 'I was so impressed by the 1/6th Gurkhas,' he told me in 1968, 'that I vowed I would join the Indian Army if I survived the war. In 1919 I joined it and served with it until 1937. I have since had three battalions of the regiment under my command in various theatres and they were all as good as the 1st Battalion was in Gallipoli, and that is saying a lot.'

There has been a great deal of speculation over the years as to who fired into Allanson's men. Did the shells come from the Navy or the Army or from a Turkish source? In effect who turned what might have been an important advantage into an actual defeat?

'Part of Cox's and Baldwin's Brigade reached crest yesterday but were shelled off by the *Bacchante*,' General Birdwood noted in his *War Diary*, 10th August 1915.

'Most of us thought the shells came from the *Bacchante*, a familiar and encouraging sight at anchor in the bay,' Colonel Phipson wrote in 1970. His opinion was shared by two midshipmen of the *Bacchante* who were on board at the time.

'I saw the flashes of the naval guns. I saw the shells exploding; and nothing will ever change my opinion,' wrote Lieutenant-General Sir Reginald Savory, whom we have already met when he was Lieutenant Reggie, 14th (K.G.O.) Sikhs.

Although the British Military Historian said categorically that 'The Navy and the shore artillery subsequently declared that the shelling was done by the Turks,' C. E. W. Bean, the Australian Historian recorded, 'These shells came, almost certainly not from the Navy but from a howitzer battery at Anzac which a few minutes before had thrown a deadly salvo among New Zealanders a little further south.' (Colonel Allanson was inclined to accept this explanation after walking over the ground between the wars.)

Opinions certainly differ, so I am wondering what you will think of this one:

I mentioned in a previous chapter that the ship's company of the *Irresistible* were marked with spots of yellow stain from the fumes of bursting Turkish shell after their ship had been mined in the Dardanelles on March 18th. Commodore Keyes also referred to the appearance of Lieutenant Sandford next morning whose 'clothes and skin [were] discoloured by the fumes of Turkish high explosive shell'. Surgeon Phipson has also told us that our wounded from Hill Q 'looked as if they had been sprayed with canary yellow colour-wash'.

'All we know for certain', wrote Captain Maurice Parkes-Buchanan, a Naval Ordnance expert, who was a sub-lieutenant in the destroyer *Wear* at Gallipoli, 'is that all H.E. [high explosive] fillings in shell are yellow in colour but when effectively detonated display black smoke. They will display yellow smoke either when they explode, as distinct from detonate, under faulty fuse action, or if the shell breaks up on impact and the filling fails to ignite due to a faulty fuse. In this case it simply crumbles into a yellow cloud.

'Although the evidence is not sufficiently conclusive to warrant any outright, positive statement absolving the Navy in absolute terms, it is reasonable to support the thought that the shells which fell among Allanson's men on Hill Q came from the Turks (whose shells were inclined to be faulty) and not from one of H.M. ships, as has been suggested.'

'A fever about Anzac' had held Sir Ian Hamilton since dawn on the 9th, so at noon he took a boat over General Godley's H.Q. above

Ocean Beach where, incredible though it may seem after all that had happened both at Anzac and at Suvla, he found his three generals – Birdwood, Godley and Shaw, in high spirits. They sat down on a spur above Godley's headquarters which gave them a grand outlook over the whole Suvla area and across to Chunuk Bair, to eat their rations and to hold an impromptu council of war.

'Godley is certain the Turks will never make us quit. Shaw is equally confident. Birdwood thinks Chunuk Bair should be safe, but not so safe as it would have been had we held on to Hill Q where Baldwin's delay lost us the crest line . . . The Anzac generals are in great form. They are sure they will have the whip hand of the Narrows by tomorrow. . . .'6

And what of the morrow?

The weary New Zealand troops at the Pinnacle and on the slopes of Chunuk Bair were relieved after nightfall on August 9th by two battalions of Shaw's 13th (Western) Division, New Army, the 6th Loyal North Lancashire and the 5th Wiltshire regiments. They had hardly settled down in their new positions when they were exposed to a tremendous attack. The whole of the Turkish 8th Division, brought from the Asiatic shore with three additional battalions, were led forward to the assault at 4.45 a.m. by Mustapha Kemal in person.

The thousand British rifles, for all of whom room could be found on the narrow summit, were overwhelmed in this first flood. Very few of the Lancashire men escaped, and the Wiltshire battalion was annihilated.

Meanwhile, on the northern side of Rhododendron Spur, the right wing of Mustapha Kemal's attack was pouring down the steep hillside to the Farm, and bitter hand to hand fighting was taking place.

Accurate details of this Turkish attack have never come to light, but the appalling British casualties bear witness to the grim struggle which took place. The detachment of the Warwickshires was killed almost to a man. The 6th Royal Irish Rifles lost half its rank and file and nearly all its officers. Brigadier-General Baldwin and his brigade-major were among those killed.

Flushed with victory, the Turks pressed on, intent on driving the invaders into the sea. But now they encountered a blast of fire from the Fleet and from every gun in the Anzac line. Under this storm the advancing Turkish masses were crushed. Of the three or four thousand men who descended the seaward slopes of the hills only a few hundred regained the crest. But there they stayed, and stayed until the end of the story.

Out of some 50,000 British troops engaged at Suvla and Anzac the casualties in three days' fighting had amounted to no less than 18,000, and the Turkish forces, still inferior in numbers though veterans in battle experience, were firmly established on every point of vantage. The Turkish strength, moreover, was increasing hourly, while Sir Ian Hamilton was nearly at the end of his resources.

On a gaunt ridge overlooking Kilia Bay in the Narrows, a massive stone obelisk can now be seen by all who make passage of the Dardanelles. This monument is on the summit of Chunuk Bair. It marks the point which was gained by New Zealand troops in the great battles for the heights. Looking up at the shining white memorial from the deck of a ship it is not difficult to recognise the vital importance of Chunuk Bair in August 1915 or the measure of the Turkish peril while the summit was in British hands.

24

The Impossible?

I tell you naught for your comfort
Yea, naught for your desire
Save that the sky grows darker yet
And the sea rises higher.
G. K. Chesterton, 1874–1936
Ballad of the White Horse

On the evening of August 10th Sir Ian wrote: 'We had Chunuk Bair in our hands the best part of two days and two nights ... The Turks are well commanded: that I admit. Their generals knew they were done unless they could quickly knock us off ... So they have done it. Never mind: never say die.'[1]

This statement is typical of the man. At the moment it was recorded the whole structure of his August plan lay in ruins. The Helles garrison had failed to prevent the Southern Group from sending reinforcements to Sari Bair; the Anzac Corps had fought itself to a standstill; a large part of IX Corps was exhausted. None of the original objectives had been gained. But the Commander-in-Chief refused to accept defeat. He counted that the Turks were as tired and disorganised as we were. He was sure their casualties had been just as severe, and with all the faith that was in him he held to his belief that victory would belong to the side with the greatest will to conquer. He knew that the Anzac troops could not attack again for several days and that even then they would have no chance of success without the help of a turning movement from Suvla, but he still had no doubt that such a turning movement was possible and would prove to be successful.

'A sanguine temperament, indomitable courage and a determination to conquer are invaluable qualities in the character of a commander-in-chief. But there can be little doubt that Sir Ian Hamilton was underestimating the difficulties that confronted him, and in particular the really serious condition in Stopford's IX Corps.'[2]

The 54th (East Anglian) Division, Major-General Inglefield,

began to reach Suvla on the afternoon of the 10th and seven of its battalions had landed by nightfall. As they would be needed for an early advance on Tekke Tepe, Sir Ian was particularly anxious that its units should not be used piecemeal. General Stopford was given instructions to that effect and also told that this division represented the last available reserve.

But at IX Corps headquarters there was anxiety for the safety of the Suvla beaches, and at 10 p.m. on the very day of their arrival six of the newly arrived battalions belonging to three different brigades were hurried inland to strengthen the defences. Soon after starting, the guide lost his way. There was much marching and counter-marching, and the troops passed a restless night to no purpose.

Early next morning (11th), orders reached Stopford from G.H.Q. that the 54th Division was to seize Tekke Tepe at dawn on the 12th. Sir Ian followed up this letter with a personal visit. In the discussion which followed he had to insist that the attack on Tekke Tepe could and must be made. Obviously, as a day had been wasted, the advance would have to be postponed for twenty-four hours, but the 54th Division must assault the crest at dawn on the 13th, and the 10th and 11th Divisions, which had taken part in the original landings on August 6th, must render as much assistance as they could.

At a conference held at IX Corps headquarters on the morning of the 12th, Stopford still found himself faced with difficulties. Poor progress had been made in the reorganisation of the whole front, and though the Turks had shown little activity on the 11th, there had been a good deal of sniping, and his troops had had a trying day. The re-sorting of units had given his men little chance of sleep, and the divisions were still so intermixed that the task of supplying rations had proved difficult.

In these circumstances he was apprehensive of launching an attack, but, if it had to be done, he wanted Lindley's 53rd (Welch) Division to advance to the foothills that afternoon, in order to give Inglefield's 54th (East Anglian) Division a shorter night march and a clear run to assault the crest at dawn on the 13th.

Major-General Lindley said at once that he did not consider his troops fit for it, but the problem was solved by Brigadier-General Inglefield, who offered to carry out the task with one of his brigades. This offer was accepted, and Brunker's 163rd Brigade was detailed to go forward to the foothills. A brigade of the 53rd would follow, and after nightfall the whole of the 54th Division would pass through to assault the crest of Tekke Tepe at dawn. The 10th and 11th Divisions were to co-operate on the flanks.

The 163rd Brigade, which consisted of the 1/5th Norfolks, the 1/8th Hampshires (Isle of Wight Rifles) and the 1/5th Suffolks, was ordered forward at 4.45 p.m. Commanding officers had never seen the ground and had doubts about the exact whereabouts of their objective. The terrain was covered with thick, prickly scrub, and it was soon evident that a mistake had been made in trying to cross this open plain in daylight. All units suffered many casualties and lost cohesion. The advance died away, and those who could do so retreated to their previous positions, with one notable exception.

Colonel Sir Horace Beauchamp, 1/5th Norfolks, known to his regiment as 'The Bo'sun' because of his love of the sea, a bold and self-confident officer who had seen service in Egypt, the Sudan and South Africa, continued to press forward with the best part of his battalion. A few men found their way back during the night, but the Colonel, 16 of his officers and 250 men went on, following the best traditions of the battalion which included the Sandringham Company and the King's agent there, Captain Frank Beck. They completely disappeared and were never seen again.

It was not until September 1919 that the mystery of their disappearance was solved: 'We have found the 5th Norfolks,' the officer commanding a British Graves Registration Unit wrote, 'but can only identify two. The others are scattered over an area of one square mile, at a distance of at least 800 yards behind the Turkish front line.'

By August 11th it was clear that the new venture – the August offensive – had failed. Major Jack Churchill wrote to his brother Winston that day, 'The golden opportunity has gone, and positions that might have been won with a little perspiration would only be gained now by blood.' In his letter Jack Churchill tried to explain what had gone wrong:

'We are all trying to understand what on earth has happened to these [Suvla] men and why they are showing such extraordinary lack of enterprise. They are not cowards – physically they are as fine a body of men as the regular army. I think it is partly on account of their training. They have never seen a shot fired before. For a year they have been soldiers and during that time they have been taught only one thing – Trench warfare . . . They landed and advanced a mile & thought they had done something wonderful. They had no standard to go by – no other troops were there to show them what was right. They seemed not to know what they should do . . . They showed extraordinary ignorance. A shell burst near a working party – at least $\frac{1}{2}$ a mile away. Officers and men stopped work, rushed to the low beach cliffs and lay down taking cover! A land mine exploded and the men near all lay flat and remained there thinking they were being shelled! . . . A few shots sent them retreating pell mell from Chocolate Hill. Blaming the senior officers must be left to the people who can give effect to their opinions. But there is no doubt that these divisions were completely out of hand.'

On August 12th Jack Churchill added a further page to his letter. 'We still hope to do a lot of good,' he wrote, 'but the chance of a real coup has gone, I am afraid.'[3]

During the forenoon of August 13th an ominous message reached Stopford from 53rd Division. 'The Turks,' Lindley said, 'were shelling his line intermittently; and one of his brigades was finding it very hard to hold on.' Hammersley, commanding the 11th Division, confirmed that a brigade of the 53rd seemed 'very shaky'.

'The tone of these messages was unwarranted,' wrote the Military Historian. But it was accepted by Stopford, who added in his telegram to the Commader-in-Chief that 'now he had only the 54th who may bolt at any minute'.

On receipt of this disturbing message Sir Ian went to Suvla where a momentous interview took place. General Stopford again asked for more time to reorganise his troops. He insisted that the 53rd Division was finished and the 54th incapable of attack. To this belief, which was plainly shared by his subordinates, he clung with determination.

Three courses were now open to Sir Ian: to agree to further delay; to insist on an attack by commanders who professed no faith in their troops and were already convinced of failure; or to appoint new commanders. Deferring his choice between these grim alternatives, he left the conference and returned to G.H.Q. where he decided, against his every inclination, to accept a further delay and to tell Lord Kitchener what he thought of the Suvla generals:

'The result of my visit to IX Corps has bitterly disappointed me. There is nothing for it but to allow them time to rest and reorganise, unless I force Stopford and his divisional generals to undertake a general action for which, in their present frame of mind, they have no heart. In fact these generals are unfit for it. With exceeding reluctance I am obliged to give them time to rest and reorganise their troops.'

Lord Kitchener's reply was received on August 15th, and it gave Sir Ian the lead he had been wanting.

'. . . I think Stopford should come home. This is a young man's war . . . Any generals I have available I will send you.'[4]

Lieutenant-General the Hon. Julian Byng was sent from France to command IX Corps, vice Stopford. Major-Generals E. A. Fanshawe and F. Stanley Maude were coming out, too. These appointments pleased Sir Ian immensely. Pending Byng's arrival, he put Major-General de Lisle from Cape Helles in temporary command of IX Corps on August 15th, and Stopford left next day.

On arrival in England Stopford was to play a dirty trick. He sent his report on Suvla, dated August 18th, direct to the War Office instead of to Sir Ian. It was drawn up less than a fortnight after the landing, before the facts could be fully known, and consequently contained inaccuracies. It also levelled a number of veiled charges against the C.-in-C.'s conduct of operations. Worse still was the behaviour of the War Office. Instead of asking the Commander-in-Chief for his comments on this report by a subordinate, the War Office accepted Stopford's memorandum at its face value and invited comments of three other generals. The War Office letter to Sir Ian inviting his remarks on the document is dated 6th November 1915. This delay was grossly unfair to Sir Ian, whose dispatch was held up in consequence.

When the Commander-in-Chief appointed Major-General de Lisle to the temporary command of IX Corps, he invited Sir Bryan Mahon (10th (Irish) Division) to waive his seniority 'at any rate for the present phase'. 'I respectfully decline,' Mahon replied, 'to serve under the officer you name. Please let me know to whom I am to hand over command of the Division.'

'A lieutenant-general in the British Army chucking up his command while his division is actually under fire is a very unhappy affair,' Sir Ian wrote, with justification. It was he who had applauded Rear-Admiral Wemyss's magnanimity in agreeing to serve under de Robeck, his junior, when Admiral Carden went sick. 'Wemyss put seniority in his pocket – fighting first, rank afterwards,' Sir Ian had said.[5]

And now the Suvla command, as we have known it, quickly disappeared. Brigadier-General Sitwell (34 Brigade) was relieved on August 18th, and on the same day Major-General Lindley resigned, recognising that he was not capable of restoring the *morale* and efficiency of his 53rd Division. Brigadier-General Hill (31 Brigade) was invalided on August 22nd, suffering from acute dysentery, and next day Major-General Hammersley, commanding the 11th (Northern)

Division, was taken off in a state of collapse from a clot of blood in his leg.

Six commanding officers, none of them below the rank of brigadier-general, packed off must surely constitute a record in British military history. And the tragedy is that the changes came too late. By August 16th the battle was already lost.

Of my own experiences in the *Bacchante*'s picket boat operating off the Suvla beaches there is little I can say, because after a couple of days there came a request from Anzac for picket boats, and we were among those sent. From Anzac we witnessed Mustapha Kemal's grand assault on August 10th and stood by for evacuation, just as we had done on the day of the original landing, while every gun in the area poured shells into the advancing enemy. Once again the Turks were held, the firing died away. Then down came the wounded to the beaches. We thought the stream would never end.

Commander Edward Cater, the Assistant Beach Master, had been killed on August 7th during a beach strafe. This gallant officer, whom I have already mentioned, was in the original landing on April 25th and had never been away.

Cater had been promoted to the rank of Commander on June 30th, exactly five weeks before his death. He is the only naval officer buried at Anzac, in the Beach Cemetery overlooking Brighton Beach. The earthly remains of Private John Simpson, 'the man with the donkey', and of Lieutenant Onslow, Birdwood's A.D.C., lie there too.

Petty Officer George Morgan, our friend of the *Ocean* and the *Triumph* was with Cater when he was killed.

'This incident happened much quicker than I can write it and it caused a depression on our feelings. We could ill afford to lose this officer, brave and fearless, who never wished men to unduly expose themselves to danger and whose object was to work hand in hand with the Army Landing Officers. I think it is my duty to say this in respect to the memory of so able an officer.

'Our party on shore,' Morgan continued, 'soon began to dwindle with wounded and sickness, and the work began to get harder and harder. Some additional officers and ratings were sent to reinforce our numbers for we had Walker's pier now to look after.

'This morning we landed guns, and hot work it was, for the horses and men, to get them into position. One awful sight I saw was when one of the horses that was taking the guns up the hill got shot through the open mouth into the back of the throat. The driver brought it down to the beach, staggering along, to be examined by the vet.

It dropped in a heap, dying fast. Another man was bringing the other horse, for they work in pairs, and when it reached its dying chum it pawed the ground and cried like a child, great tears rolling down its face. Trembling all over, it was led away at the order of a big Australian who said it was too hard to watch its grief.'

Petty Officer Morgan commented freely on the small stature of the troops in Kitchener's Army and frankly admitted his doubts about their ability to repel attacks from the Turks 'who are tidy sized men and very good fighters'. He noticed, too, giant Aussies and New Zealanders watching them with the same curiosity and wondering if England had sent her last hopes out. 'But,' he wrote, 'not long after I heard the same giants saying how proud they were of the little fellows who never knew when they were beat. What is contained in the bone comes out in the flesh. It is handed down from the warriors of old to the bank clerks, shopmen and navvies who swell the ranks of today's New Army.'[6]

At 2.20 p.m. on August 13th, when Morgan and his party were trying to salvage a boat which had been sunk by Watson's pier, a shell came over from the same direction as the one that had killed Commander Cater just a week before. The shell burst within a few feet of Morgan and riddled him with shrapnel bullets.

'I passed out for a minute or so,' he wrote, 'and on coming round found myself in a sitting position about to fall overboard. I had been struck in the right arm by one bullet. Another had passed through my right breast and lodged just under the left shoulder. A third had struck me below the right shoulder blade and had come out through my left breast. A fourth struck me lower down the back coming out at the abdomen just above the left hip; and a fifth had caught me in the small of the back paralysing the use of my legs. I was in a tidy mess.

'"Stretcher bearer! Stretcher bearer!" The call I had heard so often was for me this time.

'Officers and men alike came to visit me at the Field Dressing station. My Australian friend, my dug-out companion, and Ginger, our neighbour, all came to wish me luck. I don't know whether the boys finished off the boat we were working on. I don't expect so, as the Turks were shelling until sunset.

'On my way to the hospital ship *Rewa* I thought I would die of thirst and asked one of the bluejackets to give me a drink. He politely told me that had he wanted to kill me he would but that as he had some respect for me he wouldn't give me enough to drown a fly.'

Morgan said he received the best attention possible and that just before the *Rewa* sailed one of his officers came on board and, after seeing the surgeon, entered the ward.

'"Morgan, my boy, you are going home!"

'I thought he meant I was dying, so I said, "Aye, aye, Sir; I know, it's all right."

'He must have guessed what was going on in my mind. "No, Morgan, my lad, you're going to England instead of Alexandria!"

'How well I remember the nurse arriving and pushing him away, at the same time pushing something into my arm, saying: "Go away, please. I will not have my patient excited" . . . Then all became blank.

'I came round the following morning to find the doctor bending over me. "That bit of news did you more good than I can," he said.'

Morgan lay propped up in his cot with the words 'Going Home! Going Home!' ringing in his ears to remind him of something he had heard once before but which had not come true. 'It started me dreaming of the vessel steaming away from this cursed place where even now I can hear the noise of rapid rifle-fire and bursting shells. This place that I thought would be my last home. But now I am going to England. Homeward bound after all.

'It seemed too much for my nerves, and no wonder I didn't reply to Nurse who had asked me three times if I would have my milk.

'"Nurse, when is the ship leaving?" and she said laughingly, "When you have had your milk".

'"Hurry up then with the milk. I want to be off soon in case they alter their minds again".'

Before the *Rewa* sailed for Alexandria Morgan with other casualties for the U.K., was transferred to a troopship fitted out as a hospital carrier. 'There was not a cot to swing in,' Morgan said, 'and I missed the comfort of the *Rewa* and the kindly nurse and doctor. Plymouth was reached a fortnight later "where I had the pleasure and happiness of seeing my wife Flo and little boy again."'[7]

Considerable criticism has been levelled against the arrangements made for evacuating the sick and wounded from Gallipoli, but it was the numbers involved which made their removal so difficult.

According to a pre-arranged plan all wounded were to be taken direct to hospital ships, where they would be quickly classified on deck, the serious cases being kept on board and the lightly wounded passed across to trawlers, moored on the opposite side of the ship, for conveyance to 'hospital carriers' in Imbros harbour. The transports fitted out as carriers were not protected by the Geneva Convention and could not lie off the Peninsula as hospital ships could. Owing, however, to the requirements of the fighting troops being paramount, there were not enough lighters for the prompt evacuation of all the wounded as they streamed down from the front, and the number of trawlers available for light cases was also too small.

On August 13th the hospitals at Egypt and Malta were reported to be full, and two days later, since there were no hospital ships at Mudros, the *Aquitania* was fitted out hurriedly as a hospital carrier and sent direct from Mudros to England with no less than 2,400 wounded on board. This great Cunarder, which returned to Mudros later as a properly equipped hospital ship, was followed home by other liners carrying similar consignments. These drastic measures saved the situation.

Nursing Sisters of the Queen Alexandra's Royal Naval Nursing Service gave splendid help in the hospital ships which lay off the beaches, and their task was no less onerous and exacting than that of the doctors.

'Our chief difficulties,' wrote Nursing Sister Hilda Chibnall, 'are the endless struggles to get the patients properly clean and decently clothed, to endeavour to combat acute collapse, exhaustion and mental shock from which many of them are suffering when they reach us after lying out for hours without food, exposed to sun and tormented with flies. They all arrive on board in the clothes they have worn for many weeks or months. The dressings are done under difficulty, especially in rough weather, and the most fortunate sisters are those who are slightly built and can easily squeeze between the cots.

'Work in the operating theatres is very different from anything we have seen before. The patients have no previous preparation. They are carried straight to the table and their dirty blood-stained clothes have to be cut right off and the skin scrubbed clean before any actual surgery can begin.

'As our numbers are limited, only one night sister can be on duty at a time, and with so many cases in the ship her task is not easy. However, on one point we are all agreed – that we have never before nursed men who suffered so much and complained so little, nor seen patients show so much unselfishness towards each other and gratitude to those who are nursing them.'[8]

'It was just wonderful to see those brave nurses,' wrote Private Frank Clune, who was a patient in the hospital ship *Delta* during the August offensive. 'Some of them were mere girls, and frail-looking things, who you would think would be blown over by the least puff of wind, going around among the poor wounded boys, with a soothing word here, a glass of water there, and a draught to another who was in pain.

'When the final day of the war comes I think the greatest praise will go to those noble nurses who are working on our behalf all over the world at the present day.'[9]

We worked off the beach in our picket boat for several weeks, often sleeping in dug-outs when the *Bacchante* was out of reach. There was a noticeable change of spirit at Anzac now. Previously it had been a gay, heavily populated city, full of life and confidence in victory. All that had gone. The men knew they had given their best but that the Turks, although pushed further up the ghastly hills, still looked down from nearly impregnable positions and Constantinople was as far away as ever.

Some motor lighters, the same class as those used in the Suvla landings, had been sent to Anzac to help with the evacuation of wounded, but, because of the large numbers involved, picket boats towing large flat-topped barges were used as well. On this job we were now employed:

'*Bacchante*'s picket boat!'

'Sir?'

'Go over to Walker's Pier and take off sick and wounded Indians. They are coming down now.'

'Aye, aye, Sir!'

We had hardly got secured before the procession began to arrive, led by a stretcher case with an Indian orderly in attendance.

'Are you in charge, boy?'

'Yes, Sir,' I replied and looked down. It was the Colonel of the Regiment. His face was the colour of marble; his hands and arms were heavily bandaged. He was in great pain.

I was then to witness a sight I have never forgotten. There he lay, propping himself up on one elbow, refusing to be moved until all his men had been attended to. He had something kind to say in Hindustani to each man as he passed. '*Acchha, Colonel Sahib*,' they replied in turn, tears rolling down their cheeks. '*Bahut acchha, Sahib.*' The sepoy would then salute if he could.

Then followed a heart-breaking task of touting the wounded round the fleet. 'Sorry, old chap, full up here!' said the first ship. 'We can take three walking cases,' said the second, and so it went on. When cot cases were hoisted in, we had to wait for the stretchers to be returned, as they were urgently needed ashore.

While we were about this agonising business the wounded sepoys kept quiet. Just one screamed: '*Murgaya Sahib, murgaya!*' I'm dying, Sahib, I'm dying. His *pagri* (turban) came off and his *kangha* and *chakar* (comb and quoit-shaped hair ring, symbols of a Sikh's free masonry) became detached as he struggled for breath. Soon it was all over . . .

'All fast for'ard.' 'All fast aft!' We were back at the pier again with a load of blood-stained stretchers and the kind Indian orderly.

'*Chota Sahib*' – 'Young Sir,' he said to me when he took his leave, '*Khuda ap ka muhafiz ho* – May God preserve you.'

'*Agar Khuda ki marzi* – If it is God's wish,' I replied politely returning his salute. Whereupon the good man saluted again, turned about as if on parade and marched away into battle.

For years I had hoped to find out the name of the gallant officer, who had set such a splendid example to his men, and now, at long last I have the answer. It was none other than Lieutenant-Colonel Philip Palin, commanding the 14th (K.G.O.), Sikhs. His young adjutant, Reggie Savory, was in fact invalided a few days later desperately ill with dysentery.

'I was carried on board unconscious and not aware that there was no bunk available for me,' Savory wrote, 'but when I "came round" Colonel Palin was looking down at me: "So it's *you*, old boy! The doctors said there was a very sick man coming on board, so I volunteered to give up my bunk to him."

'Palin was surely one of the great men of Gallipoli,' Savory concluded. 'He returned to the Peninsula later and took over command of the Indian Brigade, until the Evacuation.'[10]

Savory went back too, of course.

It would be hard to imagine a more invidious task than that which befell Major-General de Lisle at Suvla. Taken on August 15th at a moment's notice from his own division, the 29th at Helles, he found himself in command of a strange corps with its organisation all to pieces. His task was to pull this IX Corps together in a very short time and to launch it against strong positions which had already resisted Stopford's attack and were getting stronger every day.

The objective allotted was the capture of W Hill and the Anafarta Spur, with the dual aim of starting a further enveloping movement and freeing Suvla Bay from enemy shell-fire.

On August 17th, in the small hours of the morning, Sir Ian sent a cable to Lord Kitchener admitting that his coup had so far failed and that the total fighting strength of his army now amounted to only 95,000 rifles against a defending Turkish garrison of some 110,000. He had hopes of eventual success, but only if he could be provided with drafts and fresh formations. He placed his immediate requirements at 45,000 reinforcing drafts, plus new formations amounting to another 50,000. 'I cannot diguise the fact,' he added, 'that a surprise will now be absent . . . my difficulties are enormously increased . . . we are up against the main Turkish army, which is fighting bravely and is well commanded.'[11]

This grave message, with its first crushing admission that the August offensive had failed, reached Lord K. at a moment when events in other theatres were causing deep concern. Several days were to pass before Sir Ian received any reply and several weeks before the Government found it possible to reach a decision.

Sir Ian visited IX Corps headquarters at Suvla on August 18th to discuss the forthcoming attack, planned for August 21st, for which de Lisle was to receive substantial reinforcements including some 5,000 Yeomanry now arriving from Egypt and three brigades of the immortal 29th Division from Cape Helles. The latter were being called upon like Caesar's Tenth Legion, or Napoleon's Old Guard, as men who could decide the fate of a battle.

Major-General de Lisle's orders were issued at 3 p.m. on the 20th. The 11th Division was to capture W Hill and the 29th Division Scimitar Hill. If these points were reached 'one strong brigade' of the corps reserve (10th Division) was to push through to establish a still more advanced line astride the Anafarta spur. No special task was allocated to the 53rd and 54th Divisions in the centre and left of IX Corps line, but they were 'to take advantage of any opportunity to gain ground'. The infantry attack, which would be preceded by half an hour's bombardment, was due to begin at 3 p.m. Once the enemy was fully engaged, the 2nd (dismounted) Yeomanry Division was to move forward across the open from Lala Baba to Chocolate Hill.

In conjunction with the attack on the Suvla front, a composite brigade from Anzac was to assault Hill 60. As all units from the New Zealand and Australian Division were so weak after the heavy fighting earlier in the month, detachments had to be drawn from British, Australian, New Zealand and Gurkha units to build up a brigade of the required strength, 3,000. They were placed under the command of Major-General Cox.

Though the Turks were believed to have 75,000 men in the northern half of the Peninsula, the greater part of this force was thought to be either on or in rear of Sari Bair or in reserve further to the north. In point of fact these figures greatly underestimated the Turkish strength available in the immediate neighbourhood under Mustapha Kemal. In consequence Major-General de Lisle was to be faced with a problem of very real difficulty.

Following a chilly night, the morning of August 21st was oppressively hot. Sir Ian came over from G.H.Q. Imbros and took up his position on the ridge above corps headquarters to watch the battle.

One of the main reasons for an afternoon attack was to enable the infantry to advance with the sun at their backs. The afternoon sun, it was hoped, would help the attacking artillery and blind the defenders with its glare. But Nature herself seemed to fight on the side of the Turks. Soon after midday the sun disappeared into banks of unseasonable cloud, and a veil of haze rose up from Suvla plain to hide the Turkish positions.

The preliminary bombardment opened at 2.30, but effected very little. The troops went forward bravely but were met everywhere with stiff resistance.

'That day I saw an unforgettable sight,' wrote Major Aubrey Herbert who was watching the battle from No. 2 Outpost, West Anzac. 'The dismounted Yeomanry attacked the Turks across the Salt Lake of Suvla. Shrapnel burst over them continuously; above their heads there was a sea of smoke. Away to the north by Chocolate Hill fires broke out on the plain. The Yeomanry never faltered. On they came through the haze of smoke in two formations, columns and extended. Sometimes they broke into a run, but they always came on. It is difficult to describe the feelings of pride and sorrow with which we watched this advance, in which so many of our friends and relations were playing their part.'[12]

In the meantime Major-General Cox's composite brigade from Anzac had begun to move forward at 3.30, after a preliminary bombardment, and their advance was also strongly contested. Partly because the scrub on the near side of the valley was set afire by enemy shells, progress was slow, and at nightfall the situation was hardly better than that of IX Corps. All that had been gained at the cost of heavy casualties was a precarious foothold on the slopes of Hill 60. The battle resumed on the 26th and continued over the 28th. By then nearly the whole network of trenches which formed the objective for the attack had been taken at the expense of a further 1,000 casualties, but the captured positions did not quite encircle Hill 60, and the summit, shutting out all view of the northern slopes, was still in enemy hands.

Later on several officers who had taken part expressed the opinion that one more thrust would have completed the capture of Hill 60, but the truth seems to be that the whole Anzac Corps was now spent. The bitter fighting on Hill 60 had added the last straw.

Lieutenant-Colonel Maurice Hankey, the Government Observer, had left Imbros for England on August 19th. His Memorandum, prepared for the Committee of Imperial Defence, is a printed document dated 30th August 1915.

'We shall be able to hold on to our position in the Southern [Cape Helles] area without achieving a substantial advance,' he said, 'while at Anzac we have a really good prospect of gaining a footing on the Sari Bair Ridges. At Suvla we are unlikely to achieve any considerable success and may find ourselves obliged to hold on in a position of some difficulty. It seems unlikely,' he warned, 'that an early and complete success can be looked for, but if adequate reinforcements are sent out and proper arrangements made to meet the deterioration of the weather which is bound to occur with the approach of autumn, the stalemate can still be broken . . .'

When writing of the newly arrived British troops, Hankey said that 'it is perhaps too early to pass judgment on them' and 'It would be difficult to exaggerate how much the efficiency of a unit depends on its commander.' He recommended 'a policy of ruthless weeding-out of inefficient commanding officers. Warfare at Gallipoli,' he concluded, 'requires exceptional stamina and nerve – qualities which are most likely to be found in young men. It is better to employ men who have reputations to make than those who have reputations to break.'

Hankey also wrote an addendum to his report headed, 'Remarks on Future Policy'. Only a few copies were made: 'The Government may well ask themselves whether they are justified in continuing a campaign which takes so tremendous toll in human life and material resources. "How much longer," they may ask, "is this running sore to continue to sap our strength? We were asked for three divisions in order to secure success, and we gave five. We deprived France of ammunition and poured it into the Dardanelles. Yet success has never come. Why should we succeed any better if we provide what is now asked?"'

To help the Cabinet make the crucial decision he put forward three possible courses of action, additional to preparing for the winter campaign. The first was 'to resume the naval attack on the Narrows', the second 'to find some pretext for withdrawal from the campaign', and the third 'to arrive at an arrangement with the Turks after obtaining the consent of Russia'.

As to the renewal of the naval attack he recognised that a group of 'responsible naval officers [by which he must principally have meant Commodore Roger Keyes] had worked out the operation in detail and believed that with proper preparation and surprise their object can be achieved'. But the Vice-Admiral (de Robeck) who 'is not lacking in dash and courage', and 'the overwhelming majority of naval officers' are 'utterly opposed' to such a plan. Thus in Hankey's view 'it would be a mistake to order an attack of this kind except in the last resort'.

Turning to withdrawal, Hankey first asked whether it is 'either tactically or politically possible, having regard to the place that prestige occupies in our system of Imperial Defence'. 'Tactically,' he continues, 'it would be a matter of the utmost difficulty; but emergency plans have been prepared.' Nor could he find any way of 'saving our face in the event of withdrawal'.

After modestly admitting his inadequacies as a critic of military doctrine Hankey managed to convey with great tact his views on why so many things had gone wrong at Gallipoli. He accepted that some mistakes have been made at home and that Sir Ian's telegraphed dispatches had fully admitted 'the mistakes made locally'. The chief point of his letter came at the end. With consummate skill he puts his finger on a great weakness in the British system in World War I, namely the vast gulf between the staff which planned operations and the men who had to carry them out. Though he fully appreciated the need for secrecy about forthcoming operations, he felt 'sure that we nearly always err on the side of excessive secrecy'.[13]

When Hankey was writing this memorandum he must have realised that Sir Ian's position was, to say the least, precarious, and that his own reports, despite their tactful wording, were not likely to enhance the C-in-C's standing in the eyes of Ministers. But it seemed clear that at the time the letter was written, Hankey believed Sir Ian would conduct the next offensive and prepare for the winter campaign. Nor does Sir Ian himself seem to have realised that the storm clouds which had been gathering about his head were about to break. 'All I will say now,' he wrote to Hankey in acknowledgement of the Memorandum, 'is that I believe I shall be able to endorse, and with enthusiasm, every single word. . . My congratulations ... It considerably strengthens my confidence in my own judgement.'[14]

Meanwhile, on August 23rd, Lieutenant-General the Hon. Sir Julian Byng had arrived from France to command IX Corps. With him came Major-Generals Maude and Fanshaw, who had also served in France, to command divisions. Maude was appointed to the 13th Division vice Shaw, invalided; Fanshaw replaced Hammersley in the 11th Division. Sir Ian, it will be remembered, had specially asked for Byng at the middle of June, when the August offensive was first projected, but his request was not approved. Now, ten weeks later, it had been granted. 'The experienced pilot had arrived, but the ship to be steered into port was already hard on the rocks.'[15]

'These fellows seem pretty cheery,' commented Sir Ian after meeting them at Imbros on their first day. 'Maude especially full of ardour which will, I hope, catch on.' But hardly a week had passed before he had to modify his views.

'Saw Byng. Everyone likes him, but he shows less keenness than I should have credited him with to have a go at the Turks. He wants to be back in France. The idea of holding on here through the winter fills him with horror, and he insists with some show of logic that we should be given means to go on or else get out forthwith. The only general whose mind seems to go beyond the needs of the moment is Maude. He is straining at the leash to have a cut at the Turks as quick as he can.'[16]

So Sir Stanley Maude, the hero of Baghdad in 1917, was already showing his metal.

At this juncture on August 30th, Lord Kitchener was informed that the French were studying the question of a landing by six French divisions on the Asiatic side of the Straits, to be made in co-operation with British troops already on the Peninsula. But few things can be more frustrating than the raising of false hopes. The whole plan collapsed under the pressure of events in the Balkans. During the last week in September Bulgaria issued orders for mobilisation, whereupon Greece and Serbia asked France and England for 150,000 men. France at once agreed, and England must follow suit. On September 25th Lord Kitchener telegraphed that two British divisions and probably one French division were to be withdrawn from Gallipoli for service at Salonika. He suggested that Sir Ian should abandon Suvla Bay.

Previously Lord Kitchener had said that there was no intention of withdrawing from the Peninsula or of giving up till the Turks were defeated. Brave words, now meaning nothing. Sir Ian's feelings are easy to imagine.

Meanwhile in France, through the determination of General Joffre and the pressure which he had exerted upon Lord Kitchener, the British Commander-in-Chief, Sir John French, was compelled to undertake the Loos-Champagne offensive before he was ready, over ground that was most unfavourable, and against his better judgement as well as that of General Haig. In the course of these operations 250,000 French and British troops were to be sacrificed.

It can well be claimed that with half that number of casualties the opening of the Straits would have been secured.

Keith Murdoch was an Australian journalist who had been sent to Egypt by the Australian Government to report on the arrangements for the receipt and delivery of letters to and from members of the Imperial Force and on other administrative matters. He also carried with him a letter of commendation signed by the Prime Minister, the Right Hon. Andrew Fisher (whom Sir Ian had met in Australia before the war). It did not in any way suggest a visit to the Gallipoli Peninsula. In short, Murdoch was not asked to report on the military situation nor, indeed, was he qualified to do so.

After a month in Cairo he applied to Sir Ian personally, in a letter dated 17th August 1915, in which he said, 'I should like to go across in only a semi-official capacity so that I might record censored impressions in the London and Australian newspapers I represent, but any conditions you impose I should of course faithfully observe.' Being granted permission, Murdoch signed the usual declaration required of war correspondents which said, 'I, the undersigned, do hereby solemnly undertake to follow in every particular the rules issued by the Commander-in-Chief through the Field Censor, relative to correspondence concerning the forces in the field, and bind myself not to attempt to correspond by any other route or by any other means than that officially sanctioned . . .'.

After visiting Mudros and Imbros and spending four days on the Peninsula, at Anzac and Suvla but not Helles, he wrote a report cruelly libelling most of the officers and other ranks (except Australian), at that time serving on the Peninsula or on the lines of communication, and also levelled a violent attack on Sir Ian and on Braithwaite, his Chief of Staff. Perhaps the meanest example of this document is its omissions.. For instance he alleged 'a want of self-sacrifice on the part of the staff' but forgot to mention the death of Doughty-Wylie at the *River Clyde* landing and that of other staff officers who took the place of slain battalion commanders and lost their own lives in so doing. But the whole paper is vile.

As soon as Murdoch reached London he sent one copy of this uncensored and defamatory report to the Australian Prime Minister and made it possible for a duplicate copy to reach the British Prime Minister. Whereupon Mr Asquith took the unusual step of raising it to the level of a State Paper.

Murdoch's report is dated 28th September 1915, and two months were to pass before Sir Ian's comments were invited, when they were too late to be of any use. Sir Ian's reply is dated December 1915, and here is his final paragraph:

'In my absence, I, a British General and a member of the Committee of Imperial Defence, have had circulated among my brother members aspersions against my honour and libels against my troops. No chance was vouchsafed me of proving the malignancy of these attacks, or of showing how far they might be inspired by personal animus. A fortnight before I ever heard of their existence they had already been passed round from hand to hand, and mouth to ear, through the most influential circles in the land.'[17]

Events were now to move quickly. From Lord Kitchener on October 4th came a cable suggesting that Braithwaite should be superseded because 'a flow of unofficial reports from Gallipoli' adversely criticised the work of the headquarters staff.

'On the face of it,' Sir Ian wrote, 'this cable seems to suggest that a man widely known as a straight and capable soldier should be given the shortest of shrifts at the instance of "unofficial reports"; i.e., camp gossip. Surely the cable message carries with it some deeper significance. What mischief was brewing at home? I realise where we stand: K., Braithwaite and I – on the verge!'

Sir Ian of course refused to sacrifice the man who had 'stood by him as a rock'.

'What is your estimate of the probable losses which would be entailed to your force if the evacuation of the Gallipoli Peninsula was decided upon?' came next from Lord K.

Sir Ian's reply, sent on the morning of October 12th, did not conceal his immediate determination that if so lamentable a decision were taken he must decline to have a hand in carrying it out. 'The loss,' he said, 'must to some extent depend upon the circumstances of the moment, but it could scarcely be less than half the men and all the guns and stores, and that possibly, with still so many raw troops at Suvla and the Senegalese at Helles, it might mean veritable disaster.'

This estimate far exceeded the worst that had been calculated at home and, together with Sir Ian's attitude, brought to a head the feeling which had been growing in Government circles for some time, that the Campaign would benefit from a change of command. In any case it was now painfully clear that, unless the change was made immediately, such a crucial decision as evacuation could not be reached with an open mind.

'Had just got into bed last night [October 15th] when I was ferreted out again by a cable "Secret and personal" from K. telling me to decipher the next one myself. Would I like to be wakened when the second message came in, I was asked. As I knew the contents as if I had written it out myself, I said "No!" – Then I fell asleep.'

The axe fell on Sir Ian early next morning as word by word he deciphered the fatal message:

'The War Council held last night decided that though the Government fully appreciate your work and the gallant manner in which you personally have struggled to make the enterprise a success in face of terrible difficulties ... (I wish they would come to the point!), they, all the same, wish to make a change in the command which will give them an opportunity of seeing you ...'[18]

General Sir Charles Monro with his own chief-of-staff was to relieve him and Braithwaite. Meanwhile Birdwood was to command.

'So long as he [Sir Ian] remained in command there was little prospect of a withdrawal,' Hankey wrote later. 'Undismayed by failure or the prospect of a winter that would isolate his forces for weeks together, this gallant soul remained firm in the belief that, in the long run, if properly supported, he could win through.'[19]

Sir Ian penned a farewell message to his troops and said his good-byes.

'The adieu was a melancholy affair. There was no make-belief; that's a sure thing. Keyes is following me in a day or two, to implore the Cabinet to let us at least strike one more blow before we haul down our flag, so there will be two of us at the task.'

Sir Ian joined the *Chatham*, Captain Drury-Lowe, in Kephalo Harbour on October 17th, and went below to his cabin where he wondered whether he could stand the strain of seeing Imbros and

G.H.Q. fade away into dreams. But he came up on to the quarter-deck at the Captain's invitation when the ship got under way and, with his two A.D.C.s, took the salute while the Fleet 'cheered ship'.

'The Navy was our father and mother,' he had written in his diary; and to his beloved Jean he cabled:

'Coming right home. Monro succeeding me. Do not be downhearted for I know I have done utmost with means given and I am quite cheerful.'

'Overjoyed at your return,' she replied. 'You have already done the impossible.'[20]

25

Evacuation

'*In that marvellous evacuation we see the national
genius for amphibious warfare raised to its highest
manifestation.*'
Sir Julian Corbett
Naval Operations, Vol. III

'*We have a lot of fellows sleeping in those valleys, and
we should never have been told to leave them.*'
Jack Churchill to Winston Churchill
22nd December 1915.[1]

Sir Charles Monro, when appointed as Sir Ian Hamilton's successor,
insisted on spending several days at the War Office to study the
Campaign before leaving for Gallipoli. He conferred with Lord K.
no less than four times but did not consult Sir Ian at all. He was a
large, stolid man, 'a blameless, sealed-pattern type of general
without much imagination, but genial and popular with his staff'.[2]
He had commanded in France with ability and distinction, but was
imbued with the principles of Western strategy and could hardly
be regarded as impartial. 'He was born with another sort of mind
from me,' Sir Ian himself wrote, adding that 'Had he been sent out
here in the first place he would never have touched the Dardanelles.
The intention of whoever selected Monro is to use him to force
K. to pull down the blinds.'[3]

Sir Charles arrived at G.H.Q. Imbros on October 28th and immediately assumed command. He brought his own Chief of Staff,
Major-General A. L. Lynden-Bell.

'I hope you will send me as soon as possible your report about
main issue at Dardanelles, viz., staying or leaving,' Lord K. telegraphed. 'Of course the general situation in the East if Turks now
held at Gallipoli were free will be considered, as well as likelihood
of Germans getting through transit to Constantinople, which seems
almost inevitable.' This message reached Imbros on the evening of
the 29th. Early on the 30th, a bright, summer-like day, the new

Commander-in-Chief proceeded to the Peninsula to see the situation for himself. His Chief of Staff had sprained a knee the night before and was unable to go, so he was accompanied by Lieutenant-Colonel Aspinall.

Never before had anyone tried to inspect all three of these widely separated fronts in the course of a single day. 'General Monro was an officer of swift decision,' Churchill wrote. 'He came, he saw, he capitulated.'[4]

Fresh from France, with its peaceful harbours and docks, and with trains and motors awaiting the arrival of steamers, Monro was not prepared for the scenes which met his gaze as he stepped ashore. The local conditions to which the Gallipoli army had long since grown accustomed – the open beach, the shelling, the crazy piers, the landing of stores by hand from bumping lighters, the strings of kicking mules (over a hundred had been killed above Suvla beach by one shell only a few days before), the heavy dust, the cramped spaces, the jostling crowds and the bathers – all within range of the enemy's guns – filled him with blank amazement. On his arrival at Anzac Cove, where conditions were even more congested, his wonder only grew. To Colonel Aspinall he remarked with a whimsical smile: 'It's just like Alice in Wonderland, curiouser and curiouser'.

Without going beyond the beaches, he familiarised himself in the space of six hours with the conditions prevailing on the 15-mile front of Helles, Anzac and Suvla. He made no attempt to inspect troops or to visit the trenches. To the Divisional Commanders summoned to meet him at their respective Corps Headquarters, he put separately and in turn a question in the following sense: 'On the supposition that you are going to get no more drafts can you maintain your position in spite of the arrival of strong reinforcements with heavy guns and limitless German ammunition?'

To this question the Divisional Commanders returned identical replies. In their present state of health the troops could not be counted on for more than twenty-four hours' sustained effort. In existing circumstances they could promise to hold their positions, but, if the Turks received unlimited ammunition, while they themselves received very little, they could only do their best.

Armed with these dubious answers the Commander-in-Chief returned to Imbros, never again to set foot on the Peninsula. His Chief of Staff, Lynden-Bell, never visited it at all. The mentality of the latter is reflected in a conversation which took place between him and Commodore Keyes:

'"You did land at Gallipoli once, Belinda, didn't you?" asked

Keyes, thinking he had accompanied Monro and not knowing at the time that he had never landed there.

'"It was not necessary to land to make up one's mind about a show like that. We made up our minds before we left England, and Wully Robertson [who had just been appointed C.I.G.S.] will soon put a stop to that other rotten show at Salonika."'[5]

On October 31st General Monro sent his telegram recommending the abandonment of the Campaign. 'The troops,' he said, 'with the exception of the Anzacs, are not equal to a sustained effort . . . We merely hold the fringe of the shores and are confronted by the Turks in very formidable entrenchments with all the advantages of position and power of observation over our movements . . . Since the flanks of the Turks cannot be attacked, only a frontal attack is possible, and no room is afforded on any of the beaches for additional divisions should they be sent . . . An attack could only be prosecuted under the disadvantages of the serious lack of depth and the absence of power of surprise, seeing that the Turkish position dominates our line throughout . . .' His survey included statements on the uncertainty of the weather and his belief that heavy guns were being sent to the Peninsula, although he had 'no information as to the influence on the situation which would be caused by complete German communication with Constantinople'.

Although it could be said that Monro was the first general on the Gallipoli Peninsula to take a realistic view of the military situation after the failure of the August offensive, he was an unsympathetic observer. 'He lacked Hamilton's resourcefulness,' said Bean, the Australian historian. In Churchill's opinion, 'He belonged to that school whose supreme conception of Great War strategy was killing Germans'. He took the view that 'these sideshows were a mistake: the troops were wanted in France'. He was to tell Admiral Wemyss that 'the occupation of Gallipoli and even Constantinople would not help us on the Western Front'.

The fatal telegram recommending evacuation fell like a thunderbolt on Lord Kitchener, and his reaction was immediate.

'Do Birdwood and other Corps Commanders agree with your opinion?' he cabled. 'I have just received letter from Maxwell [G.O.C. Egypt] in which he says the effect will be disastrous . . . It is a tremendous strain on the Turks to keep the Gallipoli Army maintained, and if we can hold I think we ought to . . .'

Monro at once ordered Generals Byng (IX Corps, Suvla) and Birdwood, to Imbros, where they arrived early next morning, November 2nd. Byng stated that he considered evacuation advisable.

Birdwood, from Indian experience, feared the result on the Muham-
medan world in India, Egypt and Persia and was 'averse to withdrawal'. He said, 'If we leave the Peninsula it is essential the whole
force must immediately be launched against Turkey elsewhere,'
but he failed 'to see where this could be done with confident hope
of success'.

Lieutenant-General Sir Francis Davies (VIII Corps, Helles,
arrived August 5th) was ill and a staff officer had been sent to obtain
his opinion. If it was favourable to the new C.-in-C.'s point of view,
only his oral assent was necessary; if unfavourable, he was to state
his reasons in writing. On being awakened in the middle of the night
to give his views on this weighty question at a moment's notice, he
picked up his pen and wrote just two words: 'I agree.'

On this same afternoon, November 2nd, General Monro telegraphed
the opinions to Lord Kitchener. In the same message he estimated
the probable losses in evacuation at between 30 and 40 per cent of
personnel and material, which revealed that if allowed to evacuate
he was prepared to sacrifice some 40,000 officers and men killed or
captured.

The following morning, November 3rd, having handed back the
temporary command of the Expeditionary Force to Birdwood,
Monro proceeded to Egypt to discuss with General Maxwell the
situation which might be created in Egypt and the Arab world by
the evacuation of the Peninsula.

Meanwhile Commodore Keyes, always confident that the Fleet
could at any time, with proper preparation, force the Dardanelles
and enter the Sea of Marmara, had, during the summer, detailed
plans for the operation with the help of officers of the naval staff.
These plans were now complete, and Keyes was confident of their
success. In this opinion he was strongly supported by Wemyss but
not by de Robeck, although the latter showed his greatness of character by giving Keyes leave to travel to London to lay his scheme
before the Board of Admiralty. He had arrived there on October 28th.

The Keyes plan was remarkable for its audacity. The Straits were
to be rushed by surprise, while the Army, with supporting naval fire,
contained the Turkish forces on the Peninsula and prevented them
from turning their mobile artillery on to the ships and the minesweepers.

Mr Balfour, who replaced Churchill as First Lord of the Admiralty,
had first of all smiled benignly on Keyes's project, but the Sea Lords
demanded definite military support, and, since the Government had

already promised the French to co-operate at Salonika, it seemed clear that all available reinforcements would now be needed for the Balkan front. Consequently the plan was turned down. As it happened Lord Kitchener had been 'immensely taken' with the plan and, when he received an unhelpful letter from Balfour, he was driven to the comment that 'the navy was afraid to wet its feet'.

In the small hours of November 4th an urgent personal telegram from Lord Kitchener arrived for General Birdwood. At that time it was customary for all telegrams to be deciphered by a special cipher officer, but this was evidently an exceptional message since the first two groups of figures represented – 'Most secret. Decipher yourself'. The cipher office therefore took it to Lieutenant-Colonel Aspinall, who was acting Chief of Staff, and asked him what to do. Aspinall replied that he would take over, but on finding that the third group spelt 'Tell no one', he, too, fought shy of ignoring Lord K's instructions and stumbled through the dark to call Birdwood. The latter, unaccustomed to the cipher and to save time, told Aspinall to get on with it.

'I shall come out to you, am leaving tomorrow night. I have seen Keyes and I believe the Admiralty will agree to making naval attempt. We must do what we can to assist them, and I think that as soon as our ships are in the Sea of Marmara we should seize the Bulair Isthmus and hold it so as to supply the Navy if the Turks still hold out. There will probably be a change in naval command, Wemyss being appointed to carry through the naval part of the work. As regards the military command, you would have the whole force . . . I absolutely refuse to sign orders for evacuation . . . Monro will be appointed to command the Salonika force.'

'Here was the true Kitchener,' Churchill later wrote. 'Here in this flaming telegram – whether Bulair was the best place or not – was the Man the British Empire believed him to be, in whom millions set their faith – resolute, self-reliant, creative, lion-hearted.'[6]

While one can agree with these sentiments, it must be admitted that not only was Lord K's suggestion impracticable but his telegram placed Birdwood in an invidious position. Although the new military appointments – but not the naval – were to be confirmed later, at the time he received this ciphered message he was merely in acting command during Monro's absence in Egypt. But Lord Kitchener, probably frustrated by the politicians, had opened his heart to Birdwood, who for many years had served on his personal staff, and I hope he felt the better for it.

Birdwood had to answer that any attempt to land near Bulair could only end in disaster. He added: 'I sincerely trust that Monro will remain in command here. He has already established confidence . . .' The soul of loyalty to his absent Commander-in-Chief, he was urging Lord K. to reverse the decision. Meanwhile he was committed to secrecy. Neither de Robeck nor Wemyss were to know of the telegram's existence.

Meanwhile in London Lord Kitchener had learnt at an interview with Commodore Keyes on the night of November 3rd that he, too, considered it hopeless to attempt to land at Bulair. He learnt, too, that the Admiralty was already cooling towards the Keyes plan. Finally, on the afternoon of the 4th at a meeting of ministers, it was decided that a naval attack on the Straits could only be sanctioned in co-operation with a new attack by the Army. In these circumstances, as no fresh troops were available to make that attack, a disappointed Lord Kitchener sent a second message:

'I am coming out as arranged,' he said. 'I fear the Navy may not play up . . . The more I look at the problem the less I see my way through, so you had better very quietly and very secretly work out a scheme for getting the troops off the Peninsula.'

At this juncture a powerful group of politicians were determined on the removal of Lord Kitchener from the War Office. Some of his colleagues believed he was clogging the direction of the war, and the most brilliant of them had not hesitated to describe him as 'a dull old man'. It was not surprising, therefore, when someone had suggested that he should go to the Near East and report, 'the proposal was received with such acclamation that, although he was under no illusion about its motive, he assented'.

Immediately after his departure there were rumours that the seals of the War Office were in the King's hands. In point of fact they were in Lord K's pocket. He had walked over from York House to inform the King of his departure and to ask leave to go. 'The support and friendship of King George was throughout Lord Kitchener's last months of life a great solace to him,' his biographer recorded, 'for he was bitterly conscious of his unpopularity with his colleages in the Government. Many were the occasions when, overworked and depressed, he strolled across late in the evening to ask an audience of the King – never refused, from which he returned comforted.'

At this crisis of his career, whatever his colleagues might be thinking or intriguing, K. had no thought of himself. He was now consumed solely with a sense of duty to his country and of responsibility for the men in Gallipoli whose fate lay in his hand. 'I pace my room at night,' he had told the Prime Minister (Asquith), whom he regarded as his only friend, 'and see the boats fired at and capsising, and the drowning men.' 'Perhaps,' he said, when the Cabinet leaped at the suggestion that he should go to the Dardanelles, 'perhaps, if I have to lose a lot of men over there, I shall not want to come back.'

En route to join H.M.S. *Chatham* at Marseilles for onward passage to Mudros, K. stepped off the train in Paris to confer with French authorities, whom he found to be just as reluctant as he was to face the problem of evacuating Gallipoli and of transferring divisions to Salonika. 'I cannot see the light,' K. told them. 'It is impossible to forecast the effect in Egypt and India.'[7]

Lord Kitchener arrived at Mudros from Marseilles late on the evening of November 9th, and there followed a long chain of conferences. At the beginning his mind appeared to be open on the question of evacuation, but the prospect of a successful offensive seemed to have been given up. The important question to decide was whether the Army could hold on, and, if it could, whether it would be serving the Allied cause as usefully in Gallipoli as if it were employed elsewhere.

Among those of Lord Kitchener's advisers on the spot, Admiral de Robeck, while insisting on the folly of any further attempt to rush the Narrows, was ready to evacuate Suvla and Anzac but wanted us to retain Helles in order to help the Navy blockade the Straits. Sir John Maxwell, G.O.C., Egypt, was resigned to complete evacuation, provided a landing could first be made at Ayas Bay, near Alexandretta. Monro was also in favour of evacuation and to secure that end was ready to support the Ayas Bay scheme. Birdwood, on the understanding that no additional troops could be spared for Gallipoli and that the Fleet would not attempt to force the Straits, was no longer strongly opposed to evacuation but was opposed to a landing in Ayas Bay. Admiral Wemyss, who shared Keyes's strong views that a further naval attempt to force the Straits must be made, was not asked for his views.

After inspecting the Helles position on November 12th from a point above the beach, Lord Kitchener moved to Anzac and Suvla.

'Though it was guessed that he was in the Mediterranean, few at Anzac anticipated such a visit. Yet when from a picket boat at the North [Walker's] Pier there climbed Birdwood's small form, together with a tall, spare, somewhat ungainly figure under a blazing red cap-band, and the two at the head of a small staff came walking down the jetty, the men nearest the shore at once realised who the visitor was.

'By the time he arrived at the beach a small crowd had collected. Some Australians – no officer leading them – called for a cheer, and at the sound the semicircle of yellow heights round the Sphinx became peopled with the distant figures of men, who came hopping down over the scrub, straight for the pier-head. The red cap was rapidly closed in among them. As he spoke to one after another, they again and again cheered him spontaneously. In the great simple man there was something closely akin to the big men who gathered round him; and they gave him a reception such as they accorded to no other man during the war.

'Under Birdwood's guidance he went with long strides straight up Walker's Ridge by the dusty semi-precipitous road to Russell's Top. Reaching the summit without a pause, he spoke to the brigadiers and then surveyed the Nek and seaward spurs from a quiet front-line position about sixty yards from the enemy trench.

'Birdwood, though never at ease until he had brought Kitchener back into safety, had fulfilled a wish of his heart in showing his old Chief the Anzac position. To Kitchener the day was one in a lifetime.'[8]

At Suvla, next day, he climbed up Karakol Dagh, with General Byng and divisional commanders, to a prominent cluster of rocks from which a wide view is obtained of the Salt Lake, the foothills, the unconquered Hill 971, Sir Ian's supreme objective in the August offensive, and the fateful bastion of Chunuk Bair.

On November 16th Lord Kitchener took Monro with him to Salonika. On the 19th he had an audience with the King of Greece in Athens. At Mudros on November 22nd he came round to Monro's way of thinking and made his long-awaited report:

'As German assistance for the Turks on the Peninsula was now practically available – and in this case British positions could not be maintained – evacuation seems inevitable,' he said. 'Anzac and Suvla should be evacuated, but Helles retained "at all events for the present".' In the course of a long discussion he revealed that he was now sure that the chance of success was thrown away by the policy, for which he himself was mainly responsible, of refusing Sir Ian Hamilton the reinforcements asked for in August and he deeply regretted that he and the Government had not made it possible for the offensive at Suvla to be resumed. By renewing the attack it might have been possible to 'turn the Kilid Bahr position and enable the Fleet to pass the Straits'. Such a success 'would have entirely changed the situation in the East'. But the operation had been prevented 'by the mistaken policy we have followed, at the dictation of France, at Salonika', and 'it was now too late'.

Lord Kitchener left for home on November 24th, but before sailing he confirmed General Monro in command of all the British forces in the Mediterranean east of Malta, excluding Egypt. Monro naturally divided these forces into the 'Salonika Army', under Lieutenant-General Sir Bryan Mahon, and the 'Dardanelles Army' under Birdwood. Monro set up his own headquarters in the *Aragon* at Mudros, where the communications were good. Birdwood, who was to carry out the evacuation, moved to Imbros, after handing over command of the Anzac forces to General Godley.

Soon after Kitchener's arrival in England Sir Ian Hamilton paid him a visit at the War Office to implore him not to agree to an evacuation.

'I believe at the bottom of his mysterious heart he would like to hang on to the Peninsula, as well as to the Balkan business,' he wrote to Churchill who was then with his regiment in France. 'But, as he says, what can he do?'[9]

At Gallipoli there had been some rain in October which had laid the dust, killed the flies and brought cooler weather. Then, in a storm on November 1st, the destroyer *Louis* dragged her anchor in Suvla Bay, grounded on a sandbank and became a total wreck, but her bows and upperworks remained visible to the Turkish gunners who daily took pot-shots at her. In the same gale the old battleship *Majestic*, which had been lying bottom up off Cape Helles since March 27th, slid down out of sight – to everyone's relief. There were a couple more storms during Lord Kitchener's absence in Greece, from November 16th–21st, when rough seas stopped boat work and caused damage to piers, while strong winds grounded aircraft. In his diary entry for November 18th Birdwood said: 'Went over to Anzac hoping to go to the trenches but found landing there impossible owing to swell and loss of boats in yesterday's storm, not one picket boat being apparently left.'

But it was on November 26th that the real trouble started. Our ship, the *Bacchante*, was at anchor in Kephalo, Imbros, when the 'gale warning' was made. We 'raised steam for slow speed to ensure safety' and set anchor watch.

The harbour is exposed to northerly winds, and, on this account the boat harbour formed at the time of the Suvla landings, by sinking an old 'dummy' battleship, had since been strengthened; and into this refuge soon came a number of small craft, mostly from Anzac, where, unlike Suvla, there is no shelter from the north.

The night of the 26th passed without incident, but on the morning of the 27th the gale-force wind suddenly veered round, driving heavy seas straight through the harbour mouth. Soon great waves, thumping against the breakwater of sunken ships, caused a wide breach. In a matter of minutes all small craft either dragged or broke adrift from their moorings, including our beloved picket boat and steam pinnace, and were thrown up on the lee shore, many being holed beyond repair. This was a serious matter with evacuation in the air.

At Anzac, thanks to the caves and underground galleries, men were able to take shelter from the storm, while the surrounding hills provided some protection for the front line. At Helles, where the trenches were mostly in sloping ground, there was only a limited amount of flooding. But in the low flat ground of the Suvla plain the state of things was indescribable. Snow descended, in a whirling blizzard. The surface of the pools and trenches froze. The men's greatcoats, being soaked through, froze, too. Many staggered down from the lines so numbed with cold that they could hardly hear or speak. Sentries left standing at their posts were found afterwards still watching from the parapet, rifle in hand, but frozen to death. The dead in IX Corps alone numbered over 200. From the Peninsula over 10,000 sick had to be removed. Many were frost bitten; many lost limbs; some lost their reason.

It is probable that the Turks suffered even worse, for prisoners said they had no blankets, no covering at all except their thin uniform and frozen greatcoats.

This storm, though it never raged again with such fury, may have hastened the approaching end to the Campaign.

On November 25th, the day following Lord Kitchener's departure, Admiral de Robeck turned over the duties of Naval Commander-in-Chief to Wemyss, and went home to England on a well-deserved leave.

The withdrawal from Suvla and Anzac was now under way. It was an operation no one concerned could contemplate without the gravest misgiving. Nothing of the kind on a scale so great or under conditions so formidable had ever been attempted before.

From beaches exposed to shell fire, without any safe natural harbour, some 90,000 men with two hundred guns had to be re-embarked in the presence of an undefeated enemy (estimated at 80,000 to 100,000 strong) whose trenches were nowhere more than three hundred yards from our own. The operation had to be carried out at a season of treacherous weather and in confined waters open to U-boat attack; and, in order to ensure secrecy, the whole operation must be undertaken under cover of darkness.

So desperately important was secrecy that the labour of working out the scheme had to be confined to the few naval and military officers to whom it was necessary to disclose what was in the wind. They had established themselves in General Birdwood's headquarters on Imbros, whence a civil notice was promulgated that 'owing to an outbreak of smallpox no Greek fishing boats are permitted to leave or approach the island'. This was Captain Sam Butler, the Intelligence Officer's ingenious idea.

Captain C. Corbett, Royal Navy, was to be in charge of the evacuation of the Suvla area from the sloop *Anemone*, while our Captain Algy Boyle took charge at Anzac from the sloop *Honeysuckle*. The *Bacchante* had no part, to our great disappointment.

From the first day which followed the warning that withdrawal was on the cards, the planning staff had got down to work. It was quickly seen that the operation must be conducted in three stages. The first, purely preparative, in which were to be evacuated all troops, animals and material not required for a defensive winter campaign, should it be decided after all to hold on. This stage was to be completed by December 10th, when the final 'go ahead' would be given. The strain of the preliminary stage had been greatly eased by the fact that 10,000 men suffering from sickness and frostbite had already been taken off following the great November storm.

The intermediate stage, the withdrawal of all men, guns and animals not needed for the tactical defence of the various positions, had to be finished by December 17th, and before this could be undertaken with any degree of safety it was vital that the breach in the Kephalo breakwater be closed. There was no time to look around for some old hulk. A start must be made while fine weather lasted. So a brave decision was taken. A fully laden collier in first-class condition was placed across the breach on December 13th. The sinking was so cleverly done that after the evacuation she was refloated and left for Mudros with her valuable cargo under her own steam.

In spite of strong winds for a couple of days the intermediate stage was completed as planned, after considerable exertion.

It was as much as the Navy could do to get the men and guns away, so it had been decided, with great reluctance, that many horses and mules, both at Suvla and at Anzac, must be destroyed. The drivers co-operated well, knowing what would happen if their charges fell into the hands of the Turks, who had a reputation for being brutal to animals in spite of Muhammed's alleged fondness for horses as well as women. It was cruel to be kind. A sharp death is preferable to prolonged torture, as the animals would be starved and then ill treated when unable to stand up to their work.

Four hundred heavy draught horses, Clydesdales, Shires, some of them prize-winners at English shows, were shot, as well as many mules. A few, however, were simply turned loose, contrary to orders. A Turkish report said later, 'Several hundred horses which had not been able to be embarked, lay dead in long rows'.

Except for the strong winds over a couple of days, the weather had been perfect, with a glassy sea and a waxing moon giving light enough to help the work of re-embarkation but not enough to reveal anything to the enemy.

Before each dawn all sight of unusual movement had ceased, beaches and roads had assumed their normal appearance and the enemy had made no move. Still there remained ashore 40,000 men, with about 60 guns and stores sufficient for four days in case bad weather should prolong the final stage.

General Birdwood had been paying almost daily visits to Anzac and Suvla during the preliminary and intermediate stages, conferring with the corps commanders, Godley and Byng, spurring on the work of preparation and heartening the men by his frequent presence.

Both at Anzac and Suvla orders for the final stage were completed by December 14th.

At Anzac on the first night, December 18th, 9,900 men were to be embarked and 10,040 on the second night. The guiding principle of the scheme was a gradual reduction of the strength of the trench garrisons, the times of withdrawal being determined by the hour at which each detachment would be required to embark and the distance from the place of embarkation. Finally a number of picked men would fall back to an inner line to cover the withdrawal of the rear guard. It was characteristic of the spirit of the Anzacs that unit commanders found great difficulty in selecting these men. When volunteers were called for by Colonel Paton of the 7th Australian Brigade every man expressed a wish to stay. Those who had served longest on the Peninsula demanded the distinction as their right, while new arrivals were equally insistent that the chance of showing their mettle should be given to them.

Large reserves of stores had to be dealt with. As it was impossible to clear these huge depots secretly in the course of ten days, vast heaps of valuable material were ruthlessly got ready to be set alight. Blankets, bayonets, boots, water bottles, socks, gloves, tarpaulin sheets and even motor-bicycles were remorselessly thrown on the fire heaps, while near A East Pier a great funeral pyre was built of a fortnight's rations for 40,000 men.

At Anzac, although evacuation was generally accepted, there were many who hated the thought of abandoning positions which they had fought so hard to capture and had laboured so long to hold. Many would have preferred to renew the attack, and among troops in the front line there was a general belief that the Turks were beaten. Up to the very last men could be seen erecting new crosses or tidying up the grave of a lost friend whom they were loath to leave. 'Christ!' one was heard to exclaim as he tip-toed down to the beach, 'I hope the dead don't hear us.'

Both at Anzac and Suvla the programme for the first night, December 18th, was carried out without a casualty and without the smallest hitch. The artillery fire was normal, and even the last minute arrival off Anzac of the old battleship *Mars*, with accommodation for 2,000 soldiers, plus other transports, raised no suspicion. A destroyer had been keeping a searchlight trained on the Turkish look-out post on Gaba Tepe for the last few nights in order to blind its occupants.

Many ingenious schemes were evolved by which rifles and guns would fire after our men had departed. Candles of varying lengths were lighted, and as they burnt down these let off explosions at intervals of time which sounded like desultory firing.

'At 6 p.m. we filed out of our trenches at Anzac without hurry,' wrote Lieutenant Reggie Savory, 14th (K.G.O.) Sikhs. Each man – besides his rifle and ammunition – carried one blanket and one waterproof sheet – no more. There was complete silence except for the sound of shuffling feet; the occasional bump of a rifle-butt; or a muffled cough. At 8 p.m. we arrived at Walker's pier, where two motor-lighters awaited us, and we filed on board almost without a check. There was one halt, very short, but long enough for its purpose. A quantity of mess stores from Fortnum and Mason had been awaiting us on the beach. It included some cases of whisky. We were determined to leave none behind and were equally determined that the Australians, who had been eyeing them, should not salvage them. Among our sick we had placed some healthy burly men with orders to extract the bottles from the cases and to hand them to us as we stepped aboard, and in the meantime to guard the precious liquid with their lives!

'This minor operation was carried out with the smooth efficiency which marked the whole of the evacuation. As I waited to step over the gunwale a mysterious figure sidled up: "Huzoor" – your honour – "ze veesky" he said handing me four bottles. Two of these I passed to my orderly; the other two I crammed into my greatcoat pockets. Other bottles were similarly distributed. We then went on board and left the soil of Anzac behind us.

'On December 23rd we disembarked at Alexandria and took the train for Suez. Our Gallipoli chapter was finished. We had acquitted ourselves to the best of our ability and had lost in the process 28 British officers, 17 Indian officers, and 1,573 men, killed, wounded or missing. It was a heavy price.'[10]

General Birdwood's order for the evacuation had ended with the instruction that hospital accommodation for 2,000 patients, together with the necessary personnel for their care, was to be organised both at Suvla and at Anzac and left on shore to the last minute.

These wise precautions were outlined in a letter signed by General Monro and held ready to be delivered by boat, under the white flag, by Captain Sam Butler, the Intelligence Officer on Birdwood's staff. It was written in French and addressed to His Excellency the Generalissimo of the Turkish Army. It asked for 'a cessation of hostilities to allow hospital ships to be anchored off the beaches so that we may embark our sick and wounded under the Red Cross flag, as well as medical personnel necessary for their care'.

Mercifully, as events transpired, it was not necessary for this letter to be delivered. At Anzac the total casualties amounted to one man wounded early in the evening and one hit in the arm by a spent bullet as his boat was leaving the beach.

At Suvla there was not a single casualty, and 'the only living thing left behind was a mule which had brought down some medical stores to the last boat to leave C Beach. As there was no room for him he was given blankets, about a month's fodder and a tank full of water. He had forgotten his strenuous past and had not learned to forecast his future. He was happy'.[11]

The success of the evacuation was due in equal measure to the perfection of the plans, the co-operation between the naval and military staffs and the admirable bearing of the rank and file. But without good weather the best-laid plans would have been of no avail. It must be realised that from the moment the evacuation was ordered the sea remained almost flat calm, yet sixteen hours after the last boat left the shore a fierce gale sprang up, which, twenty-four hours earlier, might well have led to disaster.

On December 23rd, while the Helles garrison was anxiously awaiting the news of its fate, Sir William Robertson replaced General Murray as Chief of the Imperial General Staff. Convinced that there was nothing to gain and perhaps very much to lose by attempting to remain at Helles, he was already pressing the Government for immediate evacuation. Before accepting the office, he had insisted that all orders to commanders in the field should in future be issued by him and not by the Secretary of State for War, Lord Kitchener. On December 24th the new C.I.G.S. authorised Monro to make all preparations for an immediate and final evacuation.

Admiral de Robeck returned from leave on December 31st and resumed command. General Monro departed for Egypt next day and from there to France to command the First Army. The order to evacuate Helles was now given.

The joint plan, issued by Birdwood and de Robeck, required the intermediate stage to be finished by the morning of January 8th and, weather permitting, the final stage the following night.

On January 1st the French Colonial brigade was relieved on the right of the line by the Royal Naval Division, and in the course of the next two nights the last of the French troops were taken off by the French fleet. The whole position at Helles was now under General Davies.

The progress of the intermediate stage was far more handicapped than at Anzac and Suvla, largely by unsettled weather. By January 4th it was plain that either the final stage must be postponed or large numbers of animals and vast quantities of stores must be destroyed or abandoned. Of these two alternatives General Birdwood un-hesitatingly chose the latter. By the morning of the 7th the Helles garrison had been reduced to about 19,000 men and 63 guns.

It is now known, from the memoirs of Liman von Sanders, that, having failed to stop the IX and Anzac Corps from getting away, he was determined not to fail this time.

As a prelude to a main attack along the whole of the Helles front, Liman von Sanders, unaware that evacuation had already started, had arranged that the specially trained 12th Division should carry out the preliminary operation of straightening the Turkish line. This manoeuvre was fixed for the afternoon of January 7th, when our numbers were down to a dangerous level. But, by the Grace of God the Turkish troops, in spite of the support of increased artillery and though still admirable in defence, could not be relied on to go forward *en masse*. Only at two points were half-hearted attacks delivered, which were repulsed with heavy loss, while British casualties were smaller than expected.

Aided by a quiet night, it was found possible to embark a further 2,300 men, 9 guns and nearly 1,000 animals. When daylight came on January 8th General Davies's force ashore stood at just under 17,000 officers and men.

Throughout the anxious hours of this last day on the Peninsula the Turks were exceptionally quiet. There was even less than the usual amount of shelling. But weather conditions were giving cause for anxiety. At 7 p.m. the wind began to freshen and thereafter steadily increased.

At both V and W Beaches regular harbours had been created by sinking blockships to form breakwaters which were now to prove the saving grace. Although 500 animals had to be slaughtered and 1,600 vehicles and vast quantities of stores had to be abandoned, all this was done and all personnel were brought off to safety by 5 a.m., thanks to courage and fine seamanship.

Mustapha Kemal was on leave in Constantinople when the news came through. 'Had I been there and had allowed the English to get away,' he said, 'I would have shot myself.' But Liman von Sanders was perhaps a little more realistic: 'Here again the enemy has been successful in his withdrawal despite our watchfulness. *Es war ein Meisterstueck* – It was a masterpiece!'

'No one will deny that we were glad to leave – "Oh, how glad!" Here was an end to all the weariness and suffering,' wrote Lieut-Colonel R. R. Thompson of the 52nd (Lowland) Division. 'Cape Helles had no happy memories for us; no one wanted to see the place again. But what of the men we were to leave behind us there? The good comrades who had come so gaily with us to the wars, who had fought so gallantly by our side, and who would now live for ever among the barren rocks where they had died. Never a kindly Scot would be there to tend their graves. No man was sorry to leave Gallipoli, but few were really glad.'[12]

26

Afterwards

*'We cannot undo the past, but we are bound to pass it
into review in order to draw such lessons as may be appli-
cable to the future.'*
Winston Churchill
The World Crisis

There is little doubt today that the idea of forcing the Straits, with
a view to helping Russia, eliminating Turkey from the war and
rallying the Balkan States to the side of the Allies, was one of the
few great strategical concepts of World War I. There can be
even less doubt that in the spring of 1915 the operation was not
beyond the capacity of the Entente and that a combined naval
and military attack, carefully planned in every detail before the
troops embarked and carried out with the essential advantages of
surprise, would have succeeded. Many reasons combined to
frustrate an enterprise the success of which must have altered the
course of the war, but every reason will be found to spring from one
fundamental cause, the lack of preparation before the campaign
began.

Despite this fundamental folly, it can be said with confidence that
twice during the early spring of 1915, after the naval attack of March
18th and again at the April landings the Turks were near resigning
themselves to defeat. Unfortunately the naval attack was abandoned,
never to be repeated, and, after the long warning given to the Turks,
the Mediterranean Expeditionary Force under Sir Ian Hamilton's
command, ill supplied with reserves, guns and ammunition, was not
strong enough to make success a certainty.

Britain's loss of these two opportunities is confirmed in the Turkish
official account. After pointing out that the Allies had the choice of
two methods of forcing the Straits, either a purely naval action or a
combined naval and military attack, the historian says: 'It is most
probable that the objective could have been achieved by naval
action alone had the attempt been pushed with greater vigour and

repeated several times. To win big stakes one must not shrink from big risks, or even from risking all at a crisis.'

Referring to the second possibility, a combined operation, which 'was naturally preferable and more certain', the Turkish compiler says: 'The way to do it was not as was actually done, to start with a small force and then reinforce by driblets. Sufficient strength should have been employed from the very start. If Sir Ian Hamilton had been given six divisions instead of four at the outset,' he concludes, 'the invading troops could have forced the Straits before the defenders had time to bring up reinforcements.'[1]

Whether in fact the Turks would have capitulated on the appearance of an Allied Fleet off Constantinople must remain a matter of opinion. Personally I have never once heard it discussed what was to happen next if the Fleet did break through into the Marmara. No instructions appear to have been issued by Admiral de Robeck. There seems to have been an undefined idea that the Turks would just give in.

This possibility has often been pooh-poohed by people misled by the way the Turks continued to fight the war, at Kut-el-Amara for instance, but due consideration should be given to the tremendous boost to Turkish morale which resulted from the defeat of the 'invincible' English Navy on March 18th and from the subsequent failure of the Allied Armies to reach their objectives on the Peninsula.

Fortunately we have reliable information from that discerning neutral source, the American Ambassador, who had been in Constantinople from 1913 and knew much about its people.

'In giving his assent to a purely naval expedition,' Morgenthau wrote, 'Lord Kitchener had relied on a revolution in Turkey to make the enterprise successful. Lord K. has been much criticised for his action, but I owe it to his memory to say he was absolutely right. Had the Allied fleet once passed the defences of the Straits, the administration of the Young Turks would have come to a bloody end.'

Further on in his book Morgenthau analysed the situation, showing how the Turkish Empire was about to break up into its component parts in March 1915, and he ended: 'As for Constantinople, the populace there would have welcomed the arrival of the Allied Fleet with joy, for this would relieve them of the controlling gang, emancipate them from the hated Germans, bring about peace and end their miseries.'[2]

Although no one can oppose Vice-Admiral de Robeck's decision to break off the action of March 18th because of uncertainty, there are many who were disappointed that no attempt was made to renew the attack.

Winston Churchill referred to Lord Kitchener's 'grim dilemma' and his failure to choose between a renewal of the naval attack and a pause for the arrival of military aid. 'I am sure,' he wrote, 'that Admiral de Robeck, urged by Keyes and backed, as he would have been, by the Admiralty and the Cabinet, would have resumed the naval operation if he had been ordered to do so. What the results would have been no one can declare. If he had succeeded, they must have been of supreme importance. If he had failed, at any rate there would have been no entanglement. Lord K. did not make up his mind between the two courses; he drifted into both and was unable to sustain either.'[3]

There were many who served with the Royal Navy at Gallipoli who never gave up hope that the naval attack would be resumed. 'This was especially so from April 4th onwards, a full three weeks before the Army landed and in fact the date on which the eight *Beagle* class destroyers became operational as minesweepers. With their special heavy sweep wires they could tear a passage through moored mines instead of laboriously dragging them aside into shallow water as the North Sea trawlers, which were the only sweepers available in March, had been obliged to do. The destroyers could sweep in formation, too, and so could have led a line of battleships straight through the minefields in one dramatic blow, introducing an element of surprise and shock on the Turks, who were becoming used to more cautious advances on our part.'[4]

But the chance was never taken.

Writing to Mr Balfour on 6th October 1915, when it was all nearly over, Winston Churchill reverted again to the question of the renewal of the naval attack on the Narrows. 'You should not overlook the fact,' he said, 'that Admiral de Robeck is deeply committed against this by what has taken place, and his resolution and courage, which in other matters are beyond dispute, are in this case prejudiced by the line he has taken since the beginning. Could he have seen, after March 18th, the terrible course and vast expansion of the military operations, it is inconceivable that he would not have renewed the attack . . .'[5]

Admiral de Robeck himself has kept surprisingly quiet over the whole matter. He must have had the courage of his own convictions to stand up to the pressures to which he was subjected.

'Now it is all over,' he wrote on 24th December 1915 to Admiral Sir Henry Jackson, the First Sea Lord, 'there is no doubt that the right policy has been followed, as the troops could not have gone forward, in the military opinion . . . and it was 20 to 1 against [the Navy] getting past even Chanak.'

But Commodore Roger Keyes, his Chief of Staff, never gave up. Writing to his wife on 31st December 1915, he said de Robeck's 'fear of having to do *anything* in the Straits ever since March 18th would be rather pathetic if it was not so distressing and had it not had such a ghastly effect on our whole policy and been mainly responsible for the miserable fiasco out here . . .'

Keyes and his many supporters were right. The Navy should have gone on trying. 'Contrast Admiral Beatty's attitude of mind at Jutland,' wrote Winston Churchill, 'when two of his six ships with 2,500 men had been blown out of existence in a few moments, with that of Admiral de Robeck – an officer of the highest physical courage but saddened and smitten to the heart by the loss of three obsolete vessels with small loss of life. The true war spirit of the Navy only gradually liberated itself from the shortsighted prudent housewifery of the peace-time mind.'[6]

'The consequences of the defeat of the English Fleet and of the subsequent withdrawal of the Allied armies,' wrote Ambassador Henry Morgenthau, 'had the effect of isolating the Turkish Empire from all the world, excepting Germany and Austria. For the first time in two centuries the Turks could live their national life according to their own inclinations and govern their peoples according to their own will. The first expression of this rejuvenated national life was an episode which as far as I know is the most terrible in the history of the world. New Turkey celebrated its national rebirth by murdering not far from a million of its own subjects.'[7]

Contrary to fears expressed by Lord Kitchener and General Birdwood, there were no serious repercussions in India and Egypt as a result of the Evacuation, which seems to have passed almost unnoticed in the East, possibly on account of its brilliant success.

News of the withdrawal, however, 'stunned the population of Australia and New Zealand, though intense relief was expressed at the absence of further losses. There could hardly have been a family in those two Dominions who did not have friends or relations whose remains were left on the hillsides now abandoned to the enemy.' (The Australian Force had lost 26,094, including 7,594 killed; the New Zealanders 7,571, with 2,431 killed.)

Since 25th April 1915, the first Anzac Day, 'thoughts of every man, woman and child had been centered upon those few acres, either by personal affection or interest or by a new-born pride in their nation.

Yet even had the casualties been severe during the evacuation there is little reason to believe that the reception of the tidings would have in any way changed their attitude towards the British Government and people which was one of loyal partnership and of complete trust. If Anzac troops had been sacrificed in Gallipoli, so – and equally freely – had British and French. The same qualities that invariably led the Australian and New Zealand soldier to stand by his mate caused their people to give unswerving loyalty to the partner in the struggle.'[8]

Though the forces of the two Dominions were then only in their infancy and fought with success in bigger and sometimes more costly battles elsewhere before the war was over, no campaign was so identified with them as Gallipoli was. Anzac Day, April 25th, as all the world knows, is now a National Day in both Australia and New Zealand, the day devoted to the memory of those who fell in both World Wars.

In examining the causes of our failure at Gallipoli there are some important factors which should not be overlooked, among them the brilliant leadership of Marshal von Sanders. The Turks owed much to his bold and swift decisions.

It would also be difficult to appraise too highly the help he received from Mustapha Kemal Bey, later Ataturk, ruler of Turkey. Seldom in history can the exertions of a divisional commander have exercised on three separate occasions, so profound an influence. It was his grip of the situation which contributed to the failure of the Anzac Corps to gain its objective on April 25th, the day of the landing. It was his vigorous action, when entrusted at a moment's notice with the command of the Northern Zone, that defeated General Stopford's delayed advance after the Suvla landing. And twenty-four hours later, following a personal reconnaissance, it was his brilliant counter-attack at Chunuk Bair which placed the Turks in possession of the main Sari Bair Ridge.

From the military point of view there was an unfortunate tendency to underestimate the fighting qualities of the Turk. It was wrongly imagined that his heart was not in the war against England and that he would not fight with valour. No more dangerous calculation could have been made. 'If your enemy is an ant,' an old Turkish proverb says, 'treat him as if he were a lion.'

One cause of the failure of the initial landings was the poor effect of the covering fire from H.M. ships, with the notable exception of the

Implacable. It was the paucity of fire power during the actual touch down which resulted in the appalling casualties on the beaches. Not only did bombarding ships stand too far out, whence they could see nothing, but they lifted their fire much too soon, which enabled the defenders to stand up in their trenches and pour murderous volleys into the men in the boats, while our naval shells fell harmlessly inland.

'The situation at V Beach,' wrote the Military Historian, 'was only saved from complete disaster by the machine-guns mounted in the bows of the *River Clyde*.' This is painful reading, when one reflects that H.M.S. *Albion*, mounting four 12-inch, twelve 6-inch and a number of 12-pdr guns, was on the spot for the sole purpose of providing covering fire.

That story is bad enough in itself, but the one which horrifies me most was told by Lieutenant-Commander Andrew Cunningham, later Admiral of the Fleet Lord Cunningham of Hyndhope and First Sea Lord, who was then in command of the destroyer *Scorpion*:

'After three or four sweeps for mines on the day of the landings, we destroyers lay off the beaches ready to do anything required of us, though for some incomprehensible reason we had the strictest orders not to open fire in support of the Army. I have never discovered who was responsible for this stupid edict, for many opportunities were missed of directly helping the landings by destroyers – so close inshore that they could even see the Turks bobbing up and down in their trenches.

'The *Scorpion* herself lay stopped for a considerable time off V Beach, near Sedd el Bahr, 500 yards off a trench full of the enemy firing on our troops, and unable to do anything. We could see our infantry lying flat on their faces on the beach under withering fire, and every now and then one or two men dashing out to cut the wire in front of them, only to be quickly shot down.

'It was a tragedy and a mortifying situation for a well-gunned destroyer; but a few days later it was discovered that destroyers could shoot, both rapidly and accurately, and an order that should never have been given was rescinded.'[9]

In the twenty years between the wars Combined Operations were given a back seat. The Gallipoli Campaign was fought all over again at the Staff Colleges, but that was mostly backward thinking. Many people, including even Admiral Keyes, reckoned that daylight assaults against a defended shore were suicidal. The Inter-Services Training and Development Centre, set up at Fort Cumberland,

Eastney, in 1936, received little encouragement because the Chiefs of Staff had said, in writing, that in the event of war they could see no requirement for an Amphibious Operation.

It was not till after the withdrawal from Dunkirk in June 1940 that Combined Operations Command was established at the instigation of Winston Churchill, who picked his old friend and supporter of Gallipoli days, Admiral of the Fleet Sir Roger Keyes, to be its Director. After the fighting words to Parliament: 'We shall defend our island whatever the cost may be,' Churchill directed the Chiefs of Staff to prepare measures 'for a vigorous, enterprising and ceaseless *offensive* against the whole German-occupied coastline'.

After a good start, relations between Keyes and the Chiefs of Staff became strained, and when, in October 1941, they reached breaking-point, Captain (acting Vice-Admiral) Lord Louis Mountbatten was appointed in his place.

In spite of the poor interest shown in combined operations between the wars, success of the D-day landings on 6th June 1944 may be attributed in some measure to the lessons of Gallipoli.

First in importance, perhaps, was the provision of adequate staffs from the three Services. We lived and worked together, first in barracks onshore and then afloat. Force Commanders were given specially equipped H.Q. ships with excellent communications. All three services were under the centralised direction of an impartial 'Supremo'.

Second, we had learnt that with sea power in our possession – and command of the air – we were at liberty to transport an army to a new theatre of war and to put it down at points on the coast (in scientific landing craft, not in open boats) where it was least likely to be expected.

Vice-Admiral de Robeck's gunnery officers may well salute those of 1944 and congratulate them on their achievements in Normandy. It was good to learn that technical advances had made accurate control fire possible, using much the same weapons which had proved so ineffective in 1915. Above all the Navy had learnt the value of drenching fire from small craft mounting guns and rockets and stationed close inshore, as well as from amphibious tanks which forced the enemy to keep their heads down until after the landing had been effected.

Finally, you will remember how bad weather conditions off the shore of Gallipoli had hampered boat-work and how it became necessary in the Cape Helles area and at Kephalo, Imbros, to construct boat havens with sunken ships. The grand scale of the Normandy landings called for similar protection, not only for small craft but for sea-going ships as well. Full-scale synthetic harbours provided the answer. They were towed over and brought into action shortly after D-day. They were called 'Mulberries', a code-name which certainly did not reveal to the enemy either their character or their purpose.

When the Gallipoli Campaign was over, Vice-Admiral Sir John de Robeck joined the Grand Fleet in command of a battle squadron. This was to be followed by other important appointments, including eventually that of Commander-in-Chief, Atlantic Fleet. He finally became an Admiral of the Fleet. 'A great and gallant man,' wrote Vice-Admiral Sir Gilbert Stephenson, 'admired and loved by the whole Navy.'

General Sir William Birdwood also went ahead. After Gallipoli he commanded Australian and New Zealand troops and Fifth Army in France, finally becoming Commander-in-Chief, India, in 1925–30 in the rank of Field Marshal, and Master of Peterhouse, Cambridge, 1931–8. My last glimpse of him was at the cenotaph on Anzac Day 1950, when Chief Petty Officer Main and I were presented to him. He was very weak then and had to be held up. He died on May 17th the following year, aged eighty-six.

Sir Ian Hamilton was not employed again. He accepted the decision without bitterness, although often cut in the street. In any case he did not wish for other than a fighting command. He devoted himself to the cause of ex-service men as President of the British Legion in Scotland, and accepted the picturesque sinecure of Lieutenant of the Tower of London. His other many activities included Lord Rector of Edinburgh University.

A Dardanelles Commission was appointed by the Cabinet in 1916. Its Interim Report published in March 1917 was of little value, but the full findings, which were held back till after the war, largely exonerated Sir Ian Hamilton. Would he have been treated differently had Kitchener lived to give evidence? Who can say? Yet one thing is certain: under no circumstances – even if it harmed his own position – would Sir Ian have been disloyal to his old Chief.

When the Dardanelles Commission was being convened, Churchill was among those who advised Sir Ian to be represented by Counsel,

so he consulted F. E. Smith (later Lord Birkenhead), the Attorney-
General, who suggested that his brother should act for him. As Sir
Ian was leaving F. E. Smith called out to him:

'"Of course you understand that when you attack K. I shall
defend him!"' This brought Sir Ian back into the room 'with a
round turn'.

'"Attack K? I'm not going to attack K!" "Oh yes,"' said F. E.
Smith, '"so far as I can size up the lay of your case you *must*." "I'm
sorry,"' Sir Ian replied, '"but I'm damned if I do! If that was your
assumption our deal is off!"'

'"Yes, the deal is off, but you'll be sorry some day, I more than
suspect."'

And so, 'like a bird escaping from the net of the fowler', Sir Ian
'flew back happily home'; nor did he ever regret his decision.[10]

Sir Ian's wife, Jean, died in Scotland in 1941. 'She loved flowers,'
he wrote in a tribute to her memory, 'and at her burial the grave
was covered with red poppies from the British Legion in Scotland,
lilies, spring flowers of every kind as well as delicately hued orchids
from London.'

That night it snowed and blew a gale of wind, and Sir Ian lay
awake thinking 'how sad she would be at the ruination of so many
love tokens'. But when the grave was visited next morning and the
snow had been shaken off, 'the flowers, even the delicate orchids,'
he said, 'were found to have been perfectly preserved as if they had
been put into cold storage; and for three full weeks the daffies danced
to the breeze and the tulips did not shed a petal.'[11]

Six years later, on 12th October 1947, Sir Ian passed away peacefully
at the age of ninety-four. He lies buried in his 'honeymoon suit' – as
requested in his will – beside his wife at Doune.

There is a plaque to his memory in the crypt of St Paul's Cathedral,
unveiled – as was fitting – by Sir Winston Churchill on 6th November
1957.

Lieutenant-Colonel 'Dick' Doughty-Wylie, who was awarded a
posthumous V.C. at the landing from the *River Clyde*, left a widow
Lilian Oimara, known to her intimates as Lily or Judith. She was a
member of the *Union de Dame Françaises* and had been in charge of
the English Hospital at St Valery-sur-Somme since January 1915.
News of her husband's death reached her on May 1st, from her brother-
in-law, Captain H. M. Doughty R.N., commanding H.M.S.

Agincourt, with the Grand Fleet. The telegram said 'May God comfort you'.

'The shock was terrible,' Lily recorded in her diary. 'I don't quite know what I did for the first sixty seconds. Something seemed to tear at the region of my heart. All my life was so much of his life, all his life mine. I suppose I shall have to pick up the pieces of a spoilt life, too old to start again, just a lonely widow, nothing to look forward to, nothing to work for – a blank . . .'

It is evident from her diary and from letters she wrote at the time that Lily did not accept the separation as final, even in this world, and she continued to see her husband in her dreams. She received a letter of sympathy from General Joffre as well as from Sir Ian Hamilton.

Soon afterwards she managed to get herself transferred to the R.N.A.S. Hospital at Semaria, Thasos, Greece, and while carrying on devotedly with her work there, she determined to visit Gallipoli herself. There are day-to-day entries in her diary up to August 1915, when it stops, but opens again in 1919 in the old style.

The story told by several authors that Lily Doughty-Wylie, 'the only woman to put a foot ashore during the occupation', landed at Sedd el Bahr on 17th November 1915, laid a wreath on Dick's grave and that 'the Turks fired neither bullet nor shell during the Ceremony', may only have occurred in one of her dreams. Boatwork was impossible over that period because of gales. Though this visit is not mentioned in any official report she certainly believed she had made it and there are two eye-witness accounts (Lieutenant Corbett Williamson, R.M. and F. L. Hilton, R.N.D.) of a woman seen on Cape Helles about that time. Lily wrote to the British Ambassador in Athens thanking him for 'a success I owe in some measure to you' but never posted the letter.

Anyway, I have written enough except to tell you that in the end, thank goodness, she definitely did get there. After receiving help in 1919 from Headquarters, British Army of the Black Sea, Constantinople, and from our Advanced Base, Kilia Liman near the Narrows, she was taken in a pilot boat to the *River Clyde* – still aground at 'V' Beach. Helped through a hole in the ship's side by a couple of French soldiers, she walked to the grave which she found had fallen into disrepair 'since the last time I saw it'. A cross-bred spaniel, black and tan, 'sent by Dick', joined her and she kept it, calling it Chan after Fort Chanak. She must have stayed in Turkey nearly two years as she joined the Commonwealth War Graves Commission when they came out in 1921.

Lily did not marry again. She did hospital work in Cairo in World

War II, being mentioned in dispatches and awarded the C.B.E. She died at the Lady Lampson Club, Royal Air Force, Akrotiri, Cyprus, on 24th April 1961, a very devoted and gallant war widow.

Dick's remains have never been disturbed. He still lies where he fell, in Turkish territory, the only solitary War Graves Commission grave on the whole Peninsula.

There is a stained-glass window of St George and the dragon to the memory of Colonel Doughty-Wylie in the parish church of St Peter, Theberton, Suffolk. 'I like it very much,' Lily wrote in her diary. 'St George is Dick, looking such a dear.'

Constantinople, now Istanbul, looks much the same as it did sixty years ago. It is a superb breath-taking picture when seen from a distance but dirty and shabby on closer inspection. The women are unveiled nowadays, and the ordinary working man has discarded his fez in favour of a second-hand cap sometimes worn with the peak over one ear to allow obeisance with the forehead when called to prayer. The Muezzin no longer mounts his staircase. He has advanced with the times. A switch, a loud-speaker and, some say, a tape-recorder by his bedside now save the long climb. Motor traffic has reached appalling dimensions and appears to be completely out of control. The extremes of wealth and poverty are patent everywhere. Shearwaters still fly round over the Bosphorus, skimming in a lengthened train just above the waves and never seeming to rest. Even today they are regarded with superstition. The locals call them '*Les Âmes damnées*' or 'The souls of the damned'.

On the Gallipoli Peninsula itself the cemeteries, thirty-one of them, are the real reminder of the war. Beautifully kept by the Commonwealth War Graves Commission, many of them are visible from seaward. It is untrue to say that the original graves were systematically desecrated after we had withdrawn from the Peninsula, although at some period local inhabitants and individual Turkish soldiers did dig up a few, searching the pockets and money-belts of the dead for gold coins. Many wooden crosses were also taken down and used as firewood. This behaviour was contrary to orders, but Turkish governmental control was always weak.

Sergeant G. E. Dale, late 59 Brigade, R.F.A., visited the Peninsula recently. 'The most impressive cemeteries,' he wrote, 'were Lancashire Landing (Helles), Lone Pine (Anzac), and Green Hill (Suvla). In the latter I paused over a name. For there lies quiet decent Charlie – moved from where we laid him below Chocolate Hill. Charlie never knew our brave new world of strikes and demos.

He missed the Slump, another World War, and several cold ones. Charlie never watched "telly" nor saw an honest "bob" become five new pence. . . . All that trouble and strife he missed. Ah, but life is sweet. Rest in peace, old pal.'

The total British casualties had amounted to 205,000 (115,000 killed, wounded or missing and 90,000 evacuated sick); those of the French 47,000. Owing to lack of hospital accommodation on the Peninsula large numbers were evacuated who were only suffering from light wounds or minor ailments. Of 34,000 British dead and 10,000 French dead only a small proportion have been recovered. The official Turkish estimate of their casualties was 251,000; some Turkish authorities put it as high as 350,000.

As one approaches the entrance to the Dardanelles, the 29th Division War Memorial on Cape Helles stands up boldly against the sky, although some of its grandeur has been stolen in recent years by the re-building of the lighthouse, which was demolished by the guns of the *London* in 1915. The old castle of Sedd el Bahr looks much as it did and the tongue of rocks below – where the *River Clyde* rested – are still clearly visible. This famous ship was refloated in June 1919 by the Ocean Salvage Company and taken to Malta, where, to the indignation of many, she was sold to a Spanish ship owner. First renamed *Angela*, she changed ownership in 1929 and became the *Maruja y Aurora* until sent to a shipbreaker's yard in 1966. She had a very long life, as she was built in Glasgow in 1905.[12]

Following the coast of the Peninsula in a northerly direction, the famous beaches can be easily recognised from the bones of piers and sunken ships which still show above water. What remains of the distilling plant at Anzac (destroyed by a gun from Lone Pine on the day it was landed) lies close to the water's edge. The Sphinx still grins at passing ships.

At Suvla, although the Salt Lake seems to be more thickly covered with scrub, the treacherous 'Cut' can still be seen, off which the motor lighters carrying Sitwell's 34 Brigade grounded in shoal water on August 6th, to add to the confusion. It is from Suvla Bay that the best view can be had of the Sari Bair Ridge, Koja Chemen Tepe and Chunuk Bair and of the cemeteries sited on the hillsides . . .

It is only in comparatively recent years that the exact positions in the Dardanelles of the sunken *Irresistible, Ocean* and *Bouvet* have been established. Their positions were located in 1966 by the Research Laboratory for Archaeology of Oxford, using the Proton Magnetometer. They lie in the maximum depth possible for oxygen skin-

diving, i.e. 160–180 feet. Two accomplished Turkish divers, Tosun
Sezen his partner Baskin, have been down as has also Peter Throg-
morton, an American. Much interesting material has been raised
from the *Irresistible*, where all the engine-room machinery, torpedo-
tubes and propellers have been taken. It provided a good advertisement
for naval bronzes since everything removed from her was still perfectly
polished. I have no confirmation that the paymaster's safe was found.
Sailors in 1915 were paid in gold sovereigns and half-sovereigns. The
Ocean is in deep water and it is doubtful whether much has been
salvaged from her, though propellers have been removed. Tosun
Sezen had a project, which I believe has been abandoned, of raising
one of the wrecks by blowing her up with expanded polystyrene.

On the Peninsula side opposite the Plains of Troy, two interesting
monuments have been erected overlooking Morto Bay. The first
is the French Memorial on the edge of the cliffs, symbolising *Le
Poilu*. The Turks have done much the same, except that as a rule
they only interred their dead when obliged to do so for health reasons
or because their men would not advance over their comrades' corpses.
The Turkish Memorial carries no inscription. It is simply to the
Asker, the Turkish soldier.

Carrying on up stream to the Narrows, it will be noticed that all
the old guns have been removed from the forts but that the emplacements remain. Laid on the hillside overlooking Maidos (Eceabat),
is a huge figure of a Turkish soldier made of flat stones painted
white. It was constructed in 1959 by men who lived in a camp
nearby and is said to be in memory of all Turkish soldiers who fought
for their country. Under the figure of the Soldier is this excerpt from
a poem by Mehmet Akif Ersoy:

> Stop passer by! The earth you have just trod on without knowing it
> is the spot where a period ended and where the heart of a nation
> beats.

On the opposite bank, on the Asiatic side, there is another Memorial which also cannot be missed by any passing vessel. It is simply
a date 18:3:15, and it speaks for itself.

Few memories are sadder than the memory of lost opportunities and
few failures more painful than those which, when reviewed in
retrospect were surely avoidable. The memory of Gallipoli is like
that. Yet, though the Campaign failed in its main object, it was not a
disaster.

It was largely because of the naval attacks at the Dardanelles in February and March 1915, that the Germans cancelled their offensive in the West planned for the spring of that year, also that Italy entered the war, that Greece remained neutral and that Bulgaria was content to sit on the fence until the outcome of the campaign became clear. Moreover the threat to Constantinople afforded protection to the Suez Canal as well as helping Russia. Finally it was the heavy fighting in Gallipoli that destroyed the flower of the Turkish Army and limited its activities thereafter. These were solid advantages, even if they cannot compare with the rewards that awaited the surrender of Constantinople.

We in the *Bacchante* sailed for England from Mudros on 11th January 1916. On leaving harbour we cheered ship.

'Well done *Bacchante!*' signalled the Commander-in-Chief.

Three cheers came from the *Lord Nelson* . . . from the *Cornwallis* . . . the *Prince George* . . . the *Grasshopper* . . . the *Colne* – big ships and small – all our friends. There were waves and shouts from the Merchant Navy, too, as we headed for the gate of the anti-submarine boom.

I still seem to see our Captain Algy Boyle acknowledging the cheers, with tears pouring down his cheeks.

It may not be generally known that Boyle, when a lieutenant, was in command of the Naval Guard of Honour at the funeral at Windsor of H.M. Queen Victoria on 2nd February 1901. It was he who drew his sword and cut the traces of the horses, which had become restive while drawing the gun-carriage, and replaced them with his own men. Thereafter the Royal Navy has had the privilege of manning the drag-ropes at the funeral of a monarch, as well as in 1965 that of Winston Churchill.

Captain Boyle left the *Bacchante* to join the *Malaya*, sister ship of the mighty *Queen Elizabeth*, while we midshipmen joined the *Revenge*, also Grand Fleet, just in time for Jutland. When I commanded the same 15-inch gun battleship *Malaya* (modernised) in 1944, Admiral Sir Algernon Boyle wrote of the pleasure it gave him, in his old age, to know that one of his midshipmen was in command of his old ship.

I have taken part in many naval actions in both World Wars, but, looking back now, none of them has such a place in my memory and in my heart as Gallipoli.

References

1 TO GALLIPOLI

1 Gilbert, *Winston S. Churchill*, Vol. III (Heinemann, 1971)

2 A NAVAL BEGINNING

1 Dardanelles Commission, First Report, 1917 (H.M.S.O.).
2 Churchill, *The World Crisis, 1915* (Thornton Butterworth, 1923).
3 Ibid.

4 THE GREATER STRUGGLE

1 Morgenthau, *Secrets of the Bosphorus* (Hutchinson, 1918).
2 Churchill, op. cit.

5 MARCH 18TH

1 Corbett, *Naval Operations*, vol. II (Longmans, Green & Co., 1921).
2 Keyes, *The Naval Memoirs* (Thornton Butterworth, 1934).
3 Morgan, *Experiences in the Great War* (Ms, Imperial War Museum).
4 Keyes, op. cit.
5 Morgenthau, op. cit.

6 NO GOING BACK

1 Churchill, op. cit.
2 Hamilton, *Gallipoli Diary* (Arnold, 1920).
3 Churchill, op. cit.
4 Hamilton, op. cit.
5 Ibid.
6 Ibid.
7 Godfrey, *Naval Memoirs* (Ms. Imperial War Museum, 1964).
8 Dardanelles Commission, First Report, 1917.

7 THE ARMY ASSEMBLES

1 Jerrold, *The Royal Naval Division* (Hutchinson, 1923), foreword by Churchill.
2 Ray, *The Story of XX The Lancashire Fusiliers* (Leo Cooper, 1971).
3 Hamilton, op. cit.
4 Ibid.
5 Herbert, *Mons Anzac and Kut* (Hutchinson, 1919).
6 Marsh, *Rupert Brooke, The Collected Poems with a Memoir* (Sidgwick & Jackson, 1958).
7 Churchill, op. cit.

8 THEY WENT LIKE KINGS

1 Hamilton papers (King's College, University of London).
2 Ibid.
3 Hare papers (Imperial War Museum).
4 Sanders, *Five Years in Turkey* (U.S. Naval Institute, 1927).
5 Kannengiesser, *The Campaign in Gallipoli* (Hutchinson, 1927).
6 Masefield, *Gallipoli* (Heinemann, 1917).

9 ANZAC DAY

1 Bean, *The Story of Anzac* (Angus & Robertson, 1941).
2 Louch, *In the Ranks, 1914–1915*, A Personal Record (Ms. Perth, 1970).
3 Thursby papers.
4 Birdwood papers (Australian War Memorial, A.C.T.).
5 Wemyss, *The Navy in the Dardanelles Campaign* (Hodder & Stoughton, 1924).
6 *Reveille*, March 1932, Journal of the Returned Soldiers League, Sydney.

10 V BEACH – *River Clyde*

1 Wylly, *Neill's Blue Caps* (Gale & Polden, 1923).
2 Scott, H.M.S. *Agamemnon*, letter to parents.
3 Wedgwood, *Essays and Adventures* (George Allen & Unwin, 1924).
4 Patterson, *With the Zionists in Gallipoli* (Hutchinson, 1916).
5 Wedgwood, Letter to Churchill headed Sedd-ul-Bahr, Tues. 26th (?) (Chartwell Trust).
6 Wedgwood, *Essays*, op. cit.
7 Doughty-Wylie Papers.

11 S BEACH – MORTO BAY

1 Godfrey, op. cit.
2 Lockyer papers.

12 W BEACH – LANCASHIRE LANDING

1 Godfrey, op. cit.
2 The Lancashire Fusiliers, *Annual*, 1916 (ed. Major B. Smyth).
3 Williamson, 'The 1/Lancashire Fusiliers at Cape Helles, April 25th, 1915', in Robinson and Pollock (eds) *Battle Training in Words and Pictures* (Newnes, 1939).
4 Hare papers, op. cit.
5 Ibid.
6 Churchill, *My Early Life* (Thornton Butterworth, 1930).
7 Willis, Major R. R., V.C., *The Morning Post*, 25th April 1930.
8 Foster, *At Antwerp and the Dardanelles* (R.U.S.I.).

13 X BEACH – *Implacable* LANDING

1 Lockyer papers.
2 Ibid.

14 Y BEACH AND DECEPTION

1 Hamilton, op. cit.
2 Godfrey, op. cit.
3 Churchill, op. cit.

15 DESPERATE RESISTANCE

1 Raymond, *Tell England* (Cassell, 1923).
2 Stewart and Peshall, *The Immortal Gamble* (Black, 1918).
3 Hamilton, op. cit.
4 Ibid.
5 Savory, *A Subaltern of the Sikhs* (Ms).
6 Schuyler, *Australia in Arms* (Benn, 1916).
7 Hamilton, op. cit.
8 Ibid.
9 Gilbert, op. cit.

16 LOSS OF *Goliath*

1 Eberhard von Mantey, *Auf See unbesiegt* (Lehmann, Munich, 1921–2).

17 HEROIC HEARTS

1 Bean, op. cit.
2 Nevinson, *The Dardanelles Campaign* (Nisbet & Co., 1918).
3 After Benson, *The Man with the Donkey* (Hodder & Stoughton, 1965),
     and Walsh, *Soldiers' Stories* (Ms. Auckland, N.Z.).
4 Hamilton, op. cit.
5 Herbert, op. cit.
6 Ibid.
7 Stevens (ed.), *Soldiers' Stories* (Anzac Memorial, Sydney, 1916).

18 THE FATAL PERISCOPE

1 Hersing, *U 21 rettet die Dardanellen* (Amalthea Verlag, Zurich, 1932).
2 Morgan, op. cit.

19 THE TATTERED BATTALIONS

1 Gilbert, op. cit., and Chartwell Trust.
2 Savory, op. cit.
3 Hamilton papers.

20 NO PAGE MORE WONDERFUL

1 Stoker, *Straws in the Wind* (Herbert Jenkins, 1923).
2 Corbett, op. cit., vol. III (1923).
3 Lorey, op. cit.
4 Heimburg, *U-boot gegen U-boot* (Die Woche, 1917).
5 Ibid.
6 Ibid.

21 THE NEW VENTURE

  1 Gilbert, op. cit., and Chartwell Trust.
  2 Hamilton papers.
  3 Hamilton, op. cit.
  4 Roskill, *Hankey: Man of Secrets* (Collins, 1970).
  5 Hamilton, op. cit.
  6 Hamilton papers.
  7 Hamilton, op. cit.
  8 Watkins, op. cit.

22 SUVLA BAY

  1 Aspinall-Oglander, *Military Operations, Gallipoli* (Heinemann, 1932).
  2 Hamilton papers.
  3 Aspinall-Oglander, op. cit.
  4 Ibid.
  5 Hamilton, op. cit.
  6 Aspinall-Oglander, op. cit.
  7 Ibid.
  8 Mackenzie, *Gallipoli Memories* (Cassell, 1929).
  9 Hamilton, op. cit.
10 Still, *A Prisoner in Turkey* (Bodley Head, 1920).
11 Liman von Sanders, *Fünf Jahre Türkei* (Scherl, Berlin, 1927).
12 Churchill, op. cit.
13 Hamilton, op. cit.

23 SARI BAIR

  1 Alexander Turnbull Library, N.Z.
  2 Ibid.
  3 *The Parade* (Southdown Press, 1964).
  4 Aspinall-Oglander, op. cit.
  5 Ibid.
  6 Hamilton, op. cit.

24 THE IMPOSSIBLE?

  1 Hamilton, op. cit.
  2 Aspinall-Oglander, op. cit.
  3 Gilbert, op. cit., and Chartwell Trust.
  4 Aspinall-Oglander, op. cit.
  5 Hamilton, op. cit.
  6 Morgan, op. cit.
  7 Ibid.
  8 *Journal of the R.N. Medical Services*, 1916.
  9 Stevens, op. cit.
10 Savory papers.
11 Aspinall-Oglander, op. cit.
12 Herbert, op. cit.
13 Public Record Office.

14 Hamilton papers.
15 Aspinall-Oglander, op. cit.
16 Hamilton papers.
17 Ibid.
18 Hamilton, op. cit.
19 Hankey, *The Supreme Command* (George Allen & Unwin, 1961).
20 Hamilton, Ian, B.M., *The Happy Warrior* (Cassell, 1966).

25 EVACUATION

1 Hamilton, *The Happy Warrior*, op. cit.
2 Ibid.
3 Hamilton papers.
4 Churchill, op. cit.
5 Keyes, op. cit.
6 Churchill, op. cit.
7 Esher, *The Tragedy of Lord Kitchener* (John Murray, 1921).
8 Bean, op. cit.
9 Hamilton, *The Happy Warrior*, op. cit.
10 Savory, op. cit.
11 Stewart, and Peshall, op. cit.
12 Thompson, *The 52nd (Lowland) Division, 1914–1918* (Macklehose, Jackson & Co., 1923).

26 AFTERWARDS

1 *Turkish Operations in the Great War,* vol. I (Historical Section, General Staff, Constantinople).
2 Morgenthau, op. cit.
3 Churchill, op. cit.
4 Boswell, 'The Navy's Great Chance', *Naval Review*, 1971.
5 Gilbert, op. cit., and Chartwell Trust.
6 Churchill, op. cit.
7 Morgenthau, op. cit.
8 Bean, op. cit.
9 Cunningham, *A Sailor's Odyssey* (Hutchinson, 1951).
10 Hamilton, *Listening for the Drums* (Faber, 1944).
11 Hamilton, *Jean, A Memoir* (privately printed).
12 World Ship Society.

Index